Wayne Lee examines how a society shapes, directs, restrains, understands, and reacts to violence, with particular attention to riot and war in eighteenth-century North Carolina. He links several riots, the backcountry rebellion known as the Regulation, and the War for Independence by examining each as an act of public violence, rooted in cultural practice and shaped by collective notions of legitimacy.

Beginning with public riot, Lee describes the "rules of violence" shared by rioters, authority, and the public at large and shows how those rules were observed or violated and what the consequences were for rioters and society. Moving to the larger-scale War of the Regulation, 1768-71, he examines the competing use of violence by settlers and authorities, each playing to a politicized public whose expectations of violence shaped the course of the movement from public protest to organized battlefield. He then shows how military action, like its civil counterpart, struggled for legitimacy in the Revolutionary War, the Tuscarora and Cherokee Wars, and the "militias' war" of 1780-82.

For students of collective protest, Lee provides new case studies of violence in the colonial South and a more complete explanation for the course of the Regulation. He shows that such an event cannot be understood without addressing the forces shaping choices about violence. Similarly, he establishes a new paradigm for examining behavior in war, demanding careful consideration of individual incidents and the overlapping relationship between organized fighting bodies and the civilian population. He especially insists on a subtler understanding of "military necessity," demonstrating that, in the wide landscape of violence that is war, people's choices are regulated by a broad set of cultural pressures, of which necessity is only one.

Crowds and Soldiers in Revolutionary North Carolina

Southern Dissent

Florida A&M University, Tallahassee
Florida Atlantic University, Boca Raton
Florida Gulf Coast University, Ft. Myers
Florida International University, Miami
Florida State University, Tallahassee
University of Central Florida, Orlando
University of Florida, Gainesville
University of North Florida, Jacksonville
University of South Florida, Tampa
University of West Florida, Pensacola

Southern Dissent
Edited by Stanley Harrold and Randall M. Miller

This series explores and analyzes the complexities of southern dissent on a broad, multi-ethnic plane. The series is designed to channel research in a variety of fields into a continuing reevaluation of the role of dissent in the South and what constitutes a dissenting group in any given area at any given time.

The Other South: Southern Dissenters in the Nineteenth Century, by Carl N. Degler with a new preface (2000)
Crowds and Soldiers in Revolutionary North Carolina: The Culture of Violence in Riot and War, by Wayne E. Lee (2001)

Crowds and Soldiers
in Revolutionary North Carolina

The Culture of Violence in Riot and War

Wayne E. Lee

Foreword by Stanley Harrold and Randall M. Miller, Series Editors

University Press of Florida

Gainesville · Tallahassee · Tampa · Boca Raton
Pensacola · Orlando · Miami · Jacksonville · Ft. Myers

06   05   04   03   02   01   6   5   4   3   2   1

Library of Congress Cataloging-in-Publication Data
Lee, Wayne E., 1965–
Crowds and soldiers in revolutionary North Carolina: the culture of
violence in riot and war / Wayne E. Lee; foreword by Stanley Harrold
and Randall M. Miller.
p. cm. — (Southern dissent)
Includes bibliographical references (p.) and index.
ISBN 0-8130-2095-6
1. North Carolina—History—Revolution, 1775-1783—Social aspects.
2. North Carolina—History—Regulator Insurrection, 1766-1771.
3. Violence—North Carolina—History—18th century. 4. United
States—History—Revolution, 1775-1783—Social aspects. I. Title. II.
Series.
E263.N8 L35 2001
975.6'03—dc21 00-051057

Epigraph: *Tao te Ching* translation by Stephen Mitchell
(New York: HarperPerennial, 1988), 31.

The University Press of Florida is the scholarly publishing agency
for the State University System of Florida, comprising Florida A&M
University, Florida Atlantic University, Florida Gulf Coast University,
Florida International University, Florida State University, University of
Central Florida, University of Florida, University of North Florida,
University of South Florida, and University of West Florida.

University Press of Florida
15 Northwest 15th Street
Gainesville, FL 32611–2079
http://www.upf.com

Weapons are the tools of fear;
a decent man will avoid them
except in the direst necessity
and, if compelled, will use them
only with the utmost restraint.
. . . .
He enters a battle gravely,
with sorrow and with great compassion,
as if he were attending a funeral.
Tao te Ching

Contents

Maps and Figures

All maps were created by the author with MapInfo™ unless otherwise credited.

Foreword

Turmoil gripped the peoples of North America during the second half of the eighteenth century. The French and Indian War that began in 1754 brought the British settlers on the continent's eastern fringe into conflict with the French and their American Indian allies, who controlled its interior. The British Empire's victory in 1763 led to years of dissension as many Americans challenged imperial authority, questioned their colonial status within the empire, and took up arms. By 1776, dissent had become revolution as American Patriots fought against British troops, those Americans who remained loyal to Great Britain, and those Indians who sided with the British. The war caused social dislocation, as African Americans asserted their right to freedom and poorer whites challenged the colonial elite.

Wayne Lee's *Crowds and Soldiers in Revolutionary North Carolina: The Culture of Violence in Riot and War* focuses on a central aspect of this important era in American history. His analysis of physical conflict between contending groups in colonial and revolutionary North Carolina makes a significant contribution to historical knowledge on two levels. Grounded on the most recent historiography, on broad research in primary sources, and on a close reading of those sources, *Crowds and Soldiers in Revolutionary North Carolina* establishes a framework for understanding political violence in that place and time. What he reveals about riotous behavior and the conduct of war in North Carolina between the 1750s and 1780s provides insight as well into political violence during our own time.

Lee's book raises several vital questions. How does culture encourage, shape, and limit political violence? What is the relationship between mobs and the civil authorities against whom they contend? How do riotous conditions spiral out of control? How does war sometimes degenerate into a barbarous series of reprisals? What were the rules of public violence in colonial and revolutionary North Carolina? How does an understanding of those rules help us to better understand American history?

Lee answers these and other questions concerning public violence by utilizing a structuralist approach that, during the past forty years, has become increasingly influential among scholars in Western Europe and the United States. He finds cultural patterns behind the behavior of mobs and armies in colonial and revolutionary America. But he avoids cultural determinism. Having established a context for public violence based on precedents in Europe and America, he integrates technology, historical contingency, individual variation, and calculated self-interest. The result is a shrewd understanding of the elements of public violence at a crucial time in American history. On the one hand, a desire to maintain legitimacy among both rioters and armies created a strong disposition toward limiting the use of force. On the other hand, traditions of revenge and retaliation led occasionally to spiraling violence, especially between culturally dissimilar groups.

Lee emphasizes that those who engaged in riot in colonial North Carolina had to convince the authorities, the public, and themselves that their resort to violent means was justified and that their violent tactics fell within traditional parameters. When they succeeded in this, whether the issue was disputed landownership or taxation, violent dissent was effective. But when the famous Regulators of the 1760s seemed to stretch the limits of acceptable violence, North Carolina's colonial government crushed them. Similarly, during the American Revolution, Patriot forces in North Carolina and elsewhere sought to demonstrate that their tactics fell within legitimate boundaries—that they conducted war in an honorable and moral manner. But they expected their enemies to conduct war honorably as well. When they believed that was not the case, either among Indians or Loyalists, violence transcended the battlefield to engulf prisoners and noncombatants.

North Carolinians who took the law into their own hands to rectify perceived injustices were dissenters. So were those North Carolinians who took up arms against the British Empire. Although dissent need not be violent, it often has been in the history of the South. By analyzing the interplay between protest and violent action, Lee helps us to understand why this was the case. He also helps us to understand how concepts of limited violence shaped the conflict between the new United States and Great Britain.

By linking riot and war, Lee forces readers to confront the fact that this nation's founders engaged in violent dissent and bequeathed to posterity a tradition of violent dissent. This uncomfortable legacy continues to influence the debate over the limits of dissent. Readers of Lee's book will also have to think about the cultural forces that the United States engages when it seeks to mediate violent dissent in other parts of the world. In all, *Crowds and Soldiers in Revolutionary North Carolina* is a distinguished addition to the Southern Dissent series.

Stanley Harrold and Randall M. Miller, series editors

Preface

Definitions of the appropriate use of violence have been much at issue lately in American popular and political culture. While I admit that the all-consuming effort of writing a book is apt to lead one to see connections everywhere, I nevertheless suspect that the concern is real. As evidence, witness the series of protests against the World Trade Organization in Seattle in 1999, against the IMF and the World Bank in Washington in 2000, and the ensuing public debate over the police response. Witness the tremendous international dialogue over the type of war NATO waged against Serbia during the Kosovo crisis of 1999 and the subsequent concern over ethnic Albanian retributions. Finally, to underscore the depth of popular worries about the nature of force and violence in society, a host of movies in the last five years has explored American values concerning military violence and the role of an army in society. Among others, *Braveheart* (1995), *Courage under Fire* (1996), *The Siege* (1998), *Three Kings* (1999), *Rules of Engagement* (2000), and *The Patriot* (2000) were all popular movies much invested in exploring the supposed limits of and reactions to military violence. The historical accuracy of these films is neither here nor there. What they are, however, are documents of modern American expectations. They portray both our fears of an unfeeling professional army governed only by narrow interest and our ideal that an army of citizens be ingrained with the communal values of appropriate military force.

This book is an exploration of an older, if harsher, version of those ideals and expectations as they were enacted in riot and in war. Colonial American society had a much higher tolerance for violence than we do now. In fact, to say violence was merely "tolerated" is to misunderstand and impose our values on colonial Americans' lives. Violence was considered socially functional at the same time as it was deeply feared. That contradiction resolved itself through the establishment of certain types of violence appropriate for different situations and, furthermore, corresponding norms of restraint for each type of violence. There was a spectrum of public violence that encompassed a variety of behaviors ranging from judicial punishment, through shaming parades and riots, and on up to war. For each point on the spectrum, society had defined behaviors appropriate to the situation and censured those who violated those norms. Violence enacted according to the norms was legitimate. In different societies those norms of legitimacy could hold more or less weight in individuals' decision-making processes. In colonial North Carolina, concerns about legitimacy had considerable weight, and consequently a significant impact on behavior. It may be no surprise to learn that different rules existed for crowds and for soldiers, but what may be surprising are the similarities or parallels in the ways those norms were motivated, constructed, and enforced. The link, the overarching framework unifying this study of public violence, is the powerful societal demand for violence to be culturally legitimate.

Where possible, full names are given for individuals when first mentioned in the text. Punctuation and spelling have not been updated or corrected, nor is a "sic" provided except in cases where confusion could easily result. Readers should be aware, however, that previous editors of primary sources have used different standards of modernization. Where quoting from a published edition, I have followed its editor.

As so many other authors have discovered, the process of writing a book is not a solitary one. I owe a tremendous debt to all those who contributed to the completion of this work. While my debt to them is great, they are of course absolved from any of the errors that might be found herein.

I owe much to the faculties of the department of history at Duke University and at the University of North Carolina. They provided a stimulating environment of learning and a succession of surprising new perspectives on my own work. In particular I would like to thank Alex Roland, who consistently has demonstrated a tremendous capacity to bring clarity to muddle. For many years now he has been unstinting with his time, and I am the better historian for it. Peter Wood, Cynthia Herrup, Richard Kohn, and Mary Boatwright also made outstanding contributions to this project. Additional advice and support has come from Philippe Rosenberg, Heather Streets, Elizabeth Fenn, Holly Mayer, and the anonymous readers for the University Press of Florida. And, at the very end, on short notice, Elisa Slattery proofread the entire manuscript.

This project has also benefited from the professional and financial assistance of a number of institutions and organizations. Research grants were provided by the U.S. Army Center for Military History, the David Library of the American Revolution, and the American Historical Association (through the Michael Kraus Research Grant). I'm particularly grateful to the Harry Frank Guggenheim Foundation for the Study of Violence and Human Aggression, which generously provided funds for a year of writing. During the course of my research I received exceptional service from the libraries at Duke University and at the University of North Carolina. Equally helpful was the staff at the North Carolina Department of Archives, most notably the deeply informed assistance of George Stevenson. Finally, the David Library of the American Revolution and its director, David Fowler, provided a marvelous place to research and write. I will return there often.

Last, but most certainly not least, I thank my wife, Rhonda, for her thoughtful advice, her careful editing, and her endless patience.

Introduction

Public violence in the eighteenth-century Anglo-American world was surrounded by words. Much ink was spilled as that culture sought to explain its violent acts. Why? And more importantly, at whom was all that rhetoric directed? Whom were they trying to convince? Jill Lepore has recently made a powerful attempt to answer that question for seventeenth-century New England, specifically with regard to King Philip's War.[1] She argues persuasively that the New Englanders' studious efforts to explain their often radically violent war against the Indians was an attempt to maintain their identity as Englishmen in the face of a wilderness and a native culture that were constantly undermining their sense of civilization: "If the colonists' Englishness had been compromised before the war by becoming more Indian in their ways, it was further compromised during the war by the loss of their homes and clothes and, most of all, by their killing mercilessly and abandoning the codes of 'civil nations.' By telling about the war, and most especially by writing about it, the colonists could reclaim civility, could clothe their naked war with words."[2] Although Lepore's is a powerful explanation, it nevertheless seems too chronologically and geographically specific. It depends on seventeenth-century New Englanders' tremendous fear that they were succumbing to the wilderness. While Lepore is correct in describing that fear, there were many other situations of public violence in the early modern Anglo-American world that provided very similar examples of justificatory rhetoric. Surely there must be a more universal need driving this flood of justification.

The short answer is that society demanded it. Public violence could not be enacted without reference to the cultural norms that mediated it. In some societies the public of importance, the "political public," might be restricted to a relative few. In such a society, a political elite could wage campaigns of violence without regard to the opinions of a broader range of society. A feudal baron, for example, may have felt little need to explain an attack on another local lord to any but the narrow circle of his peers. The contention here is that in the eighteenth-century Euro-American world, *especially* with regard to the use of violence, simply because it was violence, the "circle of peers" was much broader. The wrapping of violence in broadly circulated rhetoric aided in the very necessary mobilization of public opinion.[3] The rhetoric did not just "reclothe" the violence in memory; it justified action by referring to, and sometimes shifting, norms of legitimate violence.

So much for rhetoric. The next logical question is: if the weight of public opinion was so important as to require such constant justification, justification constructed according to cultural norms of appropriate violence, then how did those norms affect behavior in violent situations? Did those norms mediate behavior the same way they apparently mediated the rhetoric about that behavior? That proved a much more difficult question.

In seeking to answer that question I found myself examining two different historical literatures: one for war and one for riot. During my first undergraduate course in military history, I had been introduced to the concept of the "rules of the game" as one of the foremost forces in determining the nature of military conflict. By the "rules" the instructor meant a broad sociocultural understanding of a proper way of war. As a concrete example, he pointed out various societies' conceptions of the *jus in bello* and the *jus ad bellum*: the law of conduct in war, and the law of justifying going to war. While those categories were intellectually manageable, they did not seem to live up to their billing as among the "foremost forces" in shaping war. Most societies, after all, seemed to have ignored those formal "laws." It is certainly true, however, that different cultures have practiced war in very different ways, and the more thoughtful military historians frequently have pointed out that militaries (as institutions) reflected the society from which they came. John Keegan has recently gone even further and said that "war . . . is always an expression of culture, often a determinant of cultural forms, in some societies the culture itself."[4] Nevertheless, there still seemed to be a rather large conceptual gap between the broad notion of "culture" and the specific manifestation of "violent behavior in war."

Fortunately, there is a different literature that seemed to address the same question with regard to the violence of riot. Rioters in early modern Europe, it appeared, constructed their behavior according to their own cultural preconceptions of how such a riot should look. Their violence was an enactment of their expectations. Despite occasional improvisation, the evidence seemed clear that rioters overwhelmingly followed relatively predictable patterns. But why? Why did persons in situations of collective violence (in this case a riot), supposedly freed from psychological restraint by anonymity and chaos, cling so strongly to very specific behaviors? What was the motivation for such conservatism? The more I investigated, the more it seemed that the answer lay in legitimacy—legitimacy defined as in accordance with social norms. Rioters patterned their behavior in order to emphasize the legitimacy of their actions, and the need to appear legitimate arose from the simple fact that the tool of the rioter was *violence,* with all its implications of threatening the social order.

Violence has a way of inspiring strong reactions. It may seem somewhat banal to state such an obvious point, but consider how much scholarship has been dedicated to determining which kinds of grievances, be they political, ideological, religious, or economic, have motivated action. There is little doubt that those various grievances have moved people, even moved them to violence. But how many more people have been moved to action by that first act of violence, and so on, as one act of violence succeeded another?

Despite this awareness of the threatening implications of violence, eighteenth-century society considered riotous violence socially functional, always provided that it did not exceed the social norms or expectations of its extent and thereby become a threat to the social order. These pressures of legitimacy led early modern rioters to precede violence with petitions, to carefully select their targets, to favor proxies or even effigies as the focus for their anger. While individuals might be hurt or even beaten, Anglo-American rioters rarely killed. Property destruction was selective and carefully linked to already published grievances. Rioters protested their loyalty to the sovereign, blamed his ministers, and in general asserted that their violence was in the service of order, of maintaining the status quo rather than overturning it.

But what about war? What parallels might exist between this understanding of riot and the "rules of the game" in war? Collective behavior in war was also strongly patterned, and eighteenth-century society wrapped it, like riot, in clouds of rhetoric. That rhetoric also, whether justificatory or condemnatory, assumed common notions of acceptable behavior. In short, could not riot and war be considered as points along a spectrum of violence, each with its own set of patterns, but each also a form of social intercourse, and each also subject to cultural norms of legitimacy? There are of course many types of war, and the set of presumptions shared by both sides could narrow according to circumstance. Revolutionary, civil, and international wars, however, merely occupy different places on the spectrum—each still mediated by varying sets of norms of legitimacy.

Legitimacy of course is culturally contingent. Different societies have different sets of norms establishing "types" of violence and the norms appropriate to each. Those norms condition both rhetoric *and* behavior. One key component of those norms, for all types of public violence, was restraint. Violence did not proceed to absolutes. This restraint arose not only from political calculations of means appropriate to ends, but from deeply ingrained and widely understood cultural definitions of legitimate violence. In colonial North Carolina, the relative potency and breadth of the political public lent those norms weight; they constrained individuals and strongly patterned violence. In short, norms of legitimacy established patterns of behavior (always subject to improvisation or to changes in material conditions).[5]

Some caution is necessary here. Some readers will immediately object that it is the end goal of public violence that plays the critical role in shaping that violence. In other words, societies will discard the restraints of legitimacy in the face of necessity. Some might even object that violence might deliberately be patterned to appear legitimate as part of a practical and political calculus to gain support and achieve goals. This is exactly right. Such a deliberate calculus, however, would reflect the cultural weight of norms of violence, and the potential power of public opinion to affect the eventual outcome. Furthermore, phenomena such as war are made up of many individual violent acts; their exact character is not subject to the desires of a calculating political elite. In that landscape of violence, there is tremendous space for different groups of actors not only to have different interpretations of interest but also to cling to their own sense of the norms of violence, unaware that someone else has decided to discard or change them. Thus the claim made here is that while societal demands for legitimately enacted violence do not determine behavior, they do condition it. The extent of that conditioning depends on the strength of the consensus about the exact nature of the norms, and on the power of the public in that society.

Colonial and revolutionary North Carolina proved an ideal laboratory in which to examine and compare how norms of legitimacy in public violence were applied both in riot and in war. North Carolina experienced not only the commoner forms of riot but also a full fledged "revolt" of western farmers (the "Regulators") from 1768 to 1771. The revolt culminated in an actual battle between the Regulators and the colonial militia, thereby providing a useful glimpse at the practice of violence in the transition from protest to war. At the outset of the American Revolution, North Carolina again experienced a shift from protest to war. The fratricidal warfare that followed has often been noted, but rarely have thorough attempts been made to explain it. The virulence of the revolutionary "militias' war," particularly when analyzed in comparison to the Regulation and the more restrained Continental army, provides an opportunity to examine how the norms of restraint could break down in the face of alternative norms of legitimacy—notably the legitimacy of retaliation. In all these cases, the correspondence between public rhetoric and public behavior will reveal how communal standards moderated and shaped violence.

Riot is the subject of Part I: specifically the transmission and evolution of the cultural practice of riot, how riots were conditioned by the need to accommodate social norms, and the consequences when those norms were violated—when legitimacy became questionable. The first chapter explores the European traditions and the colonial influences on North Carolinians' practice of riot. It then reviews how North Carolinians behaved in three examples of riot: the Enfield riots, the Sugar Creek "War," and the Stamp Act disturbances. Chapters 2 and 3 look more deeply at the case of the Regulators and their opponents as rioters and then as soldiers. The amount of surviving material on the Regulator movement makes them an ideal case study in the nature of, and the negotiation over, the forms of riot. Colonial society's norms of violence significantly shaped the course of the Regulator movement. Restrained, communicative violence (the "careful riot") had cultural legitimacy, and the Regulators carefully patterned their actions according to the traditional rules of violent protest. Structural factors related to the new colonial environment (a partial slave economy, strained class relationships, geography) and circumstance, however, combined to undermine the Regulators' efforts at legitimacy and escalated the situation out of the realm of protest into a rebellion culminated by battle. It became, in fact, the War of the Regulation. This escalation helps lay the groundwork for the discussion of war in Part II.

War, too, was an accepted, "socially functional" institution, and even as riot was conditioned by expectations of legitimacy, so too was war. Breaking down that story, however, is more complex. There was a whole network of conflicting beliefs about acceptable military violence, not least of which was the simple expectation that war by its very nature would be a horribly violent event—with a *de facto* legitimate basis to kill and destroy. Riot, in contrast, from the point of view of authority was at least *prima facie* illegitimate: rioters had to assert their legitimacy through purposefulness and selectivity—in short, through *careful* rioting. War's violence did not begin with such a handicap; the question of legitimacy affected only the manner of violence, not the broader question of violence itself. In that context, legitimacy's restraints on conduct were more difficult to maintain; a fact generally obvious in the historical record of war. To complicate matters further, in the American Revolution there appeared to be contrasting examples of ways of war. The war as conducted by the militia seemed frequently out of control, although nowhere as violent as their war against the Indians, while the Continental army was more rigorously, if not perfectly, restrained. Again, upon investigation, it appeared that the question of legitimacy played a fundamental role not only in restraining the Continental army but also, paradoxically, in unleashing the bloody war of the North Carolina militias.

Chapter 4 lays out the European and colonial traditions of war that defined the web of expectations in place at the beginning of the Revolution. If, as Pauline Maier has shown, a combination of tradition and Whig ideology restrained the anti-British protest violence up to 1776, what precedents affected how the revolutionaries would conduct their war?[6] At the outset of the Revolution, North Carolinians held an ideal of "virtuous war" that encompassed the restraints and influences of popular morality, republican ideology, European military formalism, the culture of masculine honor, adaptive and reactive responses to Native Americans, and a still powerful, although declining, sense of providentialism. Chapters 5 through 7 discuss in detail the role of that ideal of virtuous war in shaping the violence of the militias. For much of the war, that violence was relatively constrained. Even early in the war, however, one finds a potential for retaliatory escalation. Questionable policies of the Whig government combined with the arrival of the British army in 1780 sparked just such a war of retaliation. Historians have often noted the role of retaliation, pointing to instances of provocation and subsequent reactions. What is often forgotten, however, is that such retaliation was culturally legitimate. Society preferred to avoid and contain such situations but again and again asserted the right of revenge. Toward the end of the war, conditions in North Carolina and the institutional weaknesses of the militia combined to unleash the law of retaliation, resulting in the bloody war that followed. Part II concludes with an epilogue that briefly outlines the more successfully restrained behavior of the Continental army, and the wellsprings of those differences.

Much of this book is about the regulation of public violence through a process of community self-censure resting on a shared set of values. This is more than punishment at law. Social ostracism, gender-based rebukes, imputations against honor—these all had power to shape behavior. Individuals might, and frequently did, violate society's aggregate set of values, but always in the knowledge that they thereby exposed themselves to censure. The capacity to restrain violence, therefore, depends on the strength of the community to censure and on the commonality of its values about violence. Public violence was usually collective, conducted by groups. And groups, particularly the eighteenth-century groups we will consider, possessed within themselves a cross section of their broader society, and therefore the potential to censure variant individual members of the groups. Some groups, however, could drift apart from society, setting up their own set of norms that deviated from those of the parent society. The most famous example of a deviant group with its own standards and its own mechanisms for enforcement would probably be the pirate communities of the same era.[7] This description is also often applied to military organizations. A standing professional army might have a tremendous capacity for self-censure, but whose values are they enforcing—the parent society's or their own?

Consider the three examples being explored here: rioters, the militias, and the Continental army. Rioters in eighteenth-century North Carolina represented a fairly broad cross section of society, the socially prominent in company with a higher proportion of the middling and common sort. Their activities thus remained susceptible to internal communal censure. In addition, since the rioters were communicating grievances and hopeful of reform, they were also mindful of the reactions of their external "audience": the wider political population. This doubly reinforced motivation to conform to expectations is what so strongly patterned, and restrained, the behavior of North Carolina's rioters. Since they expected a helpful, even paternalistic, response to their riot, they carefully patterned their behavior on precedent and thereby aspired to legitimacy. Rioters who did not really hope for a sympathetic response would lack that restraint. The truly violent rioter is one who is already hopeless.

The militia also represented a broad cross section of colonial society, although only in its peacetime structure. In practice it often deviated from that ideal, relying on the less fortunate to fill the ranks. It is worth pointing out, however, that the militia officers nearly always were drawn from the upper levels of society, and thus the institution as a whole remained at least partially representative. More important is the question of whether the militia still represented the community from which it came. That is, did the members already know each other, and thus feel psychologically as if they were still in the same community, bound by the same fear of censure? The answer varies. Equally variable was the militia's ability to conform to the expectations of their behavior.

The Continental army differed yet again. It too was a broad cross section of society, if officers are considered representative of the upper and middling orders and the soldiers the lower, but it was both more socially polarized and less geographically homogenous than the militia. Although theoretically state regiments, the smaller units within the regiments were cobbled together with individuals from all over the state, if not composed outright of individuals who would have always been considered outsiders. Once in the army, however, they formed their own community and established new sets of norms. The strict divisions between officers and men could lead to separate sets of norms, but systems of censure did exist: one within the ranks, and one enforced by the officers. Both systems defined legitimacy and sought to regulate behavior accordingly. Thus one finds the Continental soldier plundering food and provisions, legitimate within the norms of a community of soldiers frustrated at the apparent lack of support from the civilian population, but normally forbearing from the more physically violent acts of house burning, rape, and murder. The officers, moreover, were pressured by another set of norms, both international and domestic, that demanded that the Continentals fight according to conventional European standards and behave virtuously. They used their institutionally strong powers of censure to regulate soldiers accordingly, helping limit the kind of violent excesses associated with the revolutionary militias.

A number of corollary lessons arise from these forays into collective violence. The first concerns the nature of escalation. The existence of a cultural set of expectations about violence not only influenced behavior but also laid the groundwork for escalation when there was a real or perceived violation of those expectations. Because violence was such a strong motivator, if someone broke the "rules," his actions had a tendency to invoke retaliatory violence. Retribution was often "in kind"; if one side violated the norms, then the other could legitimately do the same as an act of retribution. This tendency to escalate was particularly evident in the case of two antagonists who came from different cultural milieus: for example, the Europeans and the Indians. The conflict of values led their wars against each other to escalate quickly beyond either party's original norms of appropriate violence.[8] Individuals could also use their knowledge of their own culture's expectations to accuse the enemy of violations in the service of their own personal interest. Although such rhetorical efforts may have been motivated by self-interest, they still reflected that individual's understanding of the prevailing norms of violence.

The other recurrent phenomenon in situations of collective violence is the use of demonization to legitimize violent action. Definitions of "otherness" change according to time and place, but the use of the concept to justify violence has remained fairly constant.[9] Seventeenth-century Englishmen had long been accustomed to considering the Irish or the Papists as their measures of barbarity. The colonists retained those bugaboos, but added the "savage" Indian to their repertoire of the "other." Underlying such labels was the expectation that those persons would, as a matter of course, violate the rules of violence. "Others," by their very nature, used "uncivil" violence and therefore merited no restraint in turn. Perceptions of necessity or utility might briefly alter the nature of the relationship. The English, for example, recognized the military utility or threat of the Indians and cultivated alliances or peace according to need.[10] When such a peace fell apart, however, the resultant war quickly ascended (or descended) to extreme levels of violence.

Some readers may protest the wealth of detail provided in this book, especially in the descriptions of violence. Well, if God is in the details, the devil is in the details of violence, and those details meant a great deal to those who lived through them. In short, the "how" of violence matters but is all too easily lost in simple words freighted with many possible meanings. For example, a recent article about English Protestantism included the sentence: "the nomination of a leading Puritan to the Winwick rectory in 1624 *set off a riot* between the nominee's supporters and partisans of the [other] candidate."[11] There are many such sentences in historical writing in which causes are explained (in this case the cause of a riot), but the ensuing violent behavior is ignored. How was that riot carried out? What behavior was manifested and why? This book demonstrates how to approach such questions in a variety of circumstances of public violence.

Consider another example, this one a hypothetical sentence purporting to explain the outbreak of the American Revolution: "The combination of clashing economic interest with a developing ideological perception of essential British corruption led the American colonies to rebel." Again, the immediate question that arises is *how* did they rebel? What alternatives did they perceive? In what ways did they employ violence and why? Other historians have addressed parts of these questions, particularly in regard to the early protest riots, and at the operational and organizational level of military history. Analyses of the decision to create the Continental army, for example, are common (and necessary), as are studies of how anti–standing army prejudices influenced the militia and the Continental army. But what about military violence considered more generally, on and off the battlefield? The answer lies in understanding the way cultural notions of legitimacy permeated the practice of public violence. Understanding this process in eighteenth-century North Carolina may help provide clues to its role in other societies and other times.

Part I

Careful Riot

"Riotous Disorderly Persons"

As blustering Winds disturb the calmest Sea
And all the Waters rave and mutiny:
The Billows loudly of the Wrong complain
And make an Insurrection in the Main,
The watery troops insult the lofty Clouds
And heave themselves in huge rebellious Crowds;
Tho' the tumultuous rage our Wonder draws
The Water's not to blame, the Wind's the Cause;
. . . .
So Tyrants drive the People to Extreams
And they that still stand out, it still inflames;
But when the End's obtaind, they always shew
The *honest Reasons of the Thing they do* . . .
Anonymous poem by a North Carolinian,
Printed in the *South Carolina Gazette,* June 11, 1737[1]

On February 21, 1766, the seaside towns of Wilmington and Brunswick, North Carolina, witnessed the last of a long series of tumultuous protests against the Stamp Act. Incidents had been cropping up sporadically in the colony since late October, but February found the colonists freshly determined to prevent the execution of the act on three impounded vessels. One thousand men marched into Brunswick on February 19 and commenced "negotiations" with the three royal officials charged with controlling commerce in and out of the port. Finally, on February 21, having secured the agreement of the collector of customs and the naval officer not to enforce the act, the crowd sought out the comptroller, who was taking shelter from the crowd in Governor William Tryon's residence.[2]

Tryon turned away the initial deputation requesting the comptroller's presence, and the rioters immediately dispatched a party of 400 to 500 men to the governor's house. The majority of them drew up in a rough formation, "by order," in sight of the house. They sent forward a group of 60, from which a single man emerged to request that the comptroller come out of the house. By so doing, the emissary noted, he "would not put the people to the disagreeable necessity of entering his Excellency's house . . . [and] no injury should be offered his person." The comptroller emerged and accompanied the main body of men, who then marched into town. There the various officers, in the center of a circle of protestors, took an oath that they would not in any way support the execution of the Stamp Act. According to the local newspaper account, "the people then immediately dispersed, in order to repair to their several places of abode."[3]

This event represents but one example of the kind of controlled or "careful" riots conducted in colonial North Carolina. Riot in North Carolina, as elsewhere in British North America, was a cultural practice that adhered to certain patterns. This chapter begins with the European sources of those patterns and how they interacted with the new social and cultural conditions of colonial life. But more importantly, the question at hand is how those evolving forms of violence channeled behavior along legitimate lines (the careful riot) and created a set of expectations about public violence. When those expectations were violated, escalation ensued.

A discussion of the forms of riot in colonial North Carolina must begin in Europe.[4] The colony of North Carolina began as primarily English in ethnicity, quickly incorporating Native Americans and African slaves.[5] After about 1730, other British and European ethnic groups began to arrive in significant numbers. Each brought its own cultural preconceptions and values concerning the role of violence in society. In fact, even to speak of England as a unity is to deny the efforts of a generation of English historians who have emphasized its regional variability. In the practice of riot, however, while regional details in England could vary widely, the purposes and expectations of such practices were markedly similar. In any case, English variability bolsters the argument made here that a colonial mixture of peoples with somewhat different experiences of violence made miscommunication and misunderstanding more likely, and consequently eased the escalation of violence. From this patchwork of English and European models, and the new conditions of colonial life, emerged North Carolina's way of riot.

This chapter opens, therefore, with a brief discussion of the arrival of Europeans in North Carolina, then moves to an examination of the European practice of riot. This study focuses on the period when those groups left for America but takes hints from the periods before and after the time of greatest migration. The chapter then turns to the issue of cultural transference to colonial America as other historians have perceived it, followed by a brief look at three examples of riot in North Carolina.

Immigration to North Carolina

The initial English settlement in North Carolina came mainly as an overflow from tidewater Virginia into the Albemarle Sound region, beginning in the middle of the seventeenth century and continuing throughout the eighteenth century.[6] Other ethnic groups joined the English on the coast, notably French Huguenots and Germans from the Palatinate, but there is no question of the numerical and cultural dominance of the English (among Europeans) all along the North Carolina coast by the end of the first quarter of the eighteenth century. This dominance persisted throughout the century, with the exception of an occasional cohesive pocket of Highland Scots or Scotch-Irish in the coastal plain (see map 1).[7]

This pattern of English immigration and gradual westward expansion continued, but the dramatic population increase in the piedmont counties of North Carolina occurred through the famous migrations of Scotch-Irish, Highlanders, and Germans into that region. Starting in 1730 and

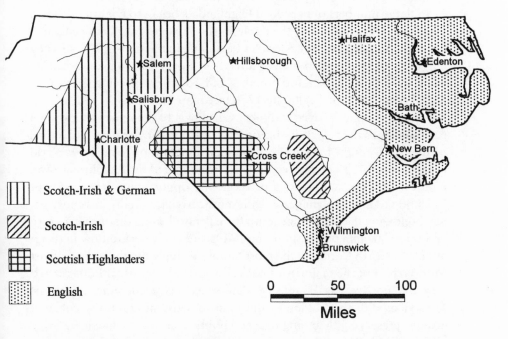

Map 1. Distribution of European ethnicities in North Carolina. (Adapted from *Colonial North Carolina in the Eighteenth Century: A Study in Historical Geography* by Harry Roy Merrens. Copyright 1964 by the University of North Carolina Press. Used by permission of the publisher.)

really getting under way after 1740, continuous streams of immigrants arrived overland from the North and transformed the piedmont counties of North Carolina. Many of these immigrants were of Scotch-Irish origin.[8] The Scotch-Irish of eighteenth-century North Carolina were descendants of Lowland Scots who had moved to northern Ireland in the seventeenth century. There they had mixed liberally with the English and probably somewhat with the Irish.[9] Early in the eighteenth century, thousands of Scotch-Irish, under economic and religious pressure in Ireland, began to depart for America. Some went directly to North Carolina, but the vast majority landed first in New England, Delaware, Pennsylvania, or Virginia.[10] The experience of the Seven Years' War in the Pennsylvania and Virginia backcountry, combined with reports of cheap land in North (and South) Carolina, impelled the move south.[11]

While the Scotch-Irish cultural legacy was complicated by the 150-year trek from Lowland Scotland to North Carolina, the colony's Highlander contingent arrived more directly. Legend holds that, following the Battle of Culloden and the suppression of the Jacobites in Highland Scotland in 1746, large numbers of pardoned Highlanders began to migrate to North Carolina. The question of their role in the Jacobite rebellion aside, it is certainly true that for three decades beginning in the mid-1730s, a steady migration of Highlanders arrived directly in North Carolina and settled in what were then Bladen and Cumberland counties, growing to an estimated population of 12,000 by 1776 (see map 1).[12]

German settlers arrived in North Carolina's backcountry following a path similar to the Scotch-Irish. Some early groups of Germans had settled on the coast, but the main wave of German immigration to the New World began around 1717 and lasted until the beginning of the Revolution. War, political turmoil, and visions of economic opportunity drove perhaps 111,000 Germans to emigrate, with most arriving initially in Pennsylvania. Following the Blue Ridge south from Pennsylvania, they began to turn up in the Carolina piedmont in the 1740s and continued to flow in thereafter.[13] In North Carolina, the most famous group were the radical pietist Moravians, but the majority of settlers were the more usual Lutherans. If they did not exactly establish bounded exclusive communities as the Moravians did, the Lutherans did tend to settle in ethnically coherent groups, preserving their language and political customs while integrating into the local economies and under local political administration.[14]

Thus North Carolina's population from 1750 to the end of the American Revolution was not only composed of an assortment of ethnicities, but it was also one that had experienced tremendous growth in recent decades, mostly in the piedmont. North Carolina's population doubled between 1730 and 1750, and then tripled again by 1770. The piedmont had expanded even more rapidly.[15] This combination of ethnic variety and explosive growth played a significant role in altering the practice of violence from what any of the various immigrants had known in Europe.

Riot in Britain

Scholars of European history have learned much about how to understand and analyze "riotous" or crowd behavior. George Rudé's pathbreaking work on early modern France and England described the crowd as a thinking organism, composed of individuals with strongly held grievances who acted with purpose and direction.[16] His insight, now seemingly so obvious, has been progressively refined as succeeding historians have looked ever more closely at the composition and motives of various "crowds." One of the principal themes that has emerged from this literature, looking particularly at the results of work on England and Scotland, is the communicative and regulatory aspect of riot.[17]

Collective popular violence in early modern Britain sought, paradoxically, *order*. Rioters sought to reestablish norms of relationships (whether economic, political, or "moral") by using various forms of violence to communicate their disapproval of a given state of affairs, and they expected that their ideal of order would be duly restored.[18] This was generally true even for violence with widely varying objectives. A charivari or shaming parade against the perceived moral violations of a neighbor was intended to correct the victim's behavior, to warn others, and to reassert the social code.[19] A riot against the exportation of grain out of an area of scarcity was intended to force authority to restrict such activity, while simultaneously forcing the immediate target to cease a particular shipment. Such a riot therefore had an immediate result as well as a projected response. Such expectations depended on at least a partial congruency in the worldview of the crowd, the audience, and the intended recipient of the message. In the case of "public" or political grievances, as opposed to moral ones, the rioters expected that at least some sector of authority would "hear" their message and react to alleviate their grievance.[20] They did not necessarily expect that the target of the riot would respond favorably; that person's perception of his interest had already led him to create the situation in the first place. The rioters did expect, however, that someone in authority would intervene. In other words, the crowd hoped that authority, considered as a group, would react in a paternalistic way.[21]

There is debate over the nature of paternalism in early modern Britain. The simplest understanding of paternalism is as a holdover from a medieval society of orders, in which the higher order of society acknowledged a moral duty to protect and care for those under its dominion. Whether such altruistic sentiments ever dominated the mind-set of the upper orders is an open question. More likely is the formulation suggested by E. P. Thompson of a "gentry-crowd reciprocity, of the 'paternalism-deference equilibrium' in which both parties to the equation were, in some degree, [through fear] the prisoners of each other. . . . [such that] the poor imposed upon the rich some of the duties and functions of paternalism just as much as deference was in turn imposed upon them."[22] Either interpretation, however, supports the notion that rioters in this period had reason to expect at least a partially benevolent upper-class response to their protests.[23] Whether rooted in true *noblesse oblige* or in fear as formulated by Thompson, an alteration in the relationship of the social orders would play a role in rewriting the use of violence.[24] In North Carolina, the changing nature of the social orders, and therefore of paternalism, fundamentally affected violence and expectations of violence.

If one accepts that popular violence had communicative and regulatory functions and expected a paternalistic response, how would that affect the forms of violent behavior? As communicators and regulators, violent actors sought (if not necessarily consciously) to present a legitimate, recognizable, indeed "not too threatening," face. This effort at constructing violence that "looked" legitimate created a relatively stable pattern of riotous behavior. To begin with, early modern riots nearly always followed an unsuccessful petition. Riots were not so much a result of a grievance as of authority's failure to resolve, or even acknowledge, the grievance once it had been articulated. Then, once acting violently, the crowd restrained that violence, particularly against persons. They selected targets appropriate to their message: enclosures, grain mills, effigies, and so on. Furthermore, the rioters' rhetoric usually acknowledged loyalty to the ultimate authority—the king or the "natural order"—preferring to blame current problems on bad royal councillors.

In addition to petitioning, targeting, and restraining, early modern rioters' behavior tended to follow from precedents that had connotations of legitimacy carried over from other contexts. Charivaris, for example, since they were a form of violence usually invoked to regulate morality, possessed a broad legitimacy across social boundaries, and so their forms were occasionally used in support of more public or political causes.[25] In a charivari, called in England variously a skimmington, a skimmety, or

riding the stang, the targets of protest had usually violated sexual or domestic codes of behavior. Common examples included wife or husband
beating, or marrying inappropriately. The target of the charivari, or a
suitably costumed effigy or neighbor proxy, was paraded through the
streets, often straddling a horse, or a board representative of a horse (the
"stang"), and usually seated backward, to the accompaniment of a ca-
cophony of "rough music."[26] One historian has pointed out "that until
late in the eighteenth century the vocabulary [of charivaris] was well
enough understood among all social classes."[27] Riots conducted in more
"political" causes, that were not charivaris *in toto*, often borrowed elements of the ritual, such as the use of effigies, parading, and mock ceremonies.

Historians of popular culture have pointed out that the forms of the
charivari were in turn modeled on yet deeper precedents. Charivaris, for
example, took their cues from English festive traditions such as harvest
ceremonies and other festivals of misrule, and from legal traditions of
shaming punishments.[28] Similarly, the frequent participation of women
(or men dressed as women) in charivaris and riots served to deflect prosecution, because, after all, women were considered to be naturally disorderly.[29] Thus the rituals of violence rested on a series of overlapping, reinforcing, legitimating precedents. The more a riot seemed to duplicate
familiar forms of behavior, the more it "looked" right, the greater its legitimacy and the less its perceived threat.

The problem remained, however, that a riot or even a charivari was still
violent, and violence could easily and quickly break out of boundaries.
Individual interest, alcohol, or passion could lead individuals to act impul-
sively in ways that their fellows might normally condemn. Equally true
was that an escalation of violence could be sparked by an excessive response by the forces of authority. If a riot was a process of negotiation, it
was a noisy, unstable one. If behavior got out of bounds, if actors of either
side exceeded the perceived "protocol of riot," they could potentially
launch what T. R. Gurr has called a frustration-aggression cycle.[30]

Gurr noted that a differential between value expectations and the
capacity to achieve those values (value capabilities) creates frustration,
which in turn can lead to a violent outburst. He worked from an assumption that the frustration proceeded from standard economic and political aspirations. He theorized that the gap between expectations and capabilities at a societal level created a state of "relative deprivation" that
could lead to revolution. In addition to Gurr's model for the outbreak of
revolution, one can add the role that the norms of violence themselves

play in perpetuating that cycle after the initial outburst. That is, violent actors have certain value expectations about the results and consequences of their violence. If those expectations are not met—if an authority, for example, has troops fire into a crowd—this further stimulates the frustration-aggression cycle independent of the original cause of the violence, dependent now on the violence itself. In formulating this understanding of frustration leading to aggression, Gurr emphasized the motivational power of anger. Anger creates action. Violence, particularly violence exceeding the protocol, violating the value expectations for violence held by the early modern population, was a great producer of anger (in addition to whatever economic or political grievances might exist). To put it in its simplest terms: illegitimate violence had a great capacity to unseat fence-sitters.

Riots in England and Scotland in the seventeenth and eighteenth centuries, therefore, generally followed certain patterns. Although less well understood than British riots, German patterns of popular unrest followed similar patterns. Eighteenth-century German resistance to aristocratic impositions in Kraichgau, later a major source of immigrants to America, used similar forms of petitioning, quiet resistance (for example, refusing to pay taxes), and finally, communally regulated acts of violence. If a difference can be detected, it might be that the German villagers exhibited a stronger sense of deference coupled with an intense localism fostered by the politically fragmented condition of Germany.[31]

Thus the riots of all of North Carolina's forebears can be said to have had a broadly similar form, with certain very distinguishable characteristics, but within which a variety of behaviors were possible according to the exact circumstances and causes of a given disturbance. One example from Scotland will suffice to show the basic pattern.[32]

On December 30, 1772, a "number of people of both Sexes" assembled in Perth, Scotland, boarded a ship lying in the harbor, and confiscated a large quantity of the barley that the ship was loading. The magistrates tried vainly to disperse the crowd, eventually falling back on the threat of military force, which led the people to go home "peaceably." At three o'clock the following morning, a number of them returned, broke into a baker's store, and carried off a considerable load of flour and bread. That same night, a group of rioters boarded another vessel and made off with some grain, which they then deposited locally "to be sold for Home Consumption." On January 1, the "mob broke out again" and attempted to release from prison two men who had been jailed as a result of the earlier riot. The magistrates assembled and brought a military party to guard the prison entrance:

> After the Riot Act was read, the Soldiers sallied out with their Guns and Bayonets twice or thrice, and drove the Mob like Sheep from their Station; but they still returning, armed with Cudgels, and pelting the Soldiers with Stones, they [the soldiers] refused to stand longer unless they were allowed to fire in their own Defence. On which the Provost allowed them to depart and delivered the Prisoners to the Mob, who went off in great Triumph, and stoned the Military, who went peaceably to their Quarters.

The crowd then broke into the house of John Donaldson, a grain merchant, caused considerable damage, and carried off the keys to his granaries. They presented the keys to the sheriff and demanded that he open the granaries and deliver the grain into Perth. Within a few days, the Perth magistrates published an advertisement encouraging the country farmers to bring what grain they could into Perth to alleviate the scarcity—specifying that it be sold in the public market.

This classic food riot encapsulates several salient characteristics of British riot forms discussed thus far. The rioters used purposeful violence against targets specific to their purpose of obtaining grain. They seized grain in order to *sell it*; they did not intend for its owners to get nothing, only that it be made available locally. They refused to acknowledge that their actions were illegal and thus contested the jailing of some of their members. In fact, in the latter stages of the incident they worked directly with the sheriff to ensure the distribution of grain. For their part, the magistrates hesitated to use force (the ready availability of military force was a relative rarity in Britain) and in the end acted to alleviate the scarcity.

Cultural Transfer

What, then, of the original problem raised at the beginning of this chapter? To what extent did British forms of riot, as cultural practice, migrate to the colonies, and how did they change once they got there? Determining the answer to that question requires a close look at violent incidents in the colonies. Those incidents, and the rhetoric surrounding them, reveal not only continuity with European usages of violence but also the impact of the new structures of life in the colonies.

Those new structures led the colonists to alter their use of violence, to improvise in response to new conditions and new needs. Unhappy people turned to old forms of protest because they were familiar and comfortable, and because the old forms carried a cachet of legitimacy that would help sway their audience, or at least not turn it against them. New problems in a new environment, however, led colonists to modify their protest reper-toire to meet immediate needs.[33] This is not to say that the various actors in question got together and articulated a conscious strategy of formulaic and familiar violence, calculated to achieve a desired response. Rather it is to say that the group, coalescing out of a coincidence of interest, already possessed a predisposition to certain kinds of behavior that arose from their past collective experience, specifically, in their experience of how power and law operated. Again, this is not to imply that the past had created a set of structures *determining* their behavior, but rather it had shaped a set of alternatives that they were likely to choose from, although always with a potential for improvisation—an improvisation shaped by the changes in material (and social) conditions created in the colonial environment.[34]

In the colonies, because of the ethnically heterogeneous population, the "collective" or aggregate had a much greater variety of experience regard-ing the relative success or failure of past violent behavior than had crowds in local communities in Europe.[35] In such circumstances, improvisation became more varied, although generally along lines reflective of such com-mon experiences as they did have. We will see, for example, how the colonial style of violent protest reflected the increased importance of mili-tary institutions in colonial society.

This work is not the first to observe that crowd behavior reflected a transfer of popular culture from Europe to the Americas. Others histori-ans have also noted the similarity between colonial crowd behavior and English practice, and a debt must be acknowledged to their work.[36] This study, however, is concerned not only with issues of cultural retention and improvisation but with the strength of those new/old forms in shaping behavior and responses to behavior.

Violence tends to produce records, and from there it often makes its way into the history books. The following three examples of riot in North Carolina are no exception. Each of them has been mentioned, if not thor-oughly discussed, by other historians, if only because they provide such gripping stories. The reader of other histories of North Carolina will par-don the repetition here, although I hope the reader will also note how the specific relevant details of violence have often been occluded in other works, to the detriment of our deeper understanding of why these people acted the way they did. As an aside, it is worth pointing out that these three examples of riots, combined with the Regulator movement covered in the following chapters, constitute virtually all of the incidents of public, collective violence in mid- to late-eighteenth-century North Carolina for which we have any records at all. Thus these case studies are more than merely exemplary.[37]

The Enfield Riots

In 1744, the Privy Council in England confirmed Earl Granville's long-standing claim, as the descendant of one of the original Lords Proprietors of Carolina, to one-eighth of both Carolinas (see map 2).[38] The area of the grant, known as the Granville District, encompassed most of the upper half of North Carolina along its border with Virginia, beginning at the Atlantic and extending indefinitely westward. The problems inherent in absentee management of such a large area fomented a series of troubles right up until the Revolution. The Enfield riot of 1759 was one such "trouble."

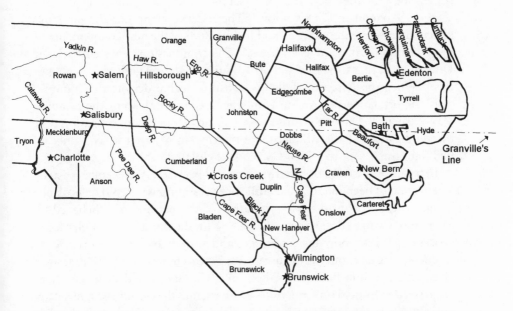

Map 2. The county boundaries in 1769. Lord Granville's line is indicated. It merges with the county boundaries beginning with Orange/Cumberland.

Granville's terms for leasing the land have been described as relatively generous; there was certainly no lack of settlers seeking to take advantage of them.[39] The problems arose not necessarily from the terms so much as from the management. Granville, who never visited his grant, worked through a pair of agents who were charged with surveying tracts, granting deeds, and collecting rents. Unfortunately, but not surprisingly, Granville's agents (and their sub-agents) were exceptionally dishonest in their dealings with the settlers. After the original agents both died in 1749, Granville appointed Francis Corbin and Thomas Child to the position. Corbin dominated the district's affairs for the next ten years, controlling or manipulating each of the series of co-agents who followed Thomas Child. Corbin's dishonesty was so flagrant that it even came to Earl Granville's attention, earning Corbin a reprimand in 1756.[40] He and his factors, however, continued their self-serving practices: double granting, excessive fee taking, and duplicitous surveying. Eventually squatters and small farmers victimized by Corbin joined forces with the more powerful individuals whom Corbin had also crossed.[41]

Matters came to a head in late 1758. At that time, a number of planters asked the colony's attorney general, Robert (Robin) Jones, to prosecute Corbin and his deputies for his corrupt practices. Jones put them off, suggesting that they petition the Assembly. They duly did so at the Assembly's November 1758 session.[42] The Assembly appointed a commission to investigate the charges, and Joshua Bodley, the new co-agent, made some efforts to alleviate grievances.[43] The commission reported back on December 22 that Corbin's land office had indeed been guilty of irregularities.[44] When the Assembly failed to censure Corbin despite the commission's report, Governor Arthur Dobbs accused him of bribing the committee chairman.[45] The one positive step resulting from the investigation was the publication of the official table of fees, an act that served only to highlight the extent to which Corbin had violated it.[46]

In terms of the rules of riot, the stage had been set. A grievance existed; a petition had been made; local authority's response was tepid or possibly bought off, and considerable sympathy for the petition was believed to exist among some of the political elite.[47] With the failure of ordinary legal processes, British popular traditions, and some have argued even legal traditions, made room for the use of riot in search of redress.[48] The arrival of co-agent Joshua Bodley in Edgecombe County provided the catalyst. He arrived in Enfield on Granville's business, and the rioters recognized an opportunity to deal with both agents at the same time. They made Bodley remain in town "upon his Parole and other Security," and during the night of January 25, 1759, a group of twenty to twenty-five men traveled to Corbin's house near Edenton.[49] There they seized him and carried him to his office in Enfield, seventy miles away.

It was no coincidence that Enfield also had been the county seat of Edgecombe County until January 1759 (by an act passed in 1758), when Halifax County was split off, taking Enfield with it.[50] Halifax was named the new county seat, but the first Halifax court was still held in Enfield. North Carolina rioters had begun to develop a tendency to situate their actions in and around the closest thing to a public center that a region of distributed settlement could boast—the county courthouse. An early example had occurred in 1730 when "a great number of people . . . [assembled in the courthouse and did] revel, drink, sing and dance stamp shout and alternately set up in the seat of Justice two mock Judges in dirission of the Admiralty," and thus succeeded in preventing the court from meeting.[51]

During the ensuing four days of Corbin's and Bodley's "captivity," the rioters extracted three statements. In the first, Corbin and Bodley posted a £2,000 bond to attend the next court session and "adjust all affairs as to paying and Accounting for all the misdemeanors of his deputies and Settle for and Refund to each person Injur'd what loss he has sustain'd by him."[52] Corbin and Bodley also signed, under duress, a list of articles setting forth guidelines for running the land office and methods of resolving future disputes. The articles included the specific demand that all the current deputies be removed.[53] Finally, the rioters had Corbin and Bodley sign a statement to "discharge, acquite [sic] all persons whatsoever from all force or violence used . . . [and] that what any persons hath done to us in order to obtain our Attendance . . . at this or any time heretofore, was only with a view to settling the Disputes between us."[54] Both men were then released.[55]

While Corbin and Bodley were no doubt considerably frightened, and the participants had demonstrated a deep commitment by marching seventy miles each way to take Corbin, the whole incident is more remarkable for its restraint. The event hardly deserves the title of "riot" at all. The protestors destroyed no property; nor did they physically harm Corbin or Bodley. Bringing Corbin to Enfield, rather than confronting him in his home, asserted the legitimate intentions of the rioters, affirming that theirs was a public dispute over the use of his office, not a private affair. It also satisfied the practical need of allowing them to demand that Corbin show them the records maintained in the Enfield office. The rioters' demand for refunds specified only the amount charged in excess of what had been established by Granville, and they generally demonstrated a willingness to work within the land office system—provided it was administered honestly. The presence of William Hurst among the crowd, a Granville County justice of the peace, further heightened the air of legality about the proceedings. This affectation of legality was confirmed by the Assembly's later accusation that the rioters had constructed a "Sham Jurisdiction."[56]

In fact, as Governor Dobbs later noted, the incident went unpursued at law until Robert Jones, the attorney general who had formerly supported the petition against Corbin, began to fear that the rioters would turn on him.[57] In May 1759, Jones informed the Council of the actions against Corbin and of threats against himself. The Council sent him to testify to the Assembly, which promptly demanded that the governor pursue measures to prosecute the offenders. The Assembly offered a £25 reward for any information leading to an arrest and characterized the incident as "Riots, Routs, Combinations, and Traterous Conspiracies."[58] The Assembly particularly condemned an apparent grave desecration that seemed to violate the norms of riot. During the period after the committee's report in December and before the kidnapping of Corbin on January 25, one of Corbin's deputies, John Haywood, died. Fearing a ruse to escape prosecution, the "rioters" had dug up Haywood's grave to confirm that he had indeed died.[59]

Governor Dobbs, while clearly believing Corbin to be guilty, nonetheless went about answering the Assembly's demands and succeeded in arresting a few of the rioters.[60] Their friends, in what was becoming another tradition of North Carolina riot, promptly broke them out of jail.[61] Corbin initiated his own effort to prosecute the rioters but was dissuaded when he realized such a trial could expose his own guilt.[62] Earl Granville for his part fired Corbin and Bodley in April 1759, citing "Divers Good Causes and Considerations . . . specially moving."[63] Governor Dobbs found the opportunity to rid himself of Corbin in January 1760. He removed Corbin from the Council for his nonattendance, his failure to apologize for said nonattendance, and his "Many prevarications and Contempts to the Council and Manifast falshoods and Endeavours to impose upon the Upper and Lower Houses of Assembly."[64]

The Assembly's response to the Enfield riot shows how the rhetoric of violence could further other political ends. There was violence, and then there was outrageous, barbarous violence, acts that exceeded all expectations. One could defame one's enemies by accusing them of unacceptable violence. Historians should read such accusations not necessarily as literal truth but as a way of understanding exactly what kinds of behavior were considered "out of bounds." Observe how the Assembly's outrage escalated to serve its own purposes. On May 18, 1759, the Assembly's resolution to prosecute used the relatively standard legal formulation cited above: "Riots, Routs, Combinations and," the somewhat more threatening, "Traterous Conspiracies."[65] But in May of the following year, the Assembly decided to use the incident in a separate struggle with Governor Dobbs and accused him of actually favoring certain leaders of the rioters with public office.[66] The rhetoric then heated up considerably. Corbin's forced bond became:

> several Mobbs, and Insurrections which for many months in Open Violation of all Law have with Impunity Assembled in great Numbers in different Counties Erected Sham Jurisdiction and restrained men of their Liberty and Broke open Goals [jails] released Malefactors dug up the Dead from the Graves and Committed other Acts of rapine and violence, but no Effectual Steps have been taken to check the Torrent of their Licentious Extravagances.[67]

The Assembly went on, in what was becoming classic colonial rhetoric, to compare the resultant internal danger to be no less than the danger of "depredations of Savages on the Frontier Settlements." These are important rhetorical changes. "Riot and Conspiracy" has become "Insurrection," with the additional evocative points about exhuming dead bodies, rapine, and comparisons to "savages"—the latter being a new colonial addition to an old set of rhetorical tools.[68] Portraying Dobbs as the friend of rioters, whose behavior was beyond the bounds, served the political ends of the assemblymen. That the Assembly could so freely portray the incident to the authorities in London in such outrageous terms, without fear of contradiction, was made possible in large part because of the now tremendous geographic distance between the original incident and the ultimate authority in London.

The Enfield riots provide an example not only of how North Carolinians used force to achieve certain ends but also how authority was expected to respond. The rioters began as petitioners. When their petition apparently failed, they carefully constructed their ensuing actions. They limited their targets and they restrained their violence while using symbols and figures of legitimacy. On the "stage" of the courthouse, presided over by a justice of the peace, they forced Corbin to post bond on a legal-seeming document.

Authority, on the other hand, found itself divided. The Assembly, swayed by Corbin, and later angry with Governor Dobbs, took a hard line against the use of violence, characterizing it as traitorous, conspiratorial, and barbarous to the point of exhuming a dead body. The governor and Earl Granville, acting in a more traditionally paternalist mode, tried to ignore the rioters and instead concentrated on the cause of their discontent, although they were ultimately unsuccessful.[69]

The Sugar Creek "War"

Another loosely connected series of incidents arose from similar motives but generated more personal violence. It began as early as 1755, finally climaxing in the miscalled Sugar Creek "War" of the spring of 1765. Henry McCulloh, Sr., residing in England, arranged to receive an enormous grant in the royal areas of North Carolina (particularly in what were then Rowan, Anson, and, later, Mecklenburg counties) provided that he settle the land.[70] He in turn had sold large portions of that land to George Selwyn (also residing in England) and to Governor Dobbs, who both labored under the same requirement to bring in colonists (see map 3).[71]

The various grantees found themselves engaged in a nearly continuous struggle with the growing wave of immigrants from Pennsylvania and Virginia. These so-called squatters were unprepared to accept that the apparently vacant land they had settled on and improved actually belonged to someone else, who expected to collect rents on the property, and who hoped to use their unsponsored arrival as credit toward the settlement requirement.[72] The as yet uncompleted boundary between North and South Carolina provided a twist to this landlord/tenant conflict; the more southerly residents played the provincial governments against each other, claiming first to be in one colony and then the other, depending on who was asking.

Resistance to the grantees' surveyors arose as early as 1755. In October of that year, the agents of Henry McCulloh, Sr., complained to the Council about the intimidation of their surveying party the previous June. Locals along the Yadkin River (in Rowan County, tract #9) had initially tried to dupe the surveyor by pointing out the wrong landmarks. When that failed, they confronted his surveying party. Fifteen men, led by Colonel George Smith, "armed with Guns, Swords, Clubs and Staves" ordered the surveyors to cease their work or they would carry them to jail and "Break their Bones."[73] The party, sufficiently frightened, complied.

The rioters' pretension to legal authority—the threat to jail the surveyors—cropped up again in the next incident in 1762.[74] On this occasion, settlers on Sugar and Reedy Creeks, land granted to Governor Dobbs

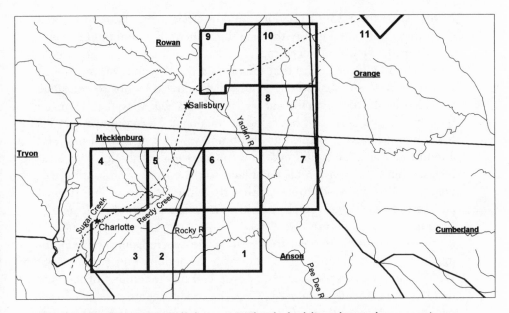

Map 3. The Selwyn/McCulloh grants. The dashed line shows the approximate route of the trading path to Virginia. County boundaries are shown as of 1769. For the time period covered here, tracts 2 and 5 belonged to Governor Dobbs, 1 and 3 to George Selwyn, and 4 and 7 to Henry McCulloh, Sr. (Tract boundaries are approximate and are based on the 1738 survey plat printed in *North Carolina Genealogical Society Journal* 4 (1978): 146, and on the map prepared by George Stevenson of the Division of Archives and History, N.C. Department of Cultural Resources, Raleigh. Further adjustments were made based on the relationship of tracts to creeklines, as noted in individual deeds.)

(tracts #2 and #5), resisted attempts to survey the area.[75] In the late spring of 1762, at least seven men "riotously contest[ed]" Dobbs's surveyors, threatening "to violently seize them and carry them to Charles Town [South Carolina]."[76] Apparently in the mid-1750s, this same group of settlers had "abused and Insulted" Sheriff Townsand of Anson County when he had tried to collect taxes. When he responded by trying to raise the *posse comitatus*, the Sugar and Reedy Creek settlement of some 150 families gathered and "beginning to behave in a riotous manner the said Sheriff in the Kings Name commanded the peace upon which they damned the King and his peace, and beat and wounded several of [the Sheriff's assistants]."[77]

Dobbs went to the frontier himself to determine what was going on. Upon his arrival in the disputed area, James Loosh, claiming to be a justice of the peace from South Carolina, and another man, claiming to be a constable, confronted him with some thirty men, of whom ten or twelve were armed. They announced that if he had come to survey, they would oppose him with force, and that they would take his companion, Sheriff Harris, to trial in Charleston. Initially, they allowed Dobbs to continue, provided he did not actually survey their lands, but they then changed their minds and surprised his camp at breakfast. Harris jumped on his horse and grabbed a pistol, but Loosh and his men restrained him and announced that they would take him to Charleston (although they later released him).[78] Dobbs, in his complaint to the governor of South Carolina, provided witnesses to swear that the settlers "have of late formed amongst themselves a Company of Militia as they pretend by Virtue of a Commission from [South Carolina]."[79]

It may be possible to measure the success of this resistance by examining the deeds issued for Dobbs's lands over the period of the riots and the succeeding two years until Dobbs's death. During the summer of the riots that Dobbs personally witnessed (1762), he and his agents were able to lay out and sell tracts to thirty-one people, at an average price of £10 10s per 100 acres in North Carolina Proclamation (N.C. proc.) money.[80] After the June 1762 confrontation with Loosh, however, with a few minor exceptions, sales in the area ceased until the spring of 1764, when Dobbs's agents surveyed and sold a large number of tracts. By the spring of 1765, they had made eighty-four sales (in addition to the first thirty-one), nearly uniformly at £10 N.C. proc. per 100 acres. Without further evidence, one cannot be certain, but it appears that the riots delayed Dobbs for two years and perhaps led him to accept a slightly lower price.[81] Whether because of Dobbs's compromise or not, there was no further conflict recorded on his lands, although significant resistance developed against other landlords.

The year 1764 saw two important events that sparked the incidents usually referred to as the Sugar Creek War. In that year, the surveyed border between the Carolinas was extended almost to the Catawba villages (south of Charlotte), making it more difficult for the southern settlers to "switch sides."[82] Equally important, the energetic Henry Eustace McCulloh took over as the agent of George Selwyn, whose lands included portions of the Sugar Creek area (tracts #1 and #3).[83] In the summer of 1764, McCulloh, anticipating resistance and hoping to simplify his task, arranged for the inhabitants to select four representatives to meet with him. McCulloh struck a deal with those representatives setting the projected rents. He planned to return in February 1765 to begin the survey.[84]

McCulloh returned in March 1765 (a month late), amidst rumors of discontent. Soon he was confronted by some 150 people assembled at Abraham Alexander's house. He later claimed they tried to terrify him into leaving, and he threatened them in return. The assemblage went away for an hour to discuss what to do and returned with an offer of rent that McCulloh found ridiculously low and insultingly offered. In a striking parallel to the prices recently paid for land in Dobbs's tracts, they initially offered by voice to pay £10 N.C. proc. per 100 acres. They then showed him a paper in which they offered to pay £10–12 N.C. proc. per 100. A letter signed by 143 people informed McCulloh that unless they got the land at a certain price they would prevent his survey. If he tried to survey anyway, "the best usage he should expect to meet with, would be to be tied Neck and heels and be carried over the Yadkin."[85]

Tying at neck and heels was a punishment used in the British military and the North Carolina militia and as such constitutes the first of several examples of how popular violence in North Carolina took cues from military traditions. The 1760 North Carolina militia law (repeated in 1764, 1768, and 1774) listed it as a punishment to be used "at discretion" for someone refusing commands during muster and was thus a punishment that did not require a court-martial to inflict. It does not appear ever to have been used as a civil punishment in England and may represent a rough and ready version of the stocks or the pillory.[86]

McCulloh was unwilling to accept this price setting, and he promised to persist with his survey. Some of the settlers followed him, and when he awoke in the morning he found two of them sitting on a fence watching him. Soon a crowd of a hundred had gathered to impede his survey. They followed him to the plantation of one of the members of the original four-man delegation.[87] When McCulloh began to work, they broke his surveying chains and compass. Thomas Polk, also one of the original four, and himself a justice of the peace, acted as spokesman for the crowd and declared that they would not allow any surveying, even on land of those who had agreed to McCulloh's terms. Polk then raised the price the settlers were willing to pay to £15 N.C. proc. McCulloh still thought the offer insulting. Polk allowed him to retire and answer their offer the next day in writing. McCulloh refused their terms.[88]

The exact terms of the disagreement over price reveal both the common problem of lack of hard currency in colonial North Carolina and the willingness of the Sugar Creek settlers to pay what they thought was a reasonable price—a price, as McCulloh put it, "they thought proper to dictate."[89] During the summer 1764 meeting, McCulloh had negotiated a price of £12 sterling per 100 acres (for good land) to as low as £5 sterling (for poor land). This was the price he claimed had been so well received in Rowan County.[90] Earlier in the spring of 1765, before this incident in Sugar Creek, he had sold a large quantity of land from his own tracts near the Rocky River at an average of £9.77 sterling.[91] The settlers during the first confrontation at Abraham Alexander's house had offered £10–£12 proclamation money. The next day, as noted above, they, through Polk, offered £15 proclamation. Since in 1765 £1 sterling was worth just over £2 proclamation, the settlers' final offer was not much lower than what McCulloh had accepted on the Rocky River.[92]

At any rate, the situation changed with the death of Governor Dobbs on March 28. He was replaced by the lieutenant-governor, William Tryon. On April 6, the new governor received a petition from John Polk, Thomas Polk's brother, on behalf of the settlers in the region, complaining of McCulloh's conduct. Tryon ordered McCulloh to cease all further attempts to survey or to dispossess the settlers until the matter could go before the Assembly.[93] Despite the order to desist, McCulloh served a writ of ejection on Polk, and his agents proceeded to try to survey a tract.[94]

On May 7, 1765, the survey party went to lay out a tract within Selwyn's grant supposed to belong to "the Widow Alexander." They were met by "several Rioters to the number of twelve or more, blacked and disguised and armed with Guns and Clubs" who "assembled in a riotous manner . . . outrageously beat and abused" the surveyors. At least one man was whipped, and another suffered a cracked skull.[95]

McCulloh knew a good piece of propaganda when he saw one. Breaking his compass and chains was one thing, particularly when that was done in conjunction with a very familiar sounding price-setting riot. Such price-fixing, for example, was quite the norm in British food riots. Actually whipping the surveyors placed the rioters on shaky ground. This is the first instance discussed thus far in which rioters whipped officials. It will not be the last. Although such practice was to become a commonplace in colonial communal violence, it was as yet an act of questionable legitimacy, particularly as perceived by newly arrived Englishmen like McCulloh and Tryon. Whipping appears to be a colonial innovation in the rituals of riot and bears explaining.

It was not unknown in England, and it was perhaps more common in Scotland, for targets of popular protest to suffer physical violence: stone throwing, beatings, clubbings, or the charivari's victim's riding the stang. I am not aware, however, of any instance in which such an individual was whipped, other than in a strictly judicial context in which it was a common form of punishment.[96] Charivari rituals took their forms from the

festive traditions of misrule combined syncretically with old penal traditions of shaming.[97] In Britain, the equally old penal tradition of whipping
may have seemed too blandly corporal—lacking the communal sense of
participating in shaming the individual. In the colonies, however, particularly the southern ones, whipping acquired new social connotations
through its frequent application to slaves and indentured servants.[98] It
retained its penal usage and thus was appropriate for a crowd asserting a
role as a kind of popular court, but it now also served to shame the victim.
Noting the frequent participation of justices of the peace in the riots discussed thus far, it is appropriate to point out that a North Carolina justice
of the peace had jurisdiction over criminal actions that could result in fines
and imprisonment and frequently inflicted corporal punishment such as
pillory whipping.[99] Whipping, therefore, was seen as a punishment meted
out at the local level.

Finally, though more tentatively, whipping was also the penalty of
choice in naval and military contexts.[100] Indeed, the South Carolina Regulators explicitly linked their use of flogging to military institutions—they
applied their vigilante justice through "courts" held by militia officers
"over the Drum Head in the Muster Field."[101] Thus whipping, in addition
to the threat to tie neck and heels, contributes to a growing impression of
the importance of military imagery in riotous behavior and its pretensions
to legitimacy. This is discussed more fully below, but for the moment consider the much higher participation ratio in military activities in the colonial environment than had been true in England. The Scotch-Irish of the
Carolina Piedmont in particular had had a long history of military or
paramilitary roles, first in Ireland and then on the Pennsylvania and Virginia frontiers.

McCulloh, therefore, duly expected to use the report of this whipping
and beating to his advantage. On May 9, he wrote to his friend Edmund
Fanning, reporting the incident. He added the inflammatory supposition
that the mob would surely have killed him had he been there; it was for
this purpose, he believed, that some of the rioters had come armed with
guns. McCulloh asked Fanning to pass this information on to the governor and the Council, who would shortly be considering Polk's petition.[102]
Six days later, the petition came before the Council along with McCulloh's
memorial (written on April 25, before the latest riot) and affidavits from
some of the surveyors. Tryon and the Council set Polk's petition aside.
Two days later, they decided to investigate the rioters instead. They offered
a pardon to any two who would come forward to act as informants.[103]

Despite this shift by the governor, the conclusion of the episode suggests that the violence, sufficiently circumscribed as it was, had worked. McCulloh's report of the riot at the Widow Alexander's might have led the government to refuse to acknowledge the settlers' petition and even to order a prosecution, but what then happened in Sugar Creek? McCulloh and his surveyors brought Polk and forty-seven others up on charges of riot in September 1765. The accused posted bond, and their cases were continued. Then in March 1766, the cases were dismissed.[104] So much for actual prosecution.

What about the land itself? There were two issues: whether to accept Selwyn's title at all, and, if so, at what price. Apparently many of the settlers in the region avoided having to acknowledge Selwyn's title at all. During the spring of the riots (1765), McCulloh's agents were able to survey and sell to only six individuals, most of whom were his allies.[105] In November 1766, the commission appointed way back in 1762 to investigate whether McCulloh had settled enough people on his tract #4 finally reported that he had not, and McCulloh acknowledged that the remaining lands must be surrendered back to the crown.[106] Note that only those settlers who had been surveyed and listed counted as "inhabitants" in determining whether the terms of the grant had been met. A "squatter" who successfully prevented survey did not count. Tryon, realizing perhaps for the first time the power of this provision to make the problem go away, promptly ordered a similar head count to be carried out for Selwyn's tracts #1 and #3, the very ones that had so recently proved troublesome. The results of that survey were reported, much more promptly this time, in April 1767. Again there were not enough legal inhabitants and the grants were surrendered.[107] Interestingly, the magistrate who validated the report was none other than Thomas Polk.[108]

In the years between the riot of 1765 and the final surrender of tracts #1 and #3 in April 1767, McCulloh had assiduously asserted title to as much land as possible, although, as with Dobbs, the riots delayed him.[109] In January 1767, he succeeded in certifying title to the land of twenty-six of the forty-eight men whom he had brought before the Salisbury court for riot, in addition to surveying in a very large number of other tracts.[110] The average price for those sales was £9.4 sterling, equivalent in 1767 to £12–£17 proclamation—equal to or marginally higher than what the rioters had offered McCulloh back in 1765.[111] At the same time, on his own lands where he had not experienced any resistance, McCulloh was selling at an average of £19.2 N.C. proc.[112] Admittedly, McCulloh arranged to gain control of a significant number of the Selwyn tracts by providing the funds via a mortgage for those settlers without cash, and those terms were particularly favorable to McCulloh. The "visible" price nonetheless reflected what Kars called a "tenuous balance of power," in much the same way that British food rioters set bread prices.[113]

In the aggregate, therefore, rioters who had petitioned, who had selected their targets, who counted officials among their members, and whose violence did not exceed certain bounds, achieved a particular kind of response. That response can be considered two-handed—what will be called here "authoritarian paternalism." With one hand Tryon deplored the violence and set up the outlines of a potential prosecution of the rioters. With the other hand he acted to remove the problem. This is not to say that Tryon, or authority generally, acted from a purely moral paternalism (à la the old *noblesse oblige*), though there was surely some of that. It was rather, as E. P. Thompson recognized in another context, a utilitarian response to a situation that those in power could not entirely control.[114] A later royal governor of North Carolina, Josiah Martin, explicitly acknowledged the government's lack of absolute control when he observed that:

> It is a principle held long and universally that it is impossible for the people in general to pay the Arrears of Rent due to my Lord Granville and that if attempt should be made to enforce payment thereof at Law, it would excite Rebellion among the Tenants.[115]

The Stamp Act

The final case study is easily the best known and also the most recognizably English in the behavior of the rioters. Most of the Stamp Act protests took place in the coastal towns, primarily Wilmington and Brunswick. It was of course the coastal towns whose interests were most affected by the Stamp Act because of its impact on trade, but also because only there, under the nose of the governor and British Navy captains, was it likely to be enforced. These areas retained a predominantly English population, accounting, no doubt, for the exceptionally traditional form of the protests there. Even these riots, however, took on a distinctively colonial flavor, particularly in their military air.

The broad outlines of the Stamp Act and the subsequent colonial protests are familiar to most historians of early America.[116] While most work has focused on Boston or New York, the details of the protest violence in North Carolina also demonstrate the degree of continuity in forms of violence between England and even this more isolated, southern region.[117]

In an effort to help recoup the costs of the vastly expensive Seven Years' War, Parliament passed the Stamp Act on March 22, 1765. The act laid a tax on a wide variety of activities that required paper, either as the object itself (newspapers, playing cards) or as documentation of something else (law licenses, legal documents, commercial papers). In the colonists' eyes, one of the most disturbing provisions in the law was that violators could be tried in the Vice-Admiralty Courts in Halifax, Nova Scotia, which had no jury.[118] During the summer before the law was to take effect on November 1, the colonists poured out a torrent of petitions and pamphlets decrying the act.[119] When Governor Tryon asked Speaker of the House John Ashe how North Carolina would react to the Stamp Act, Ashe replied that the act "would be resisted to blood and death." Tryon promptly prorogued the Assembly on May 18, 1765.[120]

While the first colonial riot took place in Boston on August 14, North Carolina remained quiet through the summer and into the fall. As the deadline for the law to go into effect approached, however, Parliament showed no signs of revoking it. Spurred on by word of resistance in New England, North Carolinians finally acted. On Saturday, October 19, some 500 people assembled in Wilmington, hanged the effigy of "a certain Honourable Gentleman," and then burned it in a bonfire.[121] They then went from house to house, brought out men to the fire, and "insisted upon their drinking, Liberty, Property, and no Stamp-Duty." The protestors continued until midnight and "then dispersed without doing any mischief."[122] A similar incident occurred again in Wilmington on October 31, although this time the effigy was of "liberty," which the mob prepared to bury. Then, claiming to find signs of life in it, the protestors returned to the town square and enthroned it in a chair. During the ensuing celebration, "not the least Injury was offered to any Person."[123]

The law took effect on November 1, but there were as yet no stamps available in the colony, nor had a stamp distributor been appointed. This deprived North Carolinians of the official who had been targeted by riots in the northern colonies. Despite the lack of stamps, Governor Tryon ordered the suspension of all activities, notably some forms of commerce, that required them. At least initially, however, he appears to have done little to enforce such a suspension. The colonists, lacking a stamp distributor on whom to focus their anger, found other targets. A militia officer who had publicly claimed that he would enforce the act had his house broken into and burglarized. A superior court judge in New Bern was dragged from his bed by a band of "Sons of Liberty" and required to take an oath that he would resume the business of the court without the necessary stamps.[124]

Meanwhile, one William Houston, apparently without his knowledge, had been appointed the stampmaster for the colony.[125] On Saturday, November 16, he ventured into Wilmington on personal business and immediately became the subject of a riot. He recalled that the townspeople "assembled about me & demanded a Categorical Answer whether I intended to put the Act . . . in force. The Town Bell was rung Drums beating, Colours flying and [a] great concourse of People [were] gathered together."[126] The *North Carolina Gazette* reported a "concourse" of 300 or 400 people and also noted the beating drums and flying colors.[127] Houston succumbed to the crowd, upon which they carried him to the courthouse and he signed a letter of resignation. The rioters paraded him in a chair around the courthouse, and then to his lodging, where they cheered and toasted him. The rioters also made a point of proceeding to the *Gazette*'s printer and gaining his assurance that he would continue to print the paper without stamps.[128] Another bonfire was lit that night, but the newspaper emphasized that "not the least Insult [was] offered to any Person." In New Bern and Cross Creek, where people were as yet unaware of Houston's resignation, an effigy of him was "try'd, condemn'd, hang'd, and burn'd."[129]

This pattern of rioting is familiar, as are the traditions behind it. They were certainly festive: parades, bonfires, toasts, and all on a market day. The rioters also pretended to legal forms, not only by trying and condemning effigies of unpopular figures but by centering activities on oath taking, even requiring that the oath be taken at the courthouse. The rioters were not threatening the social order; they wanted to maintain the status quo on their own terms. Recall the New Bern judge required to continue with the business of the court. To these forms, which lent the occasion an aura of legitimacy, the colonists added military overtones in the use of the militia's drums and colors, and in the events that followed, the outright participation of the assembled militia.

On November 18, Tryon hosted a banquet with some fifty invited local leaders. He tried to persuade them to work to prevent any such incidents of violence as had been seen in the other colonies. Tryon thus carefully avoided labeling past local incidents as violent.[130] In a spirit of compromise, he acknowledged the practical difficulties of the Stamp Act's requirement for payment in pounds sterling, a problem he thought would surely lead to its repeal.[131] He made the issue of local violence explicit, however, when he promised to represent the specie problem to London "unless his endeavours were frustrated by the conduct of the people." His guests retired from the room to consider their answer. They returned a written response that praised the governor, toasted the health of the king, but refused to acknowledge the legitimacy of the act. They did promise to "avoid and prevent, as far as our Influence extends, any Insult or Injury to any of the officers of the Crown," but they protested their general powerlessness over the public.

The stamps finally arrived on November 28, 1765, on board the *Diligence* under the command of Captain Phipps. When Phipps brought his ship into port at Brunswick, he found a large body of armed men lining the shore and filling the streets (see map 4). Hugh Waddell and John Ashe, colonels of the Brunswick and New Hanover militias, alerted to the approach of the *Diligence,* had mustered their militia and marched into Brunswick. They warned Phipps that they would fire on anyone trying to bring stamps ashore. The militia then seized one of the *Diligence*'s boats and mounted it on a cart for a procession to Wilmington followed by an "illumination" of the town.[132] The stamps remained aboard ship in Brunswick harbor.[133]

The stalemate continued peacefully until the occasion of Governor Tryon's official inauguration in Wilmington on December 20, 1765. The event, and the free food and alcohol sure to be offered, attracted a large audience, including the 2,000 militia under arms, to formally receive the governor as he was rowed in a barge upriver from Brunswick.[134] The crowd greeted Tryon with great ceremony and good humor, but the latter began to evaporate when Tryon mentioned the Stamp Act and asked his audience to receive the stamps. The discontent this comment created was further aggravated when Captain Phipps of the *Diligence* chose that moment to cling to an obscure naval custom and object to a nearby ship's flying the Irish national flag. Phipps ordered his men to seize the flag, which "so exasperated not only the sailors but the Townsmen and Militia" that they determined to seize it back.[135] The events that followed show an exceedingly thoughtful and communicative "crowd." They seized the ship's boat, which had accompanied the governor's barge, and hauled it to the courthouse. They were about to set fire to it, when some of the crowd proposed to exchange it for the flag seized by Captain Phipps. A fifteen-minute truce produced the desired compromise. The boat, spared from firing, became the object of a parade around the town and the platform from which they insulted Captain Phipps in his lodgings. Tryon tried to

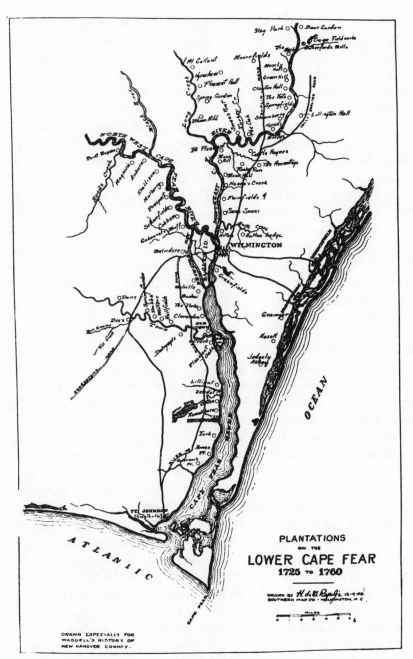

Map 4. The Cape Fear River, Wilmington, Brunswick, and Fort Johnston.
(From Sprunt, *Chronicles of the Cape Fear,* facing p. 59).

quiet the crowd from his window but succeeded only in aggravating them further, whereupon they returned the boat to the water and collected around the roasted ox and the barrels of punch prepared by Tryon for the inauguration. Instead of partaking, they stove in the barrels, allowed the punch to run in the street, pilloried the ox, and rather pointedly gave the carcass over to the slaves.[136] In a slave society, this last measure was an act guaranteed to constitute a significant insult. In fact, Samuel Johnston, an observer, noted that it was this last act that most affronted the governor's vanity; Johnston supposed that it would lead Tryon to establish the colonial capital in New Bern rather than Wilmington.[137]

Tryon's continued refusal to allow business to proceed without stamps ensured that the issue remained alive in North Carolina. In mid-January 1766, Captain Jacob Lobb of another navy vessel, the *Viper,* seized two arriving merchant ships, the *Dobbs* and the *Patience,* for failing to have their clearances on stamped paper.[138] He delivered the papers of the two ships to the customs collector, William Dry, who then asked Attorney General Robert Jones to rule on the question. His ruling, dated February 3, did not become public until February 15.[139] Jones determined that not only were the ships (plus a third, the *Ruby,* which had been seized in the meantime) in violation of the law, but the only place they could be tried was in distant Halifax, Nova Scotia.

Jones's ruling precipitated the climax of the Stamp Act resistance in North Carolina. Dry, the customs collector, was warned by a letter "from the principal inhabitants" on February 15 not to allow the ships, or their papers, to leave the harbor to be taken to Halifax. The letter warned that otherwise the dissatisfied people of the country might "come down in a body."[140] Dry tried to reassure the town that he had no intention of allowing the ships to be taken, and he reminded the people that if he were forced to leave office, his replacement might be more strict.[141]

His reassurances failed. On February 18, some of the inhabitants associated themselves as Sons of Liberty to prevent further enforcement of the Stamp Act. In their oath of association they contended, as traditional British protestors were wont to do, that they "detest[ed] Rebellion" and held "all Loyalty to Our most Gracious Sovereign."[142] It was standard practice dating all the way back to the medieval peasant rebellions to assert loyalty to the king, and to blame his ministers for whatever conditions were afflicting the populace. Such assertions of loyalty were not necessarily disingenuous, but they were certainly formulaic, part of the forms of protest designed to establish legitimacy.[143] Historians of the American Revolution rightly consider it a significant moment when Americans began to recognize the complicity of George III, and to implicate him as one of their enemies.[144]

The next day, approximately 1,000 people marched into Brunswick. They dispatched a letter and a "guard" to Tryon's house: the letter to inform him of their intentions, the guard to "protect" the governor from insult.[145] They then seized Dry and demanded the papers belonging to the impounded vessels. Dry refused to surrender them, so they, "as many as could get in," entered into his house, broke open his desk and took the papers.[146] Tryon wrote to Captain Lobb that night and asked him to assist the garrison at Fort Johnston as necessary and to "repel force with force" if the fort or its stores should be threatened.[147]

On February 20, the leaders of the rioters met the naval commander, Lobb, and the collector, Dry, who agreed to cease restrictions on trade.[148] Lobb, in a spirit of compromise, immediately released the *Ruby* and the *Patience*.[149] On February 21, perhaps determining that those two gentlemen's agreement was insufficient, the crowd sought them out again, and also the comptroller of the customs, to have them publicly swear not to enforce the act. The first two men were quickly secured, but the comptroller, after some delay, was discovered to be at Governor Tryon's house. The crowd sent a representative demanding the presence of the comptroller. Tryon informed the representative that the comptroller was "employed . . . on despatches" and that anyone wanting to see him should come to the governor's house.[150]

Tryon may have hoped to end the conflict in this way, by confronting the crowd with a choice between backing down or definitively stepping over a certain invisible boundary by breaking into the house of the royal governor. Tryon, during an earlier confrontation with his "guard," had also played with those boundaries. On February 19, when the crowd was looking for Captain Lobb at Tryon's house, he denied that Lobb was there, and when asked to give his word that Lobb was not there, he refused and: "I said they might break open my Locks & force my Doors. This they declared they had no Intention of doing." Lobb was then discovered to be elsewhere.[151] In this case, the rioters responded to Tryon's implicit challenge by sending a large body of men to the governor's residence to again demand the comptroller.[152] In the ensuing confrontation, all sides placed enormous weight on the maintenance of decorum and the adherence to certain limits. Witness the *North Carolina Gazette*'s account of the incident and its emphasis on order:

A party was then immediately despatched to fetch him [the comptroller], and marched directly to the Governour's. They halted near the house, by order; and a Gentleman was once more sent to the Comptroller, to desire he would not put the people to the disagreeable necessity of entering his Excellency's house, with a promise that if he would come out no injury should be offered his person.[153]

The comptroller, after resigning his office, came out.[154] The main body then marched to the center of town, formed a large circle around the comptroller, the naval commander, the collector, and a variety of clerks of the court and lawyers, whereupon all the officials swore that they would not enforce the Stamp Act in any way. As the *Gazette* went on to exclaim:

It is well worthy of observation that few instances can be produced of such a number of men being together so long, and behaving so well; not the least noise or disturbance, nor any person seen disguised with liquor . . . neither was there an injury offered to any person, but the whole affair conducted with decency and spirit, worthy the imitation of all the Sons of Liberty throughout the continent.[155]

A few days later, on February 26, Tryon issued a proclamation ordering the civil and military officers of the province to suppress all such illegal proceedings, conveniently ignoring the fact that most of them had themselves participated in the riots.[156] He did not call for any prosecutions, realizing the futility of such an attempt, and in fact allowed commerce again to proceed unhindered.[157] The issue dissolved on March 18, 1766, when Parliament repealed the Stamp Act.

At first glance, one could explain the restraint in the North Carolina Stamp Act riots by pointing to the failure of any forces of authority to respond decisively. Lack of a significant peace-keeping bureaucracy, and the widespread collusion of such agents of authority as did exist, prevented an escalatory cycle of violence.[158] Such an explanation is correct but does not go far enough. The very fact of restraint on the part of the rioters precluded either the authorities or the undecided from being pushed too far. The rules of violence were not clearly broken, and in that situation the rioters were able to maintain their aura of virtue and legitimacy; recall the *Gazette's* description of the event as conducted with "decency and spirit, worthy the imitation." The Stamp Act riots, confined to a small locale (the Wilmington-Brunswick nexus along fifteen miles of the Cape Fear) and clearly supported by a broad cross section of society, had a clarity of purpose and legitimacy of form that neither stepped over the line nor was muddled by rumor.

These three examples begin to suggest the norms of riot in colonial North Carolina. In all of them the rioters restrained violence, with respect to both its intensity and its target. They preceded violence (or threats of violence) with petitions to authority, and during the riots they made pretensions to legality. As part of this latter element, the county courthouse had emerged as a focal point for colonial riot. In each riot there was significant participation, if not leadership, by individuals from the political elite. While it is possible that these men hoped to use crowd action to achieve their own political/financial ends, their control of the crowd could hardly be absolute.[159] The crowd would go only as far as their sense of the norms allowed, although at the same time they used the presence of members of the upper orders as further evidence of the legitimacy of their cause.[160]

Also apparent in these examples was the willingness of authority, at one level or another, to give in or compromise to alleviate the grievance and prevent future violence. North Carolina officialdom still heeded some of the old rules of paternalism, aspiring to an "ideal of corporate communalism."[161] They set regulations to control the price and quality of bread, arranged for free distribution to the poor, and restricted the export of grain in times of potential dearth.[162] But, in general, North Carolina's brand of paternalism was probably more utilitarian than altruistic.[163] The elite recognized the necessity of acceding to public demand as much as or more than they admitted moral responsibility for the public welfare. From either motivation, the result was the same; authority responded to legitimate violence in a manner calculated to alleviate the initial grievance. Violence still worked as communication. These three riots, therefore, continued the precedent extant in Britain that controlled, communicative violence could produce favorable results.[164] In North Carolina, however, even utilitarian paternalism began to erode under the pressure of changing social conditions, a subject explored in the next chapter.

Enfield, Sugar Creek, and the Stamp Act riots have also provided evidence for emergent unique characteristics of southern colonial riot. There is, for example, a surprising lack of women in the records of these riots. There is no record or mention of a woman acting violently in any of these incidents or in the Regulator movement. This "lack" of evidence gains weight when one considers the extremely visible role women played in European riots and in some food riots in the northern colonies during the Revolution. Virtually any discussion of riot in England, Scotland, or

France will immediately turn up a variety of women occupying prominent roles.[165] Thus, in the case of riot, invisibility in the records does not merely imply that no one bothered to mention it.

How can this be explained? Although one historian has posited that the "typical" American crowd was dominated by men, historians of women in the colonial South have not explicitly addressed this issue. It may be that the prominent role of food riots in Europe highlights the role of women, and to be sure women turn up frequently in American food riots. Women had a natural authority over such issues as prices and groceries: "no one seems to have argued that women overstepped their bounds when they challenged hoarding merchants."[166] European enclosure and taxation riots that also featured women, however, might be said to roughly correspond to the surveying and customs riots of America, which often did not.

It should be admitted that all of this North Carolina "negative evidence" comes from somewhat far along in the eighteenth century, and it is during this period that some historians have pointed to a shift in the public role of women. Although women had been active in Bacon's Rebellion in seventeenth-century Virginia, Julia Spruill thought that it was surprising, and she argued that southern women were more likely to petition than northern women.[167] Even in their petitions, however, they tended to apologize for acting outside their role as women. Historians of colonial women have similarly documented the diminishing role they played in the political process, and a parallel sense of their being limited by strong notions of "appropriate" female behavior.[168] Specific to North Carolina, it has been noted that after about 1730, "women's participation in conventional male activities declined."[169] It is also possible that this may be yet another manifestation of the increasingly military character of colonial violence—while women certainly had a role in military environments, it was not normally considered to include violent participation.

The military qualities of North Carolina's riots are undeniable. We have seen, for example, how certain military punishments, such as being tied neck and heels, and whipping, were transferred to circumstances of riot. Additionally, the embodied militia played an active role in the Stamp Act riots, and even where they were not officially mustered, their visible instruments of colors and drums were present.[170] A study of urban riots in seventeenth-century France pointed to the local militias as one of three groupings around which protestors organized themselves. The other two were neighborhood solidarities and town guilds.[171] In North Carolina, not only were the latter two absent or significantly weaker, but the militia had come to play a much stronger role in colonial society than it had in Europe. Participation in the militia was more universal among white men than in Europe, in part because of its necessity against the real threat of Indian or Franco-Spanish attack. As we have seen, rioters often assumed a mantle of legitimacy through pretensions to judicial authority, and for many colonists (especially in the southern backcountry) the structures of authority found in the militia may have been the most familiar, and therefore the most amenable to symbolic reuse. Furthermore, militia musters had become festive occasions involving much drinking and carousing. They were, in fact, one of the few occasions on which large numbers of southern colonial men could be found together in one place.[172] The use of military imagery partly may reflect, therefore, the older tradition of festive symbols in riot.

All of these trends reappeared during the Regulator movement. But the violence of the Regulators occurred in circumstances that lacked the apparent clarity of these first three examples. That lack of clarity led to the radicalization of both sides, hardened by acts of violence that were perceived to have been out of bounds.

2

"To Fight the Air"

The Careful Riots of the Regulators

Mobs and Riots (that is where a number rise without Arms and only murmuring) are treated generally with Lenity as to the multitude tho' where the Offence is against Government . . . ringleaders are to suffer death without the King's pardon. But where they take up Arms to remove a Grievance or to alter the form of Movement [government] it is Treason.
Ralph McNair to Hermon Husband[1]

[Some of the other Regulators believed that since] the Governor Chose the Sword, that they were at Liberty to Defend themselves; . . . it was at length agreed . . . [that] every Man to be left at his Liberty to go to the Court as well armed or not as he Pleased; but not to use them nor offer the Least Insult, unless an Attempt was made to Massacre us; and that if they could not . . . come to an Agreement in Peace, to return home, and leave the Governor to fight the Air.
Hermon Husband[2]

On May 16, 1771, along Alamance Creek in the backcountry of North Carolina, 1,000 men of the North Carolina militia led by the royal governor confronted about twice that many of their fellow citizens, self-described "Regulators," across an open field. For almost four years the Regulators, mostly small farmers from the western counties, had petitioned, protested, rioted, and even gathered in arms, all in an attempt to bring to heel, that is to "regulate," the activities of an undeniably corrupt local officialdom. Repeated failure to reach an agreement on reform and escalating tensions over the role of violence had eventually led the governor to raise the militia, and the Regulators to mobilize in response. A series of battlefield parleys between the two sides failed to resolve matters, and finally the governor ordered the militia to advance and fire. The men advanced but hesitated at pulling the trigger. According to legend, the infuriated governor rose up in his stirrups and yelled, "fire, fire on them or on me."[3] The militia let loose, and after a two-hour battle the Regulators and their movement were crushed.

The history of the Regulation provides several examples of the "careful riot" explored in the previous chapter, but in this case the movement ended in battle. The Enfield riot, Sugar Creek, and the Stamp Act were relatively short-lived; surviving accounts are sketchy. The Regulation, however, taking its roots in a petitioning association of 1768 (if not from the Enfield riots themselves), and dominating the records for the next three years, provides a rich picture of cultural values in the practice of public violence. North Carolinians did not necessarily perceive violence as the consequence of a social breakdown. Rather, in the British tradition, they used violence as an expression of their social order and as a tool of communication. The Regulators expected that their actions would provoke a desirable response from the colonial government, and they conducted their violence not only in accord with their values but with the expectations of their audience in mind.

But the importance of the Regulator movement in illuminating values of violence does not stop there.[4] Collective violence is an unruly animal, and once unleashed it is difficult to control. Individual interest, passions, and accident all strive against the communal value of directed violence, and the particular social structure of North Carolina made it easier for the "message" of the riot to get lost in the turmoil. The Regulators' careful riot got out of control. Eventually they found themselves in a place they neither expected nor sought: across a battlefield from the muskets and artillery of a militia of their fellow citizens.

Perspectives and Causes

The quest to understand the causes of the Regulator movement has produced a number of different explanations.[5] While some have seen the Regulators as a kind of grassroots version of a growing American desire to separate from the British Empire,[6] others have denied any broadly based interpretation of the Regulation, preferring instead to label it an isolated local incident.[7] One of the earliest authoritative interpretations saw the Regulators reacting to the political domination of the tidewater over their own increasingly populous but politically hamstrung backcountry.[8] In contrast, as part of a growing historical interest in eighteenth-century social conflict, progressive historians have described the Regulator movement as rooted in class antagonisms. This thesis gained powerful support from the work of Michael Kay and Lorin Lee Cary.[9] In tracing the names and relative wealth of the Regulators and their opponents, Kay and Cary found that the majority of Regulators occupied the lower end of the socio-economic scale, while their opponents were the wealthiest men of the region.[10] They therefore posited that the Regulators' rhetoric and demands originated in their conscious perception of class differentiation.

Kay and Cary convinced many that the Regulator struggle was not about east-west sectional politics, but other historians have worried about or tinkered with their class analysis. James Whittenburg downplayed class conflict by pointing out the active leadership and participation of a number of wealthy planters, but he also acknowledged that the movement became increasingly radical and populist in its demands. Whittenburg located the source of the conflict in the clash of interests between planters and a newly arriving class of merchants, lawyers, and officials.[11]

Alternatively, Roger Ekirch has discounted class altogether, finding not an oppressed group of poor farmers but rather a vigorous and ideologically informed group of farmers frustrated by economic difficulties and particularly by corrupt officials. Ekirch's emphasis on ideology is important because he specifically showed the Regulators as proponents of country Whig thought rooted in English notions of liberty. In this interpretation the Regulators remained supportive of the overall system of government but were deeply outraged at individual corruption that they feared was undermining their "ancient rights."[12] In general, collective participation in violence against authority by a political underclass required some common ideology on which to rest. For British riots, E. P. Thompson and others have pointed to a popular culture with its own notions of ancient rights and of socially regulated economic interaction, which Thompson called the "moral economy."[13] In one sense, the brand of country Whig thought that Ekirch attributes to the Regulators was simply a more sophisticated and intellectualized version of that ideology—it too was grounded in the notion of ancient rights inviolable even by the king.

Richard Maxwell Brown has proposed yet another foundational ideology. He argued that the eighteenth-century backcountry rebellions, including the North Carolina Regulation, were founded on an ideology of the "homestead ethic," which he found uniquely American and common to the whole North American backcountry.[14] In addition to such more or less political ideologies, other historians have stressed the power of religion in defining the mental outlook of colonial Americans, and its consequent importance in providing an ideological framework for protest and in dividing up sides.[15]

These interpretations have all contributed to a fuller understanding of the causes of the Regulation. They do not, however, suffice to explain how the movement evolved over its four-year history. Whatever the initial motivation to protest, the course of the Regulation was in many ways defined by the question of the function of violence and force in society. The Regulators and their enemies possessed a set of values and expectations about the form and function of violence, and those values had dramatic consequences on behavior. Of course, violence had no absolute rules; its boundaries and legitimacy were constantly under negotiation. Indeed, the course of the Regulation movement reveals how issues such as class, economic change, and sectional division played a role in that negotiation over the boundaries and forms of violence.

The Beginning of the Regulation

The Regulator movement seen through the lens of violence demands a consideration of the nature of escalation. Historians focusing exclusively on the original causes of the movement frequently support their case with the words or deeds of various participants pulled from any point in the drama. A chronologically ordered discussion, with the rules of violence in the forefront, reveals much more about how violence (or the threat of it) engendered particular responses, and how there were both multiple types of violence and types of responses.[16] The course of the movement was governed by individuals making choices, and more often than not their decisions were made in response to issues of violence. Violence often escalates in retaliatory cycles. This is particularly true when confusion exists over the nature of the norms of violence.

Since colonial rioters always began as petitioners, the story of the Regulators begins before the violence began; specifically, it begins with the opening rounds of rhetoric. The Regulators' initial grievance was the corruption of their local officials. There had been a long history of complaints about the peculation and extortionate practices of lawyers, clerks, sheriffs, and judges, some of which were apparent in the Enfield riots. For the history of the Regulators, however, it will suffice to begin with a statement by George Sims to the "people of Granville County."[17]

Sims delivered his address to the people assembled in the courthouse for the Granville County Court session in 1765. In it he belabored the abuses they had suffered from corrupt local officials, attempted to set an agenda for reform, and in doing so revealed a set of values regarding decisions about violence. Sims first placed himself squarely in the English tradition by asserting "ancient liberties and privileges" and avowing allegiance to the king and the excellent constitution of England.[18] Then, turning to the subject at hand, he noted that if the abuses against them were sanctioned by law, "it would be enough to make us turn rebels," but since they all knew that their officials actually were acting illegally, then they should seek peaceful redress within the system. He went on to recommend that they proceed with all caution, that they be "careful to keep sober" and do "nothing rashly." They must avoid "appear[ing] as a faction endeavouring to subvert the laws, and overturn our system of government." But he concluded with a warning. "Let us behave ourselves with circumspection to the Worshipful Court . . . [and] reverence their authority both sacred, and inviolable, except they interpose, and then Gentlemen, the toughest will hold out the longest."[19]

Apparently Sims's efforts had little effect in Granville County. Accused by those same officials, Sims was taken to court for libel, and the case remained pending through 1770.[20] His sober demand for reform was taken up by Hermon Husband, who organized the Sandy Creek Association in Orange County in the summer of 1766. The association set itself the moderate goal of arranging a meeting with local officials to discuss their grievances. Of particular concern to the association was the conduct of Edmund Fanning, then the register of deeds, judge of the superior court, and colonel of the militia in Orange County. The Sandy Creek Associators published a series of petitions, and a meeting between a committee of petitioners and the county officials was agreed for October 1766. Then, on the scheduled day, Fanning declined to appear, sending word that he disapproved of certain words in the petition and of the location of the meeting. In general, he considered the association an "Insurrection."[21]

As in the Enfield case, the label of insurrection was a serious rhetorical threat. When combined with Fanning's instigating the sheriff and his minions to harass the committee, it led the Sandy Creek Association to dissolve.[22] Their grievances, however, remained, and the evidence mounted that their officials were demanding illegally high fees. The final insult was the news of a new tax to finance an official residence (quickly labeled a "palace") for the governor.[23] Thereupon, a new, more radical association formed, soon to be known as the Regulators.

The new organization advertised in January and March of 1768 that its members would refuse to pay their taxes until such time as they were "satisfied they are agreeable to Law."[24] Matters came to a head when Sheriff Hawkins seized a mare in lieu of taxes. News of the seizure, and an accompanying sense of outrage, spread through the county so quickly that a crowd of 60 to 100 angry protestors overtook the sheriff before he could return to Hillsborough with the mare. The details of what followed reveal the strong influence of British traditions of violence.

The Regulators, who later described themselves as having been armed with "Clubs, Staves &c and cloven Musquets," seized the sheriff, tied him up, and carried him into Hillsborough.[25] The sources do not say if the sheriff entered Hillsborough riding backward on the mare, but the rest of the episode had all the trappings of a traditional English "skimming-ton."[26] Certainly the Regulators "knew the rules" of such an activity. They admitted that firearms were present but claimed they were "cloven" (dys-functional). That assertion flies in the face of their later admission that some "heated unruly spirits" had fired into the roof and upper windows of Fanning's house (who was away at the time). The Regulators were careful to ground that remark, however, with the explanation that someone in the house had emerged and threatened them with pistols, and only then were shots fired into the building.[27] Even one of their enemies estimated that only "two or three bullets" had gone into Fanning's house.[28]

The parade of the bound sheriff, the selection of an appropriate house to damage, the relatively light damage to that house, and the "ill treat-ment" of sundry in town all followed English traditions of restrained dis-order. By using elements of the skimmington, the Regulators lent an aura of legitimacy to their behavior.[29] The sheriff had, in their eyes, acted ille-gally; therefore, they were punishing him in the shaming ritual of the skim-mington.[30]

In addition to their actions, it is important to note both what the Regu-lators said and what they did *not* do. The Regulators abstained from cer-tain courses of action, both in this and in later incidents. Their numbers in relation to the tiny population of Hillsborough gave them the means to destroy whatever they chose at any time. Indiscriminate violence, how-ever, would not have served their ends. Furthermore, their actions were framed by a traditional rhetoric of protest, in which they admitted the right and necessity of the government to tax, swore loyalty to King George, and appealed to their "Ancient rights."[31] The Regulators catered to the presumed expectations of their audience, whether for, against, or undecided about them. By carefully selecting the targets for damage and then limiting the extent of the damage (the "two or three shots" into Fanning's roof and windows), the Regulators again sought legitimacy in the eyes of that audience.[32] Their violence was "familiar" and recogniz-able, its purpose clear to all.

The Regulators played for legitimacy by playing fair, by observing the old rules, and therefore, according to those same old rules, they expected a positive response from authority. Their use of form and restraint to legitimate their actions was not merely in order to avoid or lessen possible retaliatory punishment. It was done to certify that their grievances were legitimate, and that if no other method obtained for gaining the attention of authority, controlled violence would. If, as one historian has put it, "popular uprisings benefited from a certain presumptive acceptability that was founded in part on colonial experience with mass action," that acceptability in part rested on the crowd's use of traditional, recognizable behavior.[33] They expected authority to react in a traditional authoritarian paternalist manner: to officially deplore the violence on one hand and to move to fix the problem with the other.

The Regulators had good reason in the early stages to expect support from some of their local leaders.[34] Husband claimed that Thomas Lloyd, an assemblyman and justice of the peace from Orange County, had supported their first petition.[35] Maurice Moore, Jr., a lawyer and assemblyman from Brunswick County, may also have been an early supporter, although he later disavowed the Regulators.[36] Husband also claimed he had an anonymous supporter among the judges during the court session of August 1767, and Thomas Person and John Pryor, wealthy and influential citizens, were themselves Regulators.[37]

The expectations that the protestors held of their own local elite were reflected in their response to word that Fanning was not coming to the meeting that had been arranged by the Sandy Creek Association in October 1766. When Fanning's messenger, James Watson, a longtime settler in the region who had served in a variety of official capacities, told them that Fanning was not coming, they immediately drew up another petition. They then "checked in" with Watson, having him listen to the new petition and certify its "just and reasonable" character.[38]

Unfortunately, it quickly became clear that the county officers, and Fanning in particular, had no interest in upholding any ideal of paternalism. Many of the officers were merchants, lawyers, and other officials with interests different from those of the farmers among whom they now lived. Ekirch described the officials in the western counties as inexperienced in public service, virtually all immigrants from other colonies, and lacking any "deeply ingrained sense of public responsibility."[39] These men generally did not see their future in the soil, and their vision of their own interest conflicted with the planters. It was a clash of economic styles if not of classes. Many of the planters in the western regions of North Carolina had arrived overland from the northern colonies; they had come seeking cheap land. The rising population led naturally to an influx of merchants, lawyers, and others whose interests diverged from those of the farmers.[40]

This divergence of interest quickly came into play. The protestors' chief enemy, Fanning, had raised the stakes of the debate very early by labeling the first mild petitions as an "Insurrection."[41] This was of course followed by Fanning's thinly disguised excuse not to attend the meeting with the Sandy Creek Association. He responded to a later petition (March 1768) by referring to the Regulators as "Rebels, Insurgents, &c., to be shot, hang'd, &c. as mad Dogs."[42] After the incident with the mare, John Gray wrote to Fanning to inform him of the damage to his house. Uncertain of what to do, Gray was inclined to raise the militia and arrest them all.[43] Fanning agreed. For the Regulators, appeal outside the county would be necessary.

Upon receipt of Gray's letter, Fanning directed the Orange County militia officers to hold a muster, suppress the riotous behavior, and arrest three presumed leaders.[44] On April 17, two of those militia officers replied that they had ordered up the seven companies but that only some 120 men had appeared, and even of those very few were inclined to help.[45] Fanning, after returning to Hillsborough, wrote to Governor Tryon and asserted that the Regulators planned to surround the town with 1,500 men and to lay it in ashes on May 3 (a charge that was to be made against the Regulators several times).[46] Fanning indicated that he would, on May 1, send out a small party under the cover of night to arrest "three or four of the principals."[47]

This was not the only report of disorder to reach the governor's ears at about this time. Protestors in Anson County, not yet in league with the Orange County Regulators, had disrupted the meeting of the county court on April 21 and 28.[48] In doing so they also were following a form of protest now traditional in North Carolina by coming to the courthouse, the one central place in a large, sparsely inhabited county, and taking it over.[49] A hostile witness described them as about forty men, armed with "Clubs and some Fire Arms." They took over the court to prevent its meeting, allowing one justice unmolested entrance to open the court long enough to adjourn it for lack of sufficient other justices.

Then on April 28, after the court had been open for some time, a much larger number of protestors appeared and proceeded to make noise sufficient to disrupt the court. Justice Samuel Spencer rebuked them and they agreed to send in representatives to set forth their grievances. A debate ensued, and eventually the protestors assumed control of the courthouse. They appointed officers among themselves and held several "Debates and Consultations." Far from being a violent incident, Spencer admitted that "they offered no direct insult to me, but told me they did not desire to hurt me, nor my Papers and records." They debated whether to burn the courthouse and the jail but resolved against it, agreeing instead to resist the collection of taxes. They then dispersed.

In the copy of their resolutions, which Spencer enclosed to Tryon, the Anson "mob" also placed itself in a traditional framework of protest, swearing loyalty to Great Britain, and avowing a willingness to pay reasonable taxes.[50] By their choice of location (the courthouse) and their behavior in it, the Anson crowd also asserted their right to be heard, even consciously deciding that further violence (burning the courthouse) was at that point unnecessary.[51]

The governor's response to even such biased reports as those provided by Fanning and Spencer was much more like what the Regulators expected. Practicing the two-handed brand of authoritarian paternalism, with one hand Tryon prepared to restore order by force and with the other he looked to redress grievances.[52] Tryon was well aware of corruption in the county officialdom; he had expressed as much to British authorities in 1767. When he wrote to the Earl of Hillsborough in June 1768 to report on the disorders of April and May, he admitted that there were just causes for popular complaint.[53] Lord Hillsborough's response was equally characteristic of authoritarian paternalism. He indicated concern about the disorder but wrote, "At the same time it will be very satisfactory to His Majesty to be fully informed of the Causes of those Disturbances, to the End that if there appears to be real Ground of Complaint, Measures may be taken to apply the proper remedy."[54]

Tryon's missives back to Fanning and Spencer were similarly restrained. He provided Fanning a proclamation to read to the Regulators, demanding that they disperse. He sympathized with Fanning's outrage but hoped that "you and your Friends may not be compelled, upon too unequal Terms, to carry Matters to Extremities before the Effect of the Proclamation [can be seen]."[55] Tryon further outlined his belief that the majority of the protestors were not troublemakers, and that he would certainly consider any petitions that were forwarded to him.[56]

In these same letters and in a message to his Council, Tryon expressed a variety of cultural values about the employment of violence. He made clear that certain kinds of violence were less acceptable than others. He referred specifically to threats to life, the burning of a house, or the use of armed force to disturb the peace.[57] Tryon also proclaimed a greater tolerance for any protestor who "openly confronts the Dangers to which he exposes himself" as opposed to the supposed unseen manipulator of the crowd.[58]

Such was one side of the governor's response. The other was to prepare to raise the militia, to authorize Fanning to call on the militia of other counties, and to provide Fanning with a sternly worded proclamation to the Regulators to disperse.[59] He wrote similarly to Spencer in Anson County.[60]

And how did the precipitate plans of Fanning, the traditional response of the governor, and the desires of the Regulators intersect? On April 30, the governor's secretary arrived in Hillsborough with the proclamation to disperse and read it publicly. The Regulators had long since been at home.[61] The next night (Sunday, May 1), Fanning proceeded with his plan to arrest the ringleaders. He seized Hermon Husband and William Butler and brought them back to the jail in Hillsborough.

Here was an act, an arrest in the dark of a Sunday night, clearly in violation of the protocols of riot and response, and the consequences were immediate and swift. As the Regulators pointed out, this act "alarmed the whole Country, Regulators or Anteregulators, all were unanimous in the recovery of the Prisoners; many who had till then opposed the prevailing measures, now went down with the foremost, as judging none were now safe, whether active, passive or neutral."[62] Word of the arrest spread with such speed that by dawn the next morning, "some Hundreds were assembled near the Town, which Number, in an Hour or two, increased to Odds of seven Hundred armed Men," all of whom were intent on freeing Husband. Fanning frantically tried to round up some militia in response to the apparent threat but was unable even to clear a path out of town to remove Husband and Butler to New Bern.[63]

Thus surrounded, Fanning sought to placate the crowd.[64] He allowed Husband and Butler to make bail, and then Fanning went to the edge of town with the governor's secretary. The two men tried to persuade the Regulators not to come into town, apparently offering some small quantities of alcohol as incentive. Most convincingly, however, the governor's secretary reread the aforementioned proclamation to disperse. He then added, on his own initiative, that the protestors should reassemble when the governor was in Orange County, for he would surely hear their petition and then redress any of their grievances against unlawful extortion by their officers.[65] This was what the Regulators expected to hear; this was what violence enacted within a legitimate framework was supposed to achieve.[66] As Husband related, "no sooner was the Word spoke, but the whole Multitude, as with one Voice, cried out, Agreed. That is all we want; Liberty to Make our grievances known."[67] The crowd quickly dispersed.

If the Regulators still had any doubts about their need to appeal beyond the county, Fanning quickly resolved them. Afraid that the Regulators' grievances might go undiluted to the governor, Fanning tried to co-opt the process by asking three Regulators to join him in drafting the petition.[68] Husband and the Regulators saw through this bald attempt to mask their true grievances. They drew up their own petitions, despite Fanning's threat to treat such an action as "High Treason."[69]

Although the Regulators had a fine sense of what constituted appropriate violence, and expected their neighbors and officials to have a similar sense, they were still carefully feeling their way forward in terms of the actual legalities. About this time, Husband received a letter from Ralph McNair, a wealthy Hillsborough merchant soon to be an assemblyman, that laid out the legal definitions of violence:

> For writing, copying, carrying about or dispersing a Libel (and anything tending to stir up a People to a dislike of a Government or even to a single Person is a Libel) the Sentence is Confiscation of goods. . . . Mobs and Riots (that is where a number rise without Arms and only murmuring) are treated generally with Lenity as to the multitude tho' where the Offence is against Government . . . ringleaders are to suffer death without the King's pardon. But where they take up Arms to remove a Grievance or to alter the form of Movement it is Treason [with its attendant punishments]. . . . However Sir, I can assure [you] with the utmost confidence that this affair if it stops here will never be represented by Colo Fanning any otherwise than as a Mob.[70]

The context of this letter hints that Husband had consulted McNair on the legal issues involved; such a deliberate consultation by protestors to determine the exact rules of riot had at least some precedent in England.[71]

In response to the promise of the governor's secretary that petitions would be heard, the Regulators stepped up their petitioning campaign. In May and June, and even into August, a blizzard of petitions and depositions arrived before the Assembly and the governor, all documenting the illegal practices of various county officials.[72] These documents were steeped in the rhetoric of traditional protest violence. The Regulators were trying to position themselves in a particular way, to show that their actions had traditional legitimacy. The petitions all indicated their contrition for the recent disorder, their loyalty to King George, and their admission of the right of the state to tax. They also carefully documented just how restrained the disorder had been, and just how much they had been provoked by the "downright roguish practices of ignorant and unworthy men [the officials]."[73]

The governor's response continued to be measured and conciliatory. In June, he wrote to the Regulators indicating his concern about the violence, noting that "if [it had been] carried but a little further [it would] have been denominated and must have been treated as high treason" but that he was sure that most of them were "actuated by honest motives." Accordingly, he promised to investigate their complaints and to prosecute any officials who had broken the law.[74] Whatever expectations the Regulators had of this promise were quickly dashed as the Orange officials in fact chose this period to *raise* their already illegal fees, and, in Husband's words, "all Hopes of the Law vanished."[75]

A cycle of escalation was well under way. The Sandy Creek Associators of 1766 had petitioned merely to meet with their local officials. Failure of that meeting, continued official abuse, and perhaps even personal violence by officials led to the skimmington-esque riding of the sheriff in April 1768.[76] While unsettling for the sheriff, the incident did not warrant Fanning's rather vociferous response in attempting and failing to raise a substantial militia force, denoting it an "insurrection," and then arresting Husband and Butler by night. His actions led to a rather more serious gathering, which, however, did not damage anything, being successfully appeased by the apparent promise of reform from an extra-county authority. The failure of that promise would lead to the next escalation in August and September 1768.

Explaining the escalation requires more than explaining the intensity or justice of the Regulators' outrage. It also requires understanding the norms of violence, and how the use of violence carried expectations. When those expectations were repeatedly dashed, the dialogue of violence intensified. Of course, *both* sides held expectations about the use of violence. The Regulators expected that they would be listened to. Authority, or at least the colonial government if not the worried local officials, expected the violence to follow certain patterns, and the breaking of those rules, or the rumor that those rules had been broken, often led authority to respond more harshly than might have been necessary. Finally, and critically, both sides were constantly aware that this process of communication was not merely between them as antagonists but was also a display to the rest of the community. Winning the approval and support of the wider audience in part depended on successfully casting their actions as legitimate. To be sure, the Regulators, like all protestors, also hoped to avoid punishment. In the English legal system, however, they were well aware that that punishment would be determined by a local jury. And that jury would be imbued with the same understanding of the appropriate uses of violence. The players in this drama were not in the grip of a determinist cultural structure of violence; they deliberately calculated their violent acts in the service of a specific interest. In this society, the role of public opinion carried weight, whether as juryman, militiaman, voter, or potential rioter, and one sure way to swing that public against you was to act violently in an illegitimate way.

The September 1768 Confrontation in Hillsborough

On July 6, 1768, Governor Tryon arrived in Hillsborough. The Regulators sent to him to complain of the continued misconduct of their officials. Tryon replied that he had ordered the prosecution of "all Public Officers in your County." He therefore hoped that they would pay when Sheriff Tyree Harris came around to collect the tax due for 1767.[77] The Regulators, however, wanted to wait until the Assembly deliberated their case. Even at this early stage of negotiation, and crucially to the creation of the coming confrontation, rumors were flying in both directions that the other side was mustering for an attack. The Regulators claimed to have heard reports that Tryon planned to bring in Indians and raise the militia to attack them. Meanwhile, Tryon was receiving reports of gatherings of hundreds of armed Regulators. The Regulators later admitted gathering but denied that they were armed.[78]

The surfacing of these deeper fears, rumors of Indian attacks on the one hand and of large-scale armed rebellion on the other, revealed how the colonial environment had added "clauses" to the norms of violence. A significant portion of the backcountry population had moved to North Carolina following the Seven Years' War. Many of them had experienced the horrors of frontier war with the Indians in the western reaches of Pennsylvania and Virginia.[79] To them, and even to those with older roots in North Carolina, the threat of using Indians was a serious violation of the social contract.[80]

In Tryon's eyes, the reports that the Regulators were assembling in arms suggested a violation of both the traditional and the strictly legal English understanding of "acceptable" protest.[81] While the myth that every man in the backcountry owned a gun has been discredited, there were certainly a great many more armed men in the population than was the case in England.[82] The ready availability of firearms in great numbers made even the threat of their use an issue of real concern to a government lacking a regular military force.[83]

Thus rumor, exaggerated by the dispersed settlement patterns in colonial North Carolina, played havoc with the rules of violence. As each side reacted to false alarms, they further heightened their own already considerable fears. Early in August, the Regulators mobilized in response to a false rumor. On August 11, the governor heard of that mobilization, which was characterized as 500 to 1,000 men assembled in arms preparing to march on Hillsborough and destroy it. He ordered up Fanning's Orange County regiment and succeeded in raising about 250 men. When the Regulators learned that the initial rumor spurring them to action had been false, they dispersed. Thereupon the governor dismissed the militia.[84] Meanwhile, members of the militia sympathetic to the Regulators had been passing along what they had heard, doubtless with their own added embellishments. Husband noted that "Alarms run Night and Day, and caused Multitudes of People to gather together."[85]

While Tryon continued to assure the Regulators that he would pursue the prosecution of local officials, and that he supported their petitioning the Assembly, he also began to adopt a harder line.[86] Husband, Butler, and some others were scheduled to be tried for the events of April and May in the Hillsborough court session scheduled for September, and Tryon anticipated an attempt by the Regulators to disrupt that court. He demanded therefore that twelve of their leaders come in and post bond that they would not disturb the court.[87] At the same time, Governor Tryon set about recruiting militia from the surrounding counties to help protect the court.[88]

The militia available to Tryon was an imperfect instrument.[89] The colony of North Carolina had always had a legally constituted militia. Initially, the right to raise it had been granted to the proprietors; the institution was naturally continued once the colony came under crown control. As in England, all adult free males were ostensibly members of the militia. Men were assigned to one of the companies of a county "regiment" and required to attend musters or pay a fine. The officers were appointed by the governor, the senior positions usually given to wealthy men with some political influence. They in turn recommended men for the junior positions. Such positions were considered socially, and potentially financially, valuable.[90] Although each male was theoretically required to serve, only rarely during the colonial period were all men actually forced to fight. Instead, North Carolina had almost always resorted to calling for volunteers from a variety of counties and then forming them into independent companies for the duration of an emergency. Occasionally, the state had funded small companies for extended periods of frontier defense, and a very tiny company had long been in service in Fort Johnston near Wilmington. Those troops, however, can hardly be considered militia as such.

Thus, the only significant force available to the state for use against the populace was the populace itself. When Tryon rode out to raise the militia, not only did he have to contend with a population potentially sympathetic to the Regulators, he had to cope with a system long in disuse and traditionally in want of coaxing.[91] In short, Tryon had to *negotiate* an army. Failure to do so would cast a long shadow over the legitimacy of the government itself.[92]

Tryon foresaw this problem. He already had laid some groundwork for support through his patronage of influential residents in Mecklenburg County.[93] Now that the time had come actually to raise a militia force, he employed every trick in the book. During the false alarm call-up of the Orange County militia on August 11–12, the governor administered an oath to those who responded, binding them to the government.[94] Then, on August 17, ignoring a scheduled meeting for that day with the Regulators, he departed for Rowan and Mecklenburg counties to sound out the militia there.[95]

Tryon arranged a general (regimental) muster of the Mecklenburg militia for August 23. As he reviewed the 900 men of the regiment, he asked them to take an Association Oath in support of the government, the same one he had administered to the Orange County militia on August 12.[96] A murmuring began in the ranks as the men of the county objected. One captain reportedly resigned his commission rather than take the oath, and one account has Tryon vainly offering a bounty to march to Hillsborough. Few men took the oath, being "unanimously determined not to fight against their countrymen."[97] The militia, at least according to the source for this story, supposedly stated that they would not fight to enforce an oppressive act, clearly demonstrating the power of the body of the militia to judge the conditions of their use.[98] Tryon, apparently unprepared for such resistance, used the coming of night to dismiss the assembly without making a public call for volunteers. Instead, he directed the company captains (of whose support he felt more confident) to hold private (company) musters and prepare lists of volunteers to bring to him on August 27.[99]

This was not the kind of muster Tryon had hoped for, and so he planned the next one much more carefully, the more so because Rowan County was closer to the heart of Regulator country. On August 26, eleven companies of the Rowan militia arrived in Salisbury for a general muster. This time Tryon began separately with the captains and other officers, dining in private with them and making his best play for their loyalty. He read them copies of his correspondence with the Regulators, judiciously leaving out their first petition to him and all its enclosures. The Rowan County colonel, Alexander Osborn, then read them a letter from four Presbyterian ministers outlining the reasons for submitting to the authority of the state, and their "abhorrence of the present turbulent and disorderly spirit."[100] The officers then retired to discuss the matter in a separate room. As in many closed-door meetings, they reached a "unanimous" decision to support the governor.[101]

It only remained to convince the troops. To that end, Tryon pulled out all the stops.[102] As the regiment stood in formation, Tryon walked along the ranks explaining the dangers of the Regulators and elaborating on the potential for a civil war. He then remarked that he sought volunteers for the mission to protect the Orange County Court, and that after the regiment had fired a volley, accompanied by the discharge of artillery, he would so solicit their support. The shooting completed, he called for volunteers, but he did so *by company*. Each company was asked to step forward en masse and join around the king's colors held by the governor. It was a masterful demonstration of how to proactively co-opt the leadership, put on a military display, and then manipulate by peer pressure. Nevertheless, one of the companies still refused to volunteer, although its captain did. Tryon had further prepared for this moment, in the finest tradition of popular politics, by providing a wagon load of beer and alcohol, to which the volunteers proceeded, after yet another discharge of artillery, and together toasted the king.[103] It was only at this point that the eleventh company, still in formation, turned and deliberately *marched* away. By maintaining formation and then marching away, the recalcitrant company made their own counterargument within the dialogue of military display begun by Tryon.[104]

In his efforts to shore up public support, Tryon also made ample use of ministers of a variety of denominations. Already mentioned was the letter of four Presbyterians to their brethren encouraging support of the governor. Tryon also enlisted the Reverend George Micklejohn, the resident Anglican minister of Orange County, to preach to the Orange and Granville militia contingents while in Hillsborough.[105] And, while in Salisbury on August 21, Tryon attended a Lutheran service where the Reverend Samuel Suther preached "due obedience to the Laws of the Country, and a union of heart to support the Peace and Tranquility of the Province." Suitably impressed with his loyalty, Tryon brought Suther along with the army and had him preach to the Rowan and Mecklenburg militia while encamped in Hillsborough.[106]

Finally, Tryon worked to cement his control over his newly raised militia force by emphasizing traditional European military forms and regulations. Other commentators on Tryon have ascribed this tactic to his experience in the British army and a personal predilection for pomp and ceremony. There is undoubtedly truth in this interpretation, but at the same time Tryon was very concerned about the public's perception of his actions. He could not afford to alienate the population further, and so now he too was playing to an audience. He was preparing to use an instrument of violence, one that, like the Regulators' protests, created expectations in the eyes of the political public. To satisfy those eyes, to lay his claim to a legitimate use of force, Tryon tried to make the militia *look* like an army. Just as rioters asserted legitimacy through familiar forms of behavior, an army too could derive legitimacy through form. He published march orders familiar to conventional European armies with an unusual amount of attention to the visual details regarding the positioning of the colors and the creation of honor companies and color guards.[107] Tryon was not doing anything new by European standards; his innovation was to use such techniques with the colonial militia, an organization that rarely aspired to such behavior. Tryon continued to stress such military formalism for the duration of the army's existence. Putting on a show of an appropriately "military" army accomplished several things. It satisfied Tryon's personal desire to reprise his time as an army officer.[108] It enhanced his demonstration of the power of the state. It enlarged his gubernatorial powers of patronage among the officer corps.[109] And, not least, it provided a legalistic means to control the soldiers as well as helping to create a strong sense of pride and fellow feeling among soldiers with potentially uncertain loyalties.[110]

As Tryon's army marched on Hillsborough, ostensibly to protect the upcoming court session, the Regulators were quick to invoke that most evocative of English rhetorical accusations: that the governor meant to create a standing army.[111] The Regulators certainly viewed his actions as provocative. Husband noted that the governor's preparations had made it difficult for the Regulator leaders to "Rule the Inconsiderate," who believed that the governor's choice of the sword left them at "Liberty to Defend themselves." Eventually the Regulators agreed that everyone could decide for themselves whether to go to the court armed, but that they would not use their weapons "nor offer the Least Insult, unless an Attempt was made to Massacre us."[112]

By the first day of the court, September 22, 1768, the potential for a major conflict had developed. Tryon had arrived late on September 19 with 1,416 men.[113] By September 22, upwards of 3,700 Regulators were encamped a half mile outside of town.[114] Battle did not follow. Violence was avoided because both sides refused to offer the other the necessary justification to fight.

On the first day, the Regulators sent word that if the governor would allow them to come into town to make their complaints against their officers, and if he would also pardon all the past breaches of the peace, then they would pay their taxes. The Regulators even allowed that the two Regulators who were under bail to stand trial would do so.[115] Upon receipt of this request, Governor Tryon, now ill, called his "war council" into session to deliberate what to do.[116] The council met apart from the governor, who was in his sickbed, and they recommended that he pardon all the Regulators save the principals, who should give bond to pay all the taxes due from the Regulators. Tryon found this recommendation too lenient and asked them to reconsider. He especially recommended that they consider whether to use the troops. The council, upon further deliberation, again recommended a pardon but also counseled that all the Regulators should take the oath of allegiance in lieu of the leaders posting bond.[117] Tryon offered these proposals to the Regulators, along with the additional requirement that they surrender their arms until the trial of their principals had been completed.[118] The Regulators requested overnight to consider. During the night, they dispersed and returned home, leaving the governor to "fight the air," and the court to proceed undisturbed.[119]

The court—which is to say, a local jury—in a manner similar to Tryon's initial response to the Regulators, acted in two ways. On one hand, they convicted two Regulators for their part in "rescuing the mare." On the other hand, they threw out indictments against nine Regulator leaders. Husband was tried and declared not guilty. Fanning was tried and found guilty, although he was fined only one penny for each of six charges. The two convicted Regulators were quickly released and pardoned, and their fines were suspended.[120] Within a few months, Tryon issued a pardon for all the Regulators, initially excepting thirteen men, and all but one of these were soon pardoned as well, with Husband the lone exception.[121]

For the moment, violence had worked. The Regulators had succeeded in bringing their grievances to the forefront of colonial politics. They had seen their chief enemy tried and convicted (if only slapped on the wrist), and none of the Regulators actually faced any significant punishment. The threat of violence had hung over the entire process. They had succeeded because of the violence, because only violence generated significant attention and popular reaction to bring about Fanning's indictment and trial. Although, by law, the Regulators could have been treated as rebels and dealt with militarily, they had successfully framed both their acts of violence and their threats of violence within a legitimate context that not only assured popular support for their cause but made it difficult for Tryon's council to justify attacking them.

Fear no doubt played a role in the governor's decision not to use force, but that fear in itself reflected the legitimacy that the Regulators had established, and the loss of legitimacy that the governor and his allies would suffer if they attacked. In addition, it seems unlikely that fear of the Regulators was the primary motive for the decision not to attack, because fear and rumor had created the confrontation in the first place. That is, rumor of the one side's mobilization kept prompting (through fear) the other side to mobilize further. This escalation was defused at the Hillsborough Court session because of a recognition that nothing had yet been *done* to warrant further violence. From the militia's viewpoint, the Regulators after all had played by the rules, and so attacking them would have been out of place. The Regulators clearly stated that they would use their arms only if attacked, and that did not happen. The violence thus remained confined within the legitimate framework of protest. Also important to defusing the situation was the close proximity of each side to the other over an extended time, which prevented rumor from getting out of control. Contrast this interpretation with, for example, William Powell's, that the Regulators, despite their numbers, were no match for "the governor's trained forces" and therefore did not attempt to interfere with the trial, and shortly dispersed.[122] Other colonists from outside North Carolina, seeing the incident from a distance, naturally interpreted it within the framework of restraint and expectation. The governor acted mildly in not calling for regular troops; the Regulators dispersed when assured their grievances would be addressed.[123] Lacking a legitimate pretext for attacking the Regulators, officialdom feared not the Regulators themselves but the reaction of the wider political public to the illegitimate use of force. The militia cheered the Regulators at the closing of the court.[124]

3

The Road to Alamance

From the Jealousie generally prevailing among the common
People, at his [Husband's] Confinement, I was apprehensive
while Husbands continued in Gaol without being brought to
Tryal, and the Courts of Law open, no vigorous support could be
relied on from the Militia.
Governor Tryon to Lord Hillsborough, April 12, 1771[1]

I hope you have no thoughts of making one [taking part] in the
Hillsborough Expedition for heavens Sake let them fight their
own battles—let them that raisd the Ferment throw in their
Blood & Vitals . . . to Abate it.
Henry Johnston to Samuel Johnston, March 1771[2]

Far from feeling crushed, the Regulators took heart from the symbolic
conviction of Edmund Fanning in a courthouse surrounded by the governor and the militia, and they proceeded both to petition the Assembly and
to bring suit against corrupt officials.[3] Feeling that their case was now
squarely before the Assembly, the Regulators also agreed to pay their
taxes.[4] The representatives at the Assembly, meeting in November, acknowledged the existence of problems in the backcountry, but they were
not inclined to pursue punishing the insurgents; neither did they enact
significant reforms.[5]

Inaction by the Assembly and the failure of attempts to prosecute corrupt officials frustrated the Regulators, and reignited an internal negotiation over the use of violence.[6] Many of the Regulators mobilized to contest
the recently called elections and continued to pursue prosecution of their
enemies, while others again resorted to popular forms of protest violence.
In November 1768, during the sitting of the Assembly, thirty men in
Edgecombe County tried to break out of jail someone whom Governor
Tryon assumed was a Regulator. The attempt was foiled by townsmen,
who shot a horse and "broke heads."[7] The Regulators threatened and then
apparently flogged Colonel Samuel Spencer with hickory switches in the

winter of 1769.[8] A March 1769 ambush attempt against Fanning failed.[9] In April, Sheriff John Lea was whipped when he tried to serve a process in Regulator country.[10] When Tryon learned of the last incident, he reported it to his superior in England but noted that he had heard "that this act of outrage is not countenanced but disapproved by the body of the people who called themselves Regulators."[11] Later that year, the Sandy Creek Baptist Church weighed in on the debate regarding violent protest, passing a resolution that "if any of our members shall take up arms against the legal authority or aid and abet them that do so, he shall be excommunicated."[12]

These violent incidents aside, for the moment the Regulators directed their main efforts at continued prosecutions and then at winning the elections of the summer of 1769.[13] The Regulators succeeded in getting several of their members (including Hermon Husband), or persons distinctly sympathetic, elected to the Assembly.[14] Freshly inspired by the results of this election, new petitions rolled into the fall session of the new Assembly.[15] At this point, the hopes of the Regulators ironically intersected with the growing conflict between the colonies and Britain. The Assembly, instead of dealing with the internal problems in the backcountry, took up Virginia's nonimportation initiative in protest of the Townshend Acts. Tryon quickly prorogued the Assembly to prevent a vote on the matter. Thus 1769 ended and 1770 began with little to no action by the Assembly. The courts, meanwhile, continued to disappoint and even to aggravate the Regulators.[16] Even the apparent success of the elections had been frustrated by the prorogation of the Assembly. This fact, combined with repeated failures at law, stoked the fires of resistance. Initially, those fires took the form of another wave of refusals to pay taxes. But then in September 1770, at a court session in Hillsborough, the flame burst forth in a fresh act of violence.

The Hillsborough Riot of September 1770

If the parading of the sheriff and the shooting of holes in Fanning's house in 1768 were like a skimmington, then what happened in September 1770 was definitely more like a riot. But to say that it was a riot is not to say that it was chaotic or uncontrolled. Riots, too, had traditional forms, and the Regulators followed the "script" almost line by line. This was not an act designed to start a war. It was an act designed to transmit a signal about the level of discontent and frustration in the western counties. Nevertheless, it did start a war. The reasons for that unexpected result lie in the expectations associated with violence, and the particular physical and social configuration of the two sides in the colonial context. But first, the riot itself.

The details of the event are available almost exclusively from anti-Regulator sources, but a certain outline of the events seems indisputable.[17] The court session opened on Saturday, September 22, and a considerable, though indeterminate, number of Regulators gathered in Hillsborough intending to disrupt the court, in much the same manner as North Carolinians had often done.[18] Nothing happened that Saturday, but when Judge Richard Henderson reopened the court on Monday the twenty-fourth, the courtroom quickly filled with Regulators, who packed the building until they were shoulder to shoulder. According to Henderson, they were armed with clubs, whips, and switches.[19] One of the Regulators asked and received permission to speak. He stated that they wanted the court to continue but that they wanted a jury selected from among themselves. Henderson recorded that approximately half an hour was spent peacefully debating the issue, when the crowd "cried out 'Retire, Retire, and let the Court go on.'"[20] The Regulators began to move outside the building and discuss what to do, when, at that moment, a lawyer, Mr. Williams, tried to approach the courthouse. For some reason, his appearance catalyzed some of the Regulators, who began to beat him. They then turned to Fanning, who was already in the courthouse, seized him, and began to beat him as well. Williams had meanwhile escaped into a nearby building. Fanning, apparently badly beaten, also managed to escape and take shelter. Henderson wrote that he then feared for his own life, but James Hunter and other Regulator leaders approached him and said they would protect him provided he continued the court until the end of the session.[21] Henderson "agreed" and held court for some hours, until the end of the day when the Regulators escorted him to his lodging in a "great parade."[22] Fanning, taken prisoner, was allowed to return to his house on his word to surrender himself the next day.

Henderson opted for caution that night and slipped out of town. Without him a proper court could not be held, and the Regulators took out their frustration on Fanning. They marched to his house, ran him out of town, and plundered and wrecked his house. Henderson indicated that some of the Regulators wanted to kill Fanning, but that others intervened, demanding only that he leave town.[23] The Regulators then made an effigy of Fanning's clothes, marched through town, broke up a church bell donated by Fanning, considered but forbore breaking up the church, and then broke the windows out of several of the merchants' houses. Henderson initially believed that the Regulators intended to lay waste the town but in his postscript noted that they left the town on Wednesday, "having done very little Mischief after Spoiling Mr. Fannings House, except breaking the Windows of most of the Houses in Town."[24] The final insult, according to the highly sensationalized and uncorroborated newspaper accounts, occurred when the Regulators "took from his chains a Negro that had been executed some time and placed him at the lawyer's bar" in the courthouse and smeared excrement in the judge's chair. The Virginia newspaper version of this story goes on to decry the Regulators: "Would a Hottentot have been guilty of such a piece of brutality! or is there the most savage nation on earth whose manners are less cultivated!"[25]

The Regulators had rioted. They had even beaten their enemies and destroyed their chief enemy's house. But at every step of the riot, they had displayed traditional characteristics of restraint and target selection. They were armed, but without firearms.[26] They struck out against their enemies but killed no one. They destroyed a house near the center of town, but only one, and not with the community-threatening option of fire. They occupied the courthouse, but not to destroy it, only to ensure that it functioned in their interest. They paraded Fanning's clothes in effigy and equally festively paraded the judge back to his lodging. All of these actions derived from a traditional understanding of the "correct" form of riotous protest. They were legitimate in a way that uncontrolled havoc was not.

The riot sent a message. Unfortunately, the version of that message received in eastern North Carolina had been transmuted into one about "turning the world upside down." Such fears had already existed, as expressed by Henry McCulloh writing from London in 1769 when he referred to the "cursed spirit of levelling" prevailing in North Carolina.[27] After the September 1770 riot, although Judge Henderson's original account of the riot revealed its traditional nature, the newspapers instead painted a highly sensationalized, even demonized, version of the Regulators' actions. According to the newspapers, the Regulators, after failing in an attempt to ambush and kill Judge Henderson while en route to Hillsborough, had instead invaded the court with "whips, loaded at the ends with lead or iron," which they "shook . . . over Judge Henderson." The following day, frustrated by Henderson's escape, the Regulators were supposed to have run Fanning out of town with dogs and "with a cruelty more savage than bloodhounds stoned him as he fled." They then turned to the contents of his cellar, where they "Gorged their more than savage stomachs with his liquors." The newspapers went on to claim that the

Regulators destroyed the homes and shops of other merchants, and one could hardly think of anything better calculated to fuel the fears of wealthy easterners than the newspapers' vivid added detail of a dead negro at the lawyer's bar and comparisons to Hottentots.[28]

Finally, just to round out the apparent list of the Regulators' offenses against the social order, one of the witnesses against them, Josiah Lyon, claimed that he had heard them "Drink Damnation to King George . . . and Success to the pretender."[29] If English tradition provided an old fear of levelling, and a somewhat newer fear of the Pretender, the colonial context put teeth in that fear by adding the specter of slave rebellion on one hand,[30] and the horror of the savage Indian on the other.[31]

Rhetorically framing the Regulator movement within the context of those fears eased the process of "othering" and delegitimating its participants. Making the Regulators into an out-group meant that they were no longer subject to the same set of rules. Violence could be enacted against them with less restraint. Whatever legitimacy the Regulators had struggled for by their restrained use of traditional forms of violence was overturned, because that legitimacy depended on being an in-group. Acts of violence that heretofore had possessed a traditional legitimacy now, in a colonial environment, rapidly appeared more threatening than they might have in England.

In part this greater unease of the political elite in the face of popular disorder derived from fears of slaves and Indians, and in part it resulted from human geography.[32] North Carolina, from the coast into the heart of the piedmont, constituted an enormous region for news to circulate through; from New Bern to Hillsborough (as the crow flies) is approximately 150 miles. It is about 170 miles from London to York. Within that area, settlement was more dispersed than in England and the road network far less complete.[33] Perhaps even more important than these physical issues was the lack of natural human lines of communication between east and west. The majority of North Carolinians living in the piedmont had arrived overland from other colonies. They were not a demographic expansion of eastern North Carolina and thus lacked family ties with the east. Furthermore, while many of the piedmonters were of English origin, many others were not. Large numbers of Scotch-Irish and Germans participated in the Regulator movement, and while no particular ethnic hatred existed between these groups and the largely English easterners, this ethnic diversity represented an additional barrier to familiarity and ease of communication.[34] Whether this created a political sectionalism is a dispute for other historians, but it certainly did *not* encourage the normal familial paths of communication to occur across the piedmont–coastal plain divide.

Of course, the demonization of the Regulators was not complete. The newspaper article was only one element of a now-growing effort among some of the political elite (from both east and west) to write the Regulators out of bounds. Sometime during this period, for example, a group of the backcountry elite publicly created a self-defense association against the "infatuated persons" who had committed "unheard of acts of Barbarity & Cruelty" and who had "demonstrate[d] to the World that they are actuated by a Spirit of Lunatics."[35] This elite, possessed of a greater sensitivity to disorder as a result of the political and demographic conditions in a southern colony, persuaded of their own interest in maintaining control, and in the midst of divesting themselves of paternalist responsibility, used newspaper accounts and rumors filtered through a disconnected human landscape to manipulate the received image of the Regulators' actions.[36] Preparing to bring military violence against the Regulators, they were again playing to an audience. They had to convince enough men in enough counties to join the militia army that would march against the Regulators. One key to that process was this effort at demonization. Against an "other," violence was legitimate, even necessary.

The Decision for War

Rumor and deliberate demonization notwithstanding, the Regulators' determined attempts to contain their violence within traditional boundaries continued to make decisive government response difficult. On October 1, North Carolina's attorney general, after reviewing the evidence from the September riot, advised the governor that it amounted only to a riot. Even toasting damnation to the king was treason only if done in direct association with violence.[37] In a few short months, the colonial government moved from this tepid legal opinion to a military campaign against the Regulators. Each stage in the escalation can, in part, be explained by action and reaction in accord with the collective understanding of the norms of violence. While the governor may already have made up his mind that military force was necessary, he could not muster such a force until he could demonstrate that the Regulators had "broken the rules" and now constituted a rebellion.[38]

While rumor and the manipulation of rumor helped Tryon in his campaign against the Regulators, they themselves contributed to their own demise. One shift in their behavior was the creation of their own judicial committees, similar to the committees of safety later created by the Whig party in the buildup to the American Revolution. A series of letters dating from late December 1770 to late January 1771 seemed to show the Regulators adjudicating local disputes and in fact banishing the guilty party.[39] If word of their decisions had leaked out back east, it would have contributed to the perception that they had overstepped the bounds by assuming judicial powers. In this context, note the difference between their need for Henderson to continue the court in September 1770 and the now apparent creation of their own courts in December 1770 to January 1771.[40] Furthermore, the Regulators were not, after all, a monolithic agency. While as a whole they had limited their behavior to long-established techniques of protest, individuals occasionally acted in a manner clearly outside the boundaries, fueling the fire against them.[41] They began by burning Judge Henderson's farm.[42]

Henderson informed Tryon late on November 18, 1770, of the burning of his farm and also reported the rumor that the Regulators planned to march on New Bern to disrupt the upcoming Assembly session. Tryon quickly alerted militia commanders to that possibility.[43] The apparent threat of a march on New Bern became a key, and recurring, component in the actions of the political elite from December through March. The importance of the belief in that threat can be in seen in the chronology of the actions of the Assembly, which began its session on December 3.

Tryon opened the Assembly with a speech emphasizing the problems in need of attention, beginning with an inquiry into the colony's finances and the practices of the officials in charge of those accounts. This effort, said the governor, would "give great and just Content to the Public." Tryon then turned his attention to the recent events in Hillsborough. He referred to the "Seditious Mob, Men who . . . have torn down Justice from Her Tribunal, and renounced all Legislative Authority. . . . These men . . . have broken through all the Bounds of Human Society." Tryon, thus quite literally framing the Regulators as out of bounds, asserted that given a little "Manly Determination" the government could "suppress these dangerous Commotions." He then asked for a resolution to raise men "under the Rules and Discipline of War."[44]

The Assembly's response admitted that the Regulators were now "too formidable for the Ordinary process of Law" and that something decisive needed to be done. Its speech also conceded that "the conduct of public officers in some parts of this Province, perhaps, has given just cause of complaint." It went on, however, to excuse the apparent corruption as not being immoral so much as mistaken given the confusing fee system.[45] Initially, in other words, a cautious sympathy for the backcountry movement remained clear. One witness even described the Assembly as being "as much Regulators in their hearts as those who had been active in the mischief," who put aside a bill to raise forces and set about punishing lawyers and clerks.[46] James Iredell, in a letter written on December 21, described the Assembly during its first two weeks as of "regulating principles." He noted that although Samuel Johnston had presented a Riot Act on December 15 (often called the Johnston Act) to simplify prosecution of the Regulators, it was ordered to lie on the table. Instead, a committee was appointed to investigate officers' fees and lawyers' practices.[47]

On December 20, Hermon Husband was ejected from the House, accused of authoring a letter printed in the *North Carolina Gazette* on December 14 that libeled Maurice Moore.[48] After Husband's expulsion, Tryon arranged to have him jailed to prevent him returning to the backcountry.[49] With Husband held without trial, the pretext now existed for the traditional jailbreak, creating a fresh alarm that the Regulators would march on New Bern. Tryon again wrote to prepare the militia against such an event and stoked the Assembly's fears by going to them on December 31 and asking for a bill of credit. "The Regulators," said Tryon, "are Assembling themselves in the neighbourhood of Cross Creek, with a large quantity of provisions, and a number of waggons in order to march down to this Town."[50]

Fear began to dominate the stage. At least one resident of New Bern believed that the Regulators intended to burn the town and even to "murder every one who shall oppose them." Invoking the language of those fearful of slave revolt or Indian attack, he professed that he was afraid to go to bed, not knowing "when I lay down in my bed but my throat may be cut before the morning."[51] It should be no surprise then that the Assembly, on January 2, picked up the Johnston Bill, passed it, and sent it to the Council.[52] The Bill passed between the houses several times, emerging on January 10, to be signed by the governor on January 15.[53]

The passage of the Johnston Riot Act formed a key moment in the escalating cycle of fear that would lead to open conflict at Alamance. The act was similar in broad outlines to the English Riot Act of 1714, but with significant added powers.[54] Like the English act, it provided that if a riotous assembly was ordered to disperse and failed to do so after an hour's grace, then authority could freely use force without fear of incurring criminal liability. The North Carolina version further specified that disrupting a court or interfering with government officials would be construed as felonies and that any person charged with such an offense could be indicted and tried in any county, not just the one where the offense had been committed. The person so indicted would have sixty days to appear for the trial. Failure to appear would constitute an automatic guilty verdict, after which "it shall and may be lawful to and for any Person or Persons to kill and destroy such Offender or Offenders" at will. Although the act was to remain in force for only one year, the sixty-day guilty clause was an extraordinary breach of the common practice of English law and had more in common with colonial statutes governing treatment of runaway slaves.[55] Legal authorities in England quickly determined that the act was illegal, and the official instructions to Tryon's recently appointed replacement, Josiah Martin, ordered him not to allow its renewal without changing that clause.[56]

This sweeping enlargement of governmental power was significant enough in itself. But the act went further still in laying the groundwork for legitimating the potential violence to come. It quite literally defined the rules of violence and response. The act specified that if any "number of Men shall be found embodied and in an armed and hostile manner, to withstand or oppose any military Forces, and [if they fail to surrender when asked] they shall be considered as Traitors." Meanwhile, the governor could make drafts from the militia and embody them according to the "Rules and Discipline as directed in case of an Insurrection."[57] And, as will be seen, the governor's behavior and rhetoric leading up to and after the Battle of Alamance precisely reflected this definition of the forms of violence available to him. The act provided a clarity of options and a preponderance of governmental legitimacy to use force that had been unavailable during the militia-Regulator confrontation in Hillsborough in September 1768.

While the Johnston Act helped define what Tryon would do when actually confronted by armed Regulators, Tryon still had to justify raising an army in the first place. As noted earlier, he had often responded to the Regulators' actions in an authoritarian paternalist manner: deploring the violence and preparing against it, while also acknowledging their grievances.[58] At some point during the winter of 1770–71, Tryon made the decision that military force would be necessary. It is difficult to determine exactly when he personally reached that decision. His actions from early December through to the beginning of his march into the backcountry, however, clearly indicate his recognition of the need to build support for that course of action. Thus his *personal* efforts, calculated as they were publicly to justify a violent response and gain the army that he needed, reveal *collective* values about the uses and limits of violence. In January and February of 1771, he continued to keep alive the increasingly likely rumors that the Regulators would march on New Bern to free Hermon Husband. He reported first to the Assembly on January 22, and then to the Council on February 7. The latter report said that the Regulators planned to "lay New Bern in ashes—and that by their advertisement had fixed on Monday the 11th [of February] to begin their march."[59] The Council and the governor moved to prevent the further sale of powder and lead to the public and also alerted several county militias to prepare to obstruct the march, to "repel force with force."[60] Tryon also arranged to have a 1,500-yard entrenchment built to protect New Bern, an act that surely did nothing to calm fears of a Regulator attack.[61]

Tryon openly worried that without a legal indictment of Husband to justify his continued imprisonment, "no vigorous support could be relied on from the Militia."[62] Tryon thus acknowledged the political sophistication of the militia. Far from being subject to either command or the lure of an enlistment bounty, he expected that the militia's collective awareness of the illegality of Husband's confinement reduced their willingness to support the government. The militiamen did not perceive a traditional jailbreak as a threat, and since it was widely known that Husband was being held without being charged, many of them probably saw such a jailbreak as legitimate. The men of the Craven County militia mustering in New Bern, for example, initially refused Tryon's personal appeal to march against the Regulators. They agreed only after he altered his request, specifying that he asked only that they fight if the Regulators "should . . . come down and destroy all your livings."[63] Here again, behavior was in part defined by notions of legitimate violence. The militia registered its acceptance of a jailbreak, as Tryon belatedly realized, but would fight to protect their homes should the Regulators step over that boundary.

Given his problems with the militia and his need therefore to solidify his legal position, Tryon held a special court on February 7, and he submitted a charge of libel against Husband to a grand jury on the eighth.[64] The grand jury rejected the indictment, and Husband was set free the same day.

The reaction of the Regulators clearly demonstrated that they were still in careful riot mode. They had been, in fact, en route to New Bern. Rumor had made them as many as 2,200 men, but one of the militia colonels who observed their camp reported their numbers as closer to 300. While some were armed, they had no cannon, which, again, rumor had reported.[65] Husband, aware of the marching Regulators, wrote to inform them of his freedom. They immediately began to disperse and march back to their separate homes. On February 16, some of the returning Regulators paraded through Hillsborough in celebration of Husband's release. Reports to Tryon of the incident revealed the Regulators employing the military air of colonial protest forms, while continuing to restrain their violence: "[the Regulators] kept Master of the Town till two O'Clock [P.M.] . . . when they Marched out in Triumph, Drums beating, without doing any Injury to the Town."[66] The threat gone, Tryon sent the militia home. When he asked the Council on February 27 to authorize raising some militia to protect the next Hillsborough court session, the Council replied that it seemed unnecessary at the moment.[67]

Passions continued to run high in the backcountry, however, particularly as word of the Johnston Act worked its way around the western counties. On March 6 and 7, a large body of Regulators met in an encampment outside Salisbury, in Rowan County, to discuss what to do next.[68] One of their main items of complaint, aside from the now well-rehearsed grievance about excessive fee taking, was that "the Assembly have gone and made a riotous Act." According to Waightstill Avery's account, the Regulators more frequently threatened to actually kill their enemies than had been true of previous Regulator meetings, and the act was the key to this new level of frustration. A Regulator orator claimed that "if they had not made that Act we might have suffered some of them to live." The speaker speculated that the idea could have come only from tyrannical (and Catholic) France, and that "they'll bring the Inquisition next."[69]

The Regulators, however, were still a long way from attacking anyone. When John Frohock and Alexander Martin, prominent officials of Rowan County and frequent targets of Regulator protests, arrived at the Regulator camp to meet them, they described the Regulators as "peaceably disposed beyond expectation." Frohock and Martin noted that some were armed and some not, and the Regulators claimed that their "Arms were not for Offence, but to defend themselves if assaulted." The Regulators asserted that they had no intention of harming any person or property and then formed a committee that would meet with a similar committee chosen by Frohock and Martin to discuss their grievances. They set a date for the third Tuesday in May, "upon which the main Body after being informed what had been done, went through the Town, gave three Cheers and returned to their home without using Violence to any Person."[70] Even the Moravians noted that aside from forcing lawyers to sign bonds to repay illegal fees, "they were guilty of no excesses."[71] This effort by two local officials to defuse the situation met with Tryon's disapproval.[72] By the time he received their letter describing the agreement, around April 5, Tryon's army was already on the march.

Tryon's frustration at the release of Husband had led him to try again for an indictment. His personal decision that military action was necessary is less important than his actions to secure sufficient support for it. He recognized the need to legitimize repressive force, and he fully intended to begin with legal authority derived from indictments of the Regulator leaders under the Johnston Act. As he wrote to Francis Nash on February 27, the indictments were necessary "to *Ground Military Operation upon.*"[73]

This time Tryon prepared the court more carefully.[74] For the new grand jury set to meet from March 11 to March 15, Tryon arranged for the selection of men of property whom he could count on as allies. That "very respectable" body quickly produced the necessary indictment.[75] The text of the indictment reveals both the jurors' fears and the kind of rhetoric they hoped would motivate others to march against the Regulators. It described the Regulators as "Wicked, Seditious [and] Evil" persons who "in great Numbers, under Arms . . . bararously [*sic*] insulted and broke up [the September 1770 court at Hillsborough]." They were also guilty of "destroying and pillaging the Houses of such Persons who were obnoxious to their Ringleaders and have lately assembled themselves in great numbers armed and arrayed in warlike manner and publickly avowing their intention of Marching to New Bern."[76] The rhetorical emphasis here is on men who have escaped ("barbarously") the bounds of civilization, and whose actions ("destroying and pillaging") have been motivated by personal vendettas ("obnoxious to their Ringleaders"). Furthermore, they have gone so far as to assemble in arms ("in a warlike manner") to march on the capital.[77]

With an indictment in hand, the very next day Tryon started firing off letters to begin the raising of his militia army.[78] Then on March 18, at a meeting of the Council, Tryon presented an intercepted Regulator letter. In it, the author, Rednap Howell, asserted that the movement had spread into Edgecombe, Bute, Halifax, and Northampton counties and could easily be raised against the government.[79] This inside look at the specter of a spreading insurgency prompted the Council to approve Tryon's request to raise the militia and march into the backcountry to "reduce them by force to an obedience to the Laws of their Country."[80]

The Alamance Army

Recruiting the army that would fight at Alamance involved serious problems.[81] Anecdotes survive of recruiting difficulties in five counties, and there is less certain evidence for others. Rednap Howell's letter (mentioned above) spoke of resistance during militia musters in Craven and Dobbs counties in the week prior to the release of Husband. According to Howell, only seven men attended the Dobbs County general muster, and the men at the Craven muster gave notice of their general dissatisfaction with the situation.[82] Craven County officials later identified a scapegoat for this murmuring in the ranks and court-martialed him on March 12. During the execution of his sentence of 150 lashes, the bystanders began to threaten to break up the proceedings, but the colonel of the regiment prevented it.[83] Bute County's muster in response to Tryon's call for troops (which began on March 19) failed to find a single volunteer out of a general muster of 800–900.[84] The Wake County militia muster of about 400 men had extreme difficulty in finding 50 volunteers and in fact succeeded only after Tryon surrounded the Wake regiment with his whole army.[85] The colonels of Chowan and Tyrell counties each asked permission to use a draft despite Tryon's initial instructions that all the soldiers be volunteers.[86] Although Tryon asked Mecklenburg County for 300 troops, it sent only 84. It had provided 310 during the crisis of 1768.[87]

Despite these difficulties, Tryon rose to the task. He used the standard financial inducements coupled with a hint of coercion and complemented those tactics with broad-brush efforts to legitimate the use of force. The measure of his eventual success can be seen by comparing the number of troops he requested from each county with the number actually raised. On March 19, Tryon sent letters to all the county colonels asking for a specific number of "hearty, Spirited" volunteers from each county.[88] Discounting the counties of the northern department because of pay problems with the northern treasurer, nearly every county eventually met its quota in full (see map 5).[89]

So what exactly were the motivations to participate? The evidence does not support the claim of some contemporaries that the army's recruits were motivated by "bounty money and high wages."[90] The privates' pay was identical to that offered for a small expedition against the Cherokees in February 1771 and was only marginally higher than the pay of frontier garrisons in 1764–66. The bounty offered to march against the Regulators was 40 shillings (£2), and while that was twice that offered to a militia force raised in 1760, it was substantially less than what then-governor Dobbs had hoped for when he claimed that a full £10 bounty would be necessary to raise sufficient troops.[91] The militia raised in 1761 for a seven-month tour with the British army outside North Carolina was offered a £5 bounty.[92] Finally, 40 shillings was the same bounty as that offered to North Carolinians to enlist in the Continental troops in 1775–76.[93] None

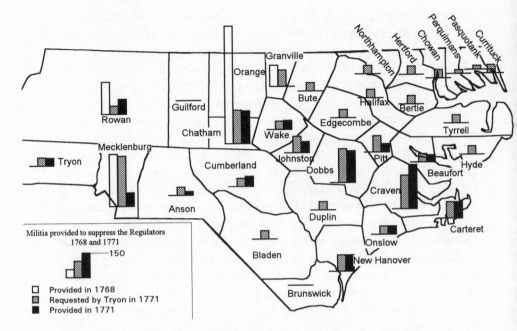

Map 5. County militia contingents of 1768 and 1771. Some figures are estimates since several specialist companies (for example, artillery, rangers, and light cavalry) were filled by more than one county. Chatham and Guilford counties are shown, but the figure therein is for Orange. Chatham and Guilford Counties were formed in 1770 (as was Wake), but Tryon did not request troops from them in 1771 either because of administrative backwardness or because they were in the heart of the Regulator movement.

of this is to discount the timeless importance of pay as a necessary factor in recruitment. Tryon himself acknowledged the problem back in 1769 when he complained to England that the lack of a local currency made it difficult to pay the troops who had supported him in 1768, and that they had made it clear that unless paid they would not be willing to help again.[94] And of course the failure of the northern treasurer to honor Tryon's warrants for pay was decisive in preventing the participation of the northern counties: no pay, no soldiers. Some pay was necessary, but its mere existence would not necessarily suffice to fill the ranks. The reluctant militia of Mecklenburg in 1768 (see chapter 2) had clearly demonstrated that further motivation was required.[95]

Tryon also hoped that laws passed in the recent Assembly promising greater toleration of dissenters in general, and Presbyterians in particular, would help solidify support for him in the backcountry.[96] He met with only partial success in this regard. Militia turnout from Mecklenburg County was lukewarm at best, although his efforts may have denied critical manpower to the Regulator army.[97]

Finally, as Tryon had done with the militia army in 1768, he took full advantage of the traditional tools of military display and discipline to solidify his control over the army, encourage or coerce recruits, and provide the appropriate message to the countryside.[98] Similarly, he used traditional military rhetoric about "honor" and "manly determination" to motivate a militia officer corps desirous of enhancing its social status with military titles and possibly military success.[99]

The resulting army has often been described as officer-heavy and composed of an unusual percentage of colonial gentry. Lacking a detailed socioeconomic study of the Alamance army, comments on its composition must remain impressionistic. It is true that several counties seem to have sent small forces of gentry, which Tryon organized into a troop of light horse.[100] But both anti-Regulator armies, the western one under General Hugh Waddell and Tryon's, had ratios of officers to men similar to later militia organizations, although Tryon's efforts to regularize the ranks may have obscured a number of men who in other circumstances might have carried a commission. Not counting clerks, surgeons, chaplains, or servants, Waddell's force of 277 men was 91 percent soldiers and 9 percent officers. Tryon's army, according to the roster put together on May 22, was 8 percent officers and 92 percent soldiers.[101] Finally, Tryon acknowledged the distinction between gentry participants and the "other ranks" when he distributed plunder after the battle. He noted in that regard to Lord Hillsborough that the plunder was divided among 1,009 men, which excluded the officers, the dead, and the 30 light horse.[102] This would imply that the whole of the army, save those enumerated exceptions, were truly "common soldiers." The army may have had a slightly larger than normal participation by the wealthier classes, but they certainly did not suffice of themselves.[103]

The March to Alamance

Tryon's march westward beginning May 4, 1771, provides us the first opportunity to observe the form of collective violence commonly recognized as conventional European war. While the particulars of that form were generally known to colonial North Carolinians, they had not often practiced it.[104] In part, Tryon aspired to this way of war because it was the

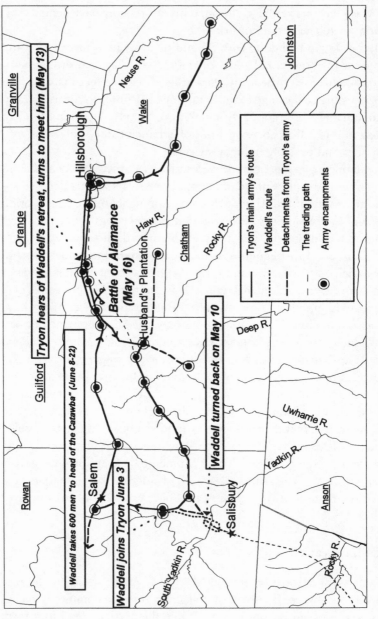

Map 6. The Alamance campaign, 1771. Each encampment of Tryon's army and the track of his army is shown. The track of his army and the trading path merge between Husband's plantation and just north of Salisbury.

Map legend:
- Tryon's main army's route
- Waddell's route
- Detachments from Tryon's army
- The trading path
- Army encampments

Map labels:

Granville

Tryon hears of Waddell's retreat, turns to meet him (May 13)

Orange

Waddell takes 600 men "to head of the Catawba" (June 8-22)

Guilford

Rowan

Salem

Waddell joins Tryon June 3

Hillsborough

Battle of Alamance (May 16)

Husband's Plantation

Haw R.

Neuse R.

Wake

Johnston

Chatham

Rocky R.

Deep R.

Waddell turned back on May 10

Uwharrie R.

Yadkin R.

Anson

Salisbury

South Yadkin R.

Rocky R.

one most familiar to him as a former British officer. He also, however, clearly believed that a rigorously controlled "conventional" army would enhance the legitimacy of his actions. Such an army, as noted previously, was more susceptible to control through military discipline and also provided a mechanism for patronage of the officers. Attention to the details of military formalism gave Tryon several advantages. It enabled the use of military display to enhance solidarity in the ranks. It provided mechanisms to control desertion, a threat doubly dangerous given that such men might well go over to the Regulators.[105] And, most importantly, Tryon hoped that a disciplined force, using eighteenth-century supply techniques, would not further aggravate an already tense countryside.[106] Tryon began his march with clear intentions both of restraining the conduct of his soldiers and of supplying them in the least intrusive manner possible. From the outset, he denied the normal subsistence allowance for the soldiers, claiming that all provisions would be supplied by the commissaries.[107] His general orders included admonitions against plundering or injuring any of the inhabitants.[108] While he frequently repeated such instructions, the repetition suggests that his efforts were not wholly successful and that the militia did in fact occasionally misbehave.[109]

Such misbehavior highlights the problem of creating a "regular army" in a colonial context. Arranging and treating the militia like a regular army was something of a two-edged sword. However much the army might try to limit its impact on the countryside, colonial anti–standing-army prejudices made it a simple matter to fuel rumors, such as were used in 1768, that Tryon aspired to create a standing army of mercenaries. Abuse and oppression, it was believed, must surely follow. A Regulator sympathizer characterized the army as "collected out of the meaner sort . . . [through] bounty money and high wages, and promises of equal share of plunder."[110] When news of misconduct by Tryon's army, real and rumored, circulated in the countryside, it naturally confirmed their fears and helped mobilize the Regulators to resist militarily. Benjamin Merrill, one of the Regulators hanged in Hillsborough after the Battle of Alamance, claimed in his gallows speech that he marched with the Regulators because of "information prevailing that the Governor was on his march to lay waste the country and destroy its inhabitants, which I now find to be false."[111] A Regulator petition of May 15 noted that "many of our common People are mightily infatuated with the horrid alarms We have heard [referring to Tryon's army's purpose and conduct]; but we still hope they have been wrong represented."[112]

Tryon moving through the countryside would be one thing, but "passing through the country, destroying houses, fields of wheat, corn and orchards, and taking from the inhabitants all manner of provisions," as one Regulator later claimed of Tryon's army, *suddenly raised the country.*[113] This of course begs the question of whether any army could ever march through a potentially hostile countryside without at least claims being made that it violated the "rules." The point, however, remains: the violation of expectations surrounding the use or threat of violence was a significant force on subsequent behavior. In this case, the apparently marauding army of Tryon "raised the country."

Once raised, how did the Regulators respond to this new threat? Frankly, they struggled and failed to arrive at a single solution. On one hand, they mobilized an army to resist; on the other, they continued to try to assert their legitimacy as protestors. Given that they in fact raised an army, what form of military violence did they choose, and how did the actions of that army reveal their attempt to straddle protest and outright rebellion? Contrary both to what one might expect and the claims of some historians, the Regulators prior to the Battle of Alamance did *not* adopt a frontier style of war dependent on ambush, raid, or surprise.[114] The sole significant act that might be described in that way has become famous as the "Black Boys of Cabarrus" incident. Nine young men of Rowan County, on their own initiative, surprised a convoy of ammunition and supplies bound from South Carolina for General Hugh Waddell's army. With blackened faces, and otherwise disguised as Indians, they stopped the wagons, searched them for military supplies, and burned those items. They then went home.[115] This act, and the later justifications for it by the relatives of these men, bore more marks of traditional "riot" violence than frontier "military" violence. Dressing as Indians, for example, can be seen as the colonial version of a long European tradition of protesting in women's dress to legitimize the violence.[116] Natalie Zemon Davis has argued that early modern rioters dressed as women in order to take advantage of women's "natural" unruliness, thereby hoping to lessen the threat of prosecution and to symbolically partake of that disorderliness. Indians provided an even more "naturally disorderly" model.[117] Furthermore, the parents of the "Black Boys," who later tried to secure them a pardon, referred to their youth and the fact that they were drunk, excuses not traditionally applied to acts of war.[118] Finally, the participant who turned king's evidence deposed that he thought "the bare burning of the Powder" would not do any harm.[119] If this was "frontier" war, then it was a very restrained version of it.[120]

It seems, rather, that the Regulators tried to have their cake and eat it too. They mobilized and acted as if they were a conventional army, but they also continued to petition the governor, that is, act as protestors, right up to the day of the battle.[121] As open conflict between the government and the Regulators began to look more inevitable, even the usually critical Moravians noted that the Regulators "resolved to establish proper military discipline among themselves, and reduce drinking and other excesses."[122] In early May, small parties of Regulators marched through the Moravian country in "good order," buying supplies, and moving on.[123] On another occasion, the Regulators stopped some Moravian wagons to search for weapons being delivered to the governor, and although they took a few tools, they "yielded to remonstrance" and did not open all the boxes.[124] It is in the actual confrontations between the Regulators and the armies under Waddell and Tryon, however, that one sees the depth of the internal conflict between the Regulators wanting to be petitioners and rioters, and those wanting to be an army.

General Hugh Waddell, marching north out of Salisbury with the militia contingents from Rowan, Anson, Tryon, and Mecklenburg counties, amounting to approximately 284 men, crossed the Yadkin River on May 5. On May 9, he found his encampment surrounded by as many as 2,000 Regulators, who demanded that he retreat back to the Yadkin. Initially, Waddell refused, and the Regulators, according to Tryon, "with many Indian shouts . . . endeavoured to intimidate [Waddell's] men."[125] Apparently they succeeded, because on May 10, a council of Waddell's officers resolved that given the superiority of the Regulator army and the general unwillingness of their troops to fight, they should retreat back across the Yadkin.[126] The Regulators perceived this as a victory and dispersed.[127]

How might the actions (and inaction) of this first Regulator army be interpreted? By gathering together in such large numbers and directly confronting a marching enemy army, they had clearly abandoned the traditional forms of riot. By remaining on the defensive and withholding from attacking Waddell's outnumbered and reluctant force, however, they showed that they had not gone all the way over into a war of rebellion. The Regulators were trying to play two sides of the legitimacy coin. On one hand, they mobilized, gathered, and confronted an enemy much as a conventional army would, demonstrating the real and potential strength of their movement. Adopting a "skulking" way of war would neither show their true numbers nor openly assert their legitimacy.[128] On the other hand, by not attacking, even in a conventional manner, they continued to try to maintain a public persona of aggrieved victims. In their eyes, after all, it was the government that was aggressively and illegally using force against them. They had mobilized to defend their homes; turning back Waddell's army was as good as a victorious battle.[129] Unfortunately, the Regulators would not be able to have it both ways. The eighteenth-century understanding of the uses and limits of violence would not allow the Regulators to demonstrate their military potential, and be "victims," *and* still avoid conflict. The confrontation with Tryon at Alamance would demonstrate that.

The Battle of Alamance

Tryon and his larger army, meanwhile, had arrived in Hillsborough on May 9. The army rested and recruited there until May 11, when it continued to march west.[130] On May 12, Tryon received reports of Waddell's retreat, and on May 13, a council of war determined that the best course of action would be to march to join forces with him near Salisbury. Tryon crossed Alamance Creek that day and established a camp. Realizing that the Regulators had gathered nearby and fearful of attack, Tryon stayed in this position through May 14 and May 15 while determining more precisely where the Regulator army lay.[131] The last negotiations before the battle began at 6:00 P.M. on the fifteenth, when Tryon received a letter from the Regulators.

In this final petition, the Regulators continued to acknowledge the fundamental political legitimacy of the Tryon regime. They still hoped to avoid violence; their petition requested only that Tryon "lend an impartial Ear" to their grievances, an act that would "promulgate such Harmony in poor pensive North Carolina, that the sad presaged Tragedy of the warlike Troops marching with Ardour to meet each other, may . . . be prevented."[132] The Regulators thus represented themselves as protestors, not revolutionaries, even while characterizing themselves as equally "warlike troops." Mobilizing and assembling, however, indicated the Regulators' awareness that their enemies had placed them beyond the pale, and that an attack was likely. They prepared to resist force with force.[133] As best as they were able, the Regulators, taken as a whole, tried to make that force conform to conventional notions of an army. If that army then fought only defensively (a preference that they had already demonstrated in front of Waddell), they would shore up their crumbling legitimacy. Their threatening, or appearing to threaten, large-scale violence had already raised much opposition against them. By fighting conventionally, by offering open battle, they could try to contain the erosion of support. To borrow the dichotomy outlined by John Keegan, the Regulators set out to employ a "western way of war," because to do otherwise would push them only further beyond the pale.[134] Their participation in the civilized manner of war, conforming to the "western way," was an effort to demonstrate their legitimacy. To fight on nonconventional terms would intensify the imagery of them as barbaric and savage.[135]

The effort of shifting from riot to conventional war and the difficulty of making that change were both demonstrated the night before the battle when the Regulators captured two of Tryon's scouts.[136] The Regulators placed the captives into the keeping of one group, but later that night some other Regulators came onto the scene, took the prisoners, tied them to a tree, and whipped them. Although such activities had been common enough throughout the early days of the Regulation, and in fact had been very publicly enacted during the September 1770 riot in Hillsborough, they were now deemed unacceptable.[137] The whipping "vexed some of the party who said they would have nothing to do with the business if such proceeding were allowed."[138] The rules of war of the day did not sanction whipping prisoners. The Regulators were too amateurish to ensure that those rules were observed but too experienced to pretend they did not know. Further evidence for the shift from rioters to soldiers, and the difficulty the Regulators had in sustaining it, occurred during the battle itself.

Tryon, on the other hand, had a similar problem, one that required that he, too, operate according to the restrained rules of war, at least until after the first battle. Like the Regulators, Tryon had to deal with public opinion. He could end up facing one of three situations. Which one he faced depended in part on public reaction to his preparation for, and use of, force. He could enjoy widespread popular support providing him with sufficient troops and a secure base to operate against relatively isolated Regulators. He could struggle through a largely passive countryside, with enough support to raise troops to fight an enemy equally troubled by passivity. Alternatively, he could be beset by thousands and thousands of hostile Regulators. As he marched to Alamance, he consistently worked to assuage public opinion, achieving in essence the second of the three possibilities. But, in the end, his political legitimacy rested on the *successful* use of force. Victory would have a significant impact on public opinion—a public opinion he had already gone to great lengths to cultivate. The countryside, it must be remembered, consisted of Regulators, enemies of Regulators, and a great number of people waiting to see which way the wind blew.[139]

For the moment then, Tryon was cautious, conservative, conventional. This need for public legitimacy had infused his recruitment strategies and his disciplining and marching of the militia, and it showed up again in his response to the Regulators' final petition. He was now in exactly the situation specified by the Johnston Act as justifying armed force. Confronted by armed resistance, he offered them an opportunity to surrender. The wording of his offer showed the extent to which the Regulators were perceived as having violated the rules of protest and laid out the last condition that would legitimize and indemnify his use of violence.[140] Addressing himself to the "People now Assembled in Arms who Style themselves Regulators," Tryon claimed that they had withdrawn themselves "from the Mercy of the Crown and the Laws of [the] Country," and he gave them one hour to "lay down [their] Arms, Surrender up the outlawed Ringleaders, and Submit . . . to the Laws of [the] Country."[141]

This message was delivered on the morning of the sixteenth, after Tryon had deployed his army from column to line about a half mile from the Regulators' camp and had begun a fresh round of negotiations.[142] For a half hour or so, an aide read Tryon's proclamation several times at different locations along the Regulators' front. All the while, Tryon continued slowly to advance until the armies were within 300 yards of each other. The Regulators responded somewhat insultingly to Tryon's aide and waved their hats at the militia to come on and attack, crying "battle, battle." Probably at this time, the Reverend David Caldwell and two Regulators, Robert Thompson and David Matear, went to Tryon as a deputation to reopen some kind of negotiation. Tryon restated his conditions and then kept Thompson and Matear as prisoners. Tryon then sent another magistrate out to read his conditions and specify that they had one hour, in accordance with the Johnston Act, to respond.

During the hour's truce, the armies continued to creep closer. Some sources claimed that they actually intermingled and that some scuffles took place, but most agreed that the two forces closed to within 30 yards of each other.[143] Samuel Cornell related that some of the Regulators actually ran "up to the mouths of our Cannon . . . [and made] use of the most aggrieving Language . . . to induce the Governor to fire on them."[144] Tryon's officers, meanwhile, had suggested that an exchange of prisoners take place. Tryon held seven Regulators and wished to exchange them for the two militiamen taken the previous evening. Some messages passed back and forth, and the Regulators eventually asked for additional time to bring the prisoners up. At about this time, Robert Thompson, the man held by Tryon from the earlier deputation, began to walk back toward the Regulator line. Ordered to stop, he apparently replied in an insulting manner and continued to walk away, whereupon Tryon shot him.[145] Tryon, at this point, may have tried to send forward a white flag, to prevent his shooting of Thompson from starting the battle. But the flag was fired on, and Tryon ordered his artillery to fire.[146] Alternative versions have Tryon sending forward another aide to indicate that the time was nearly up and that he was about to fire. The Regulators responded that "he might fire and be damned," and Tryon, according to legend, ordered his troops to fire. They initially refused, and he rose up in his stirrups and yelled, "Fire, fire on them or on me."

The opening round of artillery fire apparently caused many of the Regulators to flee the scene immediately.[147] Sufficient numbers remained, however, to contest the battle for as much as two hours. Lacking a coherent organizational structure and with only a few men willing to act as "officers," the Regulators' efforts at conventional war quickly broke down and devolved into "Indian-style" fighting: individuals firing from the cover of rocks and trees.[148] Tryon admitted in his reports that he had difficulty in driving out these men, and some Regulator accounts claimed significant initial successes. They even posited that Tryon tried to send forward a white flag in the midst of the battle. Despite one Regulator (a former soldier) crying out that it was a flag of truce and not to fire, several men fired, and the flag went down.[149] The militia having fallen back, the Regulators then supposedly charged and captured the artillery.[150] The Regulators lacked the knowledge to operate the guns, and as the cannon smoke began to clear, the militia could see that only a few Regulators held the guns. The militia charged in again, drove off the small party from the artillery, and eventually moved into the trees chasing the Regulators for perhaps a mile from the field.[151] The militia casualties were 9 killed and 61 wounded.[152] The Regulators' losses were uncertain, estimates ranging from 10 to 300 killed, 20 prisoners, and a proportionate number of wounded.[153]

The Aftermath

The events following the battle, and the public debate over the behavior of the governor, further illuminate the extent to which eighteenth-century North Carolina society felt bound by the "rules" and expectations of war.

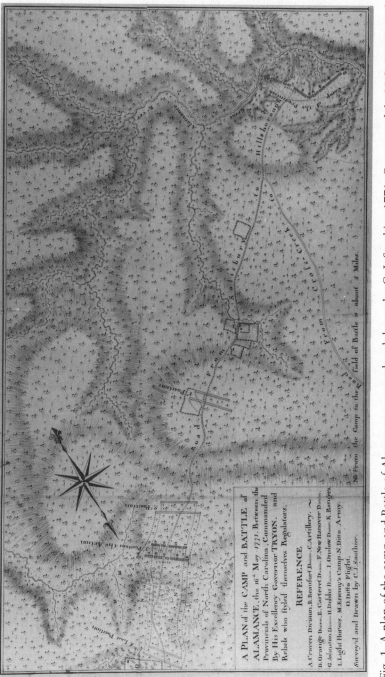

A PLAN of the CAMP and BATTLE of
ALAMANCE, the 16ᵗʰ May 1771. Between the
Provincials of North Carolina, Commanded
By His Excellency Governor TRYON. and
Rebels who styled themselves Regulators.

REFERENCE.

A Craven Division. B Beaufort D...... C Artillery.
D Orange D...... E Carteret D...... F New Hanover Division
G Johnston D...... H Dobbs D...... I Onslow D...... K Rangers.
L Light Horses. M Enemy's Camp. N Ditto Army.
O Ditto Flight.

Surveyed and Drawn by C. J. Sauthier.

Fig. 1. A plan of the camp and Battle of Alamance, surveyed and drawn by C. J. Sauthier, 1771. Courtesy of the N.C. Division of Archives and History.

The cultural practice of a particular form of violence was reached through a collective attempt to realize certain expectations. The exact nature of those expectations could be, and was, debated explicitly. The spoken and unspoken web of expectations influenced the decisions of the various actors, although very much in conjunction with the "randomizer" of their own personal predilections or interest.

Traditionally, battle in the eighteenth century carried connotations of decisiveness.[154] Alamance was no exception. Both sides experienced a marked behavioral shift in the days after Alamance. For Tryon, victory in battle released him from his previous conservatism.[155] Before Alamance, he had trod lightly, respecting the military potential of his enemy and afraid to increase it by antagonizing the countryside, acting as if, indeed, he were in a conventional war. Now he behaved as one suppressing a rebellion, with all the attendant changes in the rules. Tryon's rhetoric, both public and private, reflected the change in attitude. For the first time, Regulators, whom Tryon had always described in his correspondence as "Insurgents," became "Rebels."[156] As Rebels, the Regulators were now truly on the outside.

In the days following the battle, Tryon's actions even more clearly marked the Regulators' new status as defeated Rebels. The day after the battle, he summarily executed James Few on the battlefield.[157] Tryon then marched around the backcountry for nearly a month, destroying the farms of leading Regulators and detaching units to "apprehend any of the outlaws that may be sculking in the Neighbourhood."[158] In addition to the prisoners captured on the battlefield, the army gathered more during its march. Some were marched along with the army, roped together two by two, pending a later trial, while others were given quick trials and flogged.[159] On June 9, Tryon announced a dead-or-alive bounty on the heads of several Regulator leaders.[160] Finally, after the army returned to Hillsborough, Tryon opened a special Court of Oyer and Terminer on June 15 and tried fourteen of the prisoners. Twelve were condemned to death; six were hanged on June 19.[161]

Tryon's progress of destruction through the countryside was one half of the traditional response of English authority to a failed rebellion. The other half was to offer a way out; to allow a desperate populace an alternative to continued resistance. The pardoning of six of the condemned men was one such act of "mercy." Tryon, and Josiah Martin, who would shortly succeed him as governor, took their cue from centuries of precedent in dealing with popular rebellions.[162] They offered amnesty to those disaffected who were willing to reaffirm their loyalty, and they arranged pardons or exceptions to the laws governing treason. The major component of this program of pardons was Tryon's offer, announced on May 17, that he would grant amnesty to all who came into his camp, surrendered their arms, took an oath of allegiance, and promised to pay their taxes.[163] By December 1771, some 6,409 men had availed themselves of the pardon.[164] Over the course of the next year, the new governor, Josiah Martin, and the Assembly repeatedly shortened the list of people initially denied amnesty. Eventually only Husband, Howell, and William Butler (aside, obviously, from those already executed) were refused pardon.[165] Additionally, Tryon and Martin both wrote to the king to urge restoring the property of the executed Regulators (forfeited to the crown by the English treason law) to their families.[166] The Assembly called such mercy the "mark of his Majesty's kind and paternal attention, that he has thought fit to extend mercy to several of the offenders, unwilling to make a sacrifice to the violated laws of their Country more extensive than Exemplary vindictive justice unavoidably required."[167]

There was also a marked lack of actual pursuit, rewards notwithstanding, of those Regulator leaders still considered outlaws. Governor Martin was surprised to find that the six men who were not hanged had actually been released prior to receiving an official pardon.[168] He was even more surprised to hear that the outlawed James Hunter had attended a court session in Guilford County, and that no one there had troubled to arrest him.[169] And finally, when Martin polled the colony's justices on the propriety of pursuing further legal action against the Regulators, they responded unanimously that such action would be unnecessary. Despite the just-fought battle, Justice Thomas McGwire went so far as to say that "their offence would not amount to Treason at common Law or fall within the perview of the statute of constructive Treason . . . in which case their crimes though heinous are yet independent of the Riot Act not capital."[170]

Governor Martin's correspondence provides a perfect example of the indivisible blend of utilitarian and moral paternalism in the aftermath of rebellion. When he first arrived in North Carolina, he was convinced of the great evil of the Regulators' rebellion, but he was more than willing to pursue traditional mercy to help quiet the countryside. The utilitarian aspect of Martin's motives came out most clearly in his wish to keep secret the mercy granted to Merrill's family until he actually arrived in the back-country. There Martin would announce it publicly, "not only as a means of making my first appearance there more welcome but . . . [also] to illustrate such an emanation of his Majesty's Royal goodness by all solemnity . . . to impress a just and grateful sense of this instance of princely magnanimity."[171]

Martin eventually did travel to the backcountry to view conditions there. During his tour through Guilford County, the Regulators asked to meet with him, and he eventually agreed.[172] Their petition for mercy and explanation of their conduct aroused in him "sentiments of pity and compassion" that he had not expected. The remainder of his comments on that meeting are worth quoting at length:

> I now see most clearly that they have been provoked by insolence and cruel advantages taken of the peoples' ignorance by mercenary tricking Attorneys, Clerks and other little Officers who have practiced upon them every sort of rapine and extortion, by which, having brought upon themselves their just resentment, they engaged Government in their defence by artful misrepresentations that the vengeance the wretched people in folly and madness aimed at their heads was directed against the constitution, and by this strategem they threw an odium upon the injured people that by degrees begat a prejudice which precluded a full discovery of their grievances . . . as far as I am able to discern the resentment of Government was craftily worked up against the oppressed, and the protection which the oppressors treacherously acquired where the injured and ignorant people expected to find it drove them to acts of desperation and confederated them in violences which as your Lordship knows induced bloodshed and I verily believe necessarily.[173]

Martin went on to conclude that, given his new understanding of the Regulators, they should all be pardoned, in part (now speaking from the utilitarian side again) because of the difficulty in making exceptions "unless the criminals were in a state wherein the Royal Pleasure might operate effectually and conclusively against them."

For the Regulators, as it was for Tryon, Alamance was decisive in shaping their further decisions about violence. A number of contemporaries feared that the Regulators would continue the struggle after Alamance, perhaps resorting to a war of raid and ambush.[174] There is, however, very little evidence that the Regulators continued to resist or even considered the idea for very long. Tryon indicated that on the second night after the battle, about 300 Rebels surrounded the camp of part of his army, shot one of the sentries, and took another prisoner.[175] Then on May 22, Tryon reported that food he had requisitioned was being held up by Regulator resistance. The escort he sent retrieved the supplies without incident.[176] Such was the extent of continued resistance.

There are of course a variety of explanations for the rapid cessation of Regulator activity. Tryon's early offer of a pardon split their ranks, and as some accepted, others began to fear being turned in.[177] Some accounts of the Regulator army at Alamance indicate that many of the men present did not expect to fight and had come unarmed.[178] Clearly, those individuals would not fight on after the defeat.

Also important, however, was an understanding of eighteenth-century warfare that battle represented a decision. Regulator resistance after the battle, with the few exceptions noted above, melted away. One large contingent of about 300 Regulators, hearing of the battle, simply turned around and went home. Its leader, Captain Benjamin Merrill, apparently not feeling a need to hide out, was arrested later in his house.[179] The Moravians recorded that General Waddell met no resistance when he marched a detachment to the head of the Catawba, between June 17 and June 22, to subdue the countryside and enroll those desiring pardon.[180] Finally, Governor Martin believed, in October 1771, that the people had returned to a ready obedience to the law.[181] According to the collective understanding of conventional eighteenth-century war, defeat meant the end of resistance. Admittedly, this is a simplification. Many wars consisted of multiple battles, and, as will be seen, the American Revolution itself saw many defeats followed by continued resistance. The Regulators, however, as a popular movement, lacked the institutional resilience of a European state, which could muster another army to try for another decisive battle. They also had not achieved the kind of wide-ranging popular ideology of resistance that, in combination with emergent institutions, would sustain the brand of political revolutionary war that the American Revolution became. Lacking an institutional or ideological "fall back" position, defeat in battle, as per the understanding of the conventional form of war, was decisive.

The final example of the importance of the rules of conventional war in defining the perception of Alamance, and the post-battle discourse about it, appeared in the debate over the governor's behavior. Many people had many reasons for wanting to criticize Governor Tryon in the weeks and months that followed the Battle of Alamance. Former Regulators obviously had a very specific grievance. Northern Whigs, at a comfortable remove from the social turmoil of the Regulation, were happy to point out the "tyrannical" behavior of a royal governor. And even some of those eastern North Carolinians who had supported the suppression of the Regulators found cause to decry his methods. But the focus of all that criticism was Tryon's supposed abuse of the laws of war. Most of the accusations centered on whether Tryon had opened fire during the truce period.[182] Tryon was also accused of improperly killing Robert Thompson before the battle, of illegally hanging James Few, and then displaying insufficient mercy in his treatment of Few's and Merrill's relatives and in actually hanging six of the Rebels rather than granting them mercy as well.[183]

The specific rhetoric was revealing. Tryon's actions were "cruel . . . and unworthy a soldier."[184] How could he account for "the acknowledged Perfidy of opening on a People with a full Discharge of Artillery, &c. while under the sacred Bond of a Treaty, the Observance of which might have been expected even from a Saracen?"[185] And, in a case of turnabout being fair play, the supporters of the governor were labeled savage or "indian-like," possessing "vile and diabolical dispositions . . . [with] worse than Indian rage and fury."[186] Although one could argue that Tryon's enemies used the violations of the rules merely as a handy whip with which to flog him, his defenders countered from within the same ideological framework. They argued simply that there had been no misconduct; that it was "well known" that Tryon did not break the truce.[187]

Conclusion

This long look at the Regulators has largely ignored the causes of the Regulator movement. That subject has been exhaustively explored, although perhaps not definitively resolved. What I have shown, however, is that the course of the Regulation, in terms of the actions of both the Regulators and their opponents, and of those who might have preferred to stay neutral, can be explained to a significant degree in terms of the norms and expectations of legitimate violence. This is not to question the efforts of others to elaborate why the Regulator movement coalesced at all but rather to explain why certain events of that period took the paths that they did. Acts or threats of violence can be decisive in determining behavior, particularly collective behavior. Both sides in the Regulation struggled with the limits, styles, and consequences of violence, and they did so within strong European traditions defining the appropriate or inappropriate uses of violence. That European traditions of violence influenced colonial behavior may not sound surprising, but it is not clear that they have been given their full weight as shapers of events. The narrative of the Regulators offered here, rather than being a political, sectional, ideological, or economic explanation for the outbreak of the Regulation, is instead a cultural explanation for how the conflict worked itself out.

A significant portion of that explanation has been to emphasize the need for a group to establish a legitimate basis for the use of collective violence and then to manage violence in such a way as to reaffirm that legitimacy. If violence was so dependent upon enactment within a framework of legitimacy, who was the arbiter of that legitimacy? The Regulators represented an example of how the populace as a whole exercised significant control over that arbitration. The determination of legitimacy had always been a process of negotiation between the various levels of society but to some degree had rested finally with the political elite who dominated the mobilization of organized force. In the colonial environment, there was no ready institution of force available, and so the social center of gravity that arbitrated legitimacy shifted downward.

What drove that shift? In short, the growing potential power of the white "political public." Sociologist Roger Gould has suggested that public display of violence or violence potential communicates a message of group solidarity to the other side. It constitutes a visible symbol of that group's potential for force if its demands are not met.[188] This was surely the Regulators' intent. They were holding up their end of E. P. Thompson's "gentry-crowd reciprocity." But there was another audience. As in virtually all cases of early modern conflict, there existed a large body of the uncommitted. For that audience, the message was "our actions are legitimate." Each side sought the approval or support of, or at least to avoid condemnation by, the widest possible (political) audience. Given the tremendous capacity of violence to unseat fence-sitters, publicly establishing the legitimacy of one's violence was crucial to its success. Consequently, the Regulators went to great lengths to proactively justify their violence.

Thus widespread public opinion about the use of violence and the proper response to it came to have great power. And, as always, violence tended to demand response. It is much easier to remain emotionally neutral on issues of taxation or corrupt officials if they have not affected one personally. Violence, on the other hand, almost always created an emotional reaction. Apparent violations of the appropriate use of violence—unlike, for example, violations of tax law—had great power to lead to further violence either in retaliation or in defense of the threatened order. In the diffuse human geography of colonial North Carolina, however, the judgment of the wider public, such as that which made up the militia army in 1771, ended up resting on rumor, or in this case, on the biased report of those with established channels of communication, the very local officials of whom the Regulators complained.[189]

If the center of gravity of arbitrating legitimacy had shifted downward, by what standard was legitimacy being judged? The process of legitimation can be seen as both conscious and unconscious. That is, efforts at restraint were partly a result of rational calculations of legitimacy: "what can I get away with that the public will find acceptable?" But violence was also restrained by more ingrained cultural notions of what had proven acceptable in the past. This need for legitimation during the Regulator movement, whether rationally or culturally driven, found two methods of expression: legitimacy of form and legitimacy by demonization.

Violence is more legitimate if it is familiar, if it has the weight of custom and past acceptability. Societies are often cautious about innovation in the matter of violence.[190] Early modern Anglo-American culture had a picture in its collective mind of an acceptable riot, and the Regulators struggled to conform to that picture. Appropriately patterned violence made its purposes and limitations clear to all. Tryon aspired to a similar legitimacy of form, but for a different type of violence. He sought to suppress a rebellion, and to do so with a conventional-looking army raised on solid legal grounds.

One can also legitimate violence by constructing one's enemy as the notorious "other." The exact nature of the other is culturally contingent, changing from one time and place to another. For the colonial era, the demonization or dehumanization of Indians and African slaves is commonly pointed out in reference to the violence used against them.[191] Even with the Regulator movement, however, which involved conflict between racially if not ethnically homogenous groups, demonization was not only necessary to initiate violence but powerful in its result.[192] And in this case, the rhetoric of demonization relied on the full spectrum of early modern Anglo-colonial fears: the Regulators were treasonous Rebels, were in league with the Pretender, behaved like savages, were excessively cruel, and seemed bent on overturning a slave society.

Equally important to the nature of public violence, however, was the possibility for escalation contained within the very defining of legitimate behavior. When there are boundaries, they can be crossed. If one side violated, or was perceived to have violated, the norms of appropriate violence, then retaliation was justified. That retaliation was freed from normal restraints, and violence thereby escalated. All of these processes—adherence to form, demonization, and retaliatory escalation—also lay at the center of understanding war.

Part II

Virtuous War

Introduction

War is also conditioned by issues of legitimacy. The standards of legitimacy vary according to time and place but always arise from a broadly understood set of cultural expectations about the uses and forms of war. Therefore, to truly understand violence in war, one must first identify that society's expectations of war, found in precedent, practice, and custom. In eighteenth-century Anglo-American society (if not many others), those expectations formed a standard against which the legitimacy of violence was measured. It may be that there have been societies in which a select few determined what was acceptable violence in war, and because of their unique position in that society, they could act in a manner contrary to wider public expectations. In the eighteenth-century European Atlantic world, however, particularly in revolutionary North America, the use of military violence reflected a more broadly based sociocultural set of expectations, in part because the needs of the Revolutionary War demanded a widespread belief in its legitimacy on both domestic and international fronts.[1] In other words, the fundamental *political* legitimacy of an organization or a state depended in part on the public perception of its use of violence (or its threat).[2]

This is not to assert, however, that all aspects of warfare were determined by cultural expectations surrounding it. For example, it is a common historical understanding that the technology of the slow-firing, wildly inaccurate musket dictated the development and battlefield dominance of long thin lines of volley-firing infantry. The resulting battles could be particularly gruesome and bloody. Technology had set the parameters of this style of battle, and usage had accustomed Western society to accept its cost. It had become the "proper way," and military officers, nearly always a conservative breed, were reluctant for many years to make changes to this basic form. At the outset of the Revolution, however, Americans had been practicing a more irregular form of warfare with and against the Indians for some time. Emulating the formal battle-line tactics of the Europeans might lend legitimacy, but at a terrible cost and with great risk to the Revolution. The Americans developed a compromise solution, aspiring to military formalism with the Continental army, but also happy to use the more irregular skills of the militia where possible.

Tactical battlefield developments and strategic options have been studied by many others. The concern here is the conduct of *war,* which is a much larger phenomenon than a mere concatenation of battles. In fact, even to think of war in that way at all is a reflection of Western cultural expectations that wars are fundamentally about battles. Participants and observers in and of a war were concerned not only with the battles (and a Western society such as colonial North America was certainly concerned with them) but also with the "peripheral" activities of armies, such as the taking of food and other supplies, the taxes imposed to pay for the armies, and the violent acts of armies passing by.

This is a larger and more subtle subject than what have come to be called the "laws of war," specifically the *jus in bello*. It is about how soldiers and civilians, particularly in a North American society verging on democracy (even if it was only white male democracy), understood war, and how that understanding conditioned their behavior in it. Their definitions of legitimacy encompassed more than just restraint; they included expectations of how war should be conducted. It should "look right." There was a certain legitimacy in form. This legitimacy of form, which was not always about limiting war's overall violence, nevertheless shaped it. Battle itself, the confrontation of whole armies on an open field, was an extremely bloody way to achieve results, but Western culture had come to acknowledge it as the proper way to reach decision.[3] Although these broader issues of expectations of form will play a role in the following chapters, the primary focus will be on cultural notions about the regulation, containment, or restraint of violence in the practice of war, referring specifically to the "collateral" violence of armies: plunder/supply, treatment of prisoners, murder, rape, house burning, and so on. In other words, this study analyzes not just the violence between armies but also the violence between armies and the civilian population.

In one sense, this book is an effort to reinsert the "nonpolitical" into the historical understanding of war.[4] Standard studies of war usually begin by determining the apparent political rationale for that war and then move from there to show how that rationale dictated the course of the war. Clausewitz set the model for such considerations with his famous dictum that war is an extension of the international political process. Clausewitz argued that war, considered in the abstract, naturally tended toward totality (that is, unrestricted violence), but that since in practice war represented a violent means toward political ends, the violence was tailored to suit those ends. For Clausewitz, war was limited and shaped by rational considerations of political objective. John Keegan has critiqued Clausewitz's analysis, noting that it "implies the existence of states" and that it makes no "allowance for . . . war without beginning or end, the endemic warfare of non-state, even pre-state peoples."[5]

There is room between Clausewitz and Keegan. Even within the practice of war by European states familiar to Clausewitz, there was a deeply ingrained cultural notion of the proper way of war. That understanding shaped and constrained the violence of war; war was not merely a "rational" political act. Furthermore, cultural norms shaping war may not have helped achieve the political objective, but that did not make them less rational from a contemporary's perspective. As one obvious example, the early modern English belief in an interventionist God (providentialism) affected their acceptance of the consequences of war and even the decisions of battle.[6] As another example, anthropologist Thomas Abler has observed: "it is universally true that societies which send their men to war have rules to limit the activities of those men who are engaged in killing and maiming in furtherance of societal goals."[7] This universality of restraint is certainly rational, but it was not purely political. Furthermore, despite cultural restraint, war by definition is violent: "where emotion is paramount, where instinct is king."[8] Consequently, there is often a tension between the desire to limit and the urge to destroy—neither desire *necessarily* rational, or even political.

A brief example from the more recent past may help illuminate the importance of cultural expectations of war on its conduct. Writing about the early years of World War II, Gerhard Weinberg has shown that Adolf Hitler was consistently able to surprise and invade neutral countries in part because he had redefined the political objective of war. Hitler's "rational" calculation of political goals included the outright absorption of other nations. The majority of other European polities continued to hold to a preconception of the aims of diplomacy and war that left them unprepared for the ease with which Germany discarded those limitations. They did not anticipate that Hitler's plans encompassed such extensive goals; it was "irrational." They negotiated with him according to the old rules of limited territorial exchange, trading favors or concessions for the good will of Germany, oblivious to the fact that Hitler played by different rules and would gladly accept their concessions and then conquer them anyway.[9]

The way of war in eighteenth-century North America (and North Carolina) had developed from, and continued to be influenced by, European practices. It had been modified significantly by contact with the Indians, and also by the different geographical and socioeconomic circumstances of the colonial world.[10] At the outset of the Revolution, therefore, colonists harbored two sets of expectations about war. One was the constantly evolving European version, with which many colonists were at least intellectually familiar. The other was the developed "American" way of war that was a composite of European, native, and colonial experience. The Alamance campaign provided an example of how those different traditions could be used in a contest for political legitimacy, and it exposed some of the tensions inherent within them. Governor Tryon could never have launched such a large-scale and successful military campaign without establishing its legitimacy. Similarly, the Regulators were almost equally successful in making a case for the legitimacy of their own violence. The fractures in colonial society provided the space for this contest of legitimacy, in which the use of violence played a significant role in shifting the fence-sitters. In the end, victory was decisive and conferred its own kind of legitimacy. The American Revolution provided another example of how political legitimacy could in part depend on the legitimate use of violence, and how cultural norms of violence could shape the practice of war.

North Carolinians at the beginning of the American War of Independence aspired to fight a "virtuous war": one that encompassed the restraints and influences of traditional morality, republican ideology, European military formalism, the culture of honor, adaptive and reactive responses to Native American culture, and a still strong, although diminishing, sense of providentialism. These influences (outlined in chapter 4) constituted an aggregate value system about violence in war—a value system that not only had to be played to by policymakers (through rhetoric) but that actually influenced behavior. The ideal of virtuous war shaped North Carolinians' practice of war during the Revolution, but not perfectly. The revolutionary state and its militia, institutionally weak and struggling with the tensions between ideal and perceived necessity, allowed, if not actually encouraged, violence that violated public expectations of war and that thereby undermined its political legitimacy. This was, moreover, a particular kind of loss of legitimacy. It was a loss that had occurred through violations of the rules of violence in war, and therefore the ensuing loyalist counterrevolution began as a series of acts of retaliation. The "law of retaliation" had its own cultural legitimacy. If one's enemy acted in a fashion beyond accepted practice or social or international norms, then one could respond in kind. The rebel militia quickly responded in a like manner. Thus in war, as in riot, violated expectations could lead to an escalation of violence.

The Continental army, in contrast, had greater success than the militias in fighting a virtuous war and in restraining retaliation, in part because of its greater operational reliance on the more conventional European form of war. This emphasis arose from the Continental leadership's strong commitment to maintaining that form as an outward manifestation of the legitimacy of the army and its cause. The revolutionary ideology of virtue had to be sustained, and the colonial prejudice against standing armies overcome. Additionally, as the most visible fighting force in the American cause, the Continental army had to meet international expectations of form and conduct as part of its quest for allies. These factors, combined with the much stronger institutional structure of the Continental army and the different social composition of the soldiery, allowed the Continentals to cleave more closely, though never perfectly, to their ideal model of war.

4

Colonial Ways of War

Tradition and Development

> But the very argument for the right to kill our enemies points out the limits of that right. As soon as an enemy submits and hands over his arms we have no longer the right to take away his life. Hence we must never refuse to spare the lives of a garrison which offers to surrender. The humane manner in which war is at present waged by the majority of European Nations can not be too highly commended. If sometimes in the heat of battle, a soldier refuses quarter, it is always against the will of the officers.
> **Emmerich Vattel, *The Law of Nations*, 1758**[1]

> Our hands, which before were tied with gentlenesse and faire usage, are now set at liberty by the treacherous violence of the Savages, not untying the Knot, but cutting it: So that we . . . may now by right of Warre, and law of Nations, invade the Country, and destroy them who sought to destroy us.
> **Edward Waterhouse on the Powhatan attack of 1622**[2]

Part I showed how violence as practiced in an eighteenth-century riot was neither random, uncontrolled, nor spasmodic, but rather a complex and evolving cultural practice. The participants in a riot understood that the emotional impact of violence, along with its obvious psychological and physical consequences, rendered it *prima facie* unacceptable. That awareness on the part of incipient rioters dictated that they closely follow popular expectations of form in order to make their violence seem familiar and legitimate. Historical understanding of collective violence and the consequent impact of that violence on further behavior, therefore, must begin with an understanding of the cultural expectations that surrounded violence, and whence those expectations came. This chapter takes up this issue of precedent and development, surveying the sources and development of colonial North Carolinians' practice of war.

The American conception of war, like its forms of riot, initially came across the water from Europe. Once here, that conception, already ethnically varied, began to adjust to colonial conditions.[3] Unlike riot, however, notions of war were also occasionally directly infused with ongoing changes in Europe as the colonists participated in the Anglo-French and Spanish wars and through the transmission of a practical military literature. By the time of the American Revolution, there existed in all the colonies a complex and broadly informed set of expectations defining the nature of war: how it should be fought, who should fight it, what the rules were, and even what the probable consequences of war would be. As with riot, those expectations influenced behavior. They both set the terms of initial acts of military violence and justified outraged reaction to the violation of those expectations.

This chapter begins with the European roots of colonial notions of war. It then examines how violent interaction with the native peoples affected those notions. Finally, it considers how the institution and ideology of the militia further modified the American conception of war. The result of these three influences was a complex, *gradated* set of norms delimiting the proper application of violence in war. Most treatments of war refer to an "outrage" here or a "barbarity" there, without considering what the contemporary expectations of violence were, or that some kinds of violence were considered worse than others. An obvious example is enshrined in the penal code: murder is worse than robbery. There were similar gradations in the violence associated with war. The outline of this gradation of rules will become clearer by the end of this chapter and will be fully elaborated in chapter 7.

The European Way of War

European military practice underwent a significant shift during the colonization of North America. The sixteenth and the first half of the seventeenth centuries in Europe are often characterized as the era of religious wars, during which, some have argued, Europe experienced a "military revolution" associated with a vast increase in army size and tactical efficiency based on drill and improved gunpowder technology.[4] The rapidly expanding armies of the Wars of Religion, combined with the ideological furor created by the Reformation, led to a shockingly violent way of war. Armies, enlarged beyond the capacity of their government to regularly supply, lived at will off the countryside, taking what they needed and then taking more—as a substitute for regular pay.[5]

The conclusion of the religious wars with the Peace of Westphalia in 1648 on the Continent and Cromwell's establishment of the Common- wealth in 1650 in England marked the beginning of a shift in the European application of military violence. In part a conscious rejection of the hor- rors of the previous half century, and in part a reflection of the growing bureaucratic and financial capacity of the developing nation-states, war became more limited, both in political object and in overall viciousness.[6] By the beginning of the eighteenth century, European military practice could be broadly characterized as conducted by standing armies, usually national in character, composed of the lower orders of society enlisted for long periods, led by an officer elite who aspired to older notions of aristo- cratic military leadership, and fighting dynastic wars with restrained terri- torial ambitions. Ideally, those mostly infantry armies were supplied from magazines or depots, with provisions brought to the army by wagon and river-barge. Supplies foraged from the countryside, however, remained a frequent resort, particularly when operating in the enemy's territory. The preference for magazine-based supply in part resulted from the frequency of siege warfare in borderlands littered with large, sophisticated for- tresses. Any army that sat down to besiege such a fortress quickly denuded the surrounding area of provisions, necessitating overland or water-borne supply from friendly (or at least controlled) territory.

Despite the necessity of frequent sieges, European military practitioners recognized the decisiveness of battle and sought to create favorable condi- tions in which to wage one. In part that sense of decisiveness arose from the bloodiness of eighteenth-century battle. Replacing armies was difficult and expensive, resulting in a kind of operational tug of war between the desire to achieve victory in battle and a fear of its risks.[7] The decisiveness of battle also reflected the limited goals of war at that time. Since the destruction of a state or a people was rarely the object, a visible victory could be considered sufficient to force a peace and gain whatever objective was at issue. Ideological wars or wars of survival, on the other hand, tended to continue even in the face of defeat.[8] By the late eighteenth cen- tury, however, experience had created the expectation of the decisiveness of battle—an expectation that would rest uneasily in the context of the American Revolution. However much historical hindsight might reveal that such battles only rarely achieved a final resolution, contemporaries, believing in their decisive power, both sought them and feared them.[9]

Included in this new way of war was a developed set of rules, formal and informal, designed to (or at least thought to) limit the violence and destruction of war. As Geoffrey Parker has noted, most of those conventions had developed between 1550 and 1700, but their consistent application came more slowly, and the eighteenth century is considered to exemplify them.[10] There were essentially three sources for these conventions: the medieval Christian church, the transnational recognition of mutual self-interest among the officer class, and the juridical efforts of the Age of Reason inspired by the horrors of the early seventeenth century.[11]

Medieval Christian doctrine and the transnationalism of the feudal knightly class had bequeathed an ideal of conduct in war that protected noncombatants, preserved ransomable prisoners, and provided for the safe means of communication between enemy forces (heralds, truces, and so on).[12] In the early modern era, this tradition was reinforced by a new philosophical interest in natural law, further spurred on by widespread recognition of the costs of the religious wars, and led to several attempts to codify the laws of war. In one sense, this was merely the culmination of the efforts of Christian thinkers such as Augustine and Aquinas, but it also represented a new turn in European thought demanding that war be rational, just, and limited.[13]

The juridical works most commonly cited for the early modern period were those of Franciscus Victoria (or Vitoria), Hugo Grotius, and Emmerich Vattel.[14] Their writings began to provide a definitive list of rules that explained not only just and unjust wars (*jus ad bellum*) but also the rules of conduct within war (*jus in bello*). Many of those rules were not new but merely formal restatements of developed practice. The jurists' work, however, helped codify tradition.[15] They reinforced, for example, the more nebulous strictures of the church against the harming of noncombatants and broadened the application of officers' agreements to include the humane treatment of soldier-prisoners.

To turn more specifically to the British experience, the English Civil War provides a convenient example to illuminate the progress of the conventions of war.[16] Fortunately, there have been a series of excellent studies by Barbara Donagan, along with the work of Charles Carlton and Ian Roy, that lay out the mid-seventeenth-century British understanding of the rules of war, and how that understanding affected the conduct of the war.[17]

At the outset of the English Civil War, English men and women lived in fear that the horrors of the war on the Continent would be reenacted on their island. A whole genre of atrocity literature describing conditions in Germany had stoked those fears during the years before 1642. Eventually that literature became so formulaic as to constitute a body of tropes of what was meant by barbarity in war.[18] Atrocity narratives alerted their readers to the treatment they could expect at the hands of soldiers (especially Catholic ones), including the standard list of worries: plunder, murder, rape, and house burning, but also particularly graphic details of torture, cannibalism, and babies spitted on pikes after being torn from the mother's breast or even womb. War was also believed to weaken the natural order and the rule of law, habituating people to a world of violence that had the potential to "turn the world upside down," to say nothing of what returning soldiers were likely to do.[19]

Although these were the fears at the beginning of the war, the actual nature of the violence of the English Civil War has been disputed by historians. Long-standing tradition has asserted that the war was somehow "gentlemanly," a much restrained version of the concurrent religious wars in Germany. Ian Roy, however, has challenged that notion. He pointed out that some parts of England experienced a significant amount of wastage and that there was frequent resort to forced contribution of supplies, raiding, licensed plunder, and even demands of fire-money (a kind of extortion).[20] Donagan, in turn, documented the reality of extensive violence in England. She also emphasized, however, how English leaders "struggled to observe and enforce uncodified, unwritten rules and conventions that would set limits to personal and property damage."[21] Those limits were not always obeyed, but they did succeed in creating a kind of "rickety equilibrium . . . [in which] war crimes did not become policy, atrocities were individual and sporadic, and reprisal was precariously contained."[22]

There was thus "a clear sense of bounds beyond which action ceased to be acceptable," but what exactly were those bounds and how were they defined?[23] The English of the Civil War era recognized that the "laws of nature and nations" dictated that those who cannot harm should not be killed, but they also allowed that military necessity and the dictates of retaliation could overrule that law. There was, in addition, a large body of customary rules of war. Prisoners, no longer ransomed, should instead be exchanged with those held by the enemy on the basis of equivalent rank, or dismissed under parole not to fight again. In reality, prisoners awaiting exchange might be confined or guarded in a variety of uncomfortable ways, with only officers allowed the advantage of parole. Of course the very existence of prisoners was predicated on the notion that quarter could and should be granted in battle. Even here, however, a distinction was admitted between prisoners killed in cold blood and those killed in battle by soldiers gone wild.[24] Additionally the complex set of rules governing sieges included the provision that the garrison of a town that held out "too long" might not be granted mercy.

The rules governing the capture of a town after a siege were among the most intricate, in part because of the exasperation of attacking soldiers who might have suffered tremendous casualties in the assault, and in part because of the presence of large numbers of civilians who had a traditional claim on leniency. Besiegers were, for example, not obliged to allow women and children to leave a besieged city but might do so as an "act of grace." A town that formally surrendered was immune to sack, and the surrendering garrison traditionally marched out of the city, fully armed and prepared to defend themselves, thereby capable of enforcing the terms of the surrender. Most importantly, and most subjectively, the longer a garrison held out, the harsher became the terms of the attacker. After a certain point, the attacker would be justified, according to custom, in declaring the town beyond mercy once taken.[25] The tricky part was determining exactly when that point of no return had arrived.[26]

This is not a comprehensive list but does provide a glimpse of the "customs and usages of war" as understood during that period. As customary rules, adherence depended on each side's recognizing them as both customary and necessary, and in the ability of the other side to retaliate if provoked. Reprisal was, in fact, "legitimate if norms of conduct were flouted," and its threat served to underpin the whole system.[27]

The final restraints on the violence of the English Civil War were the "military laws"—the specific codicils adopted by an army to govern the behavior of its soldiers. The greater part of military law concerned strictly military issues, such as prohibition of desertion, sleeping on guard duty, and disrespect to superiors. But English martial law also dictated that civilians were not to be raped, murdered, or plundered (without authorization). Military concern for the availability of provisions also led to rules against the soldiers taking plough horses, destroying orchards, or letting horses graze on newly sown fields. Military law prescribed corresponding punishments for all of these offenses. In 1642, Charles I, for example, proclaimed that any soldier of his army caught "Plundring, Robbing, and Spoyling" would "be executed accordingly without mercy."[28]

The laws of nature, the customs and usages of war, and military law all naturally overlapped, each one feeding the other. An army prohibition against murder of civilians, for example, was merely a codified version of the "law of humanity," codified because violations invited retaliation by the enemy and imperiled a provisioning system often dependent on local cooperation. It should be obvious that this system of informal conventions was not completely successful in restraining violence, but it did achieve Donagan's "rickety equilibrium," preventing a total descent into the *lex talionis* (law of revenge).[29]

That the conventions had some impact on behavior is also clarified by comparing the *English* Civil War to the contemporary Anglo-Irish war. The rules were readily suspended when war was waged against "barbaric" peoples, those not possessed of a civil society as defined by the English.[30] The demonization and thus easy victimization of an "other" is an important component of the human application of violence. Edmund Leach has gone so far as to say that for killing to occur, the victims must be seen "as 'people quite unlike us,' sub-human others, people to whom *my* rules of morality do not apply."[31] Part I explored the key use of demonization even in the relatively benign situation of riot; in wartime, such rhetoric reached a shrieking pitch. To English people, the Irish had always been such an "other." After the Reformation, Catholics too formed an easy target (with the Irish doubly damned), and the exploration of the New World added yet another: the savage Indian. In Ireland, the war reached heights of savagery incomparably worse than the war in England.[32] This too was a kind of rule, a legitimate cultural expectation: less mercy, less humanity, was granted to "others."[33] Vattel explicitly acknowledged this "exception," noting that complete devastation might be acceptable when punishing "an unjust and barbarous Nation."[34]

The English Civil Wars demonstrated not only the existence of a body of conventions designed to regulate the violence of war but also how widespread awareness of those conventions had created a rhetorical arena in which one could club one's enemy with their misdeeds. Propagandistic accounts of how the other side had broken the rules were widely disseminated in attempts to rouse one's adherents and sway the fence-sitters, particularly in the context of a civil war. And the dissemination of those accounts further broadened public knowledge of the concept of rules and restrictions on the violence of war. This widening public exposure to the rules of war, combined with their increasing codification by jurists, obscured the distinction between the moral and the utilitarian imperative to adhere to the rules.[35] To be rhetorically battered for "immorally" robbing and killing civilians had practical consequences, not just in terms of potential retaliation but also in terms of public support—again, particularly in a civil war. Strictly utilitarian reasons of course remained for limiting military violence; it merely became more difficult to separate the moral from the practical. An army, or an officer, known to have committed offenses against the code could expect similar treatment in return. An officer taken prisoner and paroled, who then violated his parole and returned to the fray, not only lost honor in the eyes of others but also invited retaliation if captured again.[36] Even the protection of noncombatants, originally a relatively weak imperative derived from Christian precepts, acquired practical power—even if only conditionally—from the contemporary recognition of the need to keep the army together and to secure its supplies.[37]

In the eighteenth century, the rules became more formalized—if not ritualized—both in print and in practice.[38] Military manuals of the period, although still mostly concerned with tactics and the discipline of drill, also included numerous warnings and admonitions regarding the rules of war. Samuel Bever's *The Cadet* summed up the situation by advising that wars "should be waged with moderation—with as little killing and rancor as possible."[39]

Many of the more specific guidelines found in the military manuals were designed to prevent plundering or other excesses against the civilian population. Thomas Simes's *Military Guide for Young Officers* neatly combined the issues of honor/morality and military utility:

> Not to murder or steal is a precept as binding in the field, or winter quarters as it is in the camp or city. Marauders are a disgrace to the camp, to the military profession, and deserve no better quarter from their Officers than they give to poor peasants; nor should they find more mercy, than they shew in rifling of villages. The rapes and violences of soldiers, rebound on their indulging Commanders. Licentious armies, spread a plague, instead of giving protection; and, where terror and desolation march before the camp, a thousand imprecations of undone peasants follow.[40]

Humphrey Bland's *Treatise of Military Discipline,* probably the most widely read and reprinted manual in the British army, offered a variety of suggestions to control soldiers, noting that sending troops to destroy the enemy's countryside or lay it under contribution was no longer considered appropriate, "since they only serve to render the poor Inhabitants more miserable . . . without contributing anything to the service."[41]

Roger Stevenson's manual for European partisan warfare, which he defined as small detachments operating independently from the regular army, was a little more cavalier in its attitude toward civilians, but still restrained. He admitted, for example, the utility of holding civilian hostages in order to protect the secrecy of a march, or to prevent a village from revolting against a garrison.[42] Nevertheless, a partisan officer should "not vex the inhabitants by making them furnish too much . . . , [supplies] should be demanded in proportion to the abilities of the inhabitants; and an officer cannot be too delicate in preserving the character of a gentleman in ordering contributions, and preserving the inhabitants from being robbed, or treated ill by the soldiers."[43] Stevenson's motivations for this advice are an interesting blend of honor, utility, and morality. He claimed: "I shall not say that humanity cries out against [ill usage by soldiers] . . . because it is but too common to see war silencing the laws of humanity." But concerns that peasants might rise up and kill the soldiers, combined with the need to preserve the "character of a gentleman," should make an officer want to prevent such behavior. In another example, he advised against setting fire to a village because of the inherent inhumanity of such an act, but he also noted the utilitarian reasons against such destruction.[44]

Such prescriptive advice also found expression in British orderly books from the period. The final orders prior to the landing of the British expedition to Martinique, on January 7, 1762, included:

> Plundring and Marauding without Orders will be punish'd with Death, Disciplin'd Troops are above such Scandalous practices, which reflect dishonour upon the Nation & Sully the Glory of His Majestys Arms. The Inhabitants, Negroes, &c., that remain Quietly in their Houses, & plantations, are not to be insulted—The Inhumanity of Offering Violence to Women & Children will be punish'd with Death—No Churches, Houses, or plantations, to be burnt or destroy'd without Orders.[45]

The final line of course is the telling one: "without Orders." Despite this allowance for plunder when authorized, the public *expectation,* or as one historian has put it, "as envisioned in the parlors of London," was that foraging might be necessary but would be carried out "with as much discretion and as little disruption to the civil population as possible."[46]

The formality of siegecraft and the attendant rules of surrender also continued to crystallize in the eighteenth century. Bland tried to help the commander of a garrison in deciding when the point of no return had been reached by defining it as the point when the first breach had been made. Until then a commander could ignore the attackers' threats of violence in their summons to surrender because "the Rules of War don't authorize such Pieces of Cruelty."[47] As for prisoners, the tradition of exchange and parole continued, and in cases of confinement "it is to be expected that the Commissary's œconomy of the prisoners of war, regarding victuals and place of confinement, should be such as humanity, security, and the credit of the government require."[48]

These strictures represented an ideal—an ideal in some respects rarely lived up to. In judging their relative success or failure, however, or more particularly, in judging how a population would respond to their violation, it is critical to realize that these mostly unwritten rules also had an unwritten gradation of importance. Some rules were more important than others. Donagan provided some hints of this in her observation of the difference between the hot-blooded killing of surrendering soldiers, and their cold-blooded execution after a battle.[49] Additionally, however, the ready willingness of all sides to admit that feeding an army was a difficult business placed the prohibition against the forcible taking of food and wagons quite low on the list—that is, among the first rules to be broken. The exact nature of this gradation and its consequences for popular reactions to war's violence will be dealt with in more detail in the following chapters.

To be sure, war was still hell. One historian has interpreted Frederick the Great's conception of "limited war" merely as an attempt at limiting the total destruction wrought by the war, "not at protecting individual noncombatants."[50] And since the concern of this work is not merely the rules restraining war but the sum of the expectations of war, it is important to recognize that perhaps *the* fundamental expectation of war was its essential horror. An American minister in 1775 noted that the very "idea [of war] is shocking, the heart revolts at the prospect, and none but the *savage* and *inhuman* can consider its tragical effects without horror."[51] Such an obvious assumption hardly seems worth mentioning, but when considering popular response to the violence of war, one must acknowledge the internal contradiction of expectations. Armies were expected to restrain their behavior, but on the other hand everyone knew that war was awful. A corollary of that expectation, of particular importance during the American Revolution, was that a civil war was even more horrifying than a normal one.[52]

A second fundamental assumption about war was the overall legitimacy of war's violence. While the outset of a war might involve considerable political maneuvering, propaganda, and rhetoric designed to assert the justness of starting the war, once it was begun no one questioned the basic fact that killing the other side's soldiers in battle was an acceptable act.[53] In fact, the presumptive legitimacy of killing in battle reflected the dominance of the "battle" mentality in Western conceptions of war. The "form" of violence called battle, in the Western mind, was *a priori* acceptable; killing soldiers and civilians in other contexts, however, was a different matter.[54] As South Carolina general John Drayton wrote, "I am for preventg. every Execution, even of my enemy, by private hands, but what may be done in the Field of Battle."[55]

A third fundamental assumption about war was the recognition of justification (even of legitimation) by successful force, briefly discussed in Part I. He who wins, rules. This expectation had numerous implications. A successful army, for example, might find recruiting easier as waverers chose to side with the winner. Military success could legitimate political action, one of history's most famous examples being Lincoln's use of the near victory at Antietam to issue the Emancipation Proclamation. Furthermore, in cases of rebellion, the demonstration of successful military power on the part of rebels gave them a kind of legitimacy—*de facto* if not *de jure*.[56] This had implications in the laws of war; since technically rebels were not considered legal combatants, they were not normally granted the regular civilities.[57] From a position of success, however, a rebel movement could expect combatants' rights, much as Parliament successfully did at the outset of the English Civil War when Charles I threatened to hang rebel prisoners. Parliament's ability to retaliate quickly squashed that threat.[58] Military success by rebels also had international implications; perhaps the most famous example was the American victory at Saratoga in 1777 leading to the public alliance of France with the American Rebels.

Reinforcing this legitimacy of success was a providentialist understanding of war as God's judgment (see fig. 2). The predestinarian theology of many Protestant sects lent weight to the idea that God had already determined the victor of any given conflict, and where victory was a sign of his favor, misfortune was a sign of one's own corruption. Admittedly this could take a relatively simplistic form, such as when Cromwell replied to an envoy of the defeated Dutch in 1653: "You have appealed to the judgement of heaven. The Lord has declared against you."[59] But some thinkers pushed the concept into more legalistic directions. The English Reverend William Lloyd in 1691 published an expansive discussion on the relationship between divine judgment and international politics. In his view, since it was God who gave "one Prince a conquest over another, he thereby puts one in Possession of the other's Dominions."[60] And further, since God had ordained that transfer, "[he] hath commanded his People to give Obedience to the Kings that came in by Conquest."[61]

Finally, since the present subject is the European heritage of the American understanding of war, reference must be made to the war experiences of the non-English peoples of the British Isles. The Scotch-Irish, for example, who made up a significant part of North Carolina's population, had a long history of fighting "nontraditional" wars.[62] The old Scottish tradition of the bloodfeud, a kind of semi-legal system of justice through revenge, still thrived, although under attack by James VI and I, when the first wave of Lowlanders settled in northern Ireland.[63] Once on the plan-

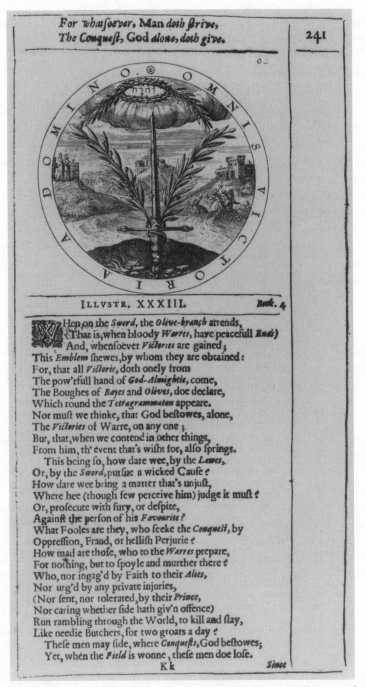

For *whatsoever*, Man *doth strive*,
The *Conquest*, God *alone, doth give.*

ILLVSTR. XXXIII.   *Book.* 4.

When on the *Sword*, the *Olive-branch* attends,
(That is, when bloody *Warres*, have peacefull *Ends*)
And, whensoever *Victories* are gained;
This *Emblem* shewes, by whom they are obtained:
For, that all *Victorie*, doth onely from
The pow'rfull hand of *God-Almightie*, come,
The Boughes of *Bayes* and *Olives*, doe declare,
Which round the *Tetragrammaton* appeare.
Nor must we thinke, that God bestowes, alone,
The *Victories* of Warre, on any one ;
But, that, when we contend in other things,
From him, th' event that's wisht for, also springs.
   This being so, how dare wee, by the *Lawes*,
Or, by the *Sword*, pursue a wicked *Cause* ?
How dare wee bring a matter that's unjust,
Where hee (though few perceive him) judge it must ?
Or, prosecute with fury, or despite,
Against the person of his *Favourite* ?
What Fooles are they, who seeke the *Conquest*, by
Oppression, Fraud, or hellish Perjurie ?
How mad are those, who to the *Warres* prepare,
For nothing, but to spoyle and murther there ?
Who, nor ingag'd by Faith to their *Alies*,
Nor urg'd by any private injuries,
(Nor sent, nor tolerated, by their *Prince*,
Nor caring whether side hath giv'n offence)
Run rambling through the World, to kill and slay,
Like needie Butchers, for two groats a day ?
   These men may side, where *Conquests*, God bestowes;
   Yet, when the *Field* is wonne, these men doe lose.
                                        K k   *Since*

Fig. 2. War as God's Justice. From George Wither, *A Collection of Emblemes.* By permission of the University of South Carolina Press.

tation in northern Ireland (starting around 1610), the Scotch-Irish found themselves engaged in a long conflict with the native Irish.[64] Many of the displaced Irish became "widcairns" or "wood-kerns" ("kern" meaning a light-armed soldier) who operated in small bands and lived by plunder. The government offered bounties for their heads, and "the colonists . . . were ferocious in dealing with any kerns who were caught."[65] The Scottish colonists used bloodhounds to hunt them out and often shot captured kerns without trial. Those kerns who were tried were paraded through the village with a halter around their neck and then hanged. The second wave of Scot immigrants arrived in Ireland just in time for the notoriously bloody war initiated by the Irish rebellion of 1641.[66] Yet another wave of Scottish emigration to Ireland was fomented by the ugly guerilla war waged against Charles II by the Covenanters of the western Lowlands in the 1660s and 1670s, an era known as the "killing times."[67] Even the decisive victory over the Irish at the Battle of the Boyne in 1690 did not end Scotch-Irish fears. Rumors and threats of risings continued to keep them on edge in the eighteenth century; many of those people would shortly embark for the New World.

This brief summary of European, and especially British, expectations of war should start to clarify the potential contradictions inherent in those expectations. Depending on situation and perspective, different rules or expectations could be brought to bear in conflicting ways. For example, demonization of the enemy could be used to justify violence that would otherwise be deemed illegitimate. Acknowledgment of the successful use of force overruled the normal expectation that when dealing with rebels the usual rules did not apply. A particularly tricky contradiction was the legitimacy of retaliation versus the broader expectation of restraint. Retrospective judgments of the relative violence of any war often involve determining the extent to which retaliation was unleashed versus merely threatened. The rules of restraint, therefore, were only one cultural force affecting the conduct of war; they conditioned rather than dominated its violence. Other broader expectations, such as the conception of war as terrible by definition or the lack of rules for "others," combined with judgments of military necessity and issues of technology and logistics, played an active role in determining the contours of military violence. The question remains, however: to what extent did the need to legitimate the use of violence in the American Revolution "condition" that use? Before answering that question, one must first examine the other influences on American conceptions of war, not least of which were the native peoples of North America.

The Cultural Exchange of War

It is a very old assumption that Euro-American methods of war were informed by those of the American Indians. That assumption, of course, is mostly about tactical methods—the classic buckskin-clad American shooting at redcoats from behind a tree. There is some truth in that imagery, and it will be examined briefly here, although it has been the subject of many other historical studies. More germane to the question of violence in war is the European *reaction* to Indian ways of war. James Axtell notes that Europeans had both "adaptive" and "reactive" responses to Indian culture.[68] With regard to war, Americans fighting from behind trees, marching in loose order, and using ambush and surprise were adaptive changes. But the American conception of war and its practice also changed *reactively* as a result of contact with the Indians. Europeans, culturally prepared to view the native peoples as uncivilized "savages," quickly believed their fears confirmed when they experienced native ways of war. The fundamental conflicts in values of violence resulted in what Adam Hirsch has called a "collision of military cultures" that led to a way of war more violent than either side normally practiced.[69] The American experience of this escalation of violence between cultures also infused itself into wars fought within the European cultural milieu. This section will explore the general question of European adaptive and especially reactive responses and will then look more closely at that experience in North Carolina.

It will be simplest to begin with the relatively settled question of European adaptation of some Indian tactics and techniques of war. Those techniques, as practiced by eastern woodland Indians, relied heavily on mobile covered fire, ambush, surprise, and raid.[70] Furthermore, while Amerindian wars varied in intensity and duration, their battles tended to be small in scale and low in casualties, although a protracted siege was not unheard of.[71] Large conventional battles between Indian groups, such as would be recognized by Europeans, were rare.[72] Describing the New England Indians during the early years of contact, Hirsch claims that "native hostilities generally aimed at symbolic ascendancy" and that the "most notable feature of Indian warfare was its relative innocuity."[73]

Such generalizations of small-scale warfare applied to the Indians of North Carolina as well as to the other eastern tribes. South Carolina governor Robert Johnson wrote in 1732 about the fighting between the Tuscaroras and Catawbas of North Carolina that "they seldom attack one another in such large bodys[;] Partys of 30 or 40 Men go out and if they can steal anything and kill 2 or 3 old Women or Men they soon return contented."[74] While Johnson's comment clearly embodied a range of European prejudices about the Indians, it also includes a grain of reality about the limited aims of Indian war.

A brief aside is necessary. This more or less standard understanding of an "innocuous" Indian style of war has been strongly challenged recently by Lawrence Keeley, writing within a debate about the true nature of "primitive war." The older historical and anthropological literature on primitive or "pre-state" warfare asserted that warfare was often ritualized, and that while individuals might be subjected to horrific treatment, the overall toll of death and destruction was relatively light.[75] Keeley uses archaeological data in an attempt to prove that primitive warfare, relative to the populations involved, was very bloody indeed.[76] The outcome of this debate remains to be seen.[77]

In the case of the eastern Indian groups, however, there is a possible solution to the apparent conflict of evidence. It is conceivable that Indian warfare at the beginning of English colonization was in a transitional moment. Devastated by disease and the resultant depopulation during the earliest phases of contact, the eastern tribes may have scaled back the intensity of their warfare from that asserted by Keeley.[78] While native societies that adopted war captives may have increased the frequency of war in response to dramatic population loss, they may at the same time have modified their tactics to reduce casualties.[79] This scaling back created the kind of war described by some early colonists as more like play than war.[80] Very quickly, however, under the influence both of the escalating savagery that characterized Euro-Indian war (discussed below) and the desire to take advantage of altered economic systems (for example, the well-known intensity of the Iroquois effort to drive out the Huron and thereby dominate the fur trade), Indian warfare regained its lethality if not its former scale.

At any rate, Indian tactics certainly differed from European expectations, and although Europeans had a general familiarity with the concept of irregular war, they recognized the value of acquiring Indian techniques as well. It must be acknowledged that recent historiography now increasingly asserts that the Europeans did not first experience irregular warfare in America. The British, for example, had fought irregular wars in Ireland and Scotland, and the border wars in southeast Europe against the Turks were primarily irregular ones.[81] Furthermore, Armstrong Starkey has challenged the notion that Americans readily adapted Indian techniques.[82] While both challenges have merit, it remains true that colonial Americans consistently insisted that there was an "Indian" style of fighting, one adopted or learned by frontiersmen, and considered necessary in fighting back against Indians.[83] In fact, the most usual method adopted for fighting Indians was to ally with other Indians. The colonists living on the frontiers indisputably adapted some native techniques, and as the frontier separated from the more settled east, that fact became a matter for comment. Robert Jones, Jr., the attorney general of North Carolina, wrote to Edmund Fanning after a tour of the western counties in 1765 that the colonists there were "in the Art of War (after the Indian Manner) . . . well skilled, . . . enterprizing & fruitful in Stratagems. . . . The Shawanese acknowledge them their superiors even in their own way of fighting."[84]

More important to the colonial way of violence in war was the early discovery that the Indians had very different cultural expectations about the usages of war and the treatment of enemies.[85] This is not to say that the Europeans were "objectively" any less violent—European wars after all were full of horrors—only that their own expectations were so massively contradicted by certain Indian practices of war that Europeans were quickly led to retaliate. Similarly, some European practices equally violated the Indians' expectations so that they too escalated the violence of their war against the white invaders. To be sure, the Europeans were already well versed with using the justification of the barbaric "other" in wreaking destruction on those unlike themselves, but the mutual detestation of the other's practices of war resurrected and fostered the mentality of retaliation that had always been just below the surface of intra-European war.[86]

From the European perspective, there were two native practices that excited the most outrage. One was the use of adoptive or "mourning" war, and the other was the torture of prisoners with the associated mistreatment of the dead. Adoptive wars, most famously as practiced by the Iroquois nations of upper New York and Canada, were intended to assuage the rage and grief of bereaved relatives but also to sustain the tribe's population at a satisfactory level.[87] Captives taken by the tribe's war parties were brought back to the village and could either be adopted or sacrificed to the grief of relatives. Among other things, mourning war made women and children legitimate targets of war—not to be killed but to be adopted, thus helping spawn a whole literary genre of captivity narratives.[88] That Europeans could also mistreat other European women and children during wartime is not at issue; the deliberate targeting of women and children to be made captives, however, outraged European sensibilities of the ways and purposes of war.[89]

Captives taken in adoptive war could not always count on adoption, and the treatment meted out to those not selected, and relayed back to the European settlements by survivors, created another source of outrage. The first experience of a captive was the return march to the home territory of the Indians, and the captors held to a ruthless, if logical, standard of killing those whom they believed could not go the distance. English captives were aware of and feared such an eventuality. Mary Jemison, captured in 1755, remembered how her mother foresaw her own doom when their captors placed moccasins on Mary's feet, thus marking Mary for adoption, but not on hers.[90] Once arrived at the home village, some surviving captives were elaborately beaten and tortured as part of a grieving process for the departed. Other Indians when taken captive expected this treatment and in quiet endurance of torture gained honor. Europeans, however, never tired of being horrified by such stories. To further reinforce that horror, in some Indian culture groups the various tortures enacted on the captives culminated in their being burned (often alive) and then ritually eaten.[91]

Even those Indian groups that did not practice adoptive war frequently did place significant emphasis on the taking of prisoners as a measure of success in war, and often those captives were subjected to various kinds of tortures, usually to death.[92] To be sure, Europeans were known to use torture, but usually in judicial contexts, and they were appalled at the full participation of the Indian community (especially women) in the torture of captives.[93] Scalps could serve as a substitute for a live prisoner, and Europeans were initially horrified by this and other mutilations of the dead.[94] As historian Bernard Sheehan put it, "the Indians' habit of scalping a slain enemy as a token of victory impressed many observers as a singularly savage way of proclaiming triumph. . . . [To them] the Indians were 'butcherly minded.'"[95] Europeans in general held a passionate concern for maintaining the wholeness of the body, even in death.[96] Such concern was strikingly visible in the eighteenth-century English and American riots to prevent the medical dissection of executed criminals.[97] Again, this should not be taken as implying that Europeans had never mutilated enemy dead or mistreated prisoners; in fact they quickly adopted scalping as a means of proving a bounty. Europeans, however, continued to use scalping and torture as a trope of outrage at the differences in Indian practice. Ian Steele noted that "while Europeans and some of their colonists accepted new and curiously humane conventions that made killing some soldiers a great victory and killing others a 'massacre' of innocents, the Indians maintained clearer definitions between themselves and their enemies. . . . Loot, scalps, and prisoners were the essential symbols of martial success for the Indians."[98] And, however much Europeans might adopt scalping or be accustomed to judicial torture, cannibalism as an accepted practice remained beyond the pale.[99]

It is of course only fair to record that certain European practices of war probably equally outraged Indians, less visibly in the records but potentially contributing to an escalation of violence. It has, for example, been convincingly argued that the eastern Indian cultures did not practice rape in war.[100] If that proscription was indeed so strong, one wonders at the probable reaction to the inevitable instances of Indian women being raped by European soldiers. Furthermore, some historians have argued that the European preference for decisive, lethal, battlefield clashes, and for war pursued with the aim of complete domination (in this age of the religious wars), initially caught the Indians by surprise. Discussing the Pequot War of 1637, Hirsch argued that when the Pequots went to war with the colonists, they did so not realizing the European need for decisive victory determined by casualties. They had calculated that if they lost, the cost of losing would be relatively light.[101] This perception is supported by the oft-cited story related by John Underhill, that the English's allied Indians at the final siege of the Pequots "came to us, and much rejoiced at our victories, . . . but cried Mach it, mach it; that is, it is naught, it is naught, because it is too furious, and slays too many men."[102]

In addition, the Europeans had particular difficulty in all their wars with Indians in coming to grips with their enemy. The elusiveness of the Indians led the Europeans to adopt or reinvent the "feed fight": a deliberate attack on the Indians' crops and villages in an effort to force them to fight.[103] It is possible that this practice was also a violation of Indian expectations of war. Francis Jennings and Patrick Malone both have argued that the natives were shocked by the Europeans' wholesale destruction of villages and crops, and their generally much more lethal way of war.[104]

It is worth observing in this context that the English did not necessarily land in America prepared to wage terrifyingly violent wars against the inhabitants. They were aware of earlier Spanish experiences and cruelties, and the English actually differentiated themselves from the Spanish in believing that *they* would establish friendly relations with the Indians.[105] The early English settlers were, in fact, armed with a dual concept of "savagism" that prepared them to expect either the best or the worst of the native inhabitants.[106] When conflict came, however, the colonists quickly discovered the differences in their ways of war, the apparent irrationality

and uncontrolled violence of which served to fix and amplify their preconceptions.[107] This collision of military cultures led to escalation. As each
side perceived apparent violations of their own expectations of war, they
retaliated. Even within the strict framework of European rules of war,
such retaliation was considered legitimate. An uncivilized enemy was not
protected by the rules.

To make matters worse, just as the colonists were already equipped
with a notion of savagism, they were also equipped with a rhetoric to
amplify their outrage. The form of the atrocity narratives so widely published during the Thirty Years' War and during the campaigns in Ireland
was quickly resurrected, replaying many of the same tropes and images
but adding American particulars such as scalping. A typical version included Indians as "Blood-Hounds" who disemboweled women and
smashed children against trees and rocks.[108] Atrocity or captivity narratives distributed as books, in newspapers, or as frontier rumor helped spur
colonists to retaliate. When they did so, they felt free of the customary
restraints of European warfare, doubly legitimated by their status as
retaliators and by the "savage" nature of their opponents.

The result of this cycle of mutual violation of expectations and subsequent retaliation was a hardening of attitudes and a preconditioned response to the outbreak of war. Every Euro-Indian war, even at its outset,
became a war of retaliation.[109] Jill Lepore has identified King Philip's War
as the decisive moment in that transformation, claiming that prior to that
war, the New Englanders had emphasized their pleasant relations with the
Indians, but that by its end their sympathy had been replaced by a contempt for the "irredeemable monsters."[110] One New Englander responded
to a 1703 raid on Deerfield, Massachusetts, by advising:

That they [the inhabitants of Deerfield] may be put into a way to
Hunt the Indians with dogs. Other methods that have been taken are
found by experience to be chargeable, hazardous, & insufficient. But
if dogs were trained to hunt Indians as they doe Bears: we should
quickly be sensible of a great advantage thereby. The dogs would be
an extream terrour to the Indians: they are not much afraid of us,
they know they can take us & leave us. . . . If the Indians were as
other people are, & did manage their warr fairly after the manner of
other nations, it might be looked upon as inhumane to pursue them
in such a manner. But they are to be looked upon as thieves and
murderers, they doe acts of hostility without proclaiming war. they
don't appeare openly in the field to bid us battle, they use those

cruelly that fall into their hands. They act like wolves & are to be dealt withall as wolves.[111]

As discussed above, the first English colonists were preconditioned to expect "good" and "bad" Indians. By the middle of the eighteenth century (at the latest), for the majority of the American colonists that dichotomy had been reduced to just "bad." Where William Wood in 1634 had been generally positive about the local Indians, his 1764 editor, Nathaniel Rogers, instead grumbled about "their immense sloth, their incapacity to consider abstract truth . . . and their perpetual wanderings. . . . The feroce manners of a native Indian can never be effaced."[112] The Indians, always a kind of "other," had evolved into the notorious other, one against whom extreme violence was justified.[113] When British general James Wolfe issued orders to his regulars during the Seven Years' War to "strictly" forbid "the inhumane practice of Scalping," he specifically excepted "when the Enemy are Indians, or Kanadians dressed like Indians."[114] There was "something different about Indians," and "most colonists . . . were unable to believe that [they] were truly like themselves—humans, possessd of both reason and the knowledge of God."[115]

Even where some Europeans, whether because of a sense of morality, or the military potential of the Indians, or the diplomatic importance of certain tribes during the imperial contest for North America, might have tried to restrain the violence of whites against Indians, such attempts were usually brushed aside. A Virginia expedition of 1610 resulted in the capture of a Paspehegh queen and her two children (despite orders not to take prisoners). On the way back to Jamestown, the men forced the expedition's leader to kill the children "by Throweinge them overboard and shoteinge owtt their Braynes in the water."[116] When the soldiers demanded that they kill the queen as well, and when ordered to do so by his superior, the commander refused to burn her alive, as he was no longer in "hot blood," so he had her executed quickly with a sword.[117] A few years later, after the celebrated Indian attack and "massacre" of 1622, the Virginia colonists retaliated by falsely agreeing to a truce and using poisoned wine and a surprise volley to kill as many as 200 Indians in one village.[118] William Shea has discussed the resultant debate over this incident, noting that Virginia Company officials in England disapproved of such dishonorable war making. The Virginians replied:

> Wheras we are advised by you to observe rules of Justice with these barberous and perfidious enemys, *wee hold nothinge injuste, that may tend to theire ruine,* (except breach of faith)[.] Stratagems were

ever allowed against all enemies, *but with these neither fayre Warr nor good quarter is ever to be held,* nor is there other hope of theire subversione, who ever may informe you to the Contrarie.[119]

The ease with which popular hatred of Indians could brush aside moral and even utilitarian arguments for restraint was also visible in the reaction to the infamous murdering of a peaceful group of Indians in Pennsylvania in 1763 by the "Paxton Boys." When Benjamin Franklin turned to the task of trying to rouse public indignation against the perpetrators, he felt obliged to go to extravagant rhetorical lengths to condemn the Paxton Boys but still failed to generate popular condemnation of them.[120] Tragically, other examples abound.[121]

This general discussion of escalation in ways of war and a hardening of attitudes toward Indians applies to North Carolina as well. For North Carolinians of the revolutionary era, whether descended from English settlers who had been in North Carolina since the seventeenth century, or from Scotch-Irish who had just arrived in the 1760s and 1770s, almost the only experience of *war* that they had known had been against Indians. The Anglo-French and Spanish wars were, with few exceptions, actually Indian wars for North Carolinians, as they had been for the future North Carolinians then living on the Pennsylvania and Virginia frontiers. And while that history of Indian wars was relatively less extensive and certainly less well known than those that took place in Massachusetts and New York, the wars were nevertheless terrifying and deeply influential experiences.

In September 1711, the Tuscaroras, with allies among several other coastal tribes, launched a series of attacks on white settlements outside New Bern and along the Neuse, Pamlico, and Trent rivers.[122] The employment of violence by both sides, and in particular the reporting of the Indians' violence, corresponded with the patterns discussed above. The initial series of Indian attacks was preceded by the capture of two prominent colonists: Baron Christoph von Graffenried, who had led a group of Swiss settlers to found New Bern, and John Lawson, the surveyor-general of North Carolina. After several days in captivity, the Indians killed Lawson but spared Graffenried, who returned to his settlement bearing the tale of Lawson's death. While Graffenried's later memoir of the events specified that he did not know exactly how Lawson had been killed, the colonists were quick to construct his death according to their expectations.[123] Christopher Gale wrote to his sister on November 2, 1711, that Lawson was "stuck . . . full of fine small splinters of torchwood, like hogs' bristles, and so [they] set them gradually on fire."[124] Ironically, in 1709 Lawson himself had published a description of exactly this kind of torture as practiced by the Sapona Indians of North Carolina.[125] In his otherwise sympathetic portrayal of the natives, Lawson negatively reflected on their practice in war. He noted that "Their cruelty to their Prisoners of War is what they are seemingly guilty of an Error in, . . . because they strive to invent the most inhumane Butcheries for them, that the Devils themselves could invent."[126]

A few days after Lawson's death, the Indians launched their attack. Colonial reports emphasized that the Tuscaroras had "without any previous Declaration of War, or show of Discontent, . . . at sun rise begun a barbrous massacre . . . killing without distinction of age or sex about sixty English, and upwards of that number of Swiss and Palatines."[127] The claim that the Tuscaroras had failed to signal their discontent is of course questionable, but it is instructive to see how quickly the colonists seized on the notion that the Indians were not playing by the rules.[128] As Sheehan has pointed out, the *reality* of the native actions was not as influential as the English expectations.[129] And sure enough, in Christopher Gale's further illustration of the barbarity of the Tuscaroras one finds echoes of the atrocity narratives of the religious and Irish wars. Gale, who had been in South Carolina during the attacks, repeated rumors about the fate of the Nevill family:

> [Mr. Nevill], after being shot, was laid on the house-floor, with a clean pillow under his head, his wife's head-clothes put upon his head. . . . His wife was set upon her knees, and her hands lifted up as if she was at prayers. . . . A negro had his right hand cut off and left dead. . . . Women were laid on their house-floors and great stakes run up through their bodies. Others big with child, the infants were ripped out and hung upon trees.[130]

The mockery of the sacred, dismemberment, impaling, and especially the violated wombs are all strikingly familiar images or even tropes from other atrocity narratives, and, like them, rumors such as these served as propaganda vehicles to motivate others to action.[131] When Gale went to the South Carolina Assembly for help, he called the attack "the grossest piece of villainy that perhaps was ever heard of in English America. . . . [the victims were] butchered after the most barbarous manner that can be expressed, and their dead bodies used with all the scorn and indignity imaginable."[132]

North Carolina's need for South Carolinian aid resulted both from an inability to rouse the militia out of their homes to aid in collective defense and from a recognition that Indian allies were the key to victory.[133] Gale again: "It is altogether impracticable to attempt such a body of men [the Tuscaroras and their allies], flushed with their first success, without Indians who are acquainted with their manner of fighting."[134] The Virginia Council also recommended trying to encourage other Tuscaroras to attack their more aggressive brethren by offering a head bounty on men, or for women and children brought in as prisoners.[135] North Carolina eventually did succeed in securing the assistance of other local tribes, and it was a force of Yamassee Indians from South Carolina that turned the tide of the war.[136]

Both the South Carolina and the Virginia governments agreed to help, but only the former provided any material assistance.[137] South Carolina dispatched a force of 33 whites and about 500 Indians, mostly Yamassees, under the command of Colonel John Barnwell. Barnwell succeeded in taking several Tuscarora forts and negotiated the surrender of Hancock's fort and the return of the white prisoners there, before marching for home.

The details of the campaign are of less interest here than are some of Barnwell's actions and observations documented in his journal of the campaign.[138] After one engagement, he was left with nine scalps and two prisoners; the latter he ordered burned alive. Immediately afterward, he marched through several Tuscarora towns and ordered everything destroyed, including 374 houses, excepting only the fruit trees.[139] Barnwell also did not hesitate to torture an enemy scout in order to obtain information.[140] During the climactic siege of Hancock's fort, Barnwell agreed to accept a negotiated surrender because the defending Indians held a number of white prisoners inside, and they "began to torture them and in our hearing put to death a girle of 8 years."[141] After the surrender, Barnwell marched through the town under a truce, and when others tried to encourage him to use the opportunity to take the fort by force, something he had promised the Indians he would not do, he replied that "I would sooner die. In truth they were murderers but if *our* Indians found that there could be no dependence on our promises, it might prove of ill consequence."[142] Barnwell thus acknowledged the necessity of observing some restraint in the face of his enemies' strong bargaining position and the continuing colonial need for native military assistance.[143]

The practices even of allied Indians, however, could further colonial fears and prejudices about their way of making war. Graffenried reported that Barnwell's Yamassee allies, after taking a Core Indian village and "killing a great many, in order to stimulate themselves still more, they cooked the flesh of an Indian 'in good condition' and ate it."[144]

Barnwell's expedition did not end the war. Raids began anew after the Tuscaroras discovered that some of their captured people had been sold into slavery in violation of the truce terms. In fact, a series of truce violations by both sides had helped keep the war hot. Graffenried arranged an early cessation of hostilities, but that truce was wrecked when a Captain Brice gathered men, attacked some Indians, and succeeded in capturing a local chief whom they then "nearly roasted alive near a fire, so much so that he died."[145] Graffenried naturally attributed the fresh outbreak of raids to this incident. A treaty was finally secured in 1713, but sporadic violence continued until early 1715.[146] The North Carolinians, deeply impressed by four years of terrible war, designated September 22 (the day of the first attack) as a "Day of Humiliation" to be observed each year by fasting and prayer.[147]

Indian wars—and more especially, fear of Indian wars—lasted throughout the colonial period in North Carolina and in the region. Just as the Tuscarora War concluded, the Yamassee War broke out in South Carolina. North Carolina played a small role in aiding that colony, spurred on by reports that the Indians had "exercised the greatest barbarities in torturing to Death most of the British Traders That were amongst them." The South Carolinians feared that they were in "imminent Danger of being massacred by Savages and perhaps of being rosted in slow Fires scalp'd stuck with Lightwood and other inexpressible Tortures."[148] Their fears notwithstanding, the South Carolinians, both black and white, were eventually able to contain the Yamassees.[149]

From the end of the Yamassee War until the early phases of the French and Indian War in the 1750s, there were no major recorded conflicts between the colonists and the Indians, but there was a relatively constant stream of reports of frontier violence.[150] The French and Indian War opened in North Carolina as an escalating series of raids—mostly by the Cherokees—on the then frontier counties of Rowan, Anson, and Orange.[151] The story of North Carolina's participation in that war has been told by others, but one incident is worth repeating here to show how North Carolinians continued to see the Indians—whom they, in common with other Americans, tended to lump together as a single group—as violators of the rules of war, who therefore merited no such consideration themselves.[152]

In June 1760, the Cherokees prosecuted a successful siege of Fort Loudoun (west of the Blue Ridge Mountains, see map 8).[153] The English garrison negotiated surrender terms as they would with a European enemy, arranging to march out with their drums and arms, and the soldiers equipped with powder and ball. Furthermore, the Indians would supply an escort who would provide food for them while they marched away. The garrison marched away for one day, and then the Cherokees ambushed the column, killed 27 men and 3 women, and took 120 prisoners. The prisoners were beaten and one was tortured to death, although eventually many were ransomed and the rest sent to the French in New Orleans. This experience of the ambush of a surrendered garrison while it marched away under truce was a common pattern in North America, and its apparent violation of the European rules aroused tremendous colonial indignation. The most famous example was the Indian attack after the siege of Fort William Henry, immortalized by James Fenimore Cooper in *The Last of the Mohicans* and analyzed as a cultural phenomenon in Ian Steele's *Betrayals*.[154]

As with the Tuscarora War, the eventual English victory in the French and Indian War did not end violence between North Carolinians and native peoples. Right up to the American Revolution, reports continued of conflict on the frontier, which served to keep alive North Carolinians' fears not just of conflict but of the particular kind of violence practiced by the Indians—or believed to be practiced by the Indians.[155] Barnwell's journal showed how utilitarian issues of allies and potential retaliation could lead to respecting at least some rules against the Indians. But even when the Cherokees had demonstrated (as they did at Fort Loudoun) the capacity to retaliate, the outrage of the colonials and their sense of violated norms drove them to continue to war against the Indians in an unrestrained manner. The violence of the Patriot war against the Cherokees in 1776, to be discussed in chapter 5, further exemplified this popular unwillingness to hold back when fighting the Indians.

In sum, colonial North Carolinians, like the other colonials, experienced a collision of military cultures resulting in Euro-Indian wars that were more violent than the normal practice either side prescribed. For many North Carolinians, this became the most familiar way of making war, a way motivated fundamentally by revenge, and reliant on "frontier" tactics of ambush, surprise, and the "feed fight." It is true that the root cause of many white-Indian conflicts can be found in the self-interested encroachments and cruelties of white settlers, leading Indians perhaps justifiably to retaliate. By the time, however, that the English settlers gathered together sufficient numbers of militia to wage war, the motivation or glue holding together such an expedition was revenge. Such a war of revenge, although increasingly subsumed in standard European notions of war, remained familiar to many colonists on the frontier from their experiences as Scottish colonists in a hostile Ireland and also correlated with the Cherokee manner of war that emphasized blood vengeance.[156] The recurrent Anglo-Indian conflicts merely served to keep alive such a way of war.

The Militia: Institution and Ideology

It was the militia that became the military instrument of revenge, but it was also the expression of much more. Its institutional structure and the ideology that Americans came to hold about the militia were fundamental forces in shaping the expectations of war held by North Carolinians at the time of the American Revolution. That structure and ideology, in conjunction with their past experience of war, would help create the notoriously fratricidal violence of the revolutionary era.

Chapter 2 briefly outlined the institutional history of the North Carolina militia, noting its existence since the inception of the colony, and its theoretically universal service requirement for white males (servants were included after 1746). This section expands on that introduction, without detailing the more or less continuous legislative efforts to update and improve the system.[157] What is more important here is the militia's actual functioning as an institution. Being in the militia meant assignment to one of the companies of a county "regiment," and the mandate to attend required musters or pay a fine.[158] The militia in this sense existed only as a pool of manpower to be tapped in emergency, with the administrative fringe benefit of providing a means to compile a list of inhabitants.

The legal and customary evolution of the militia rendered it a very problematic instrument of military force. The Tuscarora War demonstrated the difficulty of getting the militiamen to report when they felt that their own homes were threatened and needed to be defended. Worse, the colonists repeatedly demonstrated their belief that it was illegal to march them out of North Carolina, despite occasional Assembly efforts to clarify its actual legality.[159] Militiamen sometimes raised this objection even in the midst of expeditions specifically raised to leave North Carolina. The Moravians reported on the troop of about 400 who stayed in their town for several days in 1761 while bound for the Cherokee War in Virginia: "The soldiers left Sunday afternoon, but between here and Bethania some of the men mutinied, having resolved not to march out of North Carolina."[160]

The militia had other bureaucratic and legalistic weaknesses as well. North Carolina frequently had difficulty providing money to pay and feed its militia, to say nothing of furnishing arms and ammunition. Governor Dobbs stated simply in 1761 that despite a potential militia force of 16,000 men, "there are no funds to pay them or furnish them with arms Accoutrements and ammunition."[161] North Carolina expected the other provinces to pick up the tab for supplies needed for expeditions outside the colony. When that did not happen, as for example when North Carolina raised troops to aid Virginia in 1754, the troops were disbanded and sent home.[162]

The largest problem with the militia was the chronic resistance or just plain apathy displayed by both officers and soldiers.[163] In 1736, the governor complained to the Assembly that "the Penalties in the Militia Law are so slight and so inconsiderable, that it is impossible to bring them to a muster so frequently as is necessary."[164] A legislative committee in 1744 noted that the inhabitants of many counties simply failed to appoint militia officers in hopes of thereby avoiding musters.[165] Occasionally militia captains were reported to the governor as "Captains who Refuse to Act," and units sent on expeditions could melt away, taking their supplied arms with them.[166]

This unreliability in part resulted from the system of selecting officers, and the social role of officership. Theoretically all officers were appointed by the governor and held their commission at pleasure.[167] The reality was somewhat different. Governors arriving from England asked the Assembly or the Council for advice on appropriate appointments, and for officers below captain (and frequently even for the captains themselves), the governor usually sent out blank commissions to the field officers or merely rubber-stamped their recommendations.[168] When Governor Dobbs appeared to deviate from accepted practice in granting commissions, he came under fire from the Assembly and had to answer to the Board of Trade in London.[169] Dobbs also complained that he had little control over the county militia officers, because if he fired them he was unable to get replacements. He found some officers acceptable, but others were "so defective" that he could get no accounts from them.[170]

The officers themselves had different motivations for serving. Some men saw opportunities for profit in militia service through either government bounties, graft in handling militia expenses, or outright seizure and sale of Indians as slaves.[171] More pervasive, however, was the motivation of social status. Colonial society had quickly adapted the ancient European tradition of officer as aristocrat and had conferred a high social status on those with a militia commission.[172] Being a militia officer became for some a goal of social climbing, while for others, already socially "made," accepting a militia commission was a natural signal of their status.[173] Furthermore, given the officer appointment system, a field officer could use his ability to nominate subordinate officers as a form of patronage, thus further solidifying his social rank within the county. The commission as a reflection of social power was further reinforced by the occasional practice of granting rank according to how many volunteer troops an officer could raise for an expedition.[174]

With this latter characteristic, that is, the tendency to rely on social influence to raise troops, one can begin to see the role of the demands and expectations of the "soldiers" in determining the militia's overall character. The intricate patronage links between the elective assemblymen and the appointed and remunerative local positions of authority meant that militia officers (also appointive) played a significant role in influencing voters.[175] This in turn gave the soldiers some leverage over their officers. The common soldiers frequently resisted the efforts of reforming officers to discipline them and felt free to express their discontent both by voice and by action. In 1755, Captain John Sallis complained bitterly about his company going behind his back to the governor to try to remove him as captain. He assured the governor that the men did so because of his "Strictness in learning them the Discipline, and Mustering Oftener than the Law Directs," and worse, that the regiment's laxity was "wink'd at, by the Officer Commanding them, in Order to Curry favour (to get their Votes at Elections) with the People."[176] When Sallis issued warrants to fine nonattendance at muster he found that "My Serg'ts laughs at my warrants & me too."[177] On those occasions when drafts were used to fill up the ranks of an expedition, the governor found that the officers connived to avoid the call-up.[178]

All of the colonial militias, North Carolina not excepted, had difficulties imposing military discipline, whether at regular musters or while on expedition.[179] Governor Dinwiddie of Virginia noted simply that "the military Law cannot be put in force on our People but [when] conjoin'd with Regulars."[180] The old English tradition of militia musters as occasions for social interaction and festivity created an environment of familiarity that also militated against the competing tradition of strict military discipline.[181] As a final example of the democratic and intractable nature of the militia, there were of course the elaborate efforts of Governor Tryon, narrated in chapters 2 and 3, to convince, coddle, cajole, and occasionally coerce the militia into marching against the Regulators.

The militia, despite occasional resistance, did go into the field, however, and their tactics and techniques reflected both their European heritage and their increasingly American experience.[182] The militia muster had always been an opportunity to practice the more or less standard versions of European marching and firing—the parade practice.[183] And of course the social functions of the militia encouraged the maintenance of some parade as show or spectacle.[184] Even outside the muster field, the strong influence of conventional forms influenced the militia's understanding of war. When Colonel Barnwell prepared to march into Hancock's fort to accept its surrender, he arranged the occasion by drawing "the whole body up before the breach & marched them into ye Fort. 2 Trumpets, 2 Drumms, So. Carolina Standard, Yamassee & Apalatchka, Col. Boyd, Coll. Mitchell, Major Makay, Major Cole, myselfe gentelmen volunteers 2 & 2, So. Carolina men 2 & 2, ye Yamassee Capts 2 & 2."[185] Colonel James Innes, leading the North Carolina expedition into Virginia in 1754, was instructed to ensure that "all such of the Articles of War to be publiclly read as may relate to Mutiny, Desertion and the keeping up a proper Discipline among the Officers and Soldiers."[186] Many colonial militia officers also educated themselves about European war through the practical military literature of the period. Humphrey Bland's manual, cited earlier, was a standard reference work.[187]

Tryon, as has been shown, went to great lengths to incorporate standard European military practice into the militia's routine, but in general the militia brushed off such attempts and tended to settle into their own style. Governor Martin in 1772, after reviewing the militias of Orange, Guilford, and Chatham counties, remarked that "considered in a military light, nothing . . . can be imagined more contemptible in all respects . . . than those Assemblages of people in Arms, they were truly such a burlesque representation of soldiers, such a mockery of my beloved profession of arms."[188] When Timothy Pickering wrote his famous manual for the drilling of militia, he thought the showy European style unnecessary for Americans: "Away then with the trappings (as well as tricks) of the parade: *Americans* need them not. . . . 'Tis therefore preposterous, nay beyond measure absurd and ridiculous, for *them* to waste their time in learning and performing useless motions, and their money in idle parade."[189]

The North Carolinians thus adopted practices more nearly unique to America, but without completely shaking off their European heritage. Many of the militia, particularly of the western counties, preferred Indian dress, and when they brought their own weapons to muster or service, they were often hunting rifles rather than military-style muskets.[190] When outnumbered or acting defensively, the militia relied on garrisoning fortified houses or purpose-built forts. Even the semi-standing force of provincials garrisoning the frontier forts created in North Carolina during the French and Indian War relied heavily on those forts, with occasional patrolling. This was the pattern of most militia warfare: an alarm or a report of Indian incursions would lead to small numbers of militia moving to the report of the threat, gathering inhabitants in strong places, and defending them, supplemented by the occasional small, offensive patrol.[191]

Sufficiently motivated, and with adequate numbers, the colonists could and did go on the offensive. It was then that the North Carolinians, like other colonists, if fighting Indians, tended to adopt "total warfare" strategies like the feed fight. In recommending a course of action against the Cherokees in 1759, Governor Dobbs advised that

> The 3 Southern Provinces [North Carolina, South Carolina, and Virginia] . . . shou'd exert their whole force, enter into and destroy all the Towns of those at War with us, and make as many of them as we shou'd take their Wives and Children Slaves, by sending them to the Islands if above 10 years old, as the Indians use our Men &c. when taken Prisoners and not killed and scalped, and to allow £10 for every Prisoner taken.[192]

In the expedition against the Regulators, as has been shown, the militia did *not* adopt such a total offensive strategy, because of the different set of expectations that applied to that war. The post-Alamance devastation of Regulator leaders' farms and property was not a strategy of war but an act of state vengeance against defeated rebels.

Another important tradition in the colonial North Carolina militia would significantly influence fighting in the American Revolution. A number of historians have noted how the various colonial militias did not necessarily go to war in their everyday "muster" organizations. Semipermanent forces, or "provincials," were usually raised from the more mobile, less privileged segments of society rather than from the free white males that made up the militia.[193] Historians have also come to see most expeditionary "militia" forces in this way—if not outright composed of non-militia members, then at most containing only a few members of the peacetime militia, and the least privileged of those, drafted from the militia ranks. John Dederer refers to this phenomenon as a "bifurcation" in the militia, between the "universal" social institution, constantly deteriorating as a military force, and the "volunteer" branch, which relied on the dregs of society and young men, who unlike European regular armies still resisted discipline because they could go home if mistreated.[194]

The impression one gets from North Carolina is that this divide, or "bifurcation," was not as strong as Dederer argues. A better characterization might be that the militia served as a pool of manpower from which volunteers were preferred, but draftees were acceptable.[195] With the Militia Act of 1746, servants became eligible for militia service as well as free men, and, despite a growing exemption list, in 1754, of an estimated registered adult white male population of 16,400, there were only 1,000 exempt, a bare 6 percent.[196] Thus, save for black males who may have played a significant role as soldiers in expeditionary forces, the peacetime militia was in fact the total pool of military manpower available.[197] While there was a definite distinction made between units raised for expeditions and the militia that remained at home, the men came from and returned to that same pool, bringing and taking their experiences with them.[198]

While a militiaman volunteering or drafted for an expedition might lose some of his leverage with his officers if he found himself in a regionally composite unit under strange officers, that was not necessarily the most common experience in North Carolina. When the expeditionary force to South Carolina was formed in 1715, for example, three captains called for volunteers from their respective companies. They offered pay and bounty as incentive but had authority to draft, again from their own companies, if not enough volunteers were available.[199] In 1743, the North Carolina Council acted to ensure that yet another expedition to South Carolina would have local officers rather than men from South Carolina, else they doubted the chances of raising any men.[200] Governor Dobbs's and Governor Tryon's surveying expeditions on the Cherokee frontier in 1755 and 1767 were both guarded by selections from the local militia under their own officers.[201] The militia frequently turned out in small units reflecting their peacetime structure to defend locals against the Spanish raids of the 1740s or the frontier raids of the 1750s and 1760s.[202] And of course the two largest North Carolina military expeditions of the colonial era were those against the Regulators (1768 and 1771). Both of those expeditionary armies were nearly exact replicas of the peacetime militia structure, and it was those expeditions that provided the military experience of many future Patriot officers.[203]

In general then, the bifurcation in the colonial militia between the peacetime and the expeditionary versions was real, but in North Carolina there was still a strong tradition of the social peacetime version turning out relatively completely. That experience accustomed the soldiers of the North Carolina militia to maintaining some leverage over their officers, and they would continue to do so in the American Revolution.

Concomitant to the colonial militia developing its own practice of war, there had developed in America an ideology to support the continued use of the militia in preference to a regular, or standing, European-style army. The subject of the diffusion into America of the English Commonwealth Whig dislike of standing armies, and the consequent American ideological preference for a free citizen militia, is a subject that has excited a great deal of historical attention and so will be reviewed only briefly here.[204] This ideology became an important strand in the web of expectations that Americans held of the behavior of the armies that would fight the Revolution.

In England, the continued decline of the militia as an effective institution, and the growing imperial commitment, had led to an increased reliance on a more professional army even in situations of domestic disturbance.[205] This rise of a standing army led a number of opposition thinkers in England, often referred to as the Commonwealth Whigs, to intensify and justify the already traditional English dislike of professional armies. They based their opposition on an interpretation of history that saw the rise of military professionalism as "synonymous with corruption" and "inextricably entwined with the subversion of the ancient Gothic constitution by ambitious kings."[206] Their intellectual theories resonated well with the more popular English dislike, inherited from the first half of the seventeenth century, of standing armies as a source of crime, rapaciousness, and disorder.[207] Cromwell's militarily supported regime of the 1650s had only deepened that original prejudice.

The late-seventeenth and early-eighteenth-century English Whigs did more than express their dislike of a standing army; they posited the actual superiority of the militia as an institution *and* as a fighting force. Francis Hutcheson opined that a militia made up of "such reputable virtuous citizens, many of them having valuable stakes in their country, would have both greater courage and fidelity than mercenaries for life."[208]

These ideas took strong hold in America, resulting in a firm American commitment to the militia not only as a bulwark against tyranny and corruption but as an efficient military force that would not prey on the colonies' inhabitants. To cite just a few examples, Timothy Pickering wrote to the *Essex Gazette* that a well-organized militia rendered permanent professional armies unnecessary on American soil.[209] Similarly, Zabdiel Adams sermonized in 1775 that

notwithstanding the advantage a *standing army* may, on some account, have over a *militia*, yet these latter may, with more security be depended on than the *former;* because composed of men who have had their sinews strung, their limbs invigorated, and bodies hardened by daily labor, they will commonly exceed the former in strength and courage; and fighting for their estates, families and religion, will have every possible inducement to exert the most strenuous efforts in their defence.[210]

For George Mason, a "well-regulated Militia, composed of gentlemen freeholders, and other freemen" was the "natural strength, and only safe and stable security of a free government."[211] Governor Dobbs of North Carolina made a slightly different link between morality and military performance, noting that the "wantonness, luxury and neglect of the practice of . . . religious duties and moral Virtue" among the North Carolina militia was what led to their poor performance and rampant desertion.[212]

Thus, as North Carolinians entered the revolutionary era, they possessed an ideology that demanded and expected a citizen army, virtuous in its protection of the citizens, and formidable in arms. Their actual experience of war, however, was with a militia that had serious institutional flaws preventing rigorous enforcement of discipline, and whose practice of violence had been almost uniformly against Indians and therefore was of a particularly unrestrained character. The colonists were also familiar with the developing European practice of war, and the limitations on violence that that practice assumed.[213] Intellectually, Americans expected limitations to be observed, and in fact they saw the maintenance of those limitations as evidence of the virtue of the state—indeed, of the legitimacy of the state. Thus it was that the apparently illegitimate violence enacted by the British army in 1775 played such a pivotal role in motivating large numbers of colonists to support independence. And the early events of the Revolution, the battles of Bunker Hill in Massachusetts and Moore's Creek Bridge in North Carolina, seemed to bear out the virtue and efficiency of the militia as a military organization.[214] That early appearance did not last, however, and the development of the long-service Continental army reflected growing pressures of military necessity and also broader issues of international legitimacy. Those developments, and how those institutions employed violence in their particular ways, are the subject of the remaining chapters.

5

"A Fair Fight"

The Revolutionary Militias and the Struggle for Virtue, 1775–1776

> We therefore the subscribers of Cumberland County . . . thoroughly convinced that under our distressed circumstances we shall be justified before god & man in resisting force by force; Do unite. . . . And will in all things follow the advice of our General Committee, respecting the purpose aforesaid, the preservation of peace and good order, and the safety of individuals and private property.
> **Resolve of the Cumberland County Associators, June 1775**[1]

With the outbreak of fighting in 1775 and 1776, the leaders of the rebellion naturally turned to the colonial militia to provide the framework and the men to prosecute the war. While the need for collective effort led the Continental Congress to create a unified Continental army, the militia remained a crucial component of the Revolution's military arm. Much of the early fighting in North Carolina was carried out by some version of the old colonial militia institution, now freshly incarnated as the Whig, or Rebel, militia.[2]

Historical work on the Rebel militia has generally examined either its relative effectiveness as a military force or its role in the notoriously fratricidal violence of the "backcountry war." Effectiveness is not the primary concern here, although it will be seen how some of the issues of discipline and organization that related to combat performance and strategic reliability also affected the militia's use of violence.[3] This chapter and the next two focus on a version of the second issue: not just how and why the war in the countryside—the war as practiced by the militias—became as violent as it did, but how the pressures of legitimacy shaped that violence, restraining it in some contexts and unleashing it in others.

A brief note about terms is necessary. In North Carolina, the term "backcountry war" works only under an extremely broad definition of "backcountry," one that crept right up to the edge of Wilmington or New

Bern.[4] The term "militias' war" will be used instead. "Militias" is used in its broadest sense, encompassing all the non-Continental army military organizations that fought in North Carolina.[5] The word "militias," in its plural form, is also a reminder that in addition to the Whig militia, there were bands of Loyalist militia, whose behavior was conditioned by the same set of social norms and expectations of military violence.

Describing the war in the South, Ronald Hoffman expressed the standard understanding of the violence in that region following the British capture of Charleston in the spring of 1780, noting that "until the war's end, the region experienced total anarchy. Murder and banditry, brutal intimidation, and retaliation became a way of life."[6] Contemporary accounts also recognized the chaos and bloodiness of the militias' war.[7] General Nathanael Greene's comments are perhaps the most often repeated, although they were certainly not unique:

> The spirit of plundering which prevails among the Inhabitants adds not a little to our difficulties. The whole country is in danger of being laid waste by the Whigs and Torrys, who pursue each other with as much relentless fury as beasts of prey.[8]

Efforts to explain this apparently excessive military violence have often begun by blaming the British army's behavior in the South from 1780 to 1782 and the bitter resentment that it created.[9] Others have emphasized prewar class tensions, or the use of the Rebel militia as a tool for suppressing dissent.[10] Still others prefer to point out the local nature of the war, in which individuals took advantage of wartime to act on personal grudges or resentments.[11] To be sure, a wide range of motivations for violence existed, ranging, as one historian has observed, from simple "blatant greed and opportunism" to "a sadistic predisposition to violence."[12]

All of these explanations address aspects of the problem. They fail, however, to provide a comprehensive framework within which to understand the violence. Where Pauline Maier has shown how a combination of tradition and Whig ideology restrained the anti-British protest violence up to 1776, the question then arises: what happened to the nature of violence afterward?[13] Collective violence, even in the context of war, responded to social norms of legitimacy. In a military context, colonial North Carolinians were prepared to condone or at least accept certain acts and forms of violence while condemning others as illegitimate. Unfortunately, within their set of social norms lurked contradictory expectations that the new state could neither resolve nor contain. Those contradictions occasionally legitimated escalatory violence.

To restate: North Carolinians, taken as a whole, possessed a powerful set of notions about war and appropriate violence. Those notions played a significant role in shaping their behavior during the Revolution. Note the plural. North Carolinians held a number of notions about war, and those notions were founded or rooted in different values. Some had more power or greater resilience than others. The rest of this chapter and chapters 6 and 7 will explore not only exactly what those notions were but how they affected behavior, which ones endured, which ones did not, and why.

Bringing on the Revolution: The Role of Violence

The immense volume of historical work done on the question of how colonial resistance became an American Revolution precludes reviewing it all here. It is important to emphasize, however, that the role of violence in that transition may not have received its full due. In addition to the political and ideological transition from resistance to rebellion, one must add how American expectations of appropriate military violence played a crucial role in the vociferous and widely popular *reaction* to reports of British behavior in the early days of open conflict.[14] The colonists' outrage at British misbehavior, or the apparent British violation of the social norms for the use of violence (or at least the rumors of such violation), laid some of the groundwork for how the war would be fought: a war against an enemy who broke the rules.

From 1770 to 1773, a period of relative calm had descended over the relations between the colonies and Great Britain; calm, that is, in comparison to the turbulence of the 1760s and to the events to come. Parliament provided new ammunition for protest in May 1773 with the passage of what it thought was a moderate tax on tea. The ensuing events are familiar. On December 16, 1773, a great deal of tea ended up in the Boston harbor, and an angered Parliament began to pass a series of "Intolerable" Acts, beginning with closing the port of Boston.[15] The Whigs of North Carolina, while outraged and generally supportive of Boston in resisting the acts, nevertheless restrained their actions and their rhetoric. They continued to act, in short, like the careful rioters described in Part I. Several counties published resolves supporting Boston, in each case beginning their statement with the age-old affirmation of their loyalty to the best of kings.[16] The overall argument against Parliament remained political and moral, calling for resistance, not yet rebellion.[17]

The first Continental Congress's call for a ban on imports from Britain, and the arrival of more British troops in Boston to enforce the Intolerable

Acts, exacerbated tensions without initially provoking abandonment of traditional norms of behavior (at least in North Carolina). The critical moment arrived when British general Thomas Gage decided it was necessary to seize the colonial stores of powder in Concord. The resultant march of April 19, 1775, and the bloodshed it produced, dramatically changed the tone and character of colonial resistance, especially outside Massachusetts.

The various colonial committees of correspondence and safety rapidly spread news of Lexington and Concord.[18] The Whigs exploded in a rage against the British acts, calling for all Americans to fight back. They invoked that oldest rule of war: self-defense. To "repel force by force" was always acceptable.[19] In laying out the platform of resistance, the Whigs recapitulated their rationale for violence. They had petitioned the government and been ignored.[20] The king clearly had been deceived by his ministers, "the profligate part of the nobility and the corrupt majority of the house of commons."[21] Furthermore, there had been an "Increase of Arbitrary Imposition from a Wicked and despotic Ministry" that threatened the colonists' liberty and property.[22] Thus, much like the careful rioters, these incipient virtuous warriors reeled off a list of the preconditions for military violence—just war theory if you will. The list is startlingly similar to that of the rioters: war came only at the "end of a long trail of endurance—injury, petition, refusal, remonstrance, denial, warning, [and] obduracy," compounded by an ill-advised king whose corrupt ministers were threatening ancient rights and privileges.[23]

Additionally, and crucially, the British had used force illegally. The Massachusetts Provincial Congress published a broadside claiming that Gage's troops had "illegally, wantonly, and inhumanly slaughtered" Americans.[24] A circular sent to the committees in South Carolina decried the drawing of the "sword of civil war" now "stained with blood!!" It declared that

> The King's troops have at length commenced hostilities against this continent, and not confining their ungenerous attacks against men in arms defending their properties, they have slaughtered the unarmed, the sick, the helpless; having long indiscriminately oppressed they have now massacred our fellow subjects.[25]

The circular insisted, through a detailed proof, that the British had fired first. With a similar emphasis on criminal culpability, the drafters of the "Declaration on the Causes and Necessity for Taking up Arms" carefully accentuated the *illegality* of the British actions, changing words in various drafts from "attack" to "assault," and "killed" to "murdered." These revisions moved the British behavior from the realm of the military to the realm of the criminal. At the same time, the American actors were changed from "men" (the first draft) to "a soldiery" (second draft).[26] In appropriating this military language, and by emphasizing the justness of a defensive war, the drafters of the declaration asserted their legitimate transformation from rioters to soldiers. Violent American resistance was defensive, therefore just, and therefore that violence was "military," with all the connotations of legitimacy that this term implied. In such circumstances, said Zabdiel Adams, it was acceptable for a quiet people "to turn their attention to the art of war, . . . to furnish themselves with the instruments of slaughter . . . in order to their preserving themselves and property, from the hands of violence. . . . War though connected with blood and carnage, is legitimated."[27]

The incidents at Lexington and Concord also gave rise to accusations of atrocity similar to those described in chapter 4, and which would become commonplace in the years to follow. The British at Lexington had

Unmolested and unprovoked, wantonly, and in a most inhuman manner fired upon and killed a number of our countrymen, then robbed them of their provisions, ransacked, plundered and burnt their houses! nor could the tears of defenceless women, some of whom were in the pain of child-birth, the cries of helpless babes, nor the prayers of old age, confined to beds of sickness appease their thirst for blood![28]

Other accounts compared the British poorly with savages, asserting that even the savages observed some rules. The British troops, it was claimed, killed the wounded without mercy and mangled their bodies.[29]

The gaining of popular support for violent resistance demanded this kind of rhetoric to legitimate itself. Whatever the "real" motivation of radical Whigs, the rhetoric of violence (an assertion of self-defense coupled with the illegitimate violence of the British) was necessary to justify violent revolution to the broader public audience. We saw the requirement for popular mobilization in the case of the anti-Regulator militia, and James Titus has documented a similar need even for raising the Virginia expeditionary forces in the Seven Years' War. He pointed out that "the process of mobilization and war fighting [in eighteenth-century Virginia] was influenced primarily by the nature of public opinion, the precarious position of the governing elite, the absence of effective mechanisms for enforcing the laws concerning military conscription, and certain broadly shared attitudes about personal freedom that transcended social and economic categories."[30] All of those conditions recurred at the outset of the Revolution, and Michael McDonnell has recently pointed to a similar process of popular mobilization occurring in 1774–75 in Virginia.[31] As we have seen, one of the surest ways to guarantee such popular mobilization for violence is to demonize the enemy.

In the colonies, of course, there was yet another rhetorical tool of demonization available, one that tapped the great fears of the colonial mind: Indians and slaves. Whig activists in North Carolina and elsewhere were quick to use those fears. James Iredell, in June 1776, pointed out that not only were the colonists in a "state of hostility" with Britain, but that this state had been "aggravated by every possible injury the most brutal Minds could conceive." He asserted that the British did not shrink even from "the savage incitement of Indians to murder . . . , and the more than diabolical purpose of exciting our own Domestics . . . to cut our throats."[32] The British Indian superintendent in the South, John Stuart, correctly observed in the summer of 1775 that "nothing can be more alarming to the Carolinas than the Idea of an attack from Indians and Negroes."[33]

The possibility that Indians would be used against the colonies served publicists as proof of the essential corruption of Britain and was used to persuade waverers to join the struggle.[34] Southern colonists harbored significant suspicion of the intentions of the British in general, and of the Indian agents John and Henry Stuart specifically.[35] The Stuarts, and another sub-agent, Alexander Cameron, realized the potentially inflammatory consequences of using the Indians as allies. Henry Stuart may have actively tried to restrain the Cherokees, realizing that "if they should go over the Boundary Line or fall on indiscriminately to kill women and children and to attack the King's friends as well as his enemies," it would only inflame the countryside, turning potential Loyalists into enemies.[36] Despite such efforts, and despite Cameron's written promise that he would resign before he would ever be "the means of inducing [the Indians] to fall upon defenceless women and children," rumors persisted that the British planned to foment an Indian attack.[37] A speech prepared to motivate the Rowan County militia in July 1775 captured the fears and expectations of Indian violence, embodied in familiar representations of the barbaric:

> [The British intend] letting loose upon our defenceless frontier a torrent of blood, by the savage rage of Indian barbarity; who are

ordered a supply of arms and ammunition, by Lord North, immediately to attack us, and [who] resent the inhuman cruelties of the last war. Ripping infants from the wombs of their expiring mothers; roasting Christians to death by slow fire.[38]

When violence actually broke out on the frontier of the Carolinas in the early summer of 1776, Thomas Jones wrote that he hoped "a Tory will never after this open his mouth in favour of the British Government which of all Governments on Earth I believe at this time it is the most Tyrannical and bloody."[39] David Ramsay wrote immediately after the war that the Indian attack "increased the unanimity of the inhabitants. . . . Several who called themselves Tories in 1775 became active Whigs in 1776, and cheerfully took arms in the first instance against Indians, and in the second against Great-Britain. . . . Indian cruelties, excited by royal artifices, soon extinguished all their predilection for the country of their forefathers."[40]

Although some easterners may have seen the personal threat of an Indian invasion as somewhat remote, the idea still inspired a visceral reaction in them, and for those on the frontier the danger was real. In contrast, the fear of a slave rebellion was all too vivid in eastern North Carolina.[41] The summer of 1775 was alive with such rumors. That the British would seek to inspire a slave rebellion was a stock accusation in the days immediately after Lexington, but by June the rumors in North Carolina began to take on solidity. That month, Governor Josiah Martin was accused of forming "a design of Arming the Negroes, and proclaiming freedom to all such as should resort to the King's Standard."[42] On June 20, the Wilmington safety committee agreed to appoint patrols to "search for, and take from Negroes, all kinds of arms whatsoever."[43] Early July saw the Pitt County committee hardening the old system of rules governing the behavior of slaves and their freedom of movement.[44]

Then, on July 15, 1775, the safety committee of Pitt County reported that a slave in Beaufort County had confessed a projected insurrection. Forty slaves were quickly arrested, jailed, and interrogated. The examiners reportedly found "a deep laid Horrid Tragick Plan laid for destroying the inhabitants of this province without respect of person, age or sex."[45] The slaves identified a Captain Johnson as responsible for laying the plot. The committee had several slaves whipped and continued to question others. Some slaves allegedly confessed that the plan was for all of them to have risen on the eighth, to "fall on and destroy the family where they lived, and then to proceed from House to House (Burning as they went) until they arrived in the Back Country," where they would join the friends of the British government.[46] Janet Schaw noted in her journal the unifying impact that this report had on the population of Wilmington, although she later came to believe that the whole thing was fabricated as a "trick intended . . . to inflame the minds of the populace . . . to get those who had not before taken up arms to do it now."[47]

The evidence does not indicate clearly whether either the conspiracy or the governor's supposed complicity were real or simply a manifestation of colonial fears. The colonists certainly accused Governor Martin and his adherents of causing the conspiracy.[48] The Wilmington committee made out that "it was common Report" that Captain John Collet, a regular British officer commanding the small post at Fort Johnston, had "given encouragement to Negroes to Elope from their Masters" and that he had "declared openly that he would excite them [the slaves] to an Insurrection."[49] On August 2, the New Bern committee reported that it had captured a letter from Governor Martin to England. In it the governor denied any plan to raise the slaves, but he thought it would be acceptable in a state of declared rebellion. The committee (without any sense of irony whatsoever) called this a "crime so horrid and truly black" that it "could only originate in a soul lost to every sense of feelings of humanity, and long hackneyed in the detestable and wicked purpose of subjugating these Colonies to the most abject slavery."[50]

Whatever the truth of the reports, they were certainly used to encourage the militia. When a militia detachment in Anson County came to arrest James Cotton in the summer of 1775 for refusing to swear to support the committee, they saw one of Cotton's slaves start to run off to the neighbors. They warned him to stop or they would shoot. When the man stopped, "Capt Love immediately turned himself about to his Company and said now you see Gentlemen that Governor Martin and his damned officers will set the Negroes on to kill us."[51] If Governor Martin's intentions regarding the slaves had been unclear, Governor Dunmore of Virginia seemingly justified North Carolinians' suspicions when he announced in November 1775 that he would arm the Indians and free those slaves who joined his force.[52]

In addition to the volatile issues of Indians and slaves, Whig orators invoked other traditional English bugaboos about war. Had they not "been informed that the Canadians [that is, Catholics] are to be embodied?"[53] The spectre of civil war was also introduced with all its implications for Englishmen of Cromwell, military tyranny, and fratricidal strife.[54] The same Rowan County committee that spoke to its militia about the horrors of an Indian war also reminded them that the British were, in this "unnatural war,"

> declaring their intention to attack this province, by arming one part of us under British officers against the other; by which cruel means each neighborhood would be engaged in bloody massacre with its adjacent, in that bitter scourge to humanity, a civil war. Brother against brother, and son against the father.[55]

Finally, the fundamental expectation that war was naturally terrible was trotted out to encourage men to step up and do their duty. A committee of privates in Philadelphia, urging volunteers to join up, described the horrors of war that would visit them, warning that "this is the wretched conditions to which we expose our wives, our parents, and our children, and expose our own necks to the halter, . . . if we do not play the man."[56]

This rhetoric succeeded by playing to expectations of violence. In his study of propaganda during the American Revolution, Philip Davidson noted that for the instruments of propaganda "to be successful, [they] must be in line with the thinking and prejudices of the people."[57] The excessive violence of the British army, the attempt to raise the slaves, the use of Indians to inflict "indiscriminate" slaughter: these were the hot buttons after April 1775. Governor Martin complained that he did not receive an official report about Lexington until two months after the event. In the meantime, however, unofficial accounts had arrived and,

> like all first impressions [had] taken deep root in the minds of the vulgar here universally and wrought a great change in the face of things, confirming the seditious in their evil purposes, and bringing over vast numbers of the fickle, wavering and unsteady multitude.[58]

News of Lexington inspired some counties to a much more radical position than that they had adopted in 1774. Mecklenburg's militia mustered on May 19, 1775, to decide what to do about the British actions in Massachusetts. That muster led to the Mecklenburg Resolves, a document that some have called the first declaration of independence.[59] To be sure, liberty and property were still major components of Patriot rhetoric, but violence was also a powerfully emotive subject. It had a capacity to sway opinion that fine distinctions about parliamentary sovereignty did not.[60] As Samuel Johnston had predicted in 1774: "When the Sword is drawn all nice distinctions fall to the Ground, the difference between internal & external taxation will be little attended to."[61] When the North Carolina

Provincial Congress met in April 1776 to consider the question of "independency," its list of reasons for doing so was mainly composed of accusations of the use of violence by the British.[62]

Thus, the *Rage Militaire* of 1775 and 1776,[63] the filling of the ranks of the state militias, and the creation of the Continental army owed a great deal to the social norms of violence. British violations of those norms, and assertions of colonial moderation and repeated attempts to compromise, *legitimated* American defensive resistance.[64] This legitimation of resistance based on demonization of the British played a key role in broadening the base of public support. Furthermore, the fact that much of the popular resistance to Britain was founded upon visceral reactions to illegitimate violence had profound implications for the conduct of the war. The propaganda prepared the countryside to expect "out of bounds" behavior from the British and presumably, therefore, from their Loyalist allies as well. In an ironic rhetorical parallel to the condemnation of the Regulators in 1770, William Hooper declared in 1776 that "Britain has lost us by a series of impolitic, wicked and savage actions as would have disgraced a nation of Hottentots."[65] Atrocity rhetoric continued throughout the war and even survived it in postwar attempts to limit the rights of former Tories, who were called "Atrocious Monsters of Wickedness" or "turks and Canibals."[66] The Whig rhetoric may have succeeded in energizing the rebellion and temporarily filling the ranks, but it also helped lay the seeds of the bloody civil war to follow.

Military Activity in the South: 1776

Despite the inflammatory rhetoric, the North Carolina Whigs and Loyalists began hostilities conventionally. In their military activities in the first year of the war, both Whigs and Loyalists endeavored to live up to their own expectations of virtuous war. That they did not always succeed is evident, but that the situation could have been much worse is made obvious by comparing the more or less successful restraint of the early Whig war effort versus the British and Loyalists to the kind of war waged against the Cherokees in the same year.

Through the end of the summer of 1775 the Whigs employed the militia almost exclusively as an agent of internal political coercion.[67] The militia served as an organizational center, as a disseminator of news and decrees, and as an agent of enforcement for policies adopted by the committees of safety.[68] In September 1774 and again in June 1775, the Rowan County committee directed the militia companies to raise £20 for the use of the committee.[69] Three suspected Loyalists testified in August 1775 that during the summer they had been threatened by groups of armed men for failing to take the Whig oath, although in each case no one was harmed.[70] In June 1775, John Ashe, who had recently resigned his colonelcy in the New Hanover militia regiment, marched into Wilmington leading several hundred militiamen and demanded that the merchants of the town subscribe to the Patriot association oath. When asked his authority for making such a demand, Ashe merely pointed to the assembled troops.[71] A militia muster in Wilmington in June 1775 nearly led to the tarring and feathering of an English servant who had "smiled" at the militia's unmartial appearance. The officers restrained the men, but they forced him to mount a table and apologize and then drummed and fiddled him out of town.[72]

The loyalty of the militia to the Whig cause, however, could not be taken for granted. The militia was, after all, the military expression of the male population and, like it, held divided loyalties. The Cumberland County militia in the summer of 1775 held two separate musters, one for the king's friends and one for the Rebels.[73] Another militia company collectively agreed to choose sides on the basis of a fair fist fight between two of its officers, one a Tory and the other a Whig.[74] In general, however, the Whigs held the reins of administration and were largely successful in converting the old militia structure to their purposes.[75]

That administrative conversion from colonial militia to a revolutionary military began in September 1775, when the North Carolina Provincial Congress formally organized its military. On September 1, it created North Carolina's contribution to the intercolonial Continental army.[76] On September 7, it legislated a new framework for the state militia organization. The new militia law differed only slightly from its colonial antecedents.[77] First, it divided the province into six districts, allowing for a brigadier-general to organize and command the forces of each district (see map 7). Each militia company was divided into five classes or divisions. One consisted of the old and infirm; the other four served to spread the burden of service. When a call for the militia went out, theoretically only one class from each company would be susceptible to service and then usually for only three months. The law also specified that musters be held monthly rather than at the more occasional intervals of the colonial era. Finally, the Congress created a separate organization known as the minutemen. It proved to be a short-lived institution, largely collapsing by the end of 1776. It was seldom distinguishable from the general militia organization.[78]

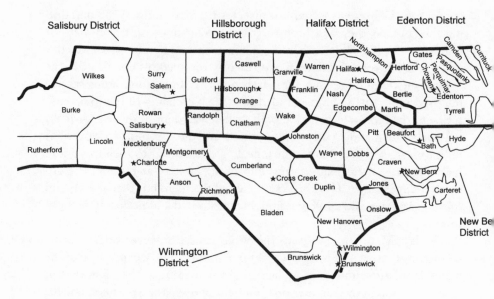

Map 7. Revolutionary militia districts, with county boundaries as of 1780.

In the course of this reshaping of the colonial militia into a Rebel militia, and the creation of its slice of the Continental line, North Carolina made a distinct effort to found those organizations on European principles of discipline. That discipline included, as chapter 4 demonstrated, formal rules of conduct. North Carolina even requested copies of Simes's *Military Guide* from the Continental Congress and duly received twelve dozen copies in August 1776, along with twenty-four copies of Simes's *New System of Military Discipline*.[79] Unfortunately, the Congress was unwilling, and probably unable, to impose a strong centralized control over the militia. For example, their instructions merely suggested that "each and every Company make such regulations as to them shall seem best, for nonattendance, disobedience, and misbehavior, at Musters by Companies."[80]

Even as it began its official military career, however, the Rebel militia continued to be an agent of enforcement, as it would throughout the war.[81] The Rowan County committee, for example, ordered the militia to bring people before the committee for examination and to confiscate gunpowder.[82] In November 1775, the New Hanover County committee directed the militia to go door to door in Wilmington and confiscate weapons, leaving one per white man in the house and a receipt for the rest.[83] The militia was also used to coerce loyalty, leading to its involvement in several unpleasant incidents in the fall of 1775. In Edenton in November, some officers and soldiers of the militia dragged suspected Loyalist Cullen Pollock from his house, marched him to the courthouse, and there tarred and feathered him.[84] Another tarring and feathering at the hands of the militia occurred in Halifax early in the fall.[85] Later in the year, Daniel Maxwell claimed that on November 27 he ran across a party of militia, who demanded that he agree to appear before the committee. He did so, but even as he voiced his agreement, a militia major came up and without explanation shot dead his companion.[86]

Despite the use of the militia as an enforcer of loyalty and an agent of confiscation, North Carolinians still expected that their citizen militia would fight virtuously and effectively. Even at this early stage of the war, the Whigs recognized that they were contending for popular support, and that to win such support they not only had to demonize the British but also had to balance the need for successful force against the requirements of legitimacy in the use of that force.[87]

Thus is framed one of the fundamental conundrums inherent in the Americans' expectations of war. Although successful force, seen as divine judgment or otherwise, might justify itself (the way John Ashe pointed to his troops as his authority for enforcing the association oath), to ensure further success required not alienating the population with inappropriate violence (the way Daniel Maxwell was alienated by the murder of his companion). Max Weber's theory on the state's monopoly of violence clearly expresses the need to resolve this contradiction. He believed that the state could legitimately expect to retain a monopoly on armed force, but that its institutions had to work "within the limits of certain accepted rules."[88] In our example, those rules were the contemporary expectations of limited, or at least justifiable, violence. If a state such as revolutionary North Carolina, which possessed only limited powers of enforcement over a relatively broadly defined political public, failed to meet those expectations, it could forfeit its political legitimacy, affecting its ability to recruit men or money, or even leading to counterrevolution. One North Carolina Whig preacher expressed exactly this view later in the war. Complaining of plundering by Rebel troops, he reminded his audience that this kind of illegitimate violence was one "of the many co-operating causes to ruin the republic of England, that the people grew weary of their own licentiousness, rejected that government which failed to protect them." He went on to specify that allowing plunder to continue "has a tendency to create disgust, not against the government which *was;* but against the government which *is.*"[89] Thus, like the rioters of Part I, the Rebel leaders included questions of legitimate violence in their political calculus. Victory required popular support. Popular support required a demonized enemy *and* appropriate (virtuous) use of violence by the state.

The Rebels believed that a virtuous soldiery, one that avoided sin or excess, obeyed their officers and the military laws, was manly and courageous, and that, in short, embodied "self and social moral regulation," would solve the conundrum.[90] Such a soldiery would be both successful *and* virtuous. As was shown in chapter 4, the colonists believed that virtue itself actually enhanced military ability.[91] A sermon to the militia of Massachusetts in 1775 listed the three necessary ingredients of victory: knowledge that the cause was just, a skillful army with soldiers of virtuous character, and trust in the Lord.[92] James Iredell, in a charge to a grand jury in 1778, called for "great public virtue, and very spirited exertions" to bring the Revolution to fruition.[93] And Samuel Johnston said that "if we have but Virtue and perserverance we may still be free."[94]

Furthermore, virtue would not only guarantee military success but would preclude excessive violence. Studies of military sermons from this period have noted how they created a "framework wherein a resort to arms could be morally justified," while simultaneously they "encourage[d] restraint."[95] Timothy Pickering had laid it out for colonial readers in his guide to training a militia:

> *Standing* armies are composed of very different men. These serve only for their pay: but that wretched pittance forms a slender motive to obedience. . . . Such soldiers . . . must be dangerous guardians of the rights of any people. . . . The militia of America is composed of men of property, and will be engaged, not to make conquests for Ambition, but merely in their own defence.[96]

Similarly, the Cumberland County Associators of June 1775 tacked on their own addendum to the standard oath being repeated all over colonies: specifically, they would ensure "the preservation of peace and good order, and the safety of individuals and private property."[97] William Drayton, in a speech to a South Carolina ranger unit in August 1775, said that he would not insult them by supposing that they had enlisted merely for gain, but on revolutionary principles. He presumed, therefore, that they would not cause trouble if forced to provide their own provisions.[98] A Loyalist preacher in New York, expressing the same value system, echoed these sentiments to a Loyalist unit in 1777. He called the soldier the "Protector of the Innocent, the Scourge and Terror of Oppressors." He interpreted biblical injunctions against violence as applicable only to unjust violence, that is, violence used "in Order to insult, oppress, or forcibly extort Money, or any sort of Property from others."[99]

Evidence comes not only from words, however, but also from actions. The playing out of this conundrum between the political need for successful military force and the cultural *and political* desire for virtue (expressed as adherence to the expectations of legitimate military violence) is clear in the campaigns of North Carolinians in 1776. The first of these was the so-called Snow Campaign against the Scovelite Tories (led by a man named Scovel) of South Carolina.[100] In late November 1775, a group of Loyalists attacked and besieged the fort at Ninety-Six. The South Carolinian Whigs then raised an army under Colonel William Richardson and asked North Carolina for help. North Carolina dispatched two companies from its newly raised Continental regiments, and much larger detachments (600–900 men) from the militia of Rowan, Mecklenburg, and Tryon counties.[101]

As Richardson marched through the backcountry en route to Ninety-Six, he "displayed the velvet hand in the mailed gauntlet," persuading Tories to go home and stay quiet.[102] When the combined armies approached Ninety-Six, most of the Loyalists scattered. The few who remained together were caught at Big Cane Break on December 22. In his autobiography, North Carolinian William Polk claimed that there were about 400 Loyalists at Big Cane Break, and that most of them were made prisoners. Polk himself participated in surprising and capturing a group of 30 men who had left the Tory camp the previous day.[103] The emphasis here is on capture. The Rebel militia used little violence, and there was no report of killing or mistreating prisoners. The captives signed an agreement relinquishing their estates if they ever again took up arms against the colony. Indeed, they agreed to assist in the defense of the province. On Richardson's recommendation, the South Carolina Provincial Congress granted them amnesty.[104] Compare this mild treatment of people whom the Whigs considered Rebels to what English tradition normally meted out to failed Rebels, or even to the punishment of the North Carolina Regulators in 1771. There were no exemplary punishments, no prisoners held (for very long), and no outright forfeitures of property. At this stage of the war, violence was restrained not only by the normal conventions of war but also by the Whig desire to capture the loyalty of the countryside.

A similar attention to the conventions of war can be observed in an incident during North Carolina's participation in the defense of Norfolk and tidewater Virginia in December and January of 1775–76.[105] Royal Governor John Dunmore had cobbled together a force of freed slaves and

British regulars and attacked a mixed force of Virginia Continentals and North Carolina militia at Great Bridge on December 9, 1775. Dunmore's regulars attacked across the bridge, only to be bloodily repulsed. Afterward, one involved British officer wrote that

> the Rebels behaved with the greatest Humanity, ceasing to fire when we were retreating with the wounded, as also to fifteen that fell into their Hands; they have since informed us that eight of them are dead. . . . They paid the greatest Respect to Fordyce's Body, burying it with all the Honors of War."[106]

The Moore's Creek Bridge campaign in the spring of 1776 was even more revealing. In it one can see not only the efforts of North Carolinians to fight in accord with the traditional European norms, aspiring thereby to the legitimacy implied by that form, but also the beginnings of their inability to control the extraneous violence of the militia.[107]

By January 1776, the now-exiled Governor Martin had convinced the British government to support him in an attempt to raise a force of Highlanders and former Regulators against the Rebels.[108] He declared the royal standard raised on January 10 and called on Loyalists to rise up against the Rebels.[109] The same day, Martin issued letters authorizing officials in eight counties to recruit militia and commission officers. The text of those letters reveals a great deal about the contemporary understanding of war. Martin authorized the named individuals to

> seize and take . . . arms, ammunition, provisions, horses and carriages . . . [for the troops you raise,] giving receipts for the same or keeping account thereof, that satisfaction may be made to the owner or owners, if they are not engaged in rebellion.[110]

He further ordered the officials to march those troops to Brunswick to take prisoners,

> taking all possible care that women and children are unmolested; that no cruelty whatever be committed to sully the arms and Honour of Britons and freemen . . . and that no violence be done against the laws of humanity but what resistance shall make necessary, to the end that the people who have been deluded into rebellion may be made sensible . . . to reclaim them to a proper sense of their duty and obedience to lawful Government, without involving the country in the horrors of war, if, by timely and dutiful submission, they make such extremities avoidable.[111]

Violence is carefully calibrated here.[112] It was expected that an army would have to take goods, but only those required by military necessity. Further, some attempt should be made to pay or account for the goods seized— *unless they were taken from Rebels.* As a royal governor, Martin could have felt justified in using extreme violence to put down a rebellion. But he directed his troops to moderation, unless the Rebels forced them to take harsher measures. Martin hoped to quiet the rebellion before it was properly begun. If that effort failed, however, "extremities" appropriate to suppressing a rebellion would have to be employed. It might be argued here that restraint was less important to Martin than success, and initial failure would lead him to drop the restraints on violence and wield fire and sword more indiscriminately. In a sense this is true, but European cultural notions of what violence was appropriate to a rebellion made room for such a response.[113] Tradition allowed a highly militarized and often very violent response to internal rebellion, provided that once successful, authority avoided widespread reprisals and pursued only limited exemplary punishments, in exactly the way Martin had acted after the Regulation.

Similarly, the Whigs potentially had legitimate access to extreme forms of violence. From their point of view it was the Loyalist rising that was an "insurgency," as was every Loyalist effort throughout the war. Nevertheless, in this initial campaign the North Carolina Whigs also strove for moderation. The potential freedom from restraint implied in cases of rebellion remained, however, and continued to lurk in the Whigs' prosecution of the war.[114]

When the Loyalists rendezvoused at Cross Creek on February 12, the turnout was something of a disappointment.[115] Many of the Regulators, who had arrived expecting to find a large force of British regulars led by the governor, simply went home.[116] Furthermore, a return of the army on the fifteenth showed 1,400 men, but only 520 with firearms.[117] On the eighteenth, the Loyalist troops, under General Donald MacDonald, began to move for the coast, hoping to rendezvous with the British fleet and the governor.[118] Meanwhile, the Whigs, alerted to the plan, had raised several forces in different parts of the province to oppose MacDonald's movement and prevent his reaching the sea.

The ensuing campaign was "regular" and "conventional" by the strictest European standards. Each side maneuvered, one to avoid battle, the other to join it. The first confrontation between MacDonald and one of the Whig contingents under James Moore was framed by an exquisitely traditional exchange of military correspondence, conducted under truce by heralds.[119] Eventually the Whigs succeeded in blocking the Loyalist army at the bridge crossing Moore's Creek. MacDonald sent a last message demanding Rebel surrender, then assaulted the bridge, only to be crushed by the Patriot forces.[120] The battle was short, sharp, and entirely conventional. In defeat, MacDonald surrendered his sword to Colonel Moore. Moore promptly returned it.[121]

A "battle," always legitimate in Western society, had been fought. Now the question was what other kinds of violence might occur in the aftermath. Of specific interest is the question of plunder and the treatment of prisoners. The evidence for plunder is mixed. The Rebels certainly scoured the battlefield itself for that traditionally allowable booty.[122] The Whigs also sent out parties to the homes of Highlanders and Regulators to confiscate weapons, an act also well within the bounds of acceptability. But many Loyalist families may have lost more than their weapons. Some Loyalists who submitted claims to the British government after the war specified that they had been plundered in the days immediately after Moore's Creek.[123] But still greater numbers of Loyalists who served in the Moore's Creek campaign did *not* report damages from the period immediately after the battle.[124]

As for official confiscation of Loyalist property, it is unclear how much may have occurred in the immediate aftermath of the battle. Whig commander James Moore indicated that the government might be considering confiscating Loyalists' estates, but such action was delayed until the Provincial Congress addressed the issue later that summer (see the discussion of Confiscation Acts in chapter 6).[125] Eli Caruthers's early-nineteenth-century collection of North Carolina revolutionary folklore included the report that Richard Caswell's Rebel militia contingent was notably restrained in its treatment of the Tories in its progress through the countryside after the battle, though Caruthers also recorded that other Whig units were not so careful.[126] Whig officers did seize the salt stored in Cross Creek and distribute it to the militia as a part of their pay.[127] The Moravians concluded that some of the returning militia had clearly been out plundering, because they were seen wearing Scottish clothing.[128] While there was certainly some official and unofficial plundering, the scale of such activities was limited, particularly in comparison to what would be seen in the 1780s. Furthermore, immediately after the battle the shops of largely Loyalist Cross Creek were open and "all was quiet and peaceful."[129]

The Whigs followed a mixed policy toward the hundreds of prisoners taken at Moore's Creek and immediately afterward. They granted the standard military parole to approximately 850 soldiers, allowing them to return home after taking an oath not to bear arms against the Rebels in the future.[130] Richard Caswell reassured Mary Slocumb immediately after the battle that no prisoners "should be hurt but such as had been guilty of murder or house burning." Slocumb, however, believed that many of the "worst" Tories were killed in the woods and swamps "wherever they were overtaken."[131] Other Tories, possibly believed to have been ringleaders, were taken to Halifax and tried. Some of those were released on their parole, and some were held prisoner for a substantial period. This latter group was composed primarily of the officers captured at Moore's Creek.[132] These men were initially confined at Halifax, with some of them paroled to the limits of the town "according to the rules and regulations of war."[133] It is worth pointing out that these were not just show trials. John Munro, despite raising men for the Loyalist army under an appointment from Governor Martin, which document the Rebels had captured, was released for lack of evidence.[134]

The Provincial Congress busied itself with the fate of the various individuals, the amount of bond they had to post to gain parole, and where they could live while on parole.[135] Some of the prisoners, tired of confinement or restriction, took the Whig oath and went home.[136] In general, the Congress tried to ensure that the prisoners were treated decently, even providing them clothing at state expense, and a cash subsistence allowance. One man was allowed to go home upon becoming ill.[137] In April, a movement began in Congress to send many of the chief prisoners out of the state, fearing that they would cause mischief where they were. Congress nonetheless scrupled to "take special care that such persons shall not be suffered to want any of the necessaries of life."[138] Some prisoners were sent to Philadelphia that summer, some to Maryland or Virginia, but others ended up remaining in North Carolina.[139] All of this was not exactly according to the strictest European conventions, but neither was it without precedent. Officers were normally the ones released on parole to await exchange, but in this case it was the officers who were held and even sent out of the state. General MacDonald noted his respectful treatment by General Moore and Colonel Caswell but was surprised that his parole was refused and that he was actually initially confined.[140] He was eventually exchanged along with other prisoners.[141]

Perhaps the most important feature of the Moore's Creek campaign and its aftermath, in terms of colonial expectations of war, was its apparent decisiveness. As after Alamance, late-arriving Loyalist units turned around and went home upon hearing news of the defeat.[142] One Loyalist unit of approximately a hundred men dissolved upon hearing of the battle, despite the pleas of their officers to continue on to Fort Johnston.[143] When the main Loyalist army conferred about what to do in the immediate aftermath of the battle, they determined to disband after learning that the Whigs had occupied Cross Creek. Most of them were captured shortly thereafter.[144]

The Rebels were equally certain of the decisive nature of this battle. One detachment marched into Cross Creek and encamped there without a thought for the possibility of any further Loyalist resistance.[145] General Moore, confident of a lack of continued resistance, reported on March 2 (a mere four days after the battle) that he had "some time ago" dismissed most of the troops under his command.[146] One Whig force en route to join the campaign was informed simply that "the matter was settled" and told to go home.[147] There were some rumors that the Tories might continue to embody, but the rumors did not pan out. Many Loyalists instead came in and took the oath of allegiance.[148] Indeed, Moore's Creek was decisive, for a time.[149]

Other incidents in North Carolina during 1776 also contribute to a picture of a Whig effort to restrain the violence of war and to meet popular expectations of virtuous military behavior. The Provincial Congress tried early to set limits on the freedom of the militia to forage or impress supplies from the countryside. On May 10, 1776, the Congress resolved that supplies could be impressed only when authorized by a warrant issued by two members of the local committee, and that those committeemen could not themselves be officers.[150] One of the few surviving documents showing a member of the North Carolina militia actually being court-martialed for plunder is from August 8, 1776. Captain Aaron Hill of the Edenton militia was stripped of his rank and discharged for plundering glass from houses in Brunswick.[151] When some violent characters broke up a tavern in Salem, a militia captain who was at a muster nearby came and arrested them. When someone suggested freeing the prisoners in order to enlist them in the army, several others, including General Griffith Rutherford, refused to accept the suggestion, noting that because of their actions they should not be enlisted.[152]

In addition to these scattered examples, the records of the Moravian communities near present-day Winston-Salem provide a focused and relatively continuous record of militia activities in the western part of the state. A brief comment about these records is necessary to understand their commentary on the violence around them. The Moravians were a pacifist German Protestant sect that had moved to North Carolina from Pennsylvania beginning in 1753.[153] Each community kept a virtually daily diary of events and comings and goings through their towns, which they then summarized at the end of the year. The diaries provide exacting detail about militia activities but must be read carefully. On one hand, the Moravians had a low standard for disorder; they were quick to label virtually any incident as a "disturbance" or "trouble." Therefore, unless the accounts provide additional details it is hard to know exactly what kind of behavior they were condemning. On the other hand, the Moravians consciously practiced an open generosity, particularly in 1776; they tried to provide help for all who needed it and took pity on hungry soldiers marching through. Their generosity and studied neutrality may have deflected violence from their communities while it continued to take place elsewhere in the region. Helpfully, however, the Moravians also usually were careful to distinguish between acts of violence committed by wandering individuals or bandits from those committed by Loyalist or Whig militias.[154] Other North Carolinians often were inclined to blame such banditry on whichever side they did not favor and use it to justify further violence.

The Moravian records for 1776 indicated that Whigs "mistreated" Tories prior to the battle at Moore's Creek, and that after the battle they treated them even "more sharply." A look at the details, however, reveals that apparently this mistreatment included simply taking away their arms and forcing "them either to take an oath to remain quiet, or to go into the field against the Governor."[155] As for the Rebel militia itself, the various Moravian communities recorded virtually no complaints against the Whigs for the whole of the year. The militia contingents marching to and from the Moore's Creek campaign or the Cherokee campaign were almost uniformly "orderly and courteous" or "gave no trouble and did not steal." They "conducted themselves according to orders."[156] The militia officers also made efforts to pay for all the supplies taken from the Moravians, a practice that would continue throughout the war, but which the Moravians would resent more and more as the Continental and North Carolina currencies lost value.[157]

The Moravians' portrait of a relatively benign militia notwithstanding, it is clear that the Whigs were not perfect. They began to set some unfortunate precedents both in their treatment of the Tories and in their leniency toward Whig violence. In August 1776, a group of Loyalists in Bladen County killed Captain Nathaniel Richardson.[158] A company of light horse captured some of those believed responsible, and Nathaniel's brother Samuel Richardson killed John Cairsy, one of the Loyalists. Samuel turned himself in to Congress, which upon examining witnesses decided that Samuel had been extremely provoked by Cairsy's behavior in front of Nathaniel's widow. Samuel was released on £500 bail to appear at the next court. Congress then immediately offered a reward for six other men believed responsible for Nathaniel's death. The proclamation announcing the award empowered the potential pursuers, in case of resistance or flight, to "kill and destroy them, any or every of them, without any Impeachment for the same."[159] Congress made a similar resolution for a group of Loyalist outliers in Chatham County, specifying a £50 reward if they were taken by the light horse designated for the job, and a £100 reward if taken by a civilian.[160]

The Whigs also continued to use the militia as political enforcers, to make arrests, administer loyalty oaths, and confiscate arms.[161] While such practices initially might seem innocuous (certainly the confiscation of arms was expected), they frequently put the militia in the untraditional position of making individuals and individuals' houses the focus for their activity.[162] Eighteenth-century Euro-American notions of war did not include warring against specific individuals. Military activity was supposed to be conducted between armies, formally constituted bodies representative of opposing states. Battles and sieges exemplified the impersonal methods of European warfare, and although individual houses could be the targets of foraging or even quartering, the individuals within those houses were not supposed to be harmed or carried away. The revolutionaries' use of the militia as enforcers—admittedly there were no alternative organizations available—placed an ostensibly military force in opposition to private persons, and at a site traditionally supposed to be secure from violence: their home.[163] As the Provincial Congress began to pass Confiscation Acts (reviewed in chapter 6), this trend worsened.

The Cherokee War: A Contrast

Such were the actions of the Rebel government and Rebel soldiers through the end of 1776, when employed against the British and Loyalists. Those actions were generally restrained but occasionally violent or of dubious precedent, and, as always, individuals and groups could be found who were willing to ignore the social norms. The government itself was inaugurating policies that would become more severe in later years. In general, however, the violence of this period, against those enemies, remained restrained and conventional.[164] It is not necessary, however, to compare the violence of the militia to later years to make this point. It needs only to be compared with the style of military violence practiced against the Cherokees in the fall of 1776.[165]

The Indian invasion expected and feared in the summer of 1775 looked to the colonists like it might be coming to pass during the summer of 1776. Rumors circulated on the frontier as early as May that the British Indian agents were indeed raising the Cherokees to attack. It was even reported that seventeen whites had been killed "and horribly mutilated," their bodies hacked into many pieces.[166] More rumors cropped up in June, and then, in July, the North Carolina council of safety received credible reports of an Indian incursion.[167] British agent Alexander Cameron was said to have instructed the Indians not to take prisoners but to kill as they went. Other reports included details of women being scalped.[168] Griffith Rutherford warned on July 13 that

> the Indins is making Grate prograce, in Distroying & Murdering, in the frunteers of this County, 37 I am Informed was killed last Wedensday & Thursday, on the Cuttaba River, I am also informed that Colo McDowel 10 men more & 120 women & Children is Beshaged. . . . I Expect the Next account to here, that they are all Distroyed.[169]

Similar reports went out to the governments of Virginia and South Carolina.

A joint expedition was quickly put together at the urging of General Charles Lee, who was then in Charleston, and the expedition's leaders expressed hope that "by the assistance of Divine Providence, [we will] crush that treacherious, barbarious Nation of Savages."[170] The North Carolina delegates to the Continental Congress were hardly more restrained when they fulminated that "the gross infernal breach of faith which [the Cherokees] have been guilty of shuts them out from every pretension of mercy," asserting that surely it would only be justice to

> carry fire and Sword into the very bowels of their country and sink them so low that they may never be able again to rise. . . . To extinguish the very race of them and scarce to leave enough of existence to be a vestige in proof that a Cherokee nation once was, would perhaps be no more than the blood of our slaughtered countrymen might call for. But . . . Women and children are not a Conquest worthy the American Arms. Their weakness disarms rage. May their blood never sully our triumphs. But mercy to their Warriors is cruelty to ourselves. We mean not to sport with their pains or to exercise

wanton acts of Cruelty upon them if the Chance of War should throw them into our hands, but to exercise that manly and generous method of pursuing them to destruction with our own Customs & the Laws of nations will vindicate.[171]

The council of safety duly advised Rutherford to "restrain the Soldiery, from destroying the women and Children" and to send all prisoners into North Carolina.[172]

Three separate columns marched over the mountains and into the Cherokee towns. The first, a combined Virginia and North Carolina force under Colonel William Christian, marched toward the Overhill villages. The second, North Carolinians under General Griffith Rutherford, proceeded against the Middle and Valley towns. Lastly, a South Carolina army under Major Andrew Williamson moved to attack the Lower towns (see map 8). The violence that these forces visited upon the Cherokees exceeded anything meted out to Loyalists and Tories in the same period, despite the fact that none of the columns met with serious resistance (Williamson's was ambushed twice and suffered some casualties).[173] In general, the great majority of the Cherokees dispersed and refused to come to close quarters with the Rebel militia. What the Whig forces did do over the course of September and October 1776, however, was destroy more than thirty-six Cherokee towns and lay waste their stores and crops.[174]

While the official accounts of the campaign are an endless litany of towns burned and crops destroyed, the less official accounts are even more disturbing. In his pension statement, Thomas Cook remembered simply that he and his fellow militia members "burnt their town, killed and destroyed as many of the Indians as we could get hold of."[175] Archibald Houston remembered marching from one place to another, destroying crops, and killing a few Indians.[176] South Carolina militiaman Arthur Fairies recorded how members of his company, having wounded a Cherokee woman, interrogated her and then, finding her unable to travel, killed her "to put her out of pain."[177] In his diary of the campaign, William Lenoir noted how one detachment "saw some Indians [and] killed & sculpt 1 Indian Squaw."[178] Captain William Moore, sent out with a detachment of light horse to destroy what he could find, succeeded after much effort in killing and scalping three Indians and capturing three others, while burning any plunder the soldiers could not carry.[179] Toward the end of their tour of duty, a dispute arose among members of his company "concerning the selling of the prisoners for slaves." Moore argued that it was their duty to deliver the Indians to prison. "The greater part [of his company] swore

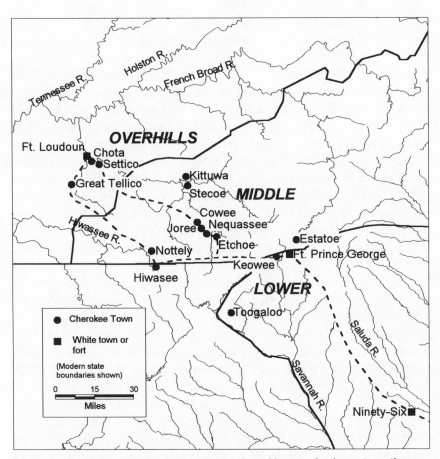

Map 8. The Cherokee towns, 1740–62. The dotted line marks the main trail across the Cherokee nation. (Adapted from *The Cherokee Frontier* by David H. Corkran © 1962 by the University of Oklahoma Press. Used by permission of the publisher.)

bloodily that if they were not sold for slaves upon the spot they would kill and scalp them immediately." Moore gave way, and the three prisoners were sold.[180]

Perhaps it is not surprising that a war against Indians should be prosecuted so violently. Similar contemporary accounts of white-Indian wars abound.[181] Nevertheless, the Cherokee War provides a kind of marker. The extraordinary violence found both in the official record of the destruction of towns and in the unofficial stories of brutal, almost casual, violence against women and prisoners reveals the kind of upper limit of violence of which the North Carolina militia was capable. The now thoroughly developed demonization of the Indians, combined with the sense that the Cherokees had struck first, and worse, that they had done so in concert with the British, legitimated this kind of violence. The demonization of the "savage Indian" was so deeply imbedded in the colonial mind that, in Arthur Fairies's journal for example, the colonists could in one breath heartily approve of a frontiersman's scalping of an Indian, and in the next justify their revenge against the Cherokees by citing how they had scalped the colonial dead.[182] As for the prisoners, the system of race slavery further contributed to this different standard of conduct by its legitimation of enslaving captive Indians (unless specified otherwise by a peace treaty). Nowhere in the annals of the Whig-Tory war does one find accounts of violence so extensive, and so presumptively justified, as in the Cherokee expeditions. This was an entirely different way of war.

The events of 1776, both in North Carolina and in the other colonies, seemed to confirm Whig expectations that a militia force by its very nature was not only restrained and virtuous but also militarily successful. Charles Lee had predicted in 1775 that the "Yeomanry of America" would have advantages over the normal peasant filler of European armies, being "accustomed from their infancy to fire arms."[183] The results of Moore's Creek, Lexington and Concord, and Bunker Hill all seemed to confirm such predictions of the efficacy of the citizen soldier. In July 1776, James Iredell spoke effusively of the undisciplined troops "just from their ploughs," and of the success of "North Carolina with 1000 militia [repulsing] 2000 Highlanders & Regulators, in whom the greatest confidence was placed."[184] As evidence of the presumed power of success, the agents sent by the Continental Congress to convince North Carolina's former Regulators to adhere to the Whig cause carried with them accounts of the Battle of Bunker Hill.[185]

The violence used to achieve those successes was shaped largely by the need of the revolutionaries to achieve consensus and consolidate support. Thus, not only did they report (and exaggerate) the illegitimacies of British violence to stir support for rebellion, all while initially continuing to use traditional techniques of riotous protests, but they also then aspired to conventional forms of war with the notions of restraint therein.[186] In these early years, the Whigs were generally successful in this effort at virtuous war, a success measurable in its contrast to the separately legitimated violence against the Cherokees. Unfortunately, the Rebel state began to undermine that conventionality through confiscation and similar acts, while also beginning to demonstrate that it could not fully control its militia when some of its members were motivated by greed, malice, or revenge. In

North Carolina, the early American successes gave way to a period of relative calm that lasted until the British capture of Charleston in 1780. During the Whig-Tory war that followed, the militias' record of military success became somewhat more dubious, and the ideal of virtuous restraint nearly collapsed. To understand that collapse, one must first examine the very real fears and tensions that persisted throughout the period after Moore's Creek and the Cherokee campaign up until the British invasion of the South.

6

Civil Consolidation

The "Peaceful" Years, 1777–1779

> A number of men of about thirty or more are combined together in this County for mischiefous purposes, they have caused four of the Drafted men to desert and declare publicly they will support them with their Guns, . . . they are daily committing acts of misprision of Treason, and persons that oppose them are always in danger of both life and property.
> **Thos. Bonner to Governor Caswell, July 6, 1778[1]**

> [250 foot and 25 horse are to be raised and ordered into Cumberland County] to seize and apprehend all such persons as shall be known to be disaffected to the American Cause and believed to be Ringleaders amongst the people called Highlanders, and that they also disarm all persons in the Counties of Cumberland, Anson, Guilford, Tryon and elsewhere from whom any injury is to be apprehended to the American Cause from thus being suffered to continue possessed of their Arms.
> **Resolution of the General Assembly, January 22, 1779[2]**

For North Carolina, the period after the end of the Cherokee campaign until the British invasion of the South, and particularly until the capture of Charleston, has been characterized as one of relative peace. That was *relatively* true. Tensions and fears, however, remained very much alive and continued to put pressure on the hopes for a virtuous war. During this period, roughly 1777 to the spring of 1780, rumored Tory conspiracies, continued reports of Indian activity on the frontier, and recurrent threats of a British invasion kept the new state government and its Whig adherents on edge. That government in turn alienated a growing number of dissidents through the passage of a series of increasingly harsh loyalty and confiscation laws, not to mention its demands for troops. Whig fears,

Loyalist outrage, and the questionable legitimacy of the acts of both sides contributed to a storehouse of frustrations that would explode with the arrival of the British in the years from 1780 to 1782.

In 1777, in part energized by the creation of the new state constitution, the General Assembly and the governor began to exert a more firm administrative control over the countryside. The Moravians noticed that taxes left uncollected since the beginning of the conflict were being taken up again in 1777.[3] The county and district courts, many of which had been in abeyance, began meeting again, in most cases replacing the less official safety committee "courts."[4] Most important to the course of violence in the state, however, were the new Confiscation Acts.

Before looking at the Confiscation Acts of 1777, it is necessary to back up and review the earlier Whig efforts in that direction. Loyalist property may have come under threat of confiscation as early as the summer of 1775, but the first official notice of such a possibility occurred in April 1776.[5] In the month after Moore's Creek, General James Moore and Colonel Nicholas Long had apparently confiscated some property and submitted lists of what had been taken to the Provincial Congress.[6] It is unclear in what context or under what pretext the property had been taken. On May 13, the Provincial Congress resolved that any person convicted by a vote in Congress of taking up arms against the Whig government, or of openly aiding the British, would forfeit all his goods and estates and be considered a prisoner of war.[7] This is, of course, a contradictory application of precedent. Rebels convicted of treason forfeited their property to the state. If they were rebels, however, they should not be considered prisoners of war. At any rate, the council of safety acted on the resolution in July, instructing Colonel Martin Armstrong of Surry County to inventory the estates of several Tories who had been in arms, making sure that their families were at least "supplied with the necessities of life."[8]

At this point in the war, however, the Whigs were not vigorously pursuing confiscation. For example, when the residents of Orange County complained that Abraham Childers, a cornet in the light horse, had taken seven rifles for the use of the army, the Congress resolved that he had "acted without authority, and with violence, evil in its example and dangerous to the security of private property."[9] Similarly, the Congress resolved in April 1776 that the Tories associated with Moore's Creek should be removed to a place of safety, but that they could dispose of their property as they saw fit.[10]

Then in November 1776, the North Carolina Congress passed a more sweeping Confiscation Act.[11] In it the Congress specified that any suspected person who took the Whig loyalty oath within ninety days of the governor's proclamation would be pardoned, and that anyone who refused the oath would forfeit his estate. Persons outside the state were exempted, provided they had not actually engaged in hostilities. In December, the Congress also passed a Treason Act, declaring that all non-prisoner-of-war residents of the state henceforth owed allegiance to North Carolina. Thereafter, any resident who levied war against the state, assisted enemies of the state, or even adhered to the king would be guilty of high treason.[12]

In the spring of 1777, the Assembly legislated that certain treasons would result in death and the forfeiture of all property, while misprision of treason would lead to imprisonment for the duration of the war and the loss of half of the offender's property.[13] That much was well within the tradition of English property law regarding acts of treason. The law also specified, however, that former officers of Great Britain or merchants with trade ties to Great Britain immediately take the oath of allegiance or leave the state. If they chose to leave, they were allowed sixty days to dispose of their property, including real estate.[14] In practice, it was expected that any persons suspected of being Tories would also be required to take the oath, not just those with obvious ties to Britain.[15] In March 1777, for example, the sheriff of Surry County ordered all who were in hiding or who had shown themselves active Tories to come in and take the oath or remove themselves from the state.[16]

In November 1777, the Assembly made that assumption official and broadened it yet further. It required all free males over sixteen to take the oath or leave, under the threat of confiscation. It also ordered the seizure of property technically confiscated but not yet seized under earlier laws. And finally, the Assembly confiscated the property of persons who had been absent from the state on July 4, 1776, or who had left since then and had not returned.[17] One Moravian noted the passage of the law but commented that it was not much enforced, although a few did leave because of it.[18] A survey of Loyalist claimants would seem to indicate otherwise. Of 113 Loyalist claims examined, 19 left North Carolina between 1777 and 1780; 12 left in 1777 alone, and of those, 7 specified that they had left because they refused to take the oath.[19] In practice, there was some flexibility in the enforcement of the oath. Several claimants indicated that they were confined for refusing the oath, sometimes on several occasions, which would indicate that the courts exercised discretionary powers in giving some individuals extra "chances" to take the oath before resorting to banishment or confiscation.[20]

The Chatham County court records provide a glimpse of this process at work, revealing not only the possibility of restraint but how the pressure was ratcheted up during this period. In May 1776 and May 1777—there were no intervening courts—there is no record of the oath being required. Then in August 1777, nine individuals who had been brought before the court as "suspected persons" refused to take the oath—although three apparently changed their minds later—and were ordered to leave the state. There was one more so ordered in November 1777, and two in February 1778. There was no record, however, of these banishments being enforced. A significant change occurred in February 1778, because at that session officials were appointed to go to "the people in general" and administer the oath, keeping lists of those who refused.[21]

The details of the continuing tightening of the Confiscation Acts through the end of the war have been summarized by others. It will suffice to say that enforcement of the acts was increasingly sweeping and unpleasant, and more frequent than for the laws of 1776 and 1777.[22] In the face of an actual conspiracy or a Tory rising, such as Moore's rising in February 1779 (see below), the Assembly was not above arrogating even more powers to its executives. On February 12, 1779, for example, the House resolved that justices of the peace be allowed to seize "all disaffected persons . . . who may be justly suspected of a disposition to carry those sentiments into execution."[23]

Unsurprisingly, the loyalty oath and Confiscation Acts provoked strong reactions.[24] Dislike of the Confiscation Acts was marked, and some Carolinians specifically observed that the acts contradicted expectations of war. Plunder, while hated, was to be expected. Judicial confiscation, however, was deemed outrageous. This attitude was even reflected in the codified laws of war as recorded by Vattel, who differentiated the seizure of privately held land from the taking of movable property as booty. The belligerent, as a sovereign state, had a right to the latter, and tradition allowed the soldiers to keep pillage on authorized occasions, particularly that found on the field of battle.[25] As for real property, however, Vattel emphasized that war was conducted between sovereigns, and thus the "conqueror take[s] possession of the property of the State and leaves that of individuals untouched."[26] Some residents of the Cape Fear region submitted a memorial to the Assembly making that same argument, claiming that in case of a war, it is contrary to the usage and custom of civilized nations to confiscate the property of private persons who may be subject to the Enemy. The most that is ever done in such cases is to secure such property, until it shall be known how the enemy behave in the like case.[27]

In making this appeal, the petitioners cited the precedent of declarations published by France, Spain, and Britain at the start of the war. In November 1779, while debating the Confiscation Act then under consideration, a significant minority of the General Assembly protested vehemently against the inconsistencies and illegalities of the proposed act. They argued that the act's elimination of an allowance for the families of men whose estates were confiscated amounted to warring "against aged parents or against Women & Children, more especially being as in this Case, our fellow Subjects."[28] Similarly, a South Carolina court ruled after the war that confiscation was neither justified by the laws of nations nor by the rules of warfare.[29]

Furthermore, the required oath of allegiance, in a society that placed great weight on one's word, was widely unpopular. Loyalists derogatorily called it the "blackjack."[30] There were certainly some who took the oath disingenuously, in a spirit of "going along to get along."[31] For many Loyalists, however, refusing the oath became a way to assert their resistance to the Whigs and to recognize each other. When one Loyalist in Salisbury accused another in 1779 of having "swalowed [sic] that black jack," they argued until the accused eventually convinced his accuser that he had not in fact taken it, whereupon they "Drank friends together with a great Shout Huraw'd for King george the third."[32]

Simply refusing the oath may not have indicated the resister's loyalty, but it almost certainly revealed an unwillingness to serve in the Whig military.[33] The demands for manpower continued throughout the "peaceful" period, not only because the war was raging in the North but because various scares in the South (discussed below) led to continual demands for troops. From 1777 to 1779, soldiers were called up both to fill the Continental regiments and to provide assistance for the increasingly difficult situation in South Carolina and Georgia.[34] North Carolina quickly fell back on the draft. Although there was precedent for drafting from the militia to fill expeditionary forces (as shown in chapter 4), in general the preference historically had been for volunteers, and the widespread Whig draft aroused considerable resentment.[35]

The Assembly usually assigned a quota to each county, set a bounty for volunteers, and provided a lower bounty for those drafted to make up the quota.[36] Theoretically, this system accommodated the division of the militia into the four classes specified in the militia law passed at the beginning of the war. The division was designed to prevent too many men from any one area being called up simultaneously. A draft supposedly would come from one of the four "classes," and that class would not be susceptible to another draft until the other three had had their turn.[37] The class system was used, but not necessarily as strictly as intended.[38] In practice, at the county level a call for troops led to a muster, at which the militia officers made their call for volunteers. When insufficient numbers came forward, the officers would arrange some kind of draft. Those arrangements varied and aroused numerous protests. There are differing accounts of how men were selected for the draft. In some units, names were "drawn," while other units, according to the law passed in April 1778, "elected" those who were to be drafted.[39] Other, probably illegal, methods further inspired resistance to the draft.[40]

Protesting the draft took two forms. One was to complain to the Assembly that the draft had been improperly managed. The other was to band together and forcibly resist it. There are any number of surviving petitions complaining of illegal or corrupt methods used to select draftees.[41] Equally many complaints by Whig officials claim that bands of men hid out in the woods, declaring their intention to violently resist the draft.[42] One group of men in Rowan County found a third way to resist. When they balloted their choices for the draft, they simply selected all the top officials of the region to fill the ranks. Most of those officials were legally exempt from the draft or were not even members of the company of those who had "selected" them.[43]

Draft resistance could lead to the third phenomenon that would enrage the Tories: Tory scouring. The Rebel militia frequently was called up—they sometimes mobilized themselves as "volunteers"—to "scour" the countryside for Tories. Tory scouring expeditions were in part an outgrowth of the civil government's requirement that adult males take the association oath, which of course the militia was required to enforce. They also occurred in response to draft resistance, and on other occasions they resulted from more specific Tory scares common to the period. The state Senate officially authorized such scouring in August 1778, declaring that the county court or any three justices of the peace could ask the ranking militia officer to call out the militia to "compel Tories or other disorderly people of their county to a due observance of the law."[44]

Most of the scourings do not appear in the narrative or legislative records of the war but are frequently mentioned by pension claimants as part of their litany of time served.[45] These little expeditions were not notable for their kindnesses. William Gipson recalled capturing several Scottish Tories in the summer of 1777; the captors promptly hanged one, although another (captured later) escaped with the connivance of some of the militia.[46] Archibald Houston participated in a similar outing in the fall of 1777, "guarding and defending the neighbourhood from the notorious rober and Tory Brown who . . . was commiting a great many outrages."[47] William Lenoir in 1778 went on three expeditions ostensibly to enforce the loyalty oath. In the first, he and his companions found no Tories in three days of searching. In the spring, however, while pursuing Tories into the Blue Ridge Mountains, they captured some who "were mostly permitted to go at large, after an examination, in which they generally made recantation, and [illeg.] promises of loyalty to the cause of independence and in some instances . . . [took] the oath." Immediately after returning, Lenoir and his company set out again in pursuit of yet more Tories. Upon capturing one, they tried to get information from the prisoner about other Tories. When the man refused, "Colonel [Benjamin] Cleveland adopted the expedient of Hanging him for a while to the limb of a tree or a bent down sapling, but which did not produce the desired effect until the dose was repeated a second time with more severity then the first."[48]

Confiscation, the draft, the requirement of an oath, and the scouring necessary to enforce that oath all contributed to keeping a large portion of the countryside at a slow boil, in some cases creating "Tories" where none had been before. But if the Tories (and some wishful neutrals) were outraged, the Whigs were scared. Real and reported Tory conspiracies, violent draft resistance, Indian scares, and projected British landings all contributed to an environment of fear. These phenomena were of course mutually reinforcing. Reports, for example, of a band of draft resisters would lead to a call for militia to hold them in check. To raise that militia, a draft might be required, and the militia would certainly need to be fed. Some of those militia units, once in the field, found it all too easy to commit acts of violence that further alienated the waverers.

In hindsight, the actual number of Loyalist risings during this period might not seem alarming, but Whigs nevertheless perceived a serious Tory threat. Of course, for some Whigs, not much was required to justify severe retaliation. Ransom Southerland, in July 1776, complained that Tory David Jackson "privately Shot & mortally wounded" a Wilmington-area Whig, and another "narrowly Escaped with his life." Southerland claimed not to be sure what response to suggest, but what he did recommend is startling in its severity:

[General Rutherford with three to four hundred men should be sent] into their Settlements & put those Rascals to death on sight & that they lay waste the Country where the inhabitants refuse to deliver the Offendors. . . . This may be thought Severe doctrine, but until something of this kind is adopted, you may rest assured no man there dare ever Say a word in favour of America.[49]

Of course the Whigs adopted no such policy of devastation, particularly in 1776. Officially sanctioned deliberate fire and sword strategies were generally reserved for the Indians.

Reports of Tory conspiracies cropped up regularly in the "peaceful" period.[50] The most famous and most frightening was the Llewelyn or gourd-patch conspiracy, revealed in the summer of 1777. The first notice the Whigs had of what turned out to be a broadly dispersed secret society bent on overturning the Whig government was an attempt by about thirty Tories to take control of Tarboro by force.[51] The attack was broken up, but revelation of the conspirators' plans proved frightening to the population. Whigs described it as "a most bloody plan" and "a most accursed plot," which had anticipated "the assassination of the leading men in every County."[52] One initiate into the conspiracy revealed that part of the plot included employing a slave patroller to "Disaffect the minds of the negroes & Cause them to run away, under the name of a Rising & Draw the Soldiers out of Halifax in pursuit of them" while the conspirators captured the magazine and the person of the governor.[53]

More plots surfaced in 1778 and 1779. A conspiracy was uncovered in Tryon County in the summer of 1778, and a meeting of the Assembly on August 15, 1778, was interrupted by apparently false rumors that the "Regulators of Guilford had risen 2,000 strong."[54] In the fall of 1778, Griffith Rutherford asserted that the Tories of Washington County were cooperating with the Indians. He reported that the whole military strength of that county was "employed in the suppression of the Savages and other inhuman hostile wretches [that is, Tories], who have their livelihood from Carnage and Rapine."[55] In January 1779, the residents of Bladen County complained to the Assembly about Tory activity in their area. They couched their accusations in the form of the classic atrocity narrative, asserting for good measure that many of the Tories were mulattos:

Your petitioners are in Constant dread & Fear of being Robbed and Murdered by a Set of Robbers and Horse Theifs, . . . Who have Commited a Great deal of mischief already. & we understand by some of them they soon Intend to ruin us Altogether. In the Borders of our District and Anson County some have had their Houses Broke and all their Cloaths Taken from Them Even their Babes and Infants were stripped naked. Women were knocked down with stakes & Tommyhakes in their Husbads Absence. . . . The most part of the Robbers are Muolattoes.[56]

Shortly after the writing of that petition, a large-scale Tory rising did occur in Tryon County. Anywhere from 100 to 1,000 Loyalists under John Moore robbed several farms of horses and guns and "did many deeds of violence."[57] Needless to say, large numbers of militia and volunteers rose up to disperse Moore's followers.[58] Governor Caswell himself went to Charlotte to aid the militia.[59] Despite the suppression of Moore's rising, conspiracies and Whig fears of conspiracies persisted throughout 1779.[60]

Equally fearsome were the recurrent rumors and reports of violence from the Cherokee frontier. The apparent success of the Cherokee campaign of 1776 and its resultant treaty had not prevented white-Indian friction; from 1777 to 1779 there were repeated Indian invasion scares, followed by predictable militia reactions. When February 1777 saw reports of white families killed on the Holston River, the government raised the militia.[61] Rumors of actual murders and projected Indian attacks continued throughout 1777 and 1778, leading the Assembly to enact a £15 bounty for Indian prisoners and £10 for Indian scalps taken by the militia; civilians would get £50 and £40 respectively.[62] Guilt was assumed. Fighting with the Indians apparently continued in 1779, and smaller expeditions moved against the Cherokees in 1780 and 1781.[63]

All of these incidents and Whig fears of Tory and Indian plots were compounded during this period by an increasingly visible British threat. In 1777, that threat was confined to several alerts and raids along the coast, both in the Chesapeake and on North Carolina's outer banks.[64] With the capture of Savannah in December 1778, the war became more threatening to North Carolinians.[65] Increased British presence not only inspired Loyalists but played into Whig fears of more conspiracies.

The point of this extended disquisition on the fears and tensions of what are usually labeled "peaceful" years is to point out the continuous pressure on the model of virtuous war aspired to by the Whigs. That model was increasingly threatened by an equally culturally powerful notion of legitimate retaliation, whether military or judicial. The Whig government contributed to that pressure by confiscating Tory property while overlooking Whig acts of violence. In 1779, for example, the Assembly willingly indemnified Colonel Benjamin Cleveland and Captain Benjamin Herndon, among others, for killing William Coyle and Lemuel Jones, and for assaulting James Harvell, presumably Tories. While the details of the incident are not clear, the close 29-to-24 vote in the House may reflect an internal debate over the appropriateness of granting the indemnity.[66] In general, the civil powers tried to construct their actions within an ideology of restraint and control over the military. In dispatching a militia force to put down a reported conspiracy, for example, Governor Caswell directed the commander to apprehend any who had assembled in arms. Only "after using every means to bring them to justice, . . . when every other means fail," said the governor, was the militia authorized "to fire upon, and, at any rate, conquer and subdue them. But . . . the spilling of human blood should at all events, be prevented if possible."[67] Furthermore, the militia, in its efforts to feed and supply itself, was required by law to obtain a warrant from two justices of the peace before impressing supplies, and a certificate had to be given showing the value of the items taken.[68] In one case during this period, a militia company that tried to take some blankets relented and took nothing when challenged to show their warrant to impress.[69]

The struggle between the desire to fight a virtuous war and the urge to retaliate, combined with the operational tendency of the militias to use the "feed fight" strategies of Indian wars against Tory outliers, is revealed in Stephen Cobb's complaint to the governor in July 1779. Cobb wrote that he had been repeatedly threatened by a Tory band led by "the Basses," and that he had tried everything in his power "to take them without killing them." He had failed. If he did not get state help soon, he wanted a warrant to "take them dead or alive, and to destroy what they have if they will not surrender themselves, and I will endeavor to get some men in whom I can confide, and encamp myself in the woods where they pass and try lives with them."[70]

Two other remarkably evocative documents produced by North Carolinians during the "peaceful years" also highlight the tensions between the military demands of the Revolution and the ideals of restrained violence. The first is a poem written by Thomas Burke, who would become the governor of North Carolina in 1781. The poem, entitled "Ruthless War," first decried British atrocities. Their behavior justified the defensive war of the colonists, but Burke also emphasized the need for clemency even in war:

Ambition proud and Avarice severe
> Invade our Land across th' *Atlantic* Main.

        *   *   *

Not ours the Crime that calls a savage Race
    From distant Wilds the murd'rous Knife to speed;
to spread relentless, unrestrain'd Distress
    Alike where Husbands, Wives, and Infants bleed.

                 *   *   *

Is it *His* Will that howling Bands in Arms
    Should tear the Consort from her Husband's Bed?
Should seize our Virgins, fair in blooming Charms,
    With hands from Blood of slaughter'd Sins still red?

                 *   *   *

Let us meantime benevolent deplore
    Necessity that kindles fierce Alarms,
Weep ev'n the Wounds wherewith our Foes we gore
    Tho' awful Justice consecrates our Arms.
Altho' his Arm the Patriot Sword should wield
    And with just Vengeance tho' his Breast should glow,
Colin's rude Soul shall to thy Numbers yield
    And learn to pity ev'n a wasting Foe.
Nor farther urge, sweet Moralist, thy Pow'r
    Than from Excess to stop the righteous Ire,
Still to mild Clemency his Breast restore
    By the soft Charms of thy melodious Lyre.[71]

The second document is the petition submitted by Samuel Richardson in September 1779. Richardson, described by his neighbors as "very ancient," had been convicted of high treason in the Salisbury District Court and was appealing to Governor Caswell for clemency.[72] What little other information that is available on Richardson indicates that he was a resident of the western county of Tryon and was a man of some property, although by no means especially consequential.[73] Richardson claimed to have been involved only in plots and never to have actually acted on them. With remarkable historical awareness, Richardson expounded on the nature of intent versus action, the legitimacy of success, the consequences of judicial vengeance, and the judgment of history:

> Plots and conspiracies, like all other human Actions, are in themselves neither good nor evil,—it is their consequences only that Stamp their Value. A Successfull resistance to Government is a Revolution, an Unsuccessful one is a Rebellion. The plot and conspiracys

antecedent to the great and Glorious Revolution of our Ancestors under King William [1688], were neither more lawfull, more honest, nor more laudable, than the plots and conspiracys under which the unfortunate Duke of Monmouth fell, with multitudes of his Adherents, only two years before: His want of success, was the only criterion, which distinguished that a Rebellion, from the other a Revolution, and the unexampled executions which followed only paved the way for more plots and conspiracys, which at the last ended in the total overthrow of the Government. I most humbly pray therefore, that your Excellency will, upon true Revolutional principles, consider me rather in the light of an unfortunate man, than that of a Criminal worthy of death; the Crime was not so unnatural, as it was unlawfull.

Richardson thus claimed that success bestowed legitimacy: a successful rebellion becomes a revolution. At the same time, however, he reminded Caswell that "unexampled" executions in the past had merely led to further rebellion. Adding to this utilitarian argument for clemency, he then appealed to "true Revolutional principles," and their ideal of protection of person and property. Despite his eloquence, and although they recommended pardon for seven other individuals convicted at the same court, the Governor's Council recommended that Richardson's sentence be executed.[74] His actual fate is not known for certain.

At the end of 1779 and the beginning of 1780, the character of the war in North Carolina was about to change. The British capture of Savannah in late 1778 was followed by a relative stalemate in Georgia and South Carolina as each side took advantage of reinforcements to successively push back the other. North Carolina participated in all of these campaigns both through its Continental troops and the expeditionary militia it sent southward. Eventually, in April and May of 1780, the British gained the upper hand and captured Charleston, including the vast bulk of the American forces in the South. This British success reenergized the Loyalists in North Carolina. The war that had been simmering quickly boiled over.

7

"The Law of Retaliation"

The War of the Militias, 1780–1782

The rebels continually fired at night on the sentinels, . . . [knowing they would do so again] a figure was dressed up with a blanket coat, and posted in the road . . . at midnight the rebels arrived, and fired twenty or thirty shot at the effigy. . . . The next day an [American] officer happening to come in with a flag of truce, he was shown the figure and was made sensible of the inhumanity of firing at a sentinel, when nothing further was intended: this ridicule probably had good effects, as . . . no [further] sentinel was fired at.

Lieut. Col. J. G. Simcoe, describing operations around Norfolk[1]

This applicant cannot forbear to relate that as cruel as this punishment might seem to be to those who never witnessed the unrelenting cruelties of the Tories of that day, yet he viewed the punishment of those two men with no little satisfaction, as they were then supposed to belong to the identical band who inhumanly inflicted corporal punishment upon his helpless [mother].

Pension Record of William Gipson[2]

British success in South Carolina, Cornwallis's subsequent entry into western North Carolina, and Major James Craig's capture of Wilmington sparked an escalation of Whig-Tory violence from 1780 to 1782 (see map 9).[3] This "pattern of raw power" was repeated all over the colonies; wherever there were British garrisons or incursions, the Loyalists were inspired to rise.[4] Some Loyalists rose because of ongoing commitment to the king, while others did so because they felt aggrieved by the Whig government's actions over the previous four years. In one sense, the presence of the British force in itself justified the resurgent Loyalist violence, both by virtue of the essential legitimacy of successful force and by the legitimacy of military formalism: the Loyalists could go to the British army, be commissioned as officers, and receive warrants to raise troops. North Carolinian

Mathew Goodson understood this "pattern of raw power" when Loyalist Nicholas Day suggested to him that the proximity of the English army meant that he must "be on one side or [the] other." Goodson replied that he would willingly be on the strongest side.[5] But the presence of the British also stimulated stories of their atrocities. For some of those inclined to be Loyalists, British violence alienated them into neutrality; for the more Whiggish, the violence spurred them to resist or retaliate.

In this stressful period, the institutional and cultural restraints on the behavior of the North Carolina militia began to break down. Violence seemed to spin out of control. Some of those Loyalists who might otherwise have felt outraged at British behavior instead turned their anger on the Whigs. Added to this volatile mix were the activities of groups of true bandits, men who made little pretense of military activity and who sought purely personal gain from the chaos. Their actions inflamed both sides as each faction tended to blame the depredations of bandits on their enemy. Contributing to the escalation of violence was the militias' reliance, especially when operating independently of either Continental army or British army control, on an operational style of war developed on the frontier, heavily dependent on raid, surprise, and ambush. In addition, when the militias believed that the other side had violated the norms of war, they seldom limited themselves to the mere threat of retribution. Instead, they applied the "Law of Retaliation."[6]

This chapter addresses first the extent to which the institutions and ideologies of restraint continued to condition the violence of the war during this period of acknowledged excesses. One must approach the violence from their perspective, not ours. North Carolinians understood military activity within a particular framework—war came with violence, but it also came with rules. Those rules also possessed a widely understood gradation of importance. Certain violent acts were worse than others and thus were less likely to be committed even during times of crisis. This chapter then explores the apparent collapse of those restraints, arguing that the new levels of violence were authorized by the cultural legitimacy of retaliation. In this sense, the rules did not collapse so much as the society shifted into another paradigm of war: the war of retaliation. That this shift occurred was in part due to the institutional structure of the militia, which proved incapable of merely threatening retaliation. They put it into effect.

To begin, it is necessary to acknowledge that there is no doubt that violence was harsh and pervasive in North Carolina from 1780 to 1782.[7] Even when reports are discounted for the inflammatory rhetoric of the

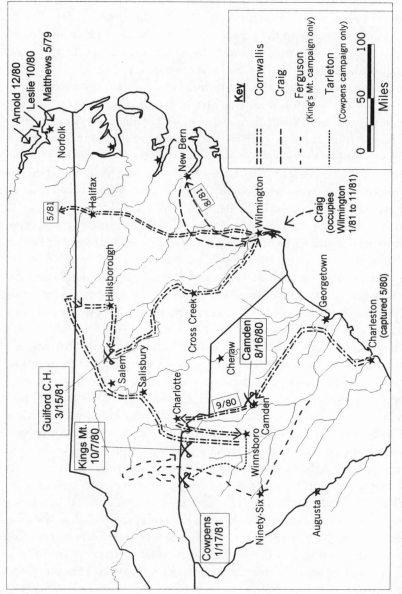

Map 9. Major British campaigns in and around North Carolina, 1780–1782.

Key

Cornwallis
Craig
Ferguson
(King's Mt. campaign only)
Tarleton
(Cowpens campaign only)

0   50   100
Miles

Arnold 12/80
Leslie 10/80
Matthews 5/79

Norfolk

Halifax

New Bern

5/81

Hillsborough

8/81

Wilmington

Cross Creek

Salem

Salisbury

Georgetown

Craig
(occupies
Wilmington
1/81 to 11/81)

Guilford C.H.
3/15/81

Charlotte

Cheraw

Camden
8/16/80

Charleston
(captured 5/80)

Kings Mt.
10/7/80

9/80

Camden

Winnsboro

Ninety-Six

Augusta

Cowpens
1/17/81

revolutionary period, the residual picture is appalling. To give one hardly isolated example, the residents of the Salisbury district complained of the misbehavior of militia, who had

> committed and perpetrated Numberless barbarities, Assassinations, Murders, and Robberies throughout the whole district. . . . and whenever they apprehended a person or more either in his own house the Woods or Highways if he was not immediately hanged, shot, or otherwise put to Death, he would be ordered under a Guard, and under pretense of sending such supposed Offender to Salisbury Jail, and then on the way thither were oftentimes murdered in Cool blood, others again have been hanged up two or three times until almost dead, and then shot by way of diversion, thus put to Death in the most torturing manner; many have been the cruel and barbarous methods. . . . Numbers of persons such as Women and Children have been tortured, hung up and strangled, cut down, and hung up again, somtimes branded with brands or other hot irons in order to extort Confessions from them. . . . and after torturing them, and practising every kind of Cruelty the most Savage heart could suggest, then would go off triumphantly, after first having plundered and rob'd the poor man's house of every Article they could lay their hands on, and sometimes set the house on fire.[8]

This account embraces many of the standard tropes of the atrocity narrative, for example, the torture of children and the hanging of women. While it may be literally true, the familiar formulaic exhortatory nature of the language makes one uncomfortable believing all of it. It also, however, contains much that reflects the reality of violence during the period as supported in other documents: the execution of prisoners under guard, the use of half-hangings to extract information, and the plundering and burning of houses. Of course, the report of an atrocity did not have to be true to spark retaliation; there are frequent instances of the report probably exceeding the reality, and in so doing inspiring further violence.

Rules and Restraint

Nevertheless, the ideal of virtuous war was still in place in 1780 and continued to condition violence through the end of the war, with admittedly decreasing success. One can still find the Whig government calling for restraint—although less so than in 1776—in order to shore up revolutionary virtue, or at least to try to calm the countryside. One can also find militiamen and officers acknowledging the force of certain traditional European customs and usages of war. And further, one can see a broader popular understanding of appropriate violence mediated through norms of gender, honor, and common morality operating on the one hand as a constraint, while unleashing retaliation on the other. Before turning to the question of why those restraints broke down, one must examine the extent to which they continued to work, always remembering that violence withheld often was not recorded, whereas violence enacted almost always was.

To understand how cultural constraints continued to function, it is important to emphasize the gradation of violence—the "some things are worse than others" principle. Although this gradation could be infinitely complex, it can be analyzed through four broad categories that contemporaries also would have recognized. They thought of plunder; the definition and treatment of prisoners; the traditional formalities of war (such as truces, commissions, messengers); and the crimes of house burning, rape, and murder. When the Moravians, for example, summed up the events of 1781, they acknowledged these categories, observing that some people had been seized, some robbed, and some wounded, but no houses had been burned, nor had anyone been killed.[9] This chapter will look at the evidence in a similar manner, analyzing both what happened and what did not, and how that reflected the social norms about the rules of violence in war.

Plunder, along with the overlapping category of military impressment, was easily one of the largest problems during the war. It encompassed a wide variety of behaviors that were judged by contemporaries on a scale of severity. Armies were expected to impress supplies. Impressment caused resentment and complaint, but it was accepted as a part of the fortunes of war provided it was executed with the appropriate formality. Advance notice was preferred, and officers were the agents of choice. They should pay where possible and offer certificates of receipt when not. Residents of the Salisbury district, for example, complained not that impressment was done, only that it was often done illegally. In their estimation, it had been too commonly done, with "insolence," and often without certificates being issued.[10] In a similar vein, Samuel Strudwick wrote to Governor Burke hoping that the governor would control the soldiers, noting that "the Contributions which the Law exacts, and the necessity of the Service requires[,] would be chearfully submitted to, if Ravage and plunder were not superaded." Strudwick admitted he was "very sensible that 'War cannot be kept to a Sett Diet,' yet there is certainly no Occasion to gorge it with the Vitals of a whole people."[11] Joseph Martin noticed while on foraging duty for the Continental army in Pennsylvania that the inhabitants seemed resigned to the necessity and never abused him (although he doubted whether his fellow New Englanders would have been equally sanguine).[12] North Carolinian Samuel McCorkle admitted that "in war every man divides his property," allowing some for the use of the state, although he believed that the state was "required to secure its . . . interest without loss to the individual."[13] The Moravians were also resigned to the inevitability of loss due to war, even going so far as to exclaim: "thank God we have no reason to complain,—it is War!"[14]

The civil government and the militia officers recognized the need to pay for provisions as much as possible. They also recognized that people preferred direct payment to a certificate, both of which remained better than the foraging of individual soldiers.[15] When the Board of War appointed George Fletcher to act as commissary in 1780, it instructed him to "lose no time in procuring [provisions], or the Soldiers will be obliged to carve for themselves, which must be avoided if possible." The board further instructed that he should try to purchase goods first, but that if a farmer would not sell, Fletcher could impress, giving certificates for what he took.[16]

The government and military officers also assumed, in accordance with military tradition, that it was acceptable to impress from one's enemies without payment. Nathanael Greene ordered General Daniel Morgan to "prevent plundering as much as possible, and be as carefull of your provision and forage as may be, giving receipts for whatever you take to all such as are friends to the independance of America."[17] In Europe, military logistics of the eighteenth century had come to depend on a system of "contributions," a kind of cash tax paid by occupied territories to avoid pillage. That cash was funneled into the state's coffers and used to fund a centralized supply system of magazines or *étapes,* that is, markets prearranged with civilian authorities along projected lines of march. The fallback system, however, remained direct foraging by the soldiers. When that system was used, it was expected that friendly residents would be paid for supplies taken and that enemy territories would be deprived only of foodstuffs or other necessities and not subjected to uncontrolled pillage.[18] Samuel McCorkle, in a sermon against plunderers in North Carolina during this period, specifically recognized that "the taking of victualls from . . . foes . . . was permitted," but the "taking of money to a considerable amount. . . . the taking of horses and cattle, and slaves, and furniture and free men Women and children" constituted a felony. McCorkle went on to observe that such plundering was even worse when taken without opposition, that is, they could not be considered trophies of war.[19]

Popular acceptance of impressment as a necessity of war was thus tied to the expectation that it be conducted by proper authority, usually officers. Soldiers not under the control of officers were more likely to plunder inappropriately. The worst possible circumstances arose on those occasions when officers were seen to direct their men in unlawful plundering.[20] In a letter to his church elders, one Moravian took some comfort in the fact that most plundering "did not take place by order of those in authority nor of the army officers, but by mob violence of a released hungry militia."[21] Governor Burke was more specific, suggesting that "Irregular troops are extremely distressing to a people where they serve—if their officer be not extremely attentive, and when the officers themselves Commit Acts of oppression they are unpardonable."[22]

Another form of quasi-legitimate plunder was the confiscation of weapons. Both Whigs and Tories considered this a lesser offense, if an offense at all. When Armand Armstrong reported on the Tory activities in and around Hillsborough in 1781, he remarked, "they are not so much charged with Plundering as disarming, and, as they say, informing the People."[23] In part, disarmament was recognized as a legitimate, military form of provisioning. In the late-war trial of two noted Loyalist officers, the court concluded that

> they had [not] on their march through a considerable part of this State . . . committed any violences more than any other Army would have done in similar circumstances, in supplying themselves with Arms, ammunitions, provisions, horses, &c., there being no proof of their having been guilty of any murders, house-burning or plundering except as above mentioned for the support of their Army.[24]

Whatever the form of plunder, both officers and soldiers can be found restraining themselves. Civil or military officials often ordered their troops not to plunder, though such orders were rarer in the militia than in the Continental army.[25] Often these orders relied on shame to deter the troops, playing to their communal notions of proper behavior. Plundering was labeled as "degrading to the name of soldier," or "unsoldier-like,"[26] while Samuel McCorkle thundered out a sermon detailing the shame, guilt, and ignominy that attached to plunderers.[27]

The Moravian diaries provide a superabundance of information about plundering, and the control of plundering, by the militias. They even reveal unofficial peer pressure within the ranks to control plundering. The Moravian towns, situated on an important crossroads, and serving as the trading centers for northwest North Carolina and neighboring Virginia, witnessed a great deal of militia activity, both Whig and Tory. In 1778 and 1779, the Moravians recorded relatively few instances of militia troops marching through, but beginning in 1780 and especially in 1781 the region was enveloped in a swirl of military activity. Their accounts reveal that the vast majority of the illicit activity in the North Carolina countryside was some variation on plunder, that least of violences on the scale of military violence. Furthermore, the majority of plundering that they recorded was relatively licit impressment, with at least some form of payment or receipt attempted.[28] Given the Moravians' relatively low tolerance of disorder, their diaries are replete with examples of militia being held, or holding itself, in good order.

Without question, in the Moravians' estimation, vigorous action by militia officers was the single most important influence in maintaining that order. Their stories often tell of officers intervening to stem disorder by soldiers. One instance arose when the Wilkes County militia, with whom the Moravians repeatedly had had troubles, was discharged in October 1780. "They were very wild" in Bethania, reports one diary, "but the wounded Captain Parris brought them to order, and ordered them to go on, which they did."[29] Similarly, officers interfered when "several scamps aimed their weapons at [Brother Meyer], to force him to give them brandy."[30] Even when trouble did not arise, the Moravians nearly always attributed the good order of any given group of militia to the care of their officers.[31]

Sometimes, however, the soldiers restrained themselves. In Friedberg, on December 15, 1778, a "Press-Master" appeared with a party of soldiers, found a crupper (part of a saddle) hidden in the chimney, and took it. According to a Moravian account, some of the soldiers with him then "went up stairs, thinking to find our living-room, but when they opened the door and started in one of them said: 'This is a Meeting House, be respectful,' and they turned back." Even in this story, however, an officer's intervention was required to return the crupper, and not everyone in town had their property restored.[32] Shame alone did not always suffice to control the militia's behavior. In an incident in Salem in September 1780, a captain and sixteen men forced their way into a house and began to take clothing and linen. At that point

> Br. Fritz found courage to speak seriously with the Captain, asking
> him whether he and his men robbed and plundered like Tories, and
> that from people whom they should protect? The Captain and some
> of his men knew Br. Fritz well, and became ashamed of the disor-
> derly conduct of their comrades, who had even torn the shirt off of
> Br. Fritz, and they begged him not to worry about the things that had
> been taken, promising that all should be restored to him, for the men
> who had taken them were drunk.[33]

The diarist noted that "finally the Captain found pluck enough to order
that all the stolen things should be brought back into the house, and this
was done." A sense of shame might stop ongoing plunder, but to restore
the status quo ante required authority.

Occasionally some groups of militia "seemed ashamed of their former
behavior" or "wished to behave better than the Virginia troops . . . who
were here some time ago."[34] In some cases, private soldiers subdued their
rowdier brethren, as when "several discharged soldiers came, and behaved so badly that one of the soldiers stationed here quieted him [sic]
with blows."[35] For every report of militiamen stealing from orchards, firing off guns, or billeting themselves in homes, there are as many descriptions of militia "well-behaved and friendly."[36]

Yet another pattern emerges in the Moravian records that deal with
plunder. When militia units made excessive demands or even freely plundered the towns, they nearly always did so on a constructed or imagined
pretext.[37] In some cases, when that pretext was refuted, the demands or
the plundering ceased. For example, the Moravians frequently had difficulties with the militia of neighboring Wilkes County, led variously by
Colonel Benjamin Cleveland or William Lenoir.[38] Even that militia, however, felt the need to accuse the Moravians of Loyalism in order to justify
their demands. The 170 Wilkes men who arrived in Salem in February
1781 "took whatever came to hand. All these demands were made with
threats, which sounded as though they sought an excuse to plunder the
town." The Wilkes men looked for evidence that the residents were Loyalists, and Lenoir "declared roundly that we were his enemies." "For the
time he would not harm us," the account continued, "except that we must
give what they needed."[39] About the same time, some other militia officers
arrived to press supplies and were initially very unpleasant, sounding "as
though the destruction of our town had been determined, since, they said,
we must have shown that we held with the English." As the Moravians
cooperated, however, the officers' attitude changed, and they proved very

"useful and ready to scatter, or to prevent the excesses [of others]."[40] On another occasion, the Moravians described "vicious men" as "seeking every opportunity to find evidence of treason, or of correspondence with the British, so that they might destroy us on that pretext."[41] The implication here is that while the militia might steal, they were reluctant to go housebreaking, a higher gradation of plundering, without a visible excuse.

This need for justification crops up again and again in accounts of the war. The Moravians protected themselves by providing no pretext to would-be plunderers. To be sure, the Moravians suffered loss, and not only from depreciated payments for impressed goods. Much was stolen, and many people were badly frightened on occasion. But officers and soldiers alike generally subscribed to a hierarchy of appropriate behavior. The confiscation of provisions was expected. It was best when paid for in cash (or salt), less good if only receipts were given, and worse yet when officially pressed without receipt. Further down the scale was the stealing of food without official sanction, followed by officer-directed, but unsanctioned, stealing, and finally, worst of all, the theft of items unrelated to military need.

The overall impression gained from the Moravian diaries is that through about the first half of 1780, the militia, while peremptory in its demands, generally confined itself to taking food, even when unauthorized stealing occurred. By the winter of 1781, however, there was a much more general breakdown in discipline within the militia. Non-food stealing increased, as did the pressing of food without giving receipts. The need for a pretext remained, and, as noted above, the Moravians never experienced the harsher sort of violence that occurred elsewhere. In 1782, the Moravian towns saw much less militia activity and virtually no violence.

The next broad category of analysis, the treatment of prisoners, is one of the most complex. It covers not only the question of granting quarter in battle but also how prisoners were treated while being held, whether they were paroled and exchanged, or whether they were tried as civil criminals. These topics will be covered in order, beginning with restraint of unlawful killing in "hot blood" (granting quarter). There follows a brief discussion of the extremely variable and complicated efforts of the Whigs to define the status of Tory prisoners, a subject that preoccupied the Whig government but never found systematic resolution. Finally, "military" prisoners will be considered, comparing their treatment to European standards of prisoner confinement, parole, and exchange.

The killing of men attempting to surrender in the midst of battle was considered more excusable than cold-blooded execution.[42] A directive from the Board of War to a militia colonel made that distinction clear, ordering him to deal severely with any who were found in arms, and then clarifying "I mean in action—and not after they are Prisoners."[43] Even hot-blooded killing, however, was still a violation of conventions of war. Most Rebel militia knew this, but many North Carolinians believed the British had set a precedent by refusing to grant quarter during the encounter between Continental general Abraham Buford and British colonel Banastre Tarleton at Waxhaws, South Carolina, in 1780 (see below). This grievance notwithstanding, the Rebels usually attempted to grant quarter to surrendering troops. Where they may not have done so, they certainly tried to make it appear that they had.[44] In July 1780, William Davie took advantage of the lack of uniforms differentiating Whigs and Tories and passed a rifle company through the sentry line of a Loyalist force. His company opened fire once inside the camp. The Loyalists immediately broke and fled and were caught by the remainder of Davie's troops and "literally cut to pieces." Davie excused the lack of prisoners by noting that "as this was done under the eye of the whole British camp no prisoners could be safely taken which may apologize for the slaughter that took place on this occasion."[45] On another outing, however, when Davie conducted a dawn attack on a Tory force at Wahab's plantation, he took thirty prisoners.[46] In another case, one Loyalist refused to continue serving as a guide for a British force after overhearing orders to "show no quarters, but to put to instant death every Whig that should be found with arms in their hands."[47]

The expected standard of behavior is revealed in the well-known incident at the Battle of King's Mountain. Major Patrick Ferguson, detached on a flanking march into western North Carolina with a force of Loyalists and a few British regulars, had taken up a defensive position on a wooded plateau known as King's Mountain. There, on October 7, 1780, a large Rebel militia force attacked and defeated him. Accounts vary as to exactly how the battle ended. When Major Ferguson was shot, the British attempted to surrender by raising a white flag. The official account submitted by the Rebel leaders a few days later asserted that "our fire immediately ceased" upon the raising of the white flag.[48] An ensign in the Rebel force remembered the event similarly, stating that as soon as the flag was seen, the firing "immediately ceased."[49] Other memories, recorded at different times, offered contrasting views. One of the Rebel commanders, Colonel William Campbell, wrote later that month that the firing stopped as soon as the troops could be notified that the British had surrendered.[50] Joseph Graham heard a different version, in which the Rebel militia saw the flag but continued firing. "Give them Buford's play," the Whigs yelled, referring to the supposed massacre of Buford's force by Tarleton at Waxhaws earlier that year. Graham wrote that eventually the Whig officers were able to stop the firing and collect the prisoners.[51] Whatever really happened, it is clear that there was concern that the soldiers may have kept on firing after the raising of a white flag. References to an earlier violation by the British appear to have fallen short of justification. In an effort to maintain the sheen of virtue, the misdeed was glossed over in initial reports and later explained away as appropriate revenge. The need to excuse the crime says more about the underlying value system, and the demand for virtuous war, than it does about the merits of the defense.

If hot-blooded killing was wrong but excusable, the question of what to do with prisoners once they were taken was even thornier. Two aspects of this problem are worth considering. The first was the debate within the Whig government and the Whig military over how to define Loyalist prisoners. The second was the more informal definitions reached by the militia in the field. The former issue is sufficiently large to deserve a separate treatment and can be touched upon only briefly here.[52]

Chapter 5 noted how, in the case of the prisoners taken at Moore's Creek, the Whig government combined conciliation (pardoning the soldiers) with relatively traditional military confinement and exchange for the leaders. Even then the Whigs felt that those guilty of nonmilitary crimes such as house burning and murder should receive harsher treatment.[53] During the course of the war, the Whig government hardened its attitudes toward the Loyalists. By 1780, there was a temptation to deal with all Loyalists captured in arms as treasonous rebels, deserving only the harsh punishments meted out by civil courts.[54] Colonel William Davie elaborated the uncertainty of the issue when he described the Loyalists he and his men had captured in 1780: "I know no particular Crime but the General one of their being *King's Militia.* . . . But on which principle they ought to be treated, I know not, whether Exchange or Punishment."[55] Many Loyalists felt that the issue was more clear cut; the Whig government had made it a policy to treat them as rebels. Robert Gray, a Loyalist officer in South Carolina, wrote in his memoir near the end of the war:

When ever a militia man of ours was made a prisoner he was delivered not to the Continentals but to the Rebel Militia who looked upon him as a State prisoner, as a man who deserved a halter and therefore treated him with the greatest cruelty. If he was not assassinated after being made a prisoner, he was instantly hurried into Virginia or North Carolina where he was kept a prisoner without friends, money, credit, or perhaps hopes of exchange.[56]

This kind of accusation certainly had some substance but was not universally true. The Whigs came to recognize the utilitarian value of counting Tories taken in arms as prisoners of war, and exchanging them for Whig militia held by the British.[57] The tension between treating a Loyalist as a civil prisoner and as an exchangeable prisoner of war was, unfortunately, probably worked out in a somewhat random fashion, but with a distinct tendency to fall back on definitions of violent acts to decide the issue. Those Tories who could be shown to have "been guilty of murder, robbery, house-burning, and offences out of the Military Line" were likely to be treated as civil criminals under the treason law.[58] Persons who had not committed such crimes could be exchanged. There was also a temptation among some Whig leaders to forcibly enlist captured Loyalists into the Continental army or into active militia service. Such service would not only earn them a pardon but would help fill the ranks. Again, an exception was made for those who were guilty of the same list of crimes, or who had been leading men among the Tories, possibly holders of British commissions. The latter were to be tried in the civil courts, while those who refused to enlist were held as prisoners of war to be exchanged.[59]

For small units of Whig militia scouring the countryside for Tories, such niceties of definition were often of little import. They improvised their treatment of captured Tories to suit the circumstance. In the aggregate, however, their behavior was restrained and shaped by norms of appropriate violence.[60] Something of a pattern emerges from the welter of accounts of the taking and subsequent treatment of prisoners, by both Whigs and Loyalists.[61] A November 1780 letter from Lord Cornwallis to General William Smallwood of the Continental army reveals many of those patterns and thus bears extended quotation. Cornwallis referred to the hanging of several Loyalist prisoners captured at King's Mountain (the hanging is discussed below) and neatly laid out the state of affairs on all sides concerning prisoners:

> I must now observe that the cruelty exercised on the Prisoners taken under Major Ferguson is shocking to humanity; and the hanging poor old Colonel Mills, who was always a fair and open Enemy to your Cause, was an act of the most Savage barbarity. It has also been reported to me that Capt. Oates, of Colo. Gray's [South Carolina Loyalist] Militia, . . . was lately put to Death without any Crime being laid to his charge. . . . I cannot suppose that you approve of

these most cruel Murders; but I hope you will see the necessity of interposing your Authority—to stop this bloody Scene, which must oblige me, in justice to the suffering Loyalists, to retaliate on the unfortunate Persons now in my power. I am not conscious that any persons have hitherto been executed by us, unless for bearing Arms, after having given a Military Parole to remain quietly at home. . . . I would willingly Exchange any of the North or South Carolina Militia, who may be prisoners with us, for those who were taken on King's Mountain.[62]

Here Cornwallis expressed a whole range of expectations: that "open enemies" not be treated as civil criminals; that execution required a criminal charge; that violation of these rules be condemned as savage and barbaric; that threatening retaliation would serve to prevent a repetition; that breaking a military parole be treated as a capital offense; and that exchange was always preferred.

Some version of these expectations informed and shaped the actual actions and reactions of the Whig and Tory militias, with the very significant addition of actual retaliation. It was true that Loyalists taken in arms were in danger of summary execution by shooting, but in general they were usually held for a more or less formal court-martial. In this way, the Whig militia aspired to a legitimacy of form, superimposing appearances of legality on what were often acts of revenge. This tension between form and revenge can be seen in William Gipson's account of his company's treatment of two Tories captured in 1779. They took the two prisoners fifteen miles to the Guilford courthouse and there held a court-martial. The Whig company condemned Hugh McPherson, a "notorious" Tory, and shot him. The other was sentenced to "be spicketed," that is, suspended over a sharp pin, with the bare foot of the victim tenuously perched on the point. This was nominally a traditional disciplinary punishment for cavalrymen, but in this instance they went beyond the norm and actually slowly drove the pin through his foot.[63] There are numerous reports of Whig militias bringing in Tories and sentencing them to be whipped, and even occasionally to be hanged or shot, after a quick court-martial.[64]

The most familiar instance was that of which Cornwallis complained, the hanging of several members of Ferguson's corps in the week after King's Mountain. A court-martial composed of field officers, instigated by reports of hangings in South Carolina, convicted thirty-six Tories (out of hundreds of prisoners) of "breaking open houses, killing the men, turning the women and children out of doors, and burning the houses."[65] Determined to inject an air of legality into the proceedings, someone had retrieved a copy of the North Carolina law that authorized two magistrates to summon a jury, and they used that as the basis for the trial.[66] Three men at a time were hanged until nine were dead; then the officers stepped in and ended it.[67] Even the manner of execution is significant. In the case of the King's Mountain prisoners, and in many of the more "informal" and illegal executions, the method of choice was hanging.[68] Hanging as a method of execution not only lent a judicial aspect to the killing (the legitimacy of form) but emphasized the supposed criminality of the victim.

Although all killing of prisoners tended to inflame the other side, these cold-blooded, drumhead executions were considered particularly egregious.[69] The Whigs and the Tories justified many executions by referring to an earlier such summary killing by the other side. While being held captive by Loyalist colonel David Fanning, Rebel militia general Herndon Ramsey was forced to write a letter to Governor Burke presenting Fanning's grievances. Fanning's party complained of a variety of cruel practices, noting especially that some prisoners had been "whipped and ill-treated, without tryal," and that a few days earlier the Rebels had supposedly taken a man on the road and "put him to instant Death." Fanning threatened, through Ramsey, that if such cruelties were not stopped, the "whole country will be deluged in Blood, and the innocent will suffer for the guilty."[70] Henry Reed, a Whig militiaman being pursued at law after the war by the friends and relatives of a Tory whom his company had killed, justified himself in this way as plainly as he could. One of his company, a certain McAdow (or McAdon), had been captured and then killed by Fanning's men. Therefore, when a Tory by the name of Alexander Shannon shortly thereafter "fell into the hands" of Reed's company, they in turn killed him. As Reed explained after the war,

> perhaps the act [killing Shannon] was not strickly consonant to the rules of law, and perhaps would not be justifiable done in a time of peace, but in the emergency of the times, when the country was almost drowned in the blood of her citizens, by barbarous murders, not done by the Brittish, but by the Tories. Therefore this fact was only a just retaliation as there was no way to subdue them except this.[71]

Similarly, David Fanning claimed in his narrative that he had killed certain men in direct retaliation for the specifically cold-blooded killing of other Loyalists.[72]

There were a number of occasions, however, when individuals acted to protect or provide for prisoners, even at risk or expense to themselves. John Arnold claimed after the war that when he had escorted thirty-four British prisoners to Hillsborough, he had spent much of his own money to provide provisions for them on the march.[73] More dramatic were efforts by individuals, sometimes officers and sometimes soldiers, to protect prisoners from the outrages of others. When, for example, a superior officer ordered the execution of a Hessian prisoner, Captain John Taylor countermanded the order.[74] Other examples abound.[75]

On balance, the record suggests that summary courts-martial and dramatic rescues aside, the experiences of most prisoners on both sides were relatively unexceptional, if never entirely pleasant.[76] In part, this was because of the extensive use of parole and eventual exchange by both sides. Many prisoners were paroled on their oath not to fight again until exchanged. Even in the midst of some of Fanning's more dramatic examples of execution, he exercised discretion. On one occasion, for example, having captured several Rebels, he had them all stand in a row "to Examine them, to see if I Knew any of them that was bad men." One such "bad man" tried to run away and was shot; Fanning paroled the remainder.[77] Throughout his narrative, Fanning reports similar instances of the capture and parole of large numbers of Rebels.[78] On the Whig side, as discussed above, "parole" continued late in the war but often took the form of impressment in the Continental army.[79]

To some, the parole oath proved remarkably binding, while others readily violated it. Breaking parole was taken very seriously, however, and some justified the poor treatment of prisoners by accusing the other side of too frequently violating parole.[80] Prominent individuals alleged to have broken their parole went to elaborate lengths to justify their actions or disprove the accusation.[81] Others went to equally elaborate lengths to avoid breaking it in the first place. Fanning reported that after he captured nine Rebel militia under Captain Thomas Kennedy, Kennedy promised not to try to escape; he even stood by observing while Fanning attacked another Rebel militia force. Impressed, Fanning immediately paroled him.[82]

Of course, parole was only one manifestation of the more formal aspects of eighteenth-century traditions of war. Others included the use of flags of truce to protect the process of negotiations, the recognition of a commission as a symbol of legitimate authority to raise troops, and the inviolability of messengers between contending armies. For the most part, both sides held closely to those rules, recognizing not only the mutual benefit that they represented but also the threat to individual honor incurred by violating them. Furthermore, to emulate European military formalism was to win legitimacy. Just as rioters channeled their behavior into certain familiar patterns in their quest for recognition, so too did militia officers seek legitimacy for their ad hoc units and operations.[83]

The actions of Loyalist colonel David Fanning were particularly revealing of this need to emulate conventional forms. In the summer of 1781, as Fanning was just beginning the most active part of his career fighting the Whigs in North Carolina, he returned to his camp after a brief absence to confront a power struggle. One of his subordinates had tried to convince the men that Fanning was trying to make them into regular troops, and many of them deserted on that basis. Fanning immediately declared that he "never would go on another Scoute, untill there was a Field Officer and the majority Chose me. They then drew up a petition to the Commanding Officer of the Kings troops," requesting a commission for Fanning.[84] He took the petition to Wilmington (then under British control) and received a commission as a militia colonel. Thus anointed, he returned to his men, ordered a general muster, and commissioned other officers in his now-official regiment. The story reflects a curious paradox within the minds of the "common sort" (in Fanning's words) between the fear of being made a regular, and their need for a "legitimate" colonel to hold them together. Fanning used his commission to raise additional men, and he also assured British major James Craig that he would "establish certain regulations for the conduct of the militia." The resulting rules required that each man take an oath of allegiance and be responsible to the officers of the unit. The rules also prohibited leaving camp, disobeying orders, plundering, and "all irregularities and disorder."[85]

Fanning carried his concern for forms into his subsequent campaigns. His narrative is full of accounts of flags being sent between contending militia parties, or truces being arranged while commanders were consulted, and of course, paroles of prisoners being accepted.[86] His narrative, in fact, functions as a near-perfect rhetorical reflection of how expectations of violence affected behavior. On one hand, he constantly reaffirms his commitment to the "rules," from the simplest of traditions of a flag of truce to a body of regulations prohibiting plunder. On the other hand, he equally constantly reminds his reader of how the Whigs had violated those rules, killing and plundering illegitimately, violating their paroles, and even conspiring to turn a truce conference into an ambush.[87] These details of form and the desire to affix blame to the Whigs are situated in a narrative that regularly admits to executing certain prisoners. Fanning's narrative is not all whitewashing; his insistence on the forms reveals their importance to him.

The truce conference he referred to was intended to be a negotiation over the establishment of a cease-fire zone in which Loyalists would be left alone and all "back-plundering would be void."[88] Believing that he had been set up for an ambush at the conference, and hearing that three of his men had been hanged and seven more sentenced to die, Fanning wrote to Governor Burke outlining his plan for retaliation if the peace (his "articles") was not accepted and the execution of his men not stayed:

> If the requisition of my articles do not arrive to satisfaction and the effusion of blood stopped and the lives of those men saved, that I will retaliate blood for blood and tenfold for one and there shall never an officer or private of the Rebel party escape that falls into my hands hereafter but what shall suffer the pain and punishment of instant death.[89]

Fanning's threat of a life (or even ten lives) for a life reaches to the top of the hierarchy of violence—murder.[90] Murder was the act most likely to inspire outrage. To avoid that charge, the militias made every effort to kill by the rules. Conversely, both sides made every effort to accuse the other of *not* killing by the rules. The rhetorical distinction between killing and murder was significant. No one said, for example, that "the British killed my friend/brother/cousin in the Battle of Guilford Court House, let's hang the next British soldier we capture." Battle, and to some extent the British army itself, carried a *de facto* legitimacy that defused vengeance.[91] Even Loyalist militia units seem to have gained that legitimacy when in actual battle.[92] As will be seen, however, the operational style of war practiced by the militias included a host of activities not directly related to battle, and it was killings committed in those situations that each side tried to justify or condemn depending on their viewpoint. It has been previously noted that the killing of prisoners was usually done in a manner intended to satisfy expectations of legality: courts-martial were held, prisoners were hanged, and so forth. Our modern vision of hanging as illegitimate vigilantism obscures their deliberate use of it to emphasize legality. In general, there are relatively few surviving accounts of out-and-out murder, of an unarmed person being peremptorily shot. It did happen, however, and all too many hangings were nearly as peremptory.[93]

There were also, however, many instances of intervention or restraint to prevent such killings. One Moravian, for example, when stopped on the road by a company of Rebel militia who threatened to shoot him if he did not give up his horse, took his chances and rode quietly away. "They let him alone."[94] On another occasion, a Whig named Ezekiel Slocumb discovered a Tory who had been hanged to a bent sapling but was still living. Slocumb immediately cut him down and restored him.[95] Robert Kincaid, with several others, was taken prisoner in 1781 by Tories "who threatened to hang them." In the end, however, he and his companions were left "tied fast and striped of every thing they had—horses and all except the wearing apparel."[96] For all the violence of the militias' war, there still existed a strong set of cultural restraints against deliberate illegitimate killing.[97]

The Breakdown of Cultural Restraint

There is little doubt, however, that many of those cultural restraints had broken down during the course of the war. Prisoners were mistreated and even killed. Houses were robbed and sometimes burned. How did the norms of restraint break down? By this point, the importance of retaliation in contributing to that breakdown should be clear. The law of retaliation, the *lex talionis,* still existed in traditional European war, where it had usually come to be threatened as a deterrent instead of indulged as revenge.[98] The same was generally true between the Continental and British armies.[99] The militias, however, were much more likely to carry out the retaliation.[100] Colonel Gray, a Loyalist, made explicit the difference between the regulars and the militia. He complained loudly that when the British took Rebel militia as prisoners, they "[being] entirely ignorant of the dispositions and manners of the people treated them with the utmost lenity and sent them home to their plantations on parole."[101] He believed that the Rebels immediately broke their paroles and "made it a point to murder every militia man of ours who had any concern in making them prisoners." He concluded that "nothing will ever be able to put our [Loyalist] Militia here on a proper footing but giving up to them all the Rebel Militia when prisoners to be dealt with according to the laws of retaliation."

A common thread running through the words and actions of officers and soldiers was the fundamental legitimacy of retaliation. As much as Governor Burke might believe that it was not acceptable practice "among *Civilized* nations" to "gratify the Vengeance of those enraged People," North Carolinians in general did not agree.[102] Retaliation was considered the appropriate method by which to "censure" those who had violated the communal standards of appropriate violence. Stories of violation inspiring retaliation, whether personal or general, are legion. For example, a

Tory who came upon the Rebel militia captain Forbes lying wounded on the battlefield after Guilford Courthouse refused him water and then kicked him. After Forbes died from his wounds, the heartless Tory was found "suspended on a tree before his own door."[103] Similarly, Jonathan Starkey explained his enlisting in the militia and his desire to kill Tories, by referring to the "inhuman and brutal capture of my old father by the Torries and British and the unheard of and cruel Treatment which he rec' from them and which resulted in his death."[104] Whig militiaman Moses Hall related a particularly evocative story of the psychological effect of violence and the equally powerful motive of retribution:

> The evening after our battle with the Tories . . . we went to where six [Tory prisoners] were standing together. Some discussion taking place, I heard some of our men cry out, "Remember Buford," and the prisoners were immediately hewed to pieces with broadswords. At first I bore the scene without any emotion, but upon a moment's reflection, I felt such horror as I never did before nor have since. . . . [The next morning] I discovered lying upon the ground . . . [what] proved to be a youth about sixteen who, having come out to view the British troops through curiousity, for fear he might give information to our troops, they had run him through with a bayonet. . . . The sight of this unoffending boy, butchered . . . relieved me of my distressful feelings for the slaughter of the Tories, and I desired nothing so much as the opportunity of participating in their destruction.[105]

The reader should note that this incident occurred during Hall's *ninth* tour of active duty as a militia soldier; nothing he had seen on earlier tours had prepared him for this particular exchange of savagery.

It is also critical to observe that Hall's desire for revenge extended to any Tories whatsoever. Retaliation could be generalized. Such a course was suggested by the residents of Guilford County who wrote to the Assembly requesting that a

> Law be enacted directing the commanding Officer in every County to take what Tories he can & keep them under a Sufficient Guard & in the mean Time publickly to notify, that for every Robery & murder afterwards committed, retaliation should be made on such Tories prisoners as you in your Wisdom Judge Proper.[106]

Similarly, British major Craig said that if the Whig government of North Carolina condoned the cold-blooded killing of prisoners, it would be "alone responsible to its subjects, for the retaliation which the Laws of War and of necessity must draw on them from their Enemy."[107]

For its part, the civil government proved all too willing to forgive ostensibly retaliatory violence committed by Whigs. While it may be true that many people accused in postwar courts of illegal violence may have claimed retaliation as a cover for self-interested plunder, it was also true that such claims carried weight in those courts. Retaliation was a successful legal defense, although one that often required special legislative pardon since apparently it would not necessarily hold up in a normal court.[108] As early as 1781, the North Carolina Senate passed a blanket indemnity resolution for all "such persons as have put to death any of the subjects of this State, being known & notorious Enemies & Opponents of the Government thereof."[109] Several examples have already been mentioned of Whigs who killed Tories and then were granted specific pardons by the General Assembly after the war.[110] In another case, William Linton's petition for pardon for his allegedly unlawful killing of Mikel Quinn claimed

> that the killing of the said Quinn was no more than what has often happened, and as often winked at by government, in all countries, when a people have contended for all that was dear and valuable to them against the Iron hand of Oppression; and ought to be considered as one of those acts incidental to and arising out of the nature of civil war, or at most an excusable and justifiable retaliation on those unfeeling and brutal ruffians who had in cold blood put to death the good subjects of the United States without regard to age or sex.[111]

In essence, the law of retaliation was a socially recognized norm of behavior that encouraged legitimate revenge in response to illegitimate violence. This was seen as socially useful violence, equally as functional, and as legitimate, as more conventionally military violence. Note, however, who was arbitrating legitimacy. It was not that an act of revenge would be accepted as legitimate by the other side. To do so was against their interest, much as the specific target of a riot was often unlikely to accept the justness of the rioters' grievances. The question is one of "release" from cultural restraint and an accompanying release from fear of censure by the wider audience. The legitimacy of retaliation provided that release. Where rioters channeled their frustrations into particular forms of violent behavior partly in order to avoid censure (social or legal), so too did soldiers point to retaliation to avoid censure (again, social or legal). It was universally acknowledged, however, that a war of retaliation was more destructive for everyone, and that restraint was preferred. The first part of this chapter detailed exactly that kind of restraint, showing that even in the worst periods of 1780 to 1782 the violence was never wholly out of control. On the other hand, there is no question that it was significantly worse than what had gone before.[112] The question, then, is what gave retaliation free rein? The answer lies in a combination of factors. The first was the presence and activities of the British. The second was the operational style of war practiced by the militia of both sides. The third was the inability of the militia as an institution to limit itself to threatened retaliation. The last was the ethnic composition of the colony.

While it was true that the British army, as a conventional European army of the eighteenth century, theoretically found the "deliberate & unnecessary shedding of blood to be repugnant," it nevertheless often failed that ideal.[113] The British did commit illegitimate violence and thereby inspired a desire for some kind of retaliation. In most situations, however, the British army was simply immune to all but large-scale military counteraction. So when Whigs were moved to retaliate for British actions, they did so against the more vulnerable Tories.

British failure to observe their own ideal resulted in part from the inability of the British high command to achieve a consistent policy with regard to the prosecution of the war. As Armstrong Starkey and Stephen Conway have pointed out, the officer corps was divided over whether to treat the Americans as Rebels and therefore subdue them with fire and sword, or to win their hearts and minds and so inspire a counterrevolution.[114] That muddle of policy led some British officers to actively pursue policies of devastation, which, as was noted above, *was worse* in the gradations of military violence than the random plunder of undirected soldiers.[115] American fear that the British would adopt the fire-and-sword policy was clear. The rumor that circulated around Rowan County after Cornwallis captured Charlotte alleged that unless everyone "[did] immediately submit to the King and take protection, every one of us were to be hanged . . . as Rebels and Traitors, our houses burnt, our lands forfeited and our other property delivered as plunder to the Army."[116] This rumor led some to go to the British camp and ask if it was true; Cornwallis and Josiah Martin, the royal governor of North Carolina, vehemently denied it.[117]

So, partly as a consequence of muddled policy, and partly because of British soldiers acting on their own, tales of British atrocity and misbehavior circulated constantly.[118] Atrocity stories had been an essential component of the Whig propaganda effort since the beginning of the war, and such tales often focused on British violations of the customs of war.[119] The

Continental Congress, for example, made a point of publishing the conclusions of a committee that investigated British conduct in 1777. They divided British behavior into four categories and claimed to have found ample evidence for each: devastation of the countryside, mistreatment of prisoners, refusal to grant quarter, and the abuse of women.[120] Captain Cogdell wrote to Governor Caswell in 1778 of the rumor that the British had thrown wounded Whig militiamen into a fire to be burned alive.[121] When the *North Carolina Gazette* eulogized General Abner Nash, it spoke of the "Depredations of bloody Tyrants, who are wasting our Country with Fire and Sword, and Spreading among us every Species of Desolation, even the brutal Violence of Female Chastity."[122]

Perhaps the most notorious incident in the southern campaign was Tarleton's "massacre" of Buford's Continentals at Waxhaws in 1780. The details were contested for many years afterward by both sides, serving as an indicator of the importance placed on a perception of having obeyed the rules.[123] What the North Carolina Whigs believed during the war, however, was that Tarleton had attacked Buford's force, refused their surrender (that is, denied them quarter), and massacred them while unarmed. Reports of the killing quickly circulated around the state; in one version, "'tis Said [Tarleton] killed at least 200 men in a most Cruel & Inhumane Manner, after piling their Arms."[124] Henry Lee, in his memoir, summed up the consequences:

> In the annals of our Indian war nothing is to be found more shocking; and this bloody day only wanted the war dance, and the roasting fire, to have placed it first in the records of torture and of death in the West. This tragic expedition sunk deep in the American breast, and produced the unanimous decision among the troops to revenge their murdered comrades whenever the blood-stained corps should give an opportunity.[125]

As mentioned previously, it was this incident that supposedly led the Rebel militia at King's Mountain to continue to fire on the surrendering British, crying: "Give them Buford's Play." Other such stories of British violations of the rules circulated freely through the countryside.[126]

Another inflammatory aspect of the British army's presence in North Carolina was the behavior and composition of the army's camp followers. It became notorious in North Carolina, and was in fact admitted by Cornwallis, that the majority of the plunderings and even other acts of violence associated with the British army were actually committed by the camp followers.[127] The Whigs particularly resented such behavior because those camp followers were composed of more than the standard soldiers' wives, dependents, and sutlers; there were also Loyalist exiles and escaped slaves.[128] Loyalist exiles felt that they had personal scores and losses to settle, as, for that matter, did former slaves. It hardly needs comment how most North Carolinians would react to the sight of escaped slaves plundering a house.

If the British leadership was at times unclear about how to treat the rebellion, the common soldiers seem to have had little doubt. To them, Rebels were rebels and deserved little mercy.[129] Additionally, they often felt that the Rebels did not fight fairly. The British soldiers came to recognize the Continentals as regulars and respected them as such but harbored resentment against the militia for the style of war it practiced.[130] The British troops who landed at Brunswick in 1776 came back from their expedition "damning the Rebels for their unmanly way of fighting, and swearing that they would give no quarter, for they took sight at them, and were behind timber, skulking about."[131] This resentment reflected a conflict in ways of war, not unlike the Anglo-Indian cultural conflict. The strong European influence on practices of war notwithstanding, Americans' previous experience of war had produced some modifications; the frontier style of war practiced by much of the militia violated British soldiers' expectations and contributed to escalation.[132]

Besides irritating the British regulars, the militias' style of war contributed more generally to the breakdown of restraint. The most famous and most often examined uses of the militia were those occasions when they were attached to the Continental or British armies. When so attached they were generally used in the same manner and in the same roles as regulars, and their success or failure in that mode has usually been seen as the measure of the quality of the institution.[133] There were some instances of large-scale battles fought exclusively by militia forces, such as King's Mountain, but those were relatively uncommon.[134] The vast majority of militia activity was either operationally less susceptible to control or restraint (ambushes, night attacks) or was aimed at individual persons.

As was outlined in chapters 5 and 6, the duties of the North Carolina Rebel militia had accustomed them to an individual or an individual's house as the focus of military activity. Tory scouring expeditions usually were mounted against specific individuals whom everyone "knew" were Tories. The experience of John Evans is instructive.[135] Sometime in 1780, the light horse militia company of Nash County arrived at his house, arrested him, carried him to the courthouse and "threatened [him] . . . with hanging, a Gallows being erected on the spot." Thus terrified, he consented to enlist for eighteen months. When he asked the reasons for his arrest, the militia told him that they had heard that he wanted to take up arms and join a Tory band in Edgecombe County, and that he had asked someone else's advice on the matter. Such was the manner in which the militia came to "know" a person's loyalties.

Even when not specifically scouring, the militia had long been used as an agency of loyalty enforcement. They looked for people at their homes, forced them to take the oath, searched houses for arms, inventoried property for possible confiscation, and so on. This focus on the house violated a fundamental Anglo-American expectation of the sacredness of the home. One historian has identified what he calls a "homestead ethic" operating in the backcountry areas of British North America. The ethic constituted a powerful set of ideals including the right to feel free of violence in the home. Although the exact roots of this belief are unclear, the evidence is that they ran, and continue to run, deep.[136] The Scottish tradition of the bloodfeud, for example, had specific conventions against harming one's enemy while he was in his house (such an offense was called *hamesucken*).[137] Atrocity narratives from the seventeenth century onward often included the formulaic accusation that families had been "turned (sometimes naked) out of doors," a phrase repeated by Loyalist claimants after the war.[138] Similarly, burning a house ranked high among military offenses. Francis Marion observed as much when he wrote to General Gates:

> I am sorry to acquaint you that Captn. Murphy's [Whig] Party have burnt a Great Number of houses on Little Peedee, & intend to go on in that Abominable work, . . . but I assure you, there is not one house Burnt by my Order, or by any of my People. It is what I detest to Distress poor Women & Children.[139]

The specialness of the home could be seen in the cases of riot as well: witness the reluctance of rioters during the Stamp Act crisis to enter Governor Tryon's house, and the importance of Fanning's home in Hillsborough as a center point for Regulator outrage. Jill Lepore, in her work on King Philip's War, also pointed out this role of the house in defining a place of safety and security, noting that the New Englanders were the most outraged by those acts that violated the home.[140]

The experience of many militiamen while in service had broken down this restraint, and since most militiamen served a number of tours, they brought that experience with them in each succeeding tour.[141] The official ordering of men into houses looking for weapons or provisions "afforded the men of dishonest propensities an opportunity of taking many things which necessity did not require."[142] This practice not only increased the opportunities for plunder but also set a precedent for violence against individuals, something that *war* was not considered to do. European notions of war defined it as a tool of the state directed against another state. In North Carolina, the militia had become a tool of the state directed against individuals, and frequently against individuals whom the militia soldiers already knew.

This personal knowledge of the enemy also contributed to another characteristic of the militias' expectations of war. When the Whig militia was called up, whether drafted or enlisted for their three-month tour, or raised as a volunteer unit in response to a specific crisis (such as the force that marched to King's Mountain), the soldiers expected to *do* something. The King's Mountain army was recruited with the promise that "they might rely on a battle before they returned home."[143] The militia did not like camp life, or marching and countermarching; when in service they expected to accomplish something, whatever that thing might be, and then go home.[144] Joseph Graham wrote of General Thomas Sumter's militia command in 1780 that

> while he kept moving, and they expected to meet the enemy, they kept with him; but whenever they came to attend only to the dull routine of camp duty, such as mounting, relieving and standing guard and enduring privations, they became discontented, and those in convenient distance went home.[145]

Lacking a more obvious target, an impatient militia often fell back on the homes of those they "knew" to be Tories. When Charles McLean of Lincoln County raised a militia force to pursue some Tories who were marching to join the king, they failed in their pursuit, whereupon

> the people employed in pershute being disappointed in overtaking them, and Being Cautious of a Reward Due them from those treators of the said State, and finding nothing else but some of the property of the saide insurgents, Laide hold of several horses.[146]

Similarly, a body of militia raised in 1776 was told that the "matter was settled" and that they could go home. One of their number, John Johnston, noted that "never were men more desirous to engage or more dejected when they found there was nothing to be done; however on our return, to keep up their spirits we . . . scowered the Country."[147]

Finally, as seen in chapter 4, the militia had developed an operational way of war that combined European and Indian precedents, resulting in a preference for night or dawn attacks, ambushes, or harassing parties.[148] Gregory Knouff has argued that this preference was reinforced by the backcountry men's investment of their masculine identity in a frontier style of war. That is, they wanted to be seen as tough, independent, even violent men who fought Indians while using an Indian style of war.[149] During the Revolution, this preference was reinforced by necessity; militia forces were usually not up to the task of open assaults on the British army.[150] Earlier in the war, Thomas Burke had expressed this operational preference and also asserted that the American way of war would triumph. He noted that experience proved that "in desultory war we [Americans] are always superior to them."[151] A purely militia force that found itself on more or less equal footing with an enemy militia unit would occasionally engage in open battle. Moore's Creek was one example and Ramsour's Mill in 1780 was another.[152] In the face of greater force, however, the militias slipped into what the modern mind would call guerilla war with a facility that the British army simply could not match.[153]

The North Carolina Rebel militia's frequent and able use of harassing, partisan warfare was particularly evident from 1780 to 1782. Colonel William Davie, observing the careless foraging of the British army around Charlotte, predicted that "a few rifle light infantry companies might perhaps be of singular service. . . . If the parties are small, [they] may lie secure among the thickets and Morasses, & annoy the Enemy very considerably."[154] John Padgett's description of his military service is also revealing. Describing his third and fourth tours with the militia since 1780, he remembered being

> constantly Employd in pursuit of Forraging Parties and in preventing communication between the British and Citizens was Frequently in Skirmishing Engagements too Tedious to mention. . . . [after enlisting again in August 1781] was in an action near that place [Wilmington] at what was Called the Brick House we were also at this time frequently in Skirmishing engagements from this place a party of us was sent on towards Georgetown [South Carolina] (I being of the number) to scour the Country and Subdue the Tories and in this Expedition we were frequently Engaged with Small parties and Suffer'd much in Consequence of the nature of the Service and Country.[155]

There were consequences to this style of warfare. Ambushes and night attacks were notoriously difficult to control once begun.[156] It was in situations like these that quarter was often refused.[157] Thomas Cummings, in his pension statement, simply noted of one of his militia tours that although no engagement was entered into, "a number of Tories were shot and cut to pieces" in the swamps.[158]

Furthermore, many accounts of the militiamen reveal that they were simply not as heavily invested in or informed about some of the conventional rules of war. William Ward, who had never seen an artillery piece before Moore's Creek Bridge, recounted that the day before that battle "a flag was brought to Genl. Caswell from the Tories . . . [and] a Captain Vance asked Genl. Caswell if he might kill the bearer of the flag, and Genl. Caswell shook his head."[159] This differing perception of war is also found in the occasional intervention of officers to prevent backcountry militiamen from sniping at sentries.[160] For many militiamen, their only knowledge of war had been of the particularly unrestrained kind practiced against Indians. Thus, the combination of a way of war already difficult to control with a heritage of unrestrained war and its consequent weaker investment in the conventional formalities eased the descent into retaliatory war.

Although the frontier style of war was itself a problem, the institutional weaknesses of the militia organizations contributed equally to the breakdown of customary restraints on war. These weaknesses, in fact, marked one of the significant differences between the militia and the Continental army and thus must account in part for the differences in their application of violence.

The first significant aspect of the structure of the militia was the question of their motivation. Although the Rebel militia was frequently filled by a draft and/or bounty money (as was the Continental army), there were many occasions when soldiers were recruited directly in response to tales of British atrocities, or to deal with a given Tory rising. In those cases, their outlook from the beginning might be one of retaliation.[161] It is a truism about wartime propaganda that often the home front acquires a hatred of the demonized enemy far in excess of that felt by the soldiers at the front.[162] In the case of the revolutionary militia, who served a tour, went home, only to be called out again, it may be that they were imbibing that kind of "home-front hatred" and then carrying it into the field with them. Jonathan Starkey so explained his service, claiming that he "fought not for money . . . But for my Country alone which was the only feling [sic] that fired my bosom, and revenge for the inhuman murder (by the enemy) of my . . . old father."[163] Reverend James Hall, a Scotch-Irish minister near the Catawba River, was "stirred . . . as he heard of the massacres, and plunderings, and battles," and he gathered his congregation together and convinced them to form a company of cavalry.[164] William Gipson explained his joining a small group of Whig volunteers as a consequence of their beating his mother and destroying "his home and patrimony."[165]

The Loyalists, for their part, were similarly motivated by continuing confiscation and Whig violence against suspected Tories.[166] Thus, Loyalist soldiers, too, were often moved to join by a hope of retaliation.[167] The Moravians explained the rising of the Tories in 1780 led by Gideon Wright as a result of their desire "to take back the things of which they had been robbed."[168] A number of Loyalist claims enumerated the injuries that led them to raise a Loyalist militia unit late in the war.[169] When Ferguson led his force into the western part of North Carolina in October 1780, he sent out a circular letter to the Tory leaders of North Carolina, using the language he thought would most effectively motivate them, including a particularly unsubtle appeal to masculine values of protecting women:

> Gentlemen:—Unless you wish to be eat up by an inundation of barbarians, who have begun by murdering an unarmed son before his aged father, and afterwards lopped off his arms, and who by their shocking cruelties and irregularities, give the best proof of their cowardice, and want of discipline; I say, if you wish to be pinioned, robbed, and murdered, and see your wives and daughters, in four days, abused by the dregs of mankind—in short, if you wish or deserve to live and bear the name of men, grasp your arms in a moment and run to camp. The Back Water men have crossed the mountains; McDowell, Hampton, Shelby and Cleveland are at their head, so that you know what you have to depend upon. If you chuse to be degraded forever and ever by a set of mongrels, say so at once, and let your women turn their backs on you, and look out for real men to protect them.[170]

This was hardly the kind of rhetoric likely to inspire restraint.

For others, the war, like militia service before the Revolution, provided an opportunity for self-aggrandizement and profit, motives little affected by the restraint of custom.[171] General Greene characterized many of Sumter's and Marion's South Carolina volunteers as "allured by hopes of plunder. . . . [They] are the dregs of the community and can be kept no longer than there is a prospect of gain."[172]

It also became a notorious fact toward the end of the war that many of the men active in the Rebel militia were Loyalists who had been forced to enlist. Men serving for fear of losing their property, or to avoid physical punishment, were hardly likely to be on their best behavior, particularly given the other institutional weaknesses of the militia.[173]

Another constantly recurring problem for the militias was the continuing inability of the state (either North Carolina or the Continental Congress) to consistently provision the troops.[174] This repeated failure to provide supplies left the soldiers to "carve for themselves."[175] The extraordinary depreciation of the American currencies starting in 1779 aggravated the situation by increasing the reluctance of producers to sell food to commissaries or army officers. North Carolina attempted to institute a tax in kind in 1780, but the lack of transport and widespread resistance rendered even that expedient only partially successful.[176] The supply system was admittedly atrocious for both the Continental army and the militia, but the militia often operated independently of the main army, with scarcely a trace of connection to any larger authority capable of supplying them.[177]

Related to this inability to provide supplies, and tied into the question of self-interest as a motivation to serve, was the occasional tendency of the Whig governments to promise plunder to the militia as a supplement to their pay. Most of the evidence for this practice comes from South Carolina, and particularly from the command of General Thomas Sumter, who instituted a policy of rewarding enlistees with a captured slave.[178] In the spirit of retaliation that was beginning to prevail late in the war, such plundering as pay began to be seen as acceptable. Whitmel Hill wrote to Burke in August 1780 of his hopes that "our distrest Militia . . . will claim to themselves some compensation for their services, which compensation they will seize on and bring home to their ruined Families. This plundering I should not generally encourage, but in the present instance I think it justifiable."[179] Troops raised on such a promise were virtually guaranteed to be less than choosy as to whom they plundered and of how much.

Finally, and perhaps decisively, if the capacity of a community to censure itself is critical to the maintenance of cultural restraints on violence, the structure of the militia undercut that capacity. Far from constituting the kind of mobile community that Holly Mayer has argued for the Continental army, the North Carolina militia units were usually all-too-temporary fraternities, lacking either a wide cross section of their home communities or sufficient permanence to develop their own sense of community.[180]

To begin with, the militia laws of North Carolina had created a system in which continuity was nearly impossible.[181] The division of the militia into four classes meant that any one company would raise one-quarter of its strength and dispatch those men to join a composite company composed of men who did not know each other. James Bartholomees's study of North Carolina revolutionary militia composition found that the divisional system, combined with the hiring of substitutes and the availability of legal exemptions, meant that "the militia in service took on a character decidedly different from the general character of its parent companies. Where the normal militia company comprised both married and single men of all economic conditions and ages, the units which took the field were almost exclusively composed of the poorer, single men from the two ends of the age spectrum, the youngest and the oldest. Many men served several tours and became almost professional substitutes."[182] Bartholomees was concerned with the consequences of this unfamiliarity on combat performance, but it had a similar impact on the restraint of violence. As a general rule, people avoid violating social norms when under the eyes of a community whose judgment matters to them, or who can punish them. The creation of non-community-based militia units who served for only three months meant that those men were unconcerned with the opinions of the others in their unit.[183]

In addition, this system further weakened the already tenuous control that the officers had on those men. In fact, despite frequent repeat service, militia soldiers rarely served under the same officers more than once; sometimes they even served under a number of different officers within the same short tour.[184] Robert Kincaid, recounting his first three-month tour in 1781, had difficulty remembering all of the different commands under whom he had served; he had "no recollection how he came to be placd under the command of so many officers."[185] Volunteer units avoided these systemic problems, as they usually were made up of neighborhood groups and officered by men whom they knew, but often those volunteers were the very ones most motivated by the hope of retaliation or profit.[186]

There are virtually no records of any courts-martial being held to discipline miscreants within the ranks, whether volunteer or regular militia, for civilian or military offenses.[187] This lack is the more remarkable given the regular use of a "court-martial" after scheduled militia musters to adjudicate fines for nonattendance or questions about who was drafted.[188] Those courts never seem to have been used as a disciplinary tool. Even if they had, the North Carolina militia law was quite lenient, specifying only a £10 fine for desertion, mutiny, or quitting one's post. The corporal punishments that had been specifically allowed under the 1774 militia law were absent from the 1777 version.[189] Fines seem to have been the preferred substitute, although the militia officers were allowed discretion in the determination of punishment (save death). The initial militia law of 1776 specified only that "each and every Company make such regulations as to them shall seem best, for non-attendance, disobedience, and misbehavior, at Musters by Companies."[190] Flaws within the militia law made it difficult to hold punitive courts at all. Governor Burke pointed out that the law required that the officers composing the court all be from the same regiment as the offender, but all too often the officers themselves were the offenders.[191] Near the end of the war, Burke complained that the militia law contained "no adequate provisions . . . for restraining or governing either men or officers when in actual service."[192] There are reports of unofficial punishment being meted out in cases of disorder; one such convict received seventeen lashes.[193] But there are as many examples of plunderers being slapped on the wrist; several such men were merely made to return the stolen items and to promise not to steal again.[194] Lieutenant Colonel Thomas Taylor of Orange County, accused of permitting "the men under his command to plunder and maraud in a most offensive and disgraceful manner," was suspended, but only after a special act of the Senate.[195] The contrast to the Continental army in this respect could not be more striking.[196]

This lack of official discipline arose in part from the fundamentally "democratic" nature of the militia organizations.[197] There was a long tradition of the soldiers weighing in with their opinions, of electing their officers, and of turning out ones they did not like.[198] General Greene's comment on the subject remains the most famous: "with the militia everybody is a general, and the powers of government are so feeble, that it is with the utmost difficulty you can restrain them from plundering one another."[199] Many of the junior militia officers were elected. When Captain William Lenoir got into a dispute with another captain over who should lead their combined venture, "they agreed to leave it to the soldiers to make choice," and once they had decided, it was "an invariable trait in the character of Militia that they will only obey their own officers in the line of action."[200] Militiaman William Ward, when refused by one officer, turned to another to arrange his transfer from a cavalry to an infantry unit when he decided that his horse had had enough.[201]

The soldiers were also able to influence operational decisions. Joseph Graham recorded how on one occasion the officers' decision not to attack a fortified brick house defended by British regulars offended their men, and "it was the constant subject of conversation with the lower grades of officers and men . . . and as an evidence of the state of discipline, and the force of public opinion, the officers were compelled, . . . to gratify them."[202] William Davie frankly acknowledged that "in those times" the approbation of the men "was absolutely necessary" before embarking on any risky venture.[203] Volunteers considered themselves exactly that and were quite willing simply to pick up and go home if they did not like the conditions under which they were living.[204] This tendency applied to the militia in general, whom Davie considered "frightened, . . . and irresolute—one day in camp, another away to save their property."[205]

Officers and soldiers in militia units did not deal with each other on a basis of equality, but there was definitely a constant tension between the officers' authority to lead and the soldiers' willingness to follow.[206] Recognition of this tension included early war regulations granting rank preference to militia officers over Continentals, and later efforts to choose Continental officers for militia commands who would not "disgust the militia."[207] Similar tensions existed in regular forces as well, but the scale was tilted much more significantly toward the soldier in the militias.[208]

There remain two factors to be considered with regard to explaining the degeneration of the war's violence in 1780–82: race or ethnicity, and class. These two categories are considered here together because in many ways the importance of the former highlights the *relative* insignificance of the latter. Encouragement of public violence frequently relied on accusations couched in the language of the barbarous "other," or the military use of the "other," or the threat of use of the "other"—whether Indians, Catholics, or slaves. This rhetorical tool was used even against fellow British subjects, people who normally would not fall outside the pale. Such "internal" demonization could take two forms. In one, the rhetor accused the enemy of using the "other" as an ally, thereby rendering the enemy susceptible to violent retaliation. More common was the imputation of inhuman characteristics to the enemy themselves, "dehumanizing" a white person into a "savage" or "barbarous" state. This too eased the process of enacting violence against an enemy so labeled. The course of the Revolution as discussed thus far has provided many examples of the importance of this process with regard to the British and their use of various out-groups (Indians and slaves).

There was yet another important, "different," ethnicity in North Carolina: the Highland Scots. There was a long-standing English discomfort with Scots, in part a result of the Jacobite rebellions of 1715 and 1745. In the Carolinas, that antipathy transmuted into a dislike of them as agents of an oppressive ministry, or for local reasons of resenting their role as merchants in the backcountry.[209] The nearly uniform Loyalism of the Highland Scot community in North Carolina, visibly evident at the Battle of Moore's Creek Bridge, contributed to Whig antipathy. Whigs often referred to the campaign as the "Scotch" insurrection, and one Rebel Scottish pensioner highlighted in his claim that he was the sole Scotsman in the Whig militia.[210] Furthermore, the massive participation of Scots in the British army (66 percent of all recruits in 1778) did not help popular suspicions of the ethnicity as a whole.[211] As a result of these suspicions, Scots occasionally figured as among the "others" in the rhetoric of colonial protest and wartime violence. One historian, in fact, blames the tarring and feathering of Cullen Pollock in part on his Scottish ethnicity, and there is evidence that the Regulators had singled out Scottish merchants for resentment.[212] A propagandist of the Revolution, addressing himself to the British army, reminded them that since the last war, "you have been despised, neglected, and treated with contempt, while a parcel of beggarly Scotchmen only have been put into every place of profit. . . . [if you fight this war and win you will] be reduced to the miserable condition of being ruled by an army of Scotch Janizaries, assisted by Roman-Catholics."[213] While ethnic hatred of Scots was relatively mild, and does not seem to have necessarily resulted in significantly more violence, the use of their ethnicity in the rhetoric of violence highlights the lack of any equivalent kind of class-based epithet.

It is a common and generally correct theme in the recent historiography of the Revolution that one subtext of the period was a tension between colonial elites and the common sort whom they tried to lead into revolution.[214] Some historians have argued specifically for North Carolina that much of the Whig-Tory violence resulted from that tension.[215] They posit that the Loyalists represented a class of small farmers who resisted Whig impositions as they had before the war. The war in this sense was an extension of an ongoing struggle and served as a release, or pretext, for violence on a larger scale in the service of that struggle. On the other hand, it has also been argued that colonial Americans, however disadvantaged by social privilege, as yet lacked a class-based ideology on which to found large-scale violence.[216] Suggested alternative ideologies on which colonists might have founded violence included country Whig notions of rights and liberties,[217] or a "homestead" ethic of individual freedom from interference—which others have called a "persistent localism."[218]

The lack of class-based epithets in the rhetoric of violence supports the argument against class divisions defining the Whig-Tory violence.[219] "Greedy landlords" or "designing capitalists" had not yet achieved the demonizing qualities of "barbarous" or "savage" in motivating popular action. In the vast majority of cases discussed here, the establishment of a foundation of legitimacy for violence rested on the alterity and misbehavior of the enemy twinned with one's own observance of the proper form. That alterity was not constructed along class divisions. Admittedly, greed or economic interest drove much activity on all sides, visible perhaps most strongly in plunder (the popular manifestation of greed) and confiscation (the elite-manipulated "state" version). The violent response to those acts, however, was more in keeping with expectations of war and violence than with class tensions. That is, violence deemed illegitimate engendered further violence. There is no such visibility of class issues in the rhetoric used to prod people to violence. Violence nevertheless was patterned. The war's violence was more than a series of individual responses to individual outrages. That patterning reflected the operation of an aggregate set of social norms.

This chapter, and the two that preceded it, made several basic points. It will be helpful to review them before going on to see how the experience of the Continental army compared to that of the militia. Military violence, or war, was widely perceived as a legitimate, socially functional activity. People assumed that war brought with it terrible costs. To begin a war required justification, although not necessarily a slavish adherence to the intellectualized *jus ad bellum*. But colonial Americans also expected that war as they fought it would be restrained in some ways. Military violence, in their estimation, could and should be contained to things truly military. War could be virtuous. That set of expectations grew out of the intellectual European tradition of the laws of war, and of the customs and usages of war (both enforced by a utilitarian notion of mutual self-interest and fear of retaliation), combined with a particularly American expectation of the virtue of a citizen army, and even more fundamentally popular notions of morality and honor. All of these expectations were reflections of a quest for legitimacy, representing Americans' assumption that violence, even military violence, was socially functional only if it was enacted in a legitimate manner. The word "legitimate" in this case implies not only political but social acceptability. This definition carries a broad meaning. For example, to label the British as barbarous for their use of Indians or slaves, or for their inappropriate use of military violence, was to legitimize the Americans' violence against them. The fundamental constraint on violence, therefore, was whether or not it could be constructed as legitimate—on several levels, politically and socially. And sure enough, that constraint of legitimacy did have an impact on the violence of the war. Throughout the war, the Whig government and the militias themselves, officers and soldiers alike, can be found reining in, or trying to rein in, the war's violence.

Unfortunately there was an alternative construction of legitimacy in the law of retaliation. Such a motive was already imbedded in the formal customs of war, and it also existed as a popular expectation of the individual's right for self-redress. The militia organization, socially and militarily undisciplined, was incapable of institutionalizing revenge. The people did not perceive that the state (or the British, depending on which side one took) was effectively redressing their grievances, and so they used the militias as an alternate means to retaliate. Such retaliation, furthermore, was culturally defined as legitimate. That such legitimacy was important is clear not only in, for example, Fanning's postwar narrative but also in the petitions for pardon for killing Tories, which were highlighted above. In all those cases, the authors attempted to persuade their audience of their fundamental innocence, based not always on the "necessities of war" but on the "Law of Retaliation."[220] Social or judicial censure for violent retaliation by the militias was virtually nonexistent. Lacking such censure, the militias' war in North Carolina spiraled out of control. The next chapter will show how the experience of the Continental army was different.

Epilogue

"Not Less Barbarous Than Impolitick": The Continental Army and Limited War

All parties are to be strictly prohibited under the penalty of capital punishment from plundering and that no violence should be offerd to any of the Inhabitants let their political sentiments be as they may unless they are found in Arms. . . . The Idea of exterminating the Tories is not less barbarous than impolitick.
General Nathanael Greene to General Andrew Pickens, June 5, 1781[1]

[The coming battle requires] our most Strenious exertion, one bold stroke will free the Land from Rapine, Devestation, & Burning; Famale Innocence from brutal Lust & Violence. . . . Glory waits to crown the brave & peace freedom & happiness will be the rewards of Victory, animated by Motives like those[,] Soldiers fighting in the Cause of Innocense humanity & Justice will never give way.
Daily Order of September 5, 1777[2]

Tho' my indignation at such ungenerous conduct of the enemy might at first prompt me to retaliation, yet humanity and policy forbid the measure. Experience proves, that their wanton cruelty injures rather than benefits their cause; that with our forbearance, justly secured to us the attachment of all good men.
George Washington to Major General Adam Stephen, April 20, 1777[3]

If the Cherokee campaign brackets one extreme of violence waged by the Americans, the Continental army marks the other. Americans had cultural access to a range of war styles. At one end was the virtually unrestricted violence of war against Indians, clearly legitimated in their minds by the alterity of the enemy, an alterity confirmed in part by their belief in the irrationality and barbarity of the Indians' "uncivilized" way of war. In the middle was the militias' war, a war style partly restrained by cultural conventions but capable of quickly escalating. Finally, marking the other end of the scale, was the Continental army. The Continental army's structure and behavior represented a more successful aspiration toward the Enlightenment ideal of limited war, reinforced by an American ideal of virtue.[4]

Exactly how successful was that aspiration? After all, in many ways the North Carolina Rebel militia was shaped by the same goals. The answer can only be comparative. The Continentals were markedly better at virtuous war than were the militia. The size of the Continental army as a subject for historical investigation precludes a detailed examination here of its practice of military violence. Fortunately, however, many historians have weighed in on the character and composition of the Continental army, and several assertions can safely be made on the basis of their work.[5] The Continental army, by and large, adhered very closely to eighteenth-century customs and usages of war, more specifically, the formalities that historians associate with limited war: siege negotiations, prisoner exchange, flags of truce, officer parole, and so on. All of those conventions, although historically arising from both moral and utilitarian motives, served to limit the application of violence. Adherence to those conventions, in marked contrast to the militia, also reduced the potential for actual retaliation. There were a number of highly volatile incidents on both sides that could easily have led to an escalation of violence, particularly in regard to the treatment of prisoners. The existence of those conventions, however, and the ability of the leadership of each side to communicate freely helped prevent such escalation.[6] As an outgrowth of a desire to adhere to European conventions of war, the Continental government and the military leadership also generally treated prisoners in a manner acceptable to the era. Continental troops accepted quarter, protected prisoners, and, within the economic constraints of the weak central government, provided for prisoners in confinement until they were exchanged.[7] Furthermore, according to historians James Martin and Mark Lender, the Continental army rarely engaged in "wanton violence against civilians, such as rape or murder."[8] Thus, we have already affirmed the generally better behavior of the Continentals in three out of the four categories of violence (prisoners, military formalism, murder) that were looked at in chapter 7. What remains is the matter of plunder and impressment.

The Continentals were not a perfectly virtuous blue-coated army that marched around the countryside paying for everything they used and ate, and treating everyone with eighteenth-century courtesy. As a number of historians have pointed out, the Continentals certainly did rob and plunder, particularly for food and firewood. This apparent contradiction between ideal and behavior warrants some response. Most portrayals of a rapacious Continental army have neither been made in the larger context of contemporary expectations nor compared to the much worse behavior of the militias. This becomes particularly clear when one analyzes the

Continentals from the contemporary perspective of a gradation or hierarchy in the seriousness of plunder.

Recall that there were several gradations within the word "plunder." The failures of the supply system often dictated that the army officially impress rather than pay for food and forage. From the point of view of the inhabitants, this was a kind of plunder, but the least violent variety.[9] The Continental army usually avoided impressment in the early years of the war (until late 1778) and, as Don Higginbotham has pointed out, "even when impressing, the supply officers under Washington's immediate control made every effort to obey state laws on the subject."[10] The Continental leadership attempted to maintain at least the pretense of reimbursement (providing receipts or certificates) and appeared committed to restraining the troops.[11]

Best intentions aside, it proved impossible entirely to prevent unauthorized foraging by the soldiers. Complaints of their stealing food and breaking up fences for firewood fill Continental orderly books and provide flesh to the perception of the Continentals as plunderers like any other period army.[12] It is instructive, however, to turn again to the Moravians and compare their experiences with the "regulars" and with the militia. Frederick Marshall put it very plainly:

> We must say for the regular troops, those belonging to the army of this country, and those belonging to the English, that their officers kept good order among them, and the excesses were committed only by camp followers, single soldiers, and especially by the militia.[13]

Part of that impression seems to have arisen from the much more extensive efforts on the part of the Continental officers to control their troops. One Continental major not only promised good behavior from his men but delivered on his promise and requested a certificate from the town affirming their restraint.[14] The Continentals were never perfect, but no one expected perfection, and the Moravians' records document that the regulars they experienced were much more likely to be controlled, and supplies much more likely to be paid for or at least receipted for.[15] The Continental officers also helped prevent abuses by their more consistent practice of sending quartering officers ahead of troops.[16] The warnings they provided allowed the town sufficient time to gather food. Even with the militia, it seems clear that it was hunger rather than greed that often led them into town to steal. Adequate food stocks tended to restrain or even forestall plundering.[17] In general, then, it seems fair to agree with Don Higginbotham's assessment that "the Continentals did a reasonably good job

... of behaving with propriety, even sensitivity, toward the noncombatant elements. . . . Not so the militia."[18]

The greater success that the Continental army had in controlling its violence, both in restraining the soldiery from abusing noncombatants and in adhering to the military formalism of eighteenth-century warfare, derived from a conscious recognition that they were being held to a higher standard of legitimacy—twice over. Considerations of international respectability weighed on their practice of war, but equally important was the leadership's recognition that the Continental army represented an ideologically suspect institution: a standing army. As such, the military leadership had to constantly reassert the virtue of that army to a domestic public and Congress predisposed to disparage them. Continental general Horatio Gates, for example, reassured the population of the Carolinas in August 1780 that they "may rely on the assurance that an army composed of their brethren and fellow-citizens cannot be brought among them with the hostile vices of plunder and depredation."[19] At least some North Carolinians got the desired message and believed in the restraint of their citizen army. In a sermon against plunder, Samuel McCorkle noted that the Continental army was "first victorious over its enemies" and "then over itself."[20] As one historian put it, "the army had not only to win the war, but the organization and its community were supposed to reflect the image Americans had of themselves and the hopes they had for their country."[21]

To be sure, following the rules was a calculated, "politick," decision, but the leadership's aspiration to follow those rules reflected their recognition of the cultural power of those rules in domestic and international society. There was an audience to be assuaged, an audience with the power to approve or condemn and in doing so make a difference. Consequently, the army's behavior came to reflect the demands of that audience. That restraint in the behavior of the army, their more virtuous war, resulted from three factors. First, the soldiers themselves came to accept the Revolution's requirement for legitimacy and the consequent demand for controlled violence. Second, the army's structure and social composition enabled greater enforcement than was found in the militia. Third, the officers themselves held strong pretensions to the cult of military honor, which motivated them to observe those rules rooted in that cult.

The senior American leadership was intimately familiar with the traditional European practice of war. Many of them had fought alongside the British during the French and Indian War, and the younger men read the appropriate military manuals of the era.[22] The desire for international respectability and military alliance helped inspire the creation of the regular army in the first place. To be diplomatically effective, that regular army had to "look" right. As John Shy put it, "Washington and other native American leaders stressed a regular army . . . because they felt a need to be seen as cultivated, honorable, respectable men, not savages leading other savages in a howling wilderness."[23] The legitimacy conferred by success, as in the victory at Saratoga, was the key to gaining the French alliance. But the French army would not fight the war on its own; it needed a recognizable and respectable American equivalent to fight alongside.

This international pressure did not necessarily exert much influence over the treatment of civilians, because the practice of European armies had rarely lived up to that ideal anyway. It did, however, affect the manner and extent to which the Continental army observed the European customs and usages of war. During the court-martial of American colonel David Henley, accused of mistreating British prisoners of war, British general John Burgoyne presented the case for the prosecution. He reminded the court (composed of Continental officers) that "the whole of this matter will be published, translated, considered, and commented upon by every nation in the world. . . . You are trustees for the honour of an infant state."[24] In addition, the observance of military conventions had come to be tied directly to the individual honor of the officers involved. Officers in the Continental army aspired to the kind of military honor extant in European armies.[25] Aware of the connection between the observance of the customs and usages of war and the maintenance of personal honor, they were thus motivated to follow those rules.

The Continental army had a further, complementary, set of motivations with regard to violence against civilians. The Continental leadership, particularly although not exclusively as personified by Washington, recognized that the revolutionary emphasis on the preservation of property and the maintenance of virtue was incongruent with an uncontrolled army. They realized that "restraint towards civilians . . . was essential to having the war effort serve as a mainspring of national legitimacy and resultant nationhood."[26]

Thus motivated by the quest for international and domestic legitimacy, and for personal honor, the officer corps of the army consistently struggled to enforce the norms of appropriate military violence and to transmit an ideology to the soldiers that would sustain it. There is simply no comparison between the efforts of the Continental army to enforce discipline and that of the North Carolina militia. Many scholars have pointed to the oft-repeated warnings to Continental soldiers to stop plundering as evidence that the soldiers were indeed plundering all the time.

While that is probably true, there is nothing quite like the volume and vociferousness of those warnings in any of the records of the militia. This does not mean the militia was innocent of plundering. It rather suggests that their officers were less interested in or diligent at restraining the men.

The Continental army took an enormous stride toward successful enforcement with the early adoption of articles of war that outlined offenses and prescribed punishments. The articles changed over the course of the war, but only in the direction of increasing severity against plundering.[27] Continental army order books are filled with warnings to the soldiers not to plunder, with dire threats of punishment and even death.[28] Those same order books often record infliction of such punishment, to include flogging and execution. One historian has argued that although George Washington often commuted sentences for various offenses, he very rarely showed mercy to plunderers.[29] Unlike the militia, courts-martial were exceedingly common, and punishment was severe.[30]

The social origins of the Continental army made possible this kind of corporal discipline. Recruits frequently were those least able to avoid service; they lacked political or financial influence. Where soldiers in the militia possessed some leverage over their officers, often local men whom they knew and dealt with regularly, Continental soldiers had no such influence. Charles Neimeyer has gone so far as to assert that the army was composed of the least powerful segments of society: escaped slaves, freedmen, vagrants, British deserters, Irish, and so on.[31] Other studies of the composition of the Continental line do not go quite so far, but they too document the relatively poor origins of the recruits. Many of them were substitutes or draftees, serving for monetary gain or because they could not afford to avoid the draft.[32] The increasingly longer terms of service also created a more stable organization, in which the men were more likely to serve under the same officers for longer periods.[33] Thus, despite ample documentation of restlessness within the ranks, protest, mutiny, or plain insubordination, the Continental army was vastly more controllable, predictable, and disciplined than the Rebel militia.[34]

Those same long terms of service, with the physical suffering that they entailed, inspired a communal sense of righteousness within the officers and soldiers of the army, who began to feel that they were the true carriers of the spirit of the Revolution.[35] The officers contributed to that sense by stressing that good behavior and success in battle would prove the virtue of the army and thus of the Revolution.[36] While the evidence for the ideological motivation of the common soldier is difficult to tease out, occasional comments or incidents reveal how soldiers may have come to see themselves as the heart of the Revolution, inspired by revolutionary principles.[37] On July 4, 1777, a Continental soldier in the camp in New York wrote that "the eyes of all our countrymen are upon us, and we shall have their blessings and praises if we are the means of saving them. . . . Let us . . . shew the whole world, that freemen contending for liberty on their own ground are superiour to any slavish mercenary."[38] Perhaps most tellingly, when the Pennsylvania line mutinied against poor pay and conditions in January 1781, the soldiers demonstrated their continuing commitment to the cause by turning over two British spies trying to take advantage of the situation, and by their restrained behavior toward the civilians along their line of march.[39]

In short, the Continental army constituted a community with a much greater capacity to self-censure than the militias. That capacity existed on two levels. One was the clear institutional ability to punish. The other was the development of attachments, social bonds, and standards of conduct specific to the military community. The army had come to consist of longer-serving soldiers, accompanied by women and civilian support staff, supervised by the socially superior officers, all of whom became invested in the maintenance of their relationships.[40] That community could therefore self-censure. That this community could also develop standards of appropriate violence different from that of the surrounding population may even help explain some of their plundering activities. The soldiers' frustration, resentment, and even self-righteousness at the lack of popular material support created an environment, or a set of norms, within which certain violence was acceptable—for example, plundering those individuals who did not support them the way they "should."[41]

A further reason for the general success of the Continental army at restraining illegitimate violence was its operational style of war. In contrast to the militia, which often fell back on a partisan style of war, the Continentals generally eschewed such tactics.[42] Admittedly, some of their greatest successes were based on night marches and surprise attacks, such as Trenton, but in general the pattern of military activity was conventional, emphasizing open-field battles, positional maneuver, and sieges. This way of war limited opportunities for violence to "get out of hand."[43]

For all of these reasons, the Continental army was more successful in conducting a more restrained form of war. If the Rebel militia was merely a continuation or outgrowth of the older colonial militia, the Continental army was an institution born of perceived need and modeled on a particular combination of ideals. Some of the Whig leadership, and particularly Washington, argued that the militia was insufficient to the demands of a long war, and that *necessity* required a standing professional army. This perception of necessity thus overruled the traditional popular distaste for such an institution. It is correct, therefore, to say that military necessity in this instance dominated cultural predilection. But, and this is a large but, this "military necessity" for a standing army was simply a judgment informed by a different set of cultural preconceptions. There were a limited number of alternatives visible to contemporaries: the colonial militia and the professional, conventional standing army. By the end of the war some soldiers, particularly Nathanael Greene, had begun to synthesize those two models into something different, but for the majority of the war those two models functioned independently, with different sets of expectations and different success in achieving them.[44]

Conclusion

In the several examples of public violence analyzed here, I have argued that such violence was patterned and restrained by cultural predispositions and expectations. Eighteenth-century North Carolinians had explicit, powerful notions about the use of violence. In meeting different circumstances, they approved of different patterns, but they maintained their right to censure violations. The importance of consensus, of the weight of communal opinion, thereby shaped violence in the direction of (if never matching exactly) their cultural assumptions and predispositions.

In colonial and revolutionary America those predispositions, and the consequent patterns of behavior, were formed from European, especially British, precedents. As a general statement this should not surprise us; cultural practice after all is a continuing process of improvisation on previous practice. The colonial environment acted as a force for improvisation and thus reshaped those traditions. We have seen, for example, how colonial rioters combined military overtones with older customs, and, perhaps partly as a result, the visibility of women in colonial riots declined. The colonists also developed new and virulent notions of who the "other" was, derived from real fears of Indian invasions and slave insurrections. The constant physical proximity of those "others" lent them salience in the rhetoric of violence.

These newer manifestations of a language and practice of violence eventually formed their own patterns, identifiably American, which were repeated with surprising specificity. Why did persons in situations of collective violence, supposedly freed from psychological restraint by anonymity and chaos, cling so strongly to specific behaviors? Why were riots so careful, and why was so much effort put into making war virtuous? The argument made here is that the rationale was legitimacy. The introduction to this book began by asking what all the fuss was about: to whom was the justificatory rhetoric that surrounded public violence in early modern Anglo-America directed? In one sense, the answer points to utilitarian motivations. Policymakers, writers, and orators felt the need to sway the opinion of the masses (in this case the white masses) and used the rhetoric of violence to justify their position or execrate the enemy.[1] If successful, they could claim consensus or even (literally) win recruits. But to label the rhetoric utilitarian begs the question by ignoring the power of the values that were being appealed to. The very volume of rhetoric employed in eighteenth-century North Carolina suggests that it must have reflected a deep-seated and widespread set of values about the use of violence. Those values, if so powerful as to require constant rhetorical reference, must have affected more than rhetoric; they also affected action. Cultural norms about violence, in conjunction with the deliberate reference to those norms by others, patterned violent behavior. Those patterns acquired their own aura of legitimacy and could be used to make a given act of violence legitimate. Even when the violence had radical intent, if it *looked* familiar, if it partook of the legitimacy endowed by form, it was more likely to be accepted.

Thus restraint was not necessarily about individual conceptions of morality. After all, much of the evidence presented here has been about preserving the appearance (even if after the fact) that a particular violent act was just. The apparent necessity of public justification, however, indicated a fear of legal or social censure, a fear that the actors would be condemned for breaking the rules. While individuals may have been motivated for personal reasons in a variety of directions, usually beyond the reach of historians, their actions, especially when so visibly and publicly violent, tended to reflect their sense of the aggregate value system. Collective public violence was very much a compromise between individual desire and the social norm.

There was of course no universality in perception or even in expectation. That is, although one individual might try to justify his violence by reference to expectations, another might not accept that justification. Or, as was likely in the colonial era, the *reported* version of a given violent act might have little relation to reality, since violence was so often translated into a series of standard tropes or images. Because violence was such a powerful motivator of behavior, incidents or reports of incidents that violated the expectations of form and legitimacy tended to inspire a violent reaction.

All of this means that for eighteenth-century Americans the question of adherence to an appropriate form of violence carried significant weight. Appearance conferred legitimacy. The desire for legitimacy affected violent behavior.

The process of analysis developed in this work can be used for other periods of history. The key is to establish what expectations a given society has of a particular kind of violence, make a reasoned conclusion about the extent and power of the political public, and then track not only how those expectations shaped behavior initially but how the violation of those expectations created shifts in behavior, and may in fact have established new precedent. This is one way to consider the tension between cultural predilection and "necessity." The former patterns behavior while the latter acts as a force for improvisation and in the end may establish new precedent. A couple of references to the recent history of the United States may clarify the utility of this analysis.

During the Civil Rights movement, part of the genius of the leadership of Martin Luther King, Jr., was his recognition (from the model provided by Mahatma Gandhi) that rigidly peaceful marches could not transgress societal expectations of behavior appropriate to a protest. The sight of such protests being broken up violently by the state, however, would violate fundamental American values about the appropriate use of force. Eventually, the televised images of such illegitimate violence would inspire reaction. That the process was so difficult and so painful reflected the depth of racist notions of "otherness" that had for so long legitimated violence against African Americans. Note the power of the audience, in this case literally the television audience. King's insistence on peaceful protest made their legitimacy clear; no miscommunication of violence could occur. This was a calculated utilitarian decision about methods of protest. King and his followers were not people in the grip of a cultural structure that dictated their protest behavior. Nevertheless, their behavior reflected an aggregate value of legitimate violence.[2]

In cases of protest, the role and power of the audience is much clearer than it is in war. Consider, however, the role of American norms of military violence in shaping the Vietnam War, and more recently, the post–Gulf War bombing of Iraq and the bombing of Serbia and Serb forces in Kosovo. It seems clear, for example, that the limitations observed (imperfectly) by American policymakers with regard to international borders— there would be no invasion of North Vietnam—resulted from a recognition of domestic and international expectations of legitimate war. South Vietnam's war of self-defense did not justify invasion of the north. Furthermore, domestic doubts about the legitimacy of the war itself and concerned reaction to the televised images of destruction were critical to American policymakers' decisions about how to conduct the war. Those pressures led eventually to "Vietnamization" and withdrawal. Post-Vietnam American concerns for casualties, and a belief that economic sanctions are somehow less violent than full-scale military intervention, in part shaped the application of military force in Iraq and Serbia in 1998 and 1999. The American military's extensive efforts to avoid civilian casualties, and the frankly ironic limitation of options to missiles and bombs, reflected the American public's expectations of legitimate violence and their desire to avoid American casualties.

Admittedly, these were complex historical events, and there were other forces and sets of expectations in play (notably American policymakers' worries about Arab notions of legitimacy, specifically for violence as used by the United States against an Arab state). Of crucial importance to all of these modern examples is the role of communication technology and the media. Where the normative locale of legitimacy for the militia was the rural neighborhood, within which communication occurred mostly on a face-to-face basis, in the twentieth century that zone of interaction has greatly expanded.

These short examples are hardly definitive treatments of the role of cultural legitimacy in shaping violent behavior; nor are they complete explanations of the events themselves. Nevertheless, they are suggestive. "Interest" may move a person to act, but once decided, *how* will that person act? When discussing violence, it seems to me that the "how" matters. When the violence is collective, the "how" is often patterned in response to the requirements of legitimacy. Often. Not always. Individuals remain a force unto themselves. They break the rules, ignore the patterns. When they do, however, or if they are rumored to have done so, there are consequences. Sometimes it is the loss of political legitimacy, and sometimes it is simply more violence.

Notes

Abbreviations

DLAR—The David Library of the American Revolution, Washington Crossing, Pa.

DUSC—Duke University Special Collections, Durham, N.C.

ER—English Records, North Carolina Department of Archives, Raleigh.

Evans—Evans, Charles. *American Bibliography.* New York: Peter Smith, 1941. An Evans "#" is sometimes given in the citation to clarify the edition used.

Gates Papers (microfilm ed.)—Horatio Gates Papers, 1726–1828. Microfilm edition prepared by the New York Historical Society and the National Historical Records and Publications Commission.

Granville District Records—Granville District Records from the Marquis of Bath's Library in Longleat, Warminster, Wiltshire, England, 1729–80; microfilm copy at NCA.

Gray's Narrative—Gray, Robert. "Observations on the War in Carolina by Colonel Robert Gray, Officer of Provincial Troops," Military Collection, War of the Revolution, British and Loyalist Papers (a manuscript copy of an original "in the Chalmers Mss. Belonging to Mr. Bancroft"), NCA.

Greene's Papers—Greene, Nathanael. *The Papers of General Nathanael Greene.* Edited by Richard K. Showman, Dennis M. Conrad, Roger N. Parks, and Elizabeth C. Stevens. 11 vols. Chapel Hill: University of North Carolina Press, 1976–.

JCC—Library of Congress. *Journals of the Continental Congress, 1774–89.* 34 vols. Washington: GPO, 1905–37.

Loyalist claim—Refers to either the Records of the American Loyalist Claims Commission, 1776–1831 (AO 12), PRO or the Papers of the American Loyalist Claims Commission, 1780–1835 (AO13), PRO, both on microfilm at the DLAR. Notes will indicate name of claimant and from which numbered series the citation is made.

Moravian Records—Fries, Adelaide L. *Records of the Moravians in North Carolina.* Raleigh: North Carolina Historical Commission, 1922–69.

NCA—North Carolina Department of Archives and History, Raleigh.

NCCR—Saunders, William L., ed. *The Colonial Records of North Carolina.* 10 vols. Raleigh: various publishers, 1886–90.

NCSR—Clark, Walter, ed. *The State Records of North Carolina.* 16 vols. Winston and Goldsboro: Various publishers, 1895–1907.

Pension Record—Revolutionary War Pension and Bounty-Land-Warrant Application Files. National Archives, Washington (citations to individual claims include the pension record number in parentheses.)

PRO—Public Record Office, Kew, Great Britain.

Regulator Documents—Powell, William S., James K. Huhta, and Thomas J. Farnham, eds. *The Regulators in North Carolina: A Documentary History, 1759–1776.* Raleigh: State Department of Archives and History, 1971.

SHC—Southern Historical Collection, University of North Carolina, Chapel Hill.

TC—Tryon, William. *The Correspondence of William Tryon.* Edited by William S. Powell. 2 vols. Raleigh: North Carolina Division of Archives and History, 1980–81.

All other references to published sources are given in author/short title format. For complete bibliographic information, refer to the bibliography. Manuscripts, newspapers, court records, and some published broadsides are fully cited in the endnotes for ease of reference.

Introduction

1. Lepore, *The Name of War.*

2. Ibid., 94.

3. Lepore also acknowledges this role of rhetoric, ibid., 106ff. See also Titus, *Old Dominion at War,* 142–43; Conway, "To Subdue America," 381.

4. Keegan, *History of Warfare,* 12.

5. This theory of patterned behavior (*habitus*) based on precedent but subject to improvisation and changes in conditions is derived from Bourdieu, *Outline of a Theory of Practice,* 72, 79, 81, 85.

6. Maier, *From Resistance to Revolution.*

7. Rediker, *Between the Devil and the Deep Blue Sea,* 254–87.

8. This is part of the subject of chapter 4, but also has been noted by several students of European and Native American contact. See, for example, Abler, "Scalping, Torture"; Hirsch, "Collision of Military Cultures."

9. Leach, *Custom, Law, and Terrorist Violence,* 30.

10. This is not to say that the Indians automatically were considered "others" from the outset of English colonization. See chapter 4.

11. Foster, "The Godly in Transit," 194. Emphasis added. No criticism of Foster is implied; his sentence merely provided an example of a "riot" left hanging.

1. "Riotous Disorderly Persons"

1. Davis, "Three Poems from Colonial North Carolina," 34–35. Emphasis in original.

2. For most of the events discussed in Part I of this book, North Carolina was governed by a royal governor. The legislative body consisted of the Governor's Council appointed by the ministry in England (with considerable input from the governor), and an elective Assembly.

3. This account, discussed more completely below, is derived from the *North Carolina Gazette*, February 26, 1771; and Governor Tryon to Secretary Conway, February 25, 1766, NCCR 7:169–74.

4. I use the term *riot* as the most convenient way to refer to a large-scale, public incident that used or threatened to use violence. Similarly, I use the terms "crowd" or "rioters" without implying any negative connotations.

5. "England" or "English" refers to Great Britain exclusive of Scotland and Wales.

6. For discussions of the settling of North Carolina, see Ashe, *History of North Carolina*, 1:58–60, 276–79; Lefler and Newsome, *North Carolina*, 50, 65, 69–81; Kars, "Breaking Loose," 4–10; Merrens, *Colonial North Carolina*, 18–31, 53–81.

7. One attempt to identify ethnic populations in the early United States showed North Carolina having a white population of 66 percent English, 15 percent Scots, 6 percent Scotch-Irish, and a further mixture of Irish, German, Dutch, French, and Swedish (this compilation does not include the African or Indian population). U.S. Department of Commerce, *Historical Statistics*, 2:1168. These statistics have been much disputed, particularly the differentiation of Scots and Scotch-Irish. Additionally, numbers of English probably should have been counted in one of the two Scots groups. For a discussion of these statistics as they relate to the Scotch-Irish, see Jackson, *A Social History of the Scotch-Irish*, xi; Jones, "The Scotch-Irish in British America," 286–87. One has to be careful not to get carried away by the impression that the entire backcountry was settled by non-English ethnicities. It was incontestably an extremely mixed region, and the Scotch-Irish and German presence was very strong, but the English were also present in significant numbers. Merrens, *Colonial North Carolina*, 61, 68; Ramsey, *Carolina Cradle*, 201–2.

8. For the Scotch-Irish migrations, see Blethen, *From Ulster to Carolina*; Davidson, *Colonial Scotch-Irish*; Hanna, *Scotch-Irish*; Jackson, *A Social History of the Scotch-Irish*; Jones, "The Scotch-Irish," 284–313; and, especially, Leyburn, *Scotch-Irish*.

9. Leyburn is careful to point out that the Ulster community in the late seventeenth century had received a significant English influx, particularly from northern England, but also from London. After 1685, there were also some French Hugue-

nots (*Scotch-Irish*, 127–28). He also addresses the thornier issue of Scottish inter-marriage with the Irish (133–39). See also Fischer, *Albion's Seed*, 605–8, who calls this a migration from the "borderlands" to the backcountry, thereby encompassing as one the people who came to America from northern Britain and those from northern Ireland.

10. The Scotch-Irish who went directly from Ireland to North Carolina formed communities closer to the coast, such as the group settled by Henry McCulloh in Duplin County in 1736. Foote, *Sketches*, 159.

11. The truth of such reports about the cheapness and availability of land is another matter. The rumors certainly persisted. See Kars, "Breaking Loose," 63–65.

12. Dobson, *Scottish Emigration to Colonial America*; Graham, *Colonists from Scotland*; Meyer, *Highland Scots of North Carolina*. Meyer debunks the "pardoned Jacobites" legend (23), noting that most of the North Carolina arrivals came from Argyll, which had been strongly pro-Hanoverian during the 1745 rebellion. The population estimate is also from Meyer (84–85).

13. Fogleman, *Hopeful Journeys*, 1–9; Wokeck, *Trade in Strangers*, 53.

14. Fogleman, *Hopeful Journeys*, 11, 131–32; Ramsey, *Carolina Cradle*, 87–93, 146–51. Aside from the Moravian sect, which has generated an extensive literature because of its well-preserved records, there has been only limited work done on the influence of German culture in North Carolina. See Hammer, *Rhinelanders on the Yadkin*; Bernheim, *History of the German Settlements*; the Reverend G. William Welker, "Early German Reformed Settlements in North Carolina," partially reprinted in NCCR 8:727–58.

15. Merrens, *Colonial North Carolina*, 53–54. See also Kars, "Breaking Loose," 5–6.

16. Rudé wrote a variety of works on the subject of crowd activity, notably *Paris and London in the Eighteenth Century* and *The Crowd in History, 1730–1848*. Rudé is considered the founder of this kind of study, although a number of other scholars before him laid some of the groundwork. For England, that group includes notably Beloff, *Public Order and Popular Disturbances*, and Darvall, *Popular Disturbances and Public Order*.

17. The following discussion is based on a reading of a wide variety of works on the subject of riot, disorder, rebellion, and charivari in England and Scotland from the late medieval through the early modern eras. Instead of a large note here, see the section in the bibliography labeled "European Riot and Charivari." Citations from specific sources will be made where appropriate.

18. See Charles Tilly's categorization of types of European collective violence, in which he labels much of early modern violence "conservative." "Collective Violence in European Perspective," 84–85, 87.

19. The word "charivari" was not commonly used in England, but it has come to be the word of choice in scholarship on the subject.

20. Admittedly there were many circumstances in which a "moral" issue could be a public or political one.

21. It is important to note that a given individual in a position of authority might possess no paternalistic impulses whatsoever and conduct his affairs accordingly. The hope of the rioters would be to activate such impulses (whether through fear or altruism was irrelevant; see below) in other members of the ruling order. It is also essential, however, to recognize, as E. P. Thompson has so famously stated, that the rise of a capitalist economy in place of an older moral economy made such conflicts between the orders more frequent and more difficult to resolve. See Thompson, "The Moral Economy of the English Crowd," 76–136, and "The Moral Economy Reviewed," 259–351.

22. Thompson, "The Patricians and the Plebs," 71, 85. John Bohstedt offers a similar formulation of paternalism as a utilitarian response to pressures from below in "The Moral Economy and the Discipline of Historical Context," 273–74.

23. See especially Manning, *Village Revolts*, for his discussion of the government's response to enclosure riots.

24. Thompson, "The Patricians and the Plebs," 42. See also Gilmour, *Riot, Risings, and Revolution*, 236–37.

25. The notion of charivaris as acceptable across social classes is of course disputable depending on the period and place one examines. Martin Ingram, for example, has shown how English elite culture continued to acknowledge, if not condone, "moral" charivaris well into the seventeenth century and even to treat them with tolerance in the eighteenth century. Ingram, "Ridings, Rough Music, and 'the Reform of Popular Culture,'" 100–101, 105. See also Burke, *Popular Culture in Early Modern Europe*, 207–86. For examples of charivari forms employed in "political" causes, see Ingram, "Ridings, Rough Music," 91; Thompson, "Rough Music," 516–19; Connolly, "Violence and Order in the Eighteenth Century," 54; Stevenson, *Popular Disturbances*, 60.

26. It is worth mentioning that a version of "riding the wooden horse" was a punishment in the British military through the eighteenth century and was retained as such in the North Carolina militia law through 1774. NCSR 23:943. For further evidence of its survival in North Carolina, see Hermon Husband, "An Impartial Relation (1770)," 319; Kay and Price, "'To Ride the Wood Mare,'" 362.

27. Thompson, "Rough Music," 524–25.

28. Ingram, "Ridings, Rough Music." A festival of misrule involved the temporary inversion of authority, as, for example, when servants assumed the role of master for the day.

29. Davis, *Society and Culture*, 97–151.

30. Gurr, "Psychological Factors in Civil Violence," 37–38. The "protocol of riot" phrase is from Bohstedt, "The Discipline of Historical Context," 272.

31. Fogleman, *Hopeful Journeys*, 47–51. In addition to Fogleman's work, see Luebke, *His Majesty's Rebels*, 180–81, 184–85, 196; Friedrichs, *Urban Society in an Age of War*, 201-4, 221.

32. The following story is recounted in Purdie and Dixon's *Virginia Gazette*, April 1, 1773.

33. Alfred F. Young makes a similar argument about cultural innovation in "English Plebeian Culture," 187–88.

34. For the theoretical background to this position, see Bourdieu, *Outline of a Theory of Practice*, 72, 79, 81, 85.

35. Although British and German traditions of riot were broadly similar, violence is a ticklish enough enterprise that even minor variations in expectations could create confusion and misapprehension. Not enough work has been done on the differences between the two to make solid conclusions, but whatever the exact extent of differences in the culture of riot between Britain and Germany, as with regional variability in England, the German presence further complicated the heterogeneity of the colonial population, and hence its experience and traditions of violence.

36. Young, "English Plebeian Culture," is a sophisticated treatment of this process, although he works with a relatively limited repertoire of violence (charivari in New England). There is of course an enormous literature on the transmission and impact of "True Whig" thought on the development of an ideology of resistance and eventually revolution in the colonies. Maier's *From Resistance to Revolution* is the most outstanding example in applying this literature to the actual use of violence. For further work on the nature of crowd activity in the colonies and their European origins, see Smith, "Anglo-Colonial Society and the Mob"; Countryman, "'Out of the Bounds of the Law'"; Countryman, "The Problem of the Early American Crowd"; Gilje, *Road to Mobocracy*, 1–43; Gilje, *Rioting in America*, 12–59; Palmer, "Discordant Music"; Wood, "A Note on Mobs in the American Revolution"; Wyatt-Brown, *Southern Honor*; Greene, "From the Perspective of Law"; Shaw, *American Patriots and the Rituals of Revolution*; Slaughter, "Crowds in Eighteenth-Century America"; Hoerder, *Crowd Action in Revolutionary Massachusetts*.

37. Political factionalism in the late seventeenth century and early eighteenth century had sparked two "rebellions." Rankin, *Upheaval in Albemarle*; Dill, "Eighteenth-Century New Bern, Part III." Other small-scale incidents occurred throughout the century, some of which will be mentioned in passing. And of course it must be acknowledged that North Carolina's records are notoriously incomplete.

38. One-eighth of both Carolinas equated to the northern half of North Carolina. For a summary of the history of Earl Granville's claim, see Ekirch, *"Poor Carolina,"* 127–33. See also Saunders's preface in NCCR 5:lvi–lix; Coulter, "The Granville District," 35–61; Whittenburg, "Backwoods Revolutionaries," 81–83.

39. Ekirch, *"Poor Carolina,"* 129–30.

40. Ibid., 133–41; Granville was explicit in explaining the reprimand; he wrote to Corbin and (then co-agent) Benjamin Wheatley: "great & frequent complaints are transmitted to me of . . . [illeg.] you employ to receive entries & make surveys in the back Counties." Granville noted their extortionate fees and ordered them to proceed to the back counties to take "effectual Methods . . . for redressing a

Grievance that reflects a Scandal upon my Office, as well as the Honesty of the persons employed in it." Granville to Corbin and Wheatley, April 18, 1756, Granville District Records.

41. Ekirch, "*Poor Carolina*," 141.

42. Dobbs to Granville, February 5, 1759, Granville District Records. Dobbs's language is unclear, but some 500 people appear to have been involved with the petition in some way, either in signing it or presenting it.

43. Dobbs to Granville, February 5, 1759, Granville District Records; Assembly Journals, November 25, 1758, NCCR 5:1042–43. Bodley had been appointed co-agent with Corbin in 1756. Ekirch, "*Poor Carolina*," 137.

44. Assembly Journals, December 22, 1758, NCCR 5:1088–94.

45. Dobbs to the Board of Trade, August 3, 1760, NCCR 6:294.

46. Coulter, "The Granville District," 45. There were a variety of fees payable by a settler who wanted to claim a tract of land (a surveyor's fees, a clerk's fee for entering the deed, etc.). Granville had transmitted to his agents a table of such fees, but they had "neglected" to publish it, enabling them to charge whatever fees they pleased.

47. Attorney General Robert Jones had encouraged the petition. During that December, Governor Dobbs had removed Corbin from his judgeship and colonelship. Dobbs to Granville, February 5, 1759, Granville District Records. As Ekirch has pointed out, of the eight known participants in the incident described below, most were "middling planters and one, William Hurst, was a Granville County Justice of the Peace." Ekirch, "*Poor Carolina*," 141. The other seven were Alexander McCulloch, David Crawley, Joel Lane, David Lane, Barnaby Lane, David Cooper, and John Farrell. See Warrant to Sheriff of Halifax, Colonial Court Records, Civil Papers, Supreme Court, 1759, 3, NCA.

48. Pauline Maier has outlined the English and colonial notion of the importance, usefulness, and even essentialness of riot to their vision of a free society. Maier, *From Resistance to Revolution*, 21–24. In Maier's interpretation, it remains extralegal. John Paul Reid has gone further, arguing in several works that legal tradition allowed for popular enforcement of the law. See Greene's discussion in "From the Perspective of Law," 61.

49. Dobbs to Granville, February 5, 1759, Granville District Records. Corbin initially refused to go, so they placed him on a horse with a man behind him. He then consented to go if they would let him use his carriage.

50. Corbitt, *Formation of the North Carolina Counties*, 114–15.

51. Narrative of Edmond Porter, May 15, 1733, NCCR 3:511. See also Tilley, "Political Disturbances in Colonial Granville County," 342–45; Isaac, *Transformation of Virginia*, 88–92. Other examples of the use of the courthouse will be seen below and in chapter 2.

52. Bond from Halifax County, January 27, 1759, Records Received from Other Than Official Sources, 4, NCA. Interestingly, William Hurst, later charged with riot in this case, served as one of the securitors of Corbin's bond.

53. Articles of Agreement between Francis Corbin . . . , Miscellaneous Collections, Granville District Papers, Land Office Records, 1744–63, NCA. The first article, like the bond, demanded a refund of fees that were in excess of those established by Lord Granville. Bodley was excepted from this article as he had only recently become an agent. Dobbs says that they initially demanded that Corbin himself resign, but Corbin persuaded them to let him stay on as long as he worked in conjunction with Bodley. Dobbs to Granville, February 5, 1759, Granville District Records.

54. Articles dated January 26, 1759, Miscellaneous Collections, Granville District Papers, Land Office Records, 1744–63, NCA. This document was apparently a draft and so is not signed.

55. In addition to the documents cited above, see Dobbs to the Board of Trade, August 3, 1760, NCCR 6:292–95.

56. Assembly Journals, May 23, 1760, NCCR 6:411–12. One study of an English charivari suggests that the participation of local officials lent the affair greater legitimacy: "[the constable's] neighbours may well have believed, as the Cripples [the victims] suggested, that an official presence would lend greater legitimacy to their actions, that they 'might doe and effect [the punishment] under color of his . . . office.'" Kent, "Folk Justice," 78. Edward Countryman found similar "counter-governments" in the land riots he studied in the northern colonies. "'Out of the Bounds of the Law,'" 43.

57. Dobbs himself apparently ignored the riot, as he knew of it by February 6. Dobbs to Granville, February 5, 1759, Granville District Records (postscript dated February 6). Jones began to fear the crowd because Corbin persuaded him to act as his attorney in bringing charges against the rioters. See Statement of Charges in Colonial Court Records, Civil Papers, Supreme Court, 1759, 3, NCA.

58. Assembly Journals, May 18, 1759, NCCR 6:113; Council Journals, May 14, 1759, NCCR 6:79–80. See also the Assembly's address to Governor Dobbs, May 15, 1759, NCCR 6:106–7.

59. Governor Dobbs to the Board of Trade, August 3, 1760, NCCR 6:294. The exact timing of this incident is not clear. It may have occurred before the commission's report had been released. If so, the exhumation evidences the Enfield rioters' confidence that a prosecution would result from their petition and thus highlights the extent of their frustration when that did not happen.

60. It must be noted that Dobbs had an older, personal grievance with Corbin, who had attempted to implicate Dobbs in illegally making grants from Granville's district. Council Journals, December 4, 1758, NCCR 5:996.

61. Dobbs to the Board of Trade, August 3, 1760, NCCR 6:295. The freeing of prisoners had precedent in England and Scotland but achieved a certain regularity in North Carolina. During 1737, some 500 people of Bertie and Edgecombe counties marched to free a man they believed had been imprisoned for failing to pay the then controversial quitrents. Officials countered that he was actually in jail for insulting the marshal "in the Execution of his Office." At any rate, he paid his fine

and was released before the mob came into town, and they all went home. Gabriel Johnston to the Board of Trade, October 6, 1732, NCCR 4:267. Countryman's study of northern land riots also found numerous examples of jail breaking but notes that it was practiced selectively. "'Out of the Bounds of the Law,'" 46. Gilje includes it as one of the most common types of colonial riot. *Rioting in America*, 28. Other instances will be seen in the following chapters.

62. Dobbs to the Board of Trade, August 3, 1760, NCCR 6:295. In the statement of charges against the rioters, we see another example of how to construe violence to appear as bad as possible: "Why with Force and Arms At Chowan County . . . they made an Assault upon him Francis Corbin and him Beat wounded imprisoned and evilly treated and him long detained in Prison against the Law and Custom of the Kingdom . . . and did to him other Enormities to the great Damage of him . . . and wherefore the said Francis Corbin by Robert Jones Jun. his Attorney Complains that they the aforesaid . . . [on January 25, 1759, with force and arms] to wit, Swords Staves & Daggers . . . ," Statement of Charges, Colonial Court Records, Civil Papers, Supreme Court, 1759, 3, NCA. The trial docket shows the charges being dropped in the November 1759 court session.

63. Granville's Instructions, April 25, 1759, NCCR 6:30. Granville reinstated Thomas Child, who proved little better, and he too was fired in 1761. Granville's Instructions, April 6, 1761, NCCR 6:547.

64. Council Journals, December 22, 1759, NCCR, 2d ser., 9:66–67.

65. Assembly Journals, May 18, 1759, NCCR 6:113. Similarly restrained rhetoric is used in their note to Dobbs on May 15, 1759, NCCR 6:106–7. Each of these items was a separate offense at common law, but they were often used together in cases of riot, although the inclusion in this case of "Traitorous Conspiracies" could potentially elevate the case to high treason. See below for a discussion of the statutory legalities of riot.

66. Dobbs called for new elections for an Assembly to meet on April 22, 1760. This new Assembly session was marked by a series of bitter conflicts with the governor over a variety of issues. The conflict was particularly marked during May 1760, when the Assembly's missive discussed in the text was written. See Ashe, *History of North Carolina*, 1:297–90.

67. Assembly Journals, May 23, 1760, NCCR 6:411–12. Dobbs's response to this accusation fills in many of the details of the whole incident and at least partially verifies that not much of importance had happened in Enfield between May 1759 and May 1760 to warrant the Assembly's sense of outrage. Dobbs to the Board of Trade, August 3, 1760, NCCR 6:292–95. Dobbs explains at length why he thinks the Assembly made these accusations.

68. There was a significant difference in the British legal system between "riot" and "insurrection," and this distinction was known to the colonists. See Ralph McNair to Hermon Husband, May or June 1768, NCCR 7:767–70. By common law, riots of more than eleven persons were felonious but were not so severely punished as "insurrection" or "making war against the King," which was treason.

The Riot Act of 1715 created new conditions for identifying an unlawful assembly as a riot, but the North Carolina colonists seem to have continued to function according to the common law definition until the Assembly passed its own riot act in response to the Regulators in 1771. See Blackstone, *Commentaries*, 4:81–82, 142–43, 146; Hayter, *The Army and the Crowd*, 9; Brownlie, *The Law Relating to Public Order*, 37–39.

69. Dobbs and Granville each had a variety of reasons for being unhappy with Corbin, but they were also clearly displeased by his treatment of the settlers. Granville to Corbin and Wheatley, April 18, 1756, Granville District Papers, NCA; Dobbs to Child, February 5, 1759, Granville District Papers, NCA; Dobbs to Granville, December 29, 1755, Granville District Papers, NCA. A fuller discussion of the nature of paternalism in North Carolina society is in chapter 2.

70. For a fuller discussion of the history of McCulloh's grants, see Sellers, "Private Profits and British Colonial Policy," 535–51. I would like to thank George Stevenson of the North Carolina Archives for his assistance with McCulloh's tracts.

71. McCulloh received twelve tracts. He sold tracts #1 and #3 to John Selwyn and tracts #2 and #5 to Governor Dobbs. The remainder went to business partners and family members of McCulloh. See Kars, "Breaking Loose," 14.

72. In order to secure the grant, the grantees were required to bring a certain number of settlers onto the tract within a given time. The "unsponsored" arrival of settlers provided an opportunity for the grantees to claim them toward the requirement.

73. Council Journals, October 13, 1755, NCCR 5:493–94. The names of the accused rioters were Colonel George Smith, Captain Jonathan Hunt, John Hunt, Benjamin Merritt, Benjamin Drake, John Drake, Samuel Drake, Sr., John South, Benjamin Roundsopher, Josiah Roundsopher, Zebulon Stout, Josiah Barton, John McGivul, David Harry, and "one" Vanclift.

74. There are no further reports of significant resistance to surveyors in Rowan County. In 1761, Henry Eustace McCulloh (Henry McCulloh's son) arrived in North Carolina to act as his father's agent. He claimed that his work settling the Rowan County tracts proceeded quite peaceably. H. E. McCulloh's Memorial to William Tryon, April 25, 1765, NCCR 7:15–17. Kars mistakenly locates this in Mecklenburg County. "Breaking Loose," 23. Conflicting claims of landownership continued to plague the region, however. For example, the records of the Moravian settlement at Wachovia (now Winston-Salem) mention a number of occasions when their "regularized" titles conflicted with squatters. *Moravian Records*, 1:32–33, 451–52, 2:652. See also Whittenburg, "Backwoods Revolutionaries," 103–4.

75. Dobbs's correspondence concerning these incidents repeatedly lumps together his and Selwyn's tracts, as the "Sugar and Reedy Creek" settlements appear to have crossed the dividing line between them.

76. Dobbs to Governor Boone of South Carolina, May 17, 1762, NCCR 6:779–80. Dobbs names James Loost (or Loosh), David Adams, Andrew Logan, Patrick Gibson, Benjamin Patten, John Logan, and Moses Shelly.

77. Testimony of John Frohock et al., December 10, 1762, NCCR 6:795. The exact timing of this incident is uncertain but is related as if it took place a few years before 1762. Kars argues on good evidence that it must have taken place before 1758. Kars, "Breaking Loose," 27. The "damning" of the King's Peace was a potentially serious breach with traditional forms of riot. Frohock made this claim, however, in testimony designed to impugn the rioters. Unfortunately there are not enough records to clarify this question.

78. Dobbs to Governor Boone of South Carolina, July 6, 1762, NCCR 6:781. The South Carolina governor, in his response to Dobbs, confirmed that Loosh was a justice of the peace and therefore, while blamable for the excesses of his behavior, had not acted criminally since the border was unsettled. NCCR 6:791.

79. Dobbs to Governor Boone of South Carolina, July 6, 1762, NCCR 6:784; testimony of John Frohock et al., December 10, 1762, NCCR 6:795. Dobbs complained that the dispute had begun as early as 1755 when he had first started to survey out his lands (later interrupted by the outbreak of war) and had decided a dispute against one Laverty. Laverty then used the South Carolina bureaucracy to press his one claim, thus inspiring others to emulate him. Dobbs to Governor Boone of South Carolina, July 6, 1762, NCCR 6:783–84.

80. This discussion is based on the deeds issued from Dobbs's grants in Mecklenburg and Anson counties. Holcomb, *Anson County, N.C. Deed Abstracts, vol. 2*; Holcomb and Parker, *Mecklenburg County Deeds*.

81. It may seem dubious to base this argument on a mere 10s change in price. The case gains weight, however, from the tremendous uniformity in price in both periods of sales. Nearly all of the first thirty-one sales were exactly £10 10s, while the later eighty-four were equally consistently £10 even. This uniformity is particularly marked in comparison to McCulloh's deeds discussed below. Furthermore, the continuous depreciation of proclamation money over the two-year hiatus combined with an actual drop in price constituted a significant savings for the settlers.

82. Merrens, *Colonial North Carolina*, 30; Lefler, *Colonial North Carolina*, 96. The first east-west line on North Carolina's border with South Carolina was surveyed in the summer and fall of 1764. The survey stopped just short of the Catawba territory on September 28, 1764. Upon completion of this survey, the governor of South Carolina issued a proclamation that all inhabitants should abide by its division. See Skaggs, "North Carolina Boundary Disputes," 39–44, 46–49, 73–74.

83. Henry Eustace McCulloh was the son of absentee landlord Henry McCulloh. He had served as agent for his father since 1761, successfully settling many claims in their own tracts in Rowan County (see above). Henry Eustace

claimed that he did not want the job of Selwyn's agent, knowing that any attempt to survey the area would meet resistance. He recorded that his father (in England) offered his services to Selwyn behind his back. McCulloh's Memorial, NCCR 7:18. According to the Mecklenburg deed books, Henry Eustace was appointed Selwyn's agent on November 21, 1763. Holcomb and Parker, *Mecklenburg County Deeds*, 56.

84. The four representatives were James Norris, Thomas Polk, James Flannigin, and George Allen. Virtually all of the details we have on the Sugar Creek War come from McCulloh's descriptions of it in a memorial to the governor and Council and in his letter to Edmund Fanning (it was in fact McCulloh who called it a war). The former is in NCCR 7:12–31; the latter NCCR 7:32–34. A few additional details are provided in the Council Journals for May 17, 1765, NCCR 7:37–38.

85. McCulloh's Memorial, NCCR 7:22.

86. For "tying neck and heels" in the British military, see Ivers, *British Drums on the Southern Frontier*, 180; Fielding, *Tom Jones*, 215; Claver, *Under the Lash*, 12–13. For its use in early Jamestown, see Morgan, "The First American Boom," 194; and Morton, "The Origins of American Military Policy," 77. For the North Carolina militia law, see NCSR 23:520, 598, 763, 943. For civil punishments in England, see Melling, *Crime and Punishment*, and Andrews, *Old-Time Punishments*.

87. The plantation belonged to James Norris. McCulloh hoped to avoid confrontation by beginning his survey there because Norris continued to agree with the original terms and had in fact asked McCulloh to survey his lands on that basis. McCulloh's Memorial, NCCR 7:24. Norris continued to support McCulloh, as evidenced by his acting as a surveyor for McCulloh during the incident at the "widow Alexander's tract" in early May (see below).

88. Only the first sentence of his reply to Polk has been preserved. Eight pages following that sentence are missing from the manuscript. McCulloh's Memorial, NCCR 7:25.

89. McCulloh's Memorial, NCCR 7:25.

90. McCulloh's Memorial, NCCR 7:16.

91. Data extracted from Holcomb and Parker, *Mecklenburg County Deeds*.

92. Franklin, "Agriculture in Colonial North Carolina," 546. Alternatively, Tryon in 1767 claimed that £1 sterling was legally worth £1.33 proc., but in reality it fetched as much as £1.8 proc. NCCR 7:491. See also McCusker, *Money and Exchange in Europe and America*, 215–19. Of course the pure exchange rate was not so much the issue as the almost total lack of pounds sterling in the backcountry. Governor Tryon to Seymore Conway, December 26, 1765, NCCR 7:144.

93. Council Journals, April 6, 1765, NCCR 7:6. It was the petition and Tryon's order to desist which produced McCulloh's long memorial explaining what had happened.

94. McCulloh wrote on April 27, 1765, that he intended "to proceed with

survey on Shugar Creek & also with scattering the Grae [sic] of God among them" hoping that the settlers would "begin to doubt wrangle and dispute among themselves." Henry E. McCulloh to Edmund Fanning, *Regulator Documents*, 19–20.

95. Henry E. McCulloh to Edmund Fanning, May 9, 1765, NCCR 7:32; Council Journals, May 17, 1765, NCCR 7:37–38.

96. This is an impression based on wide reading of materials covering the seventeenth through the end of the eighteenth century. Whipping was not, at any rate, as common as it would come to be in North (and South) Carolina.

97. Ingram, "Ridings and Rough Music," passim.

98. Gilje's survey of rioting in colonial America noted only two instances of whipping in the northern colonies, but he does not specify whether they were exceptional. *Rioting in America*, 29. Whipping was a premier form of vigilante punishment meted out during the South Carolina Regulator movement. Klein, "Ordering the Backcountry," 661; Brown, *South Carolina Regulators*, 38–52, 55.

99. Tryon's "A view of the polity," NCCR 7:480. For example, a person convicted of petty larceny in Rowan County in May 1769 received 25 lashes, and another petty larceny case netted 39 lashes. Journal of Waightstill Avery, July 28, 1769, the Draper Manuscript Collection, North Carolina Papers (series KK).

100. The eighteenth-century British military flogged its soldiers and sailors at a tremendous pace. Punishments of 600–1,500 lashes were not uncommon (usually meted out over several days). The colonial militia also used flogging as a punishment, though generally in much smaller doses. See Anderson, *A People's Army*, 131–35; Selesky, *War and Society*, 186–89.

101. Charles Woodmason, "Memorandum [on the Regulators]," Sermon Book No. 4, p. 15 quoted in Brown, *South Carolina Regulators*, 52.

102. Henry E. McCulloh to Edmund Fanning, May 9, 1765, NCCR 7:32.

103. Council Journals, May 17, 1765, NCCR 7:37–38.

104. Salisbury District Trial and Minute Docket, 1761–90, in September 1765 and March 1766, NCA. Kars does not find an explanation for the dismissal, although she hints that Fanning (as judge) may have played a role in it, possibly after the reconciliation of Polk and McCulloh (see below). Kars, "Breaking Loose," 38–40.

105. Extracted from Holcomb and Parker, *Mecklenburg County Deeds*. James Norris and three of the Alexander family made up four of the six.

106. For the original appointment of this commission, see NCCR 6:773–92; for the report in November 1766, see NCCR 7:275–78.

107. Council Journals, April 24, 1767, NCCR 7:451–54. This is not to say that McCulloh was losing money. He retained the grants for all the deeds for which he had succeeded in registering people as "his" (or Selwyn's). Kars, "Breaking Loose," 17–18. In tract #4, for example, H. E. McCulloh succeeded in registering 24,482 acres out of 100,000. Extracted from Holcomb and Parker, *Mecklenburg County Deeds*. H. E. McCulloh later wrote that at his best guess, most of the 100,000 acre tracts contained only about 50,000 acres of "valuable" land. H. E.

McCulloh to Conway Richard Dobbs, May 2, 1770, Dobbs Papers (typescript), SHC. Tryon himself noted that the grantees received quite a sufficient reward given that they had not actually brought in settlers; they had merely taken advantage of those arriving on their own. Tryon to the Earl of Shelburne, October 31, 1767, *TC* 1:586. The advantage to McCulloh (and other grantees) in surrendering was to avoid having to pay quitrents to the crown for the full acreage of the grant. Once the "unsettled lands" were surrendered, McCulloh would owe quitrents only on the registered portions.

108. Polk was also brought back into the circle by granting him (with John Frohock and Abraham Alexander, two of the men beaten at the Widow Alexander's) the oversight of the public buildings for the future Charlotte—an office with significant potential for profit. Polk also subsequently worked as an agent for McCulloh. Kars interprets this as McCulloh "breaking" Polk and suggests that McCulloh probably offered to drop his prosecution against him in exchange for accepting his terms. Kars, "Breaking Loose," 41–42, 44.

109. Henry McCulloh to Edmund Fanning, January 10, 1766, and February 27, 1766, and April 3, 1766, all printed in *Regulator Documents*, 30–34. Recall that this activity was done in Selwyn's name.

110. Holcomb and Parker, *Mecklenburg County Deeds*. I found twenty-nine names from the prosecution list who also purchased Selwyn's land in the winter of 1767. Kars also notes that family members of several other rioters purchased land through McCulloh at this time. In total, between January 5 and February 3, 1767, he sold 192 tracts of Selwyn's land. I should acknowledge a tremendous debt here to Kars's excellent work in the Mecklenburg Deed books in determining who purchased land from McCulloh, and on what terms.

111. Holcomb and Parker, *Mecklenburg County Deeds*. It is interesting to note how John Frohock, McCulloh's agent on site, purchased large quantities of Selwyn's tracts for a significantly lower price (approximately half) than most of the other settlers. See above for conversion rates. Kars arrived at a slightly higher average price and used a higher N.C. proc. value conversion rate.

112. This is not a converted figure. While not every deed specifies whether in proclamation or sterling, the general patterns are clear. In the winter/spring of 1767, McCulloh set the prices for his own land in N.C. proc., but Selwyn's land in sterling.

113. Kars, "Breaking Loose," 35. The settlers may not have anticipated the difficulties that those terms would cause in the future. As a lender, McCulloh set the mortgage in proclamation money, at a level usually between two and three times higher than the sterling price listed on the deed. Part of the difference reflected the conversion rate, part reflected the lender's profit.

114. Thompson sees the helpful responses of authority in violent situations as their recognition of the even greater potential (violence) of the plebs. He offers a notion of a paternalism-deference equilibrium in which "there is a sense in which rulers and crowd needed each other, watched each other, performed theatre and

countertheatre to each other's auditorium, moderated each other's political behaviour." Thompson, "Patricians and the Plebs," 57, 71, 85.

115. Governor Josiah Martin to Isaac Wilkinson, February 10, 1775, Granville District Records. Martin had made a similar comment in the less revolutionary year of 1773. Josiah Martin to Samuel Martin, July 20, 1773, ibid.

116. Morgan and Morgan's *Stamp Act Crisis*, while dated, is still the best starting point. Much of the historiography about the Stamp Act revolves around whether the colonists were being disingenuous about their rationale for protesting.

117. For other works covering the Stamp Act in North Carolina, see Lee, "Days of Defiance"; Spindel, "Law and Disorder"; Sprunt, *Chronicles of the Cape Fear River*. The various surveys of North Carolina colonial history also outline the Stamp Act protests.

118. See Morgan, *Stamp Act Crisis*, 35–43, for details on the act.

119. Many of these pamphlets are collected in Morgan, *Prologue to Revolution*. North Carolina's Maurice Moore wrote a pamphlet in this vein, which is available in Boyd, ed., *Some Eighteenth Century Tracts*, 157–74.

120. Waddell, *A Colonial Officer*, 82. Tryon initially set the next Assembly for November 30, but then in late October he delayed it again until March 12. This prorogation prevented North Carolina from participating in the intercolonial Stamp Act Congress.

121. The parading, hanging, and burning of an effigy is of course familiar from English practice, but one should not discount the possibility that North Carolinians were taking their cue in this from newspaper accounts of similar doings in Boston. Although there are no surviving issues of North Carolina newspapers from this period to demonstrate this possibility, the *South Carolina Gazette*, on September 14, 1765, reported the details of the effigy burnings in Boston and New London. Given the propensity of colonial newspapers to reprint each other's stories, it is likely that they also appeared in the Virginia and North Carolina papers. Samuel Johnston, at least, was informed of riots taking place in Annapolis. Samuel Johnston to ———, October 2, 1765 (preserved as an enclosure with a letter of January 9, 1766), Hayes Collection, SHC.

122. *North Carolina Gazette*, November 20, 1765, NCCR 7:123–25. Note that in 1765, Wilmington probably had only some 800 residents (not taxables, residents). Lennon and Kellam, *Wilmington Town Book*, xxxv. It being a Saturday (market day), there would have been a great many people from the surrounding counties in town. A Wilmington town ordinance set market days as Thursday and Saturday. *Wilmington Town Book*, 18.

123. *North Carolina Gazette*, November 20, 1765, NCCR 7:123–25.

124. Both incidents appear in a letter from a Pitt County man dated November 18, 1765, and printed in the *Connecticut Courant* on January 6, 1766. It should be noted that in all of the riots and disturbances discussed in this book, this is the only report of a house being burglarized by protestors. During the Regulation, the report that money had been taken from Edmund Fanning's house was disputed by

participants, though other property certainly was. Property was frequently damaged, but usually as a public expression of grievance, not "robbed" for private gain.

125. Houston was appointed on July 9, 1765, but for whatever reason the news did not arrive until November. Warrants for Stampmasters, July 9, 1765, PRO T54/39 copied in ER 18–6.

126. William Houston to William Tryon, April 21, 1766, PRO CO5/299; William Houston to John Brettell, November 20, 1765, House of Lords Records Office, London, Main Papers, January 27, 1766, both cited by Spindel, "Law and Disorder," 8.

127. *North Carolina Gazette*, November 20, 1765, NCCR 7:123–25.

128. The printer (Andrew Stuart) claimed that he had not printed the paper for some weeks before the beginning of the Stamp Act because of a fever. *North Carolina Gazette*, November 20, 1765, NCCR 7:123–25.

129. Ibid.

130. The dinner is described in *North Carolina Gazette*, November 27, 1765, NCCR 7:127–30. Tryon sent a copy of this article to England along with a cover letter, which indicated the number of guests. See also Samuel Johnston to ———, January 9, 1766, Hayes Collection, SHC.

131. Tryon actually went further in expressing his sympathy with the colonists by offering to pay personally any tax on any legal instruments for which the governor received a fee. He also agreed to pay for a number of wine licenses for various towns.

132. Waddell, *A Colonial Officer*, 87–88.

133. At any rate, no replacement stamp distributor had yet been appointed, and Tryon may have ordered Phipps to keep them on board. Tryon to Commissioners of the Treasury, April 5, 1766, NCCR 7:195–96.

134. There are three accounts of various phases of this incident: two different accounts in the *Maryland Gazette* (Annapolis), February 20, 1766 (bylined from Wilmington), and March 13, 1766 (dated from Norfolk, January 8, 1766). The other is in a letter from Samuel Johnston to ——— (enclosure), January 9, 1766, Hayes Collection, SHC. See also Spindel's narrative of the event, "Law and Disorder," 10–11.

135. Quote from Samuel Johnston to ——— (enclosure), January 9, 1766, Hayes Collection, SHC.

136. It is an interesting side note that the nineteenth-century historian John Wheeler preferred to report that the ox was thrown in the river. Wheeler, *Historical Sketches*, 1:52.

137. Samuel Johnston to ———, January 9, 1766, Hayes Collection, SHC. See also Spindel, "Law and Disorder," 11. The act to establish the capital at New Bern was duly passed in November 1766.

138. Tryon to Conway, February 25, 1766, NCCR 7:174. The *Diligence* received orders to depart Brunswick for repairs on February 6, although it did not

actually leave for some time. Phipps transferred the stamps to the care of Captain Lobb aboard the *Viper*. Tryon to Jacob Lobb, February 6, 1766, *TC* 1:237.

139. NCCR 7:176–77. Jones's ruling was printed in the *North Carolina Gazette* on February 26, 1766 (as found reprinted in the March 21 *Virginia Gazette*). The letter written to Dry (see following note) on February 15 indicated that Jones's ruling had only just been received.

140. "Principal Inhabitants of the Town of Wilmington" to William Dry, February 15, 1766, NCCR 7:177–78.

141. *Virginia Gazette*, March 21, 1766.

142. Association signed by the principal Gentlemen . . . , February 18, 1766, NCCR 7:182.

143. Countryman also noted this in his study, "'Out of the Bounds of the Law,'" 56.

144. Maier, *From Resistance to Revolution*, 198–227.

145. John Ashe, Thomas Lloyd, and Alexander Lillington to William Tryon, February 19, 1766, NCCR 7:178.

146. William Dry to Commissioners of the Customs, February 24, 1766, PRO T1/453, copied in ER 16–74.

147. Tryon to the Commander of the *Viper* or the *Diligence*, February 19, 1766, NCCR 7:179. Lobb soon thereafter ordered the guns at Fort Johnston to be spiked, believing he could not defend it. Jacob Lobb to John Dalrymple, [February 20, 1766], NCCR 7:181. Lobb later explained his actions by citing a rumor that Colonel Hugh Waddell was marching on the fort with 300–400 men with the intent to seize it. Jacob Lobb to William Tryon, February 24, 1766, *TC* 1:253–54. Fort Johnston is located at the mouth of the Cape Fear, downriver from both Wilmington and Brunswick. It is variously spelled Johnston or Johnson in the sources (see map 4).

148. *North Carolina Gazette*, February 26, 1766; Tryon to Conway, February 25, 1766, NCCR 7:170.

149. Two separate letters of Jacob Lobb to William Dry, February 20, 1766, NCCR 7:183. Lobb used the excuse of perishable commodities aboard the *Patience*, and his uncertainty about the legality of the seizure of the *Ruby*. This was done despite an apparent promise made to Tryon the morning of February 20 to hold on to the *Patience*. Governor Tryon to Secretary Conway, February 25, 1766, in NCCR 7:169–74. Lobb's actions were in part motivated (as Tryon assumed) by the stoppage of provisions to his ship. In fact, one of his provisioning parties had been seized and jailed by the townspeople on February 5, and on February 20 he had only three days' worth of bread remaining. NCCR 7:184; *TC* 1:249, 250, 261. See also Dry's account of Lobb's decision: William Dry to Commissioners of the Customs, February 24, 1766, PRO T1/453, copied in ER 16–74.

150. *North Carolina Gazette*, February 26, 1766. Tryon's account reveals that the comptroller (William Pennington) had already left the house at the first request for him, but Tryon went out and called him back inside, using the excuse of "dispatches." Tryon to Conway, February 25, 1766, NCCR 7:171.

151. Tryon to the Commander of the *Viper* or the *Diligence*, February 19, 1766, NCCR 7:179.

152. Tryon says there were 400–500 men drawn up in sight of the house, from which a detachment of about 60 came down the avenue, sending in one representative to talk. Tryon, like most of those in authority who describe colonial crowds, was careful to note that in the course of the entire episode, there were so many men armed, and so many unarmed (in this case about 580 armed, 100 unarmed). In most particulars, Tryon's account (Tryon to Conway, February 25, 1766, NCCR 7:169–74) agrees with that found in the *North Carolina Gazette*, February 26, · 1766. For other examples of attention paid to armed/unarmed status (prior to the Regulators, which are covered in the next chapter), see NCCR 3:511; 6:781; and McCulloh's comment about the Sugar Creek rioters (discussed above), NCCR 7:32.

153. *North Carolina Gazette*, February 26, 1766.

154. The protestors considered this resignation of some importance. They had wanted the comptroller to execute his office, but to ignore the issue of stamps. Therefore, when they took him into town they asked him to go aboard the *Patience* to certify its contents. He refused, having resigned the office. Tryon to Conway, February 25, 1766, NCCR 7:169–74.

155. *North Carolina Gazette*, February 26, 1766.

156. Tryon's Proclamation, February 26, 1766, TC 1:259–60. Spindel, "Law and Disorder," 15, notes that two militia colonels, nine justices of the peace, and the mayor of Wilmington were all active in the riots.

157. William Tryon to Henry Seymour Conway, March 3, 1766, TC 1:264–65; William Tryon to the Commissioners of the Treasury, April 5, 1766, NCCR 7:195–96.

158. Spindel, "Law and Disorder," 15–16.

159. Ekirch argues that the Enfield riots arose in part as a result of a dispute between McCulloh and Corbin. "*Poor Carolina*," 141. For Sugar Creek, Kars believes that Thomas Polk's ambitions motivated him in the riots against H. E. McCulloh's surveyors. "Breaking Loose," 42–44. Finally, Spindel shows the extent of elite participation in the Stamp Act riots. "Law and Disorder," 15. A similar argument is made regarding food riots in England in Shelton, "The Role of Local Authorities," 50–66.

160. Hermon Husband noted as much in one of his sermons: "A few men may rise in a riot without a Cause; and disaffected lords and great men may have such ambitious views, encouraged by some enemy prince;—but for the generality of the poor of a Province to rise, there must be some cause." Husband, "An Impartial Relation (1770)," 318.

161. The phrase is from Gilje, *Road to Mobocracy*, vii.

162. For poor laws, see Lennon and Kellam, *Wilmington Town Book*, 14, 151–52; Senate Journals, May 7, 1777, NCSR 12:83. See also the records of the overseers of the poor in Edenton in Saint Paul's Parish Records, SHC. For control of

exports, see Proclamation by Governor Tryon, January 21, 1771, NCCR, 2d ser., 9:247–48; Governor Josiah Martin to Earl Hillsborough, August 21, 1772, NCCR 9:323–24.

163. Kay, "'To Ride the Wood Mare,'" 377.

164. As evidence of such a precedent, see Josiah Martin to Isaac Wilkinson, February 10, 1775, Granville District Records. In that letter, Martin noted how unlikely it was that they would ever be able to collect all the back quitrents from the inhabitants of the Granville District. He suggested a compromise of having them pay two or three years' arrears, noting that "if attempt should be made to enforce payment thereof at Law, it would excite Rebellion among the Tenants." Martin went on to emphasize how the residents were confident of their own strength to prevent the execution of the law and would set any legal decision at naught. Martin then referenced the Enfield riots and the Regulator troubles as evidence.

165. See virtually any entry in the section in the bibliography: "European Riot and Charivari." For women's role in northern colonial food riots, see Smith, "Food Rioters," 3, 26.

166. Smith, "Food Rioters," 27–28.

167. Spruill, *Women's Life and Work*, 233ff., 243–44.

168. Berkin and Norton, *Women of America*, 39; Norton, *Liberty's Daughter*, xiv; Wilson, "The Illusion of Change," 414ff.; Lewis, *Pursuit of Happiness*, 188.

169. Spindel, "Women's Civil Actions," 173.

170. Recall also the claim by some of the early Sugar Creek rioters that they were a militia company from South Carolina. See also the very military looking riots in Georgia in 1766 and in Salem, Massachusetts, in 1774, in, respectively, Johnson, *Militiamen*, 59, 63; *Pennsylvania Gazette*, February 9, 1774. Richard Maxwell Brown has also noted how colonial backcountry rebellions frequently drew their organizational structure from the militia. "Backcountry Rebellions," 86.

171. Beik, *Urban Protest*, 45.

172. See the description of a militia muster from October 30, 1754, in the *Moravian Records*, 1:110, in which the soldiers, according to the strict Moravian standard, "behaved better than is usual on such occasions, though this does not apply to Captain Hampy and his men. [They beat drums during dinner, when asked to stop, they started shooting off guns] . . . after the Muster the men were so full of whiskey that they fought each other until they were covered with blood." See also Isaac, *Transformation of Virginia*, 104–10, for a discussion of militia musters as social events in colonial Virginia.

2. "To Fight the Air"

1. Ralph McNair to Hermon Husband, May or June 1768, *Regulator Documents*, 121–24.

2. Husband, "Impartial Relation (1770)," 280.

3. Foote, *Sketches of North Carolina*, 60.

4. The recognition of North Carolina rioters as purposeful and restrained is not a new one. William Saunders in editing the Colonial Records observed as much about them in 1890. NCCR 9:x–xi. The emphasis here is not just on the matter of restraint but on the existence of a *form* of violence, one that had rules that affected behavior, the violation of which could lead to escalation.

5. Regulators, although of significant interest to some colonial historians, have remained on the fringes of most historical work given the normal interpretation of them as off the track leading to the Revolution. Whig historians were uncertain how to treat the Regulators because there was long a perception (now disputed) that the majority of the Regulators became Loyalists during the Revolution. More importantly, however, to the place of the Regulation in the history of the Revolution, the leadership of the forces that crushed the Regulators, save the governor himself, were almost invariably the same ones who later led the Whig party into revolution in North Carolina. The revolutionary loyalties of the Regulators are outside the scope of this work. See Johnson, "The War of the Regulation"; Kay, "The North Carolina Regulation," 105.

6. See Adams, "The Carolina Regulators," 346–47, for a discussion of the nineteenth-century Whig historians' views on the Regulators. More recently, see Powell, *War of the Regulation*, 26–28. This is of course in line with the oft-mentioned claim that the Battle of Alamance was the "first battle of the American Revolution"; a phrase still present on the memorial plaque at the battle site. For an example of a North Carolina historian making the "first battle" claim, see Fitch, *Some Neglected History*, 262.

7. Ashe, *History of North Carolina*; Alden, *The South*, 152–63; Dill, *Governor Tryon*.

8. Bassett "The Regulators of North Carolina." The primary modern exponent of this thesis has been Hugh Lefler in a variety of books on North Carolina. The most commonly cited are Lefler and Newsome, *North Carolina*; and Lefler and Wager, *Orange County*. See also William Powell's introduction in *Regulator Documents*, xv–xxvii; Morgan, "Conflict and Consensus," 293–97. Again, see Adams, "The Carolina Regulators," 350, for a further discussion of the "sectional" school.

9. Bassett, although the originator of the sectional interpretation of the Regulation, also first introduced the possibility of class conflict. He characterized the Regulation as a kind of conservative peasant uprising. We will see later the value that this interpretation has in understanding the forms of violence taken by the Regulation. The progressive school historians who have discussed the Regulators include Douglass, *Rebels and Democrats*, 71–100; Morris, *The American Revolution Reconsidered*, ix–x, 70. Kay and Cary's work is available in a variety of forms: Kay, "An Analysis of a British Colony"; Kay, "The North Carolina Regulation"; Kay and Cary, "Class, Mobility, and Conflict"; Kay, "The Institutional Background to the Regulation."

10. They used two indices of wealth: slave ownership, and position in the tax rolls from eight and eleven years after the Regulation. They found "almost all wealthy westerners" opposed to the Regulators, and that the Regulators were "poorer than average." Kay and Cary, "Class, Mobility, and Conflict," 127–31.

11. Whittenburg, "Planters, Merchants, and Lawyers," passim, especially 220; and Whittenburg, "Backwoods Revolutionaries."

12. Ekirch, "*Poor Carolina*" and "The North Carolina Regulators." In framing his argument in this way Ekirch was of course following the lead of Bernard Bailyn in finding the roots of revolution in the country Whig ideology of resistance, and of government by contract. Bailyn, *Ideological Origins*. This thesis was further modified in respect to the use of violence by Pauline Maier in *From Resistance to Revolution*.

13. See the discussion in chapter 1.

14. Brown, "Back Country Rebellions," passim.

15. Denson, "Diversity, Religion"; Kars, "Breaking Loose."

16. While most works on the Regulators supply a narrative summary of some kind, there was no truly detailed narrative of the Regulation until the recent dissertation of Marjoleine Kars, "Breaking Loose," 252–424. Gaps in the narrative provided in this and the next chapter can be filled out in her work.

17. Not much is known about George Sims. His family appear to have been early settlers in Granville County, and a George Sims appears on the 1790 census in Caswell County. See the editor's introduction to George Sims, "An Address to the People of Granville County," in Boyd, ed., *Some Eighteenth Century Tracts*, 179; the speech follows on 182–92. The choice to begin with Sims is not a random one. It was with a version of Sims's statement that Hermon Husband, the chief apologist for the Regulators, and one of their foremost leaders, began his tract, "An Impartial Relation of the First Rise and Cause of the Recent Differences in Publick Affairs." Husband quoted this address, with some variation, in the opening pages of "An Impartial Relation (1770)." Hermon Husband was born in 1724 in Maryland and migrated around midcentury to Orange County along the Deep River. He was a Quaker, although that organization disowned him in 1764. For a full biography, see Jones, "Herman Husband."

18. Sims, "An Address," 184–85.

19. Ibid., 190–91.

20. Husband, "A Fan for Fanning (1771)," 347. While this work is still usually attributed to Husband, Archibald Henderson argues for a different unknown author in "Hermon Husband's Continuation."

21. Husband, "Impartial Relation," 259.

22. Ibid., 261.

23. Ibid., 262–63; *Boston Chronicle*, November 7–14, 1768, in *Regulator Documents*, 195–96. For a complete account of the history of Tryon's palace, see Dill, *Governor Tryon*.

24. Regulator Advertisement No. 4, January 1768, *Regulator Documents*, 76; Regulator Advertisement No. 5, March 22, 1768, ibid., 79. The name "regula-

tors" had been used by other protesting associations in England. See, for example, Thompson, "The Moral Economy of the English Crowd," 111–12.

25. This incident is described in a letter of the Regulators to Governor Tryon, not dated, NCCR 7:759–66; Husband, "Impartial Relation," 267; and John Gray to Edmund Fanning, April 9, 1768, NCCR 7:705.

26. Bertram Wyatt-Brown has found a number of examples of charivaris in the colonial South. *Southern Honor*, 440–43, 450, 452.

27. Regulators' Advertisement No. 11, May 21, 1768, *Regulator Documents*, 115–21.

28. John Gray to Edmund Fanning, April 9, 1768, NCCR 7:705.

29. This is in line with the use of charivari in "public" cases rather than moral ones as discussed in chapter 1.

30. Kars, "Breaking Loose," 264n.18, notes that the sheriff's act of distraint while the owner was riding the horse may have increased the sense of outrage, since by tradition an object that was in use could not be seized for taxes.

31. For examples, see Advertisement, August 1766, NCCR 7:249–50; Articles adopted by Regulators and Associators, April 30, 1768, NCCR 7:732; Regulator Advertisement No. 11, May 21, 1768, NCCR 7:760.

32. Nicholas Rogers discusses similar limitations to crowd behavior in terms of choosing houses, breaking windows, "jostling" their opponents, and then generally moving on in "Popular Protest in Early Hanoverian London," 263–93. For a more theoretical discussion of the tradition of legitimate violence as protest, see Kittrie, *War against Authority.*

33. Maier, *From Resistance to Revolution*, 21.

34. Apparently, in the early stages they believed that Fanning himself would be their ally. Regulator Advertisement No. 11, May 21, 1768, NCCR 7:760.

35. Husband, "Impartial Relation," 258.

36. Ibid., 281–82.

37. Ibid., 261; Whittenburg, "Planters, Merchants," 221; Tilley, "Political Disturbances," 356–57. Whittenburg provides a list of wealthy, prominent planters who were generally pro-Regulator. "Backwoods Revolutionaries," 111. See also Ekirch, "*Poor Carolina*," 165–66.

38. Husband, "Impartial Relation," 259–60.

39. Ekirch, "*Poor Carolina*," 168–74.

40. This is Whittenburg's interpretation in "Planters, Merchants," 222.

41. Husband, "Impartial Relation," 259.

42. Ibid., 265. Fanning's rhetoric showed no signs of letting up. When he reported to Governor Tryon after the firing on his house, he referred to "Dark Cabals" and "traitorous Dogs" and said they must be termed "Rebels & Traitors." Edmund Fanning to William Tryon, April 23, 1768, NCCR 7:713–16.

43. John Gray to Edmund Fanning, April 9, 1768, NCCR 7:705–6.

44. Edmund Fanning to John Gray, April 13, 1768, NCCR 7:706–7.

45. Thomas Hart and Francis Nash to Edmund Fanning, April 17, 1768, NCCR 7:710. Seven companies represented a theoretical minimum of 350 men.

46. The likelihood that the Regulators intended such drastic action is small. The minutes of their April 30 meeting indicated that they did plan to go to town soon, but they had been persuaded by the Reverend Micklejohn to delay until May 11, provided there were no further distrainments. On that day, they planned to send but twelve men to town "to propose and deliberate on such matters as shall be conducive to the preservation of our public and private interest." NCCR 7:716.

47. Edmund Fanning to Governor Tryon, April 23, 1768, NCCR 7:713–16.

48. The Anson County men wrote to the Orange County Regulators to associate in their common cause on May 14. Jno. Stringer to ———, May 14, 1768, *Regulator Documents*, 111.

49. The only account of this incident is the letter of Colonel Samuel Spencer to Governor Tryon, April 28, 1768, NCCR 7:722–26.

50. The Resolves were sent to Tryon in Spencer's letter, NCCR 7:726.

51. A similar incident almost occurred in Johnston County in August. There a group of about eighty men tried to take over the courthouse, but the justices heard of their approach and collected some others and drove them off with clubs. Tryon to Lord Hillsborough, December 24, 1768, NCCR 7:884–86.

52. This interpretation of Governor Tryon's response is supported by research on the early modern English legal system, which, while rigid in theory, practiced flexibility through the provision of "loopholes" at several levels of the system. This flexibility allowed for consideration of the context of actions under prosecution. Samaha, "Hanging for Felony"; Herrup, "Law and Morality." I have interpreted Tryon's response as more moderate than others have concluded (see, for example, Kars, "Breaking Loose," 283–84). His reaction was, as I say in the text, "two-handed": prepared to be quite harsh in suppressing disorder but equally prepared to address grievances.

53. Governor Tryon to Earl of Shelburne, July 4, 1767, NCCR 7:497; Governor Tryon to Earl of Hillsborough, June 16, 1768, NCCR 7:791–93. See also Kars's discussion of how both Tryon and his predecessor Governor Dobbs tried to deal with the corruption of the sheriffs in remitting taxes back to the central government. "Breaking Loose," 285–87.

54. Lord Hillsborough to Governor Tryon, August 13, 1768, NCCR 7:799–800.

55. Tryon to Fanning, April 27, 1768, NCCR 7:718.

56. Ibid., 7:720; Tryon to Spencer, May 1768, NCCR 7:727–28.

57. Tryon to the Council, April 29, 1768, NCCR 7:730–31. He also specified as unacceptable anyone who committed any "Treasons, Felonies, Poysonings, Enchantments, Sorceries, Art Magick Trespasses and Extortions." While the last is potentially open ended, the others constitute a common expression of fear of disorder, particularly the reference to magic and poisoning.

58. Tryon to Spencer, May 1768, NCCR 7:728.

59. Tryon's proclamation is available in Council Journals, April 27, 1768, NCCR 7:720–21. His alerting the other militias is in NCCR 7:719, 722.

60. Tryon to Spencer, May 1768, NCCR 7:727–28.

61. Husband, "Impartial Relation," 267.

62. Regulator Advertisement No. 11, May 21, 1768, *Regulator Documents*, 120.

63. Fanning supposedly threatened to send the two prisoners to New Bern and indicated they would surely be hanged. Husband, "Impartial Relation," 268, 284; Captain John Paine to Fanning, May 1, 1768, NCCR 7:743. The writs of arrest and imprisonment of Husband are in Military Collection, War of the Regulation, Box 1, NCA. They accused him of "traitorously and feloneously Conspiring . . . in starting up an Insurrection." Thomas Lloyd, a justice of the peace whom Husband previously thought a supporter, executed the writ to commit Husband to the New Bern jail.

64. Several descriptions of Fanning's meeting with the crowd exist. Husband discusses it in "Impartial Relation," 268–69. Eli Caruthers conducted a variety of interviews with local people early in the nineteenth century, related in *Caldwell*, 122–23. Finally, an interview with former Regulator Joseph Macpherson in 1819 survived in the Orange County Court records and is reprinted in *Regulator Documents*, 566–67. See also how the governor described the incident in his letter to Samuel Spencer, May 1768, NCCR 7:727–28.

65. See the previous note. That same day, Fanning published a proclamation similar to the governor's, which also promised that there would be no prosecutions provided that everyone went home (although it carefully reserved the right to prosecute if they continued "in their seditious, riotous and tumultuous Practices"). NCCR 7:739–40.

66. Although it is worth noting that Husband, a Quaker, generally disapproved of even such "traditional" violence as this.

67. Husband, "Impartial Relation," 268.

68. Fanning to Jacob Fudge, May 1, 1768, NCCR 7:741.

69. Husband, "Impartial Relation," 269.

70. Ralph McNair to Hermon Husband, May or June 1768, *Regulator Documents*, 121–24.

71. Bohstedt, "The Moral Economy," 272.

72. NCCR 7:771–82 reprints a series of depositions outlining supposed illegal practices by county officials. Interestingly, as an indicator of continued hope for a paternalistic response, the depositions were all made before various justices of the peace, who in turn faithfully transmitted them to the Assembly.

73. These are four separate advertisements or petitions to the governor: NCCR 7:758–59, 759–67, 770–71, 806–9.

74. Tryon to the Regulators, Council Journals, June 20, 1768, NCCR 7:793. He wrote similarly to the Anson Regulators in August, NCCR 7:809–10. See also his proclamation against excessive fee taking on July 21, 1768, NCCR 7:795–96.

75. Quote from Husband, "Impartial Relation," 274; Husband, "Fan for Fanning," 375. The exact date of the fee raising is not recorded, as it was an unofficial and technically illegal act. Husband's account indicates that it was sometime before August 1768.

76. Eli Caruthers recorded one provocative incident in which the sheriff supposedly distrained the dress right off a farmer's wife and then slapped her when she objected. He does not record the date of this incident. *Old North State*, 3.

77. Tryon to the Regulators, August 1, 1768, in Council Journals for August 13, 1768, NCCR 7:801.

78. Husband, "Impartial Relation," 275; Husband, "Fan for Fanning," 379; Deposition of Tyree Harris, August 3, 1768, NCCR 7:798.

79. Jones, "The Scotch-Irish in British America," 296–97; Hanna, *Scotch-Irish*, 2:40.

80. For more details, see the discussion of colonial fears of Indians in chapter 4.

81. See the discussion in chapter 1. Also note that North Carolina legal precedent included a provision for distinguishing between arms carried for offensive versus defensive purposes. The distinction seems to have been based not on the actual weapon carried but the way it was used. Court records for 1728 reprinted in NCCR 2:824–25. Thus, the Regulators' later claim (see below) to have carried their firearms only for defensive purposes had legal precedent. Similarly, see the legal emphasis laid on the offensive use of weapons in the English charivari recorded by Kent, "Folk Justice," 72–73.

82. Alan Watson's study of wills in Edgecombe County, for example, found that two-thirds of the population had guns. "Society and Economy," 237–38. The percentage was likely less since not everyone in the county possessed enough property to justify making a will. A series of militia musters from 1754 and 1766 that listed how many were unarmed provides conflicting evidence. Some cases support the two-thirds or more with weapons, while others said there were "but few fitted with arms." NCSR 22:332, 367–68, 382, 392–93, 397–98. John Morgan Dederer concluded that the Americans were relatively the most "heavily armed people in the world." *War in America*, 116n.11. Michael Bellesiles's recent book *Arming America* has ignited a controversy over the extent of the weapon-owning colonial population. It remains to be seen how that debate will be resolved. But consider Tryon's recent experience with the Stamp Act riots, where he counted 580 armed and 100 unarmed men in the crowd. Tryon to Conway, February 25, 1766, NCCR 7:169–74. There has recently been a serious effort to discredit the idea that the English population was as unarmed as perception has had it. Joyce Lee Malcolm argues convincingly that efforts to restrict the ownership of guns in England in the late seventeenth century were rarely enforced and generally ineffective. *To Keep and Bear Arms*, 77–93. From Tryon's perspective of firearms being generally illegal in England, their number and open legality in America would still have been a significant contrast. Malcolm admits as much later in her book by noting the qualitative difference in arms ownership in the colonies in that it was not just a right, it was a requirement. *To Keep and Bear Arms*, 138–39. Charles Carlton notes that prior to the English Civil War, approximately one household in fifteen possessed a firearm. *Going to the Wars*, 98.

83. Although seemingly self-evident, this lack is yet another colonial factor that would tend to make the governor touchier about armed protest. A number of

works address the use of the army to suppress or contain disorder in eighteenth-century England; one good overview is Hayter, *The Army and the Crowd*.

84. The minutes of the Governor's Council (August 13, 1768, NCCR 7:800–806) differ on the numbers both of Regulators and of militia from the governor's journal (*Regulator Documents*, 128). The former claimed that there were 1,000 Regulators "assembled in arms" and that 400 militiamen took the oath. The governor, however, recorded only 500 Regulators and that but 250 militiamen were raised. Tryon may have realized that such a small force could not defend the town and that its very existence would serve to provoke the Regulators. He certainly began very shortly after this (August 17) to raise the militia in other counties.

85. Husband, "Impartial Relation," 275.

86. Governor Tryon to Regulators, August 13, 1768, *Regulator Documents*, 159.

87. Ibid., 160. In the same sentence (written August 13), he noted that he would be in Salisbury on August 25, thus revealing that he may already have decided to raise the Rowan county militia.

88. Kars, "Breaking Loose," 294, concludes that Tryon reached this decision after the August 11–12 incident during which Fanning could summon only about 250 of the militia, and that he was made yet more nervous by a letter from some of those same men who indicated that they were not willing to serve against the Regulators. See Husband, "Impartial Relation," 281.

89. The prerevolutionary militia organization of North Carolina has received scant attention, although a number of works introduce their study of the revolutionary militia by discussing its colonial roots. See Gobbel, "The Militia of North Carolina"; Wheeler, "Development and Organization," 307–23. Also useful are Wheeler, "The Role of the North Carolina Militia"; Kay and Price, "'To Ride the Wood Mare'"; Bartholomees, "Fight or Flee." The following is adapted from all of these sources and from my own research. More details on the development of the militia are outlined in chapter 4.

90. In 1762, Governor Dobbs explained the appointment system, claiming that he appointed some from former experience in the regulars or earlier military service, and because one was a "gentleman of good fortune." Dobbs to the Board of Trade, August 3, 1760, NCCR 6:282–84. For the generally wealthy character of senior militia officers, see Kay and Price, "'To Ride the Wood Mare,'" 385–88; Johnson, *Militiamen*, 46–47, 82. For profit taking by militia officers, see Ekirch, "*Poor Carolina*," 117–18. For the use of officership as socially enhancing, see Isaac, *Transformation of Virginia*, 104–10; Boucher, "The Colonial Militia," 125–30.

91. For examples of the intractability of the militia, see Council Journals, November 27, 1759, NCCR 6:119, and *Moravian Records*, 1:237. Also see the discussion in chapter 3 regarding the militia's pay and bounty. For evidence of pro-Regulator sympathies in the Orange and Granville militia, see Husband, "Impartial Relation," 281, 284; Spencer to Tryon, April 28, 1768, NCCR 7:725,

and of course all of the above-mentioned incidents of low turnouts by the Orange County militia. The Rowan and Mecklenburg militias are discussed below.

92. This is the same shadow that would fall over royal Governor Josiah Martin in the opening months of the American Revolution. His failure to raise a sufficient force contributed to the Whigs' ability to take over the reins of the bureaucracy. See chapter 5.

93. Preyer, *Hezekiah Alexander*, 54–56; Husband, "Fan for Fanning," 349.

94. Council Journals, August 13, 1768, NCCR 7:806.

95. Tryon's Journal (1768), *Regulator Documents*, 129; Husband, "Impartial Relation," 276. Tryon sent a representative to the meeting bearing a letter rescinding much of the compromise reached during the crisis of August 11–12 and requiring twelve of their leaders to post bond that they would not try to interrupt the September court session. NCCR 7:804–6. The Regulators replied that they had always managed to contain the violence of the "multitude" before and that they would continue to do so. James Hunter et al. to Tryon, August 19, 1768, NCCR 7:810–11.

96. *South Carolina Gazette*, October 3, 1768. This newspaper account noticed that there should have been as many as 1,900 men present at the muster instead of the 900–1,000 actually there.

97. During Bacon's Rebellion in Virginia, Governor Berkeley found himself in a similar situation. He raised the Gloucester County militia, but when they found he intended to use them against Bacon, they refused to serve. Morgan, *American Slavery*, 266.

98. *South Carolina Gazette*, October 3, 10, 1768.

99. Tryon's Journal (1768), *Regulator Documents*, 130. On August 27, they met with Tryon and indicated that around 300 volunteers would turn out, and in fact the September army list shows 310 men from Mecklenburg. Ibid., 133; Return of Troops, September 22, 1768, *Regulator Documents*, 169.

100. NCCR 7:813–14.

101. Tryon's Journal (1768), *Regulator Documents*, 130–31.

102. Ibid., 131.

103. Military forces in this era often expected that alcohol would be available as a part of their ration, although by the late eighteenth century it was by no means a certainty. Tryon on this occasion would not disappoint that expectation. He ordered two wagons of liquor prepared for the march on Hillsborough. Tryon's Journal (1768), *Regulator Documents*, 134. Despite all his efforts, Rowan ended up providing only 168 men (from six companies, nominally 300 men). Return of Troops, September 22, 1768, *Regulator Documents*, 169.

104. Some of the incidences of mutiny in the Continental army followed similar practices in the soldiers' use of formation and marching. Joseph Martin described the beginning of one such mutiny in which one soldier stamped the butt of his musket on the ground and "called out, 'Who will parade with me?' The whole regiment immediately fell in and formed." Martin, *Ordinary Courage*, 109. For

similar displays of behavior during mutinies or "soldiers' protests," see Anderson, *People's Army*, 189–94.

105. The Presbyterians' letter is available in NCCR 7:814–16. Micklejohn's sermon was ordered printed and thus has survived in full. It is a classic defense of authority, asserting that the temporal powers are derived of God, and, even more secularly, defending the British constitution as the best in existence and therefore less open to challenge. It is reprinted in *Regulator Documents*, 170–84.

106. Tryon's Journal (1768), *Regulator Documents*, 129, 142. For Suther's background, see *TC* 2:161n.7.

107. Compare, for example, Tryon's journal of the expedition to Hillsborough in 1768, and his journal of the Alamance campaign in 1771, with Colonel Waddell's journal of his separate command during the Alamance campaign. *Regulator Documents*, 136–45, 410–50; NCCR 8:600–607. Waddell was a militia officer with many years' experience of active campaigning with North Carolina troops. For further evidence that such display was considered uncommon, see the critical letter of "Atticus" to Tryon published in the *Virginia Gazette*, November 7, 1771, *Regulator Documents*, 520. Also see Governor Martin's impression of the militia muster he attended in 1772. Martin to Hillsborough, October 25, 1772, NCCR 9:349.

108. Tryon to Hillsborough, August 7, 1769, *TC* 2:352.

109. Colonial militia officers saw their position as one which certified their place in the social strata. Achieving a militia commission was a way to enhance status. During this campaign, Tryon furthered that sense of status by having, for example, six lieutenant generals and two major generals for an army of 1,416 men (in the original document, the clerk transposed this number to 1,461). In total, he had 126 officers (excluding the surgeons and the chaplain), a full 9 percent of the army. Return of Troops, September 22, 1768, *Regulator Documents*, 169; Tryon's Journal (1768), *Regulator Documents*, 140.

110. Tryon's efforts at discipline and drill were unusual enough to lead the Regulators to conclude that he was trying to create standing regiments, although, admittedly, this could have been a rhetorical device on the part of the Regulators. Regulators to Tryon, undated, NCCR 7:811–12. Armies continue to use drill, discipline, and uniformity to create group cohesion and instill obedience. For a history of such practices, see McNeill, *Keeping Together in Time*.

111. NCCR 7:811–12. Anti–standing army ideology had a long history in post–Civil War England and in America. See, for example, Schwoerer, *No Standing Armies!*; Cress, "Radical Whiggery"; Kohn, ed., *Anglo-American Antimilitary Tracts*; Halbrook, *That Every Man Be Armed*, 32–33. Although Don Higginbotham has expressed concern over whether American anti–standing army prejudices had deep popular roots, the behavior and rhetoric of the Regulators would seem to indicate that they did. "Early American Way of War," 279–82. See also the discussion in chapter 4.

112. Husband, "Impartial Relation," 280. Compare this to the New Jersey land rioter of 1749 who "wis'd they [meaning the authority] had fired upon them

the said Rioters, for if they had they never should have seen such work, for . . . they would have destroy'd them [the militia] all and drove them into the sea." Quoted in Countryman, "'Out of the Bounds of the Law,'" 47. Without the provocation of being fired upon, neither this New Jersey rioter nor the Regulators were prepared to resort to *armed* violence, even if they had come so armed.

113. A roster of Tryon's troops is printed in *Regulator Documents*, 169.

114. Husband, "A Fan for Fanning," 386. Tryon claimed there were only 800 Regulators outside town. *Regulator Documents*, 135. Report in Wilmington supported the lower number. Ann Hooper to Dorothy Murray, October 7, 1768, *TC* 2:200.

115. Husband, "Impartial Relation," 282. The Regulators had also continued to employ the traditional rhetoric of protest asserting their loyalty to king and country, and even excluding Tryon from their "list" of enemies. See, for example, Regulators to Tryon, undated, NCCR 7:811–12. Possibly of equal importance was the decision of Husband and Butler to stand trial. They wavered on the issue, and we know that Husband at one point had decided to avoid it but was persuaded by John Wilcox to stand trial in order to help avoid violence. Husband, "Impartial Relation," 280; Deposition of William McPherson, April 23, 1770, NCCR 7:848.

116. The war council consisted of all the field and general officers in the army plus all the assemblymen who happened to be in town. The list is reprinted in *TC* 2:185. The proceedings of the war council are available there and also in NCCR 7:840–42.

117. Is this a more or less lenient recommendation from their perspective? The monetary squeeze on the leadership replaced by an oath from the multitude? If more lenient, it is an interesting commentary on the desire of the Council to avoid violence, especially given the governor's demand that they consider using the troops. If less lenient, then it is strong evidence for the presumed power of an oath in colonial society.

118. The final, complete terms were that nine leaders were to be delivered for eventual trial, the Regulators should surrender their arms until the conclusion of the present court session, and they should promise to pay their taxes. If they did all that, the governor would pardon all of them, save the nine, and of course the two already scheduled for trial.

119. Husband, "Impartial Relation," 280, 282; Tryon's Journal (1768), *Regulator Documents*, 135. Approximately thirty men came in and surrendered their arms.

120. The best summary of the court proceedings is in Kars, "Breaking Loose," 311–12.

121. Tryon's Proclamation, October 3, 1768, NCCR 7:850–51; Tryon to Hillsborough, December 24, 1768, NCCR 7:886; Hillsborough to Tryon, March 1, 1769, NCCR 8:17.

122. Powell, *War of the Regulation*, 15. John Alden's interpretation was that the Regulators "were awed by his [Tryon's] display of strength and melted away." Alden, *The South*, 158.

123. Such was the view expressed in Boston in November 1768, reprinted in the *Virginia Gazette*, January 19, 1769, *Regulator Documents*, 217.

124. Husband, "Impartial Relation," 295. Husband thought the cheering an attempt not to look foolish in the face of the results of the court. While the officers may have felt foolish, it seems unlikely that the cheers of the soldiers were less than genuine.

3. The Road to Alamance

1. *Regulator Documents*, 396.

2. Hayes Collection, SHC.

3. See Kars's discussion of the petitions submitted for consideration by the November Assembly. "Breaking Loose," 317.

4. Sheriff of Orange County to Tryon, October 29, 1768, NCCR 7:863–64.

5. The Assembly acknowledged the legitimacy of the complaints of the Regulators, but only rhetorically. Assembly Journals, November 12, 1768, NCCR 7:931. An attempt by the Council to pass a strong bill for the trial of rioters, however, failed. The Assembly described it as "expressly contrary to the sentiments of this House." Assembly Journals, November 30, 1768, NCCR 7:965–66. Kars argues that the bill failed only because of the House's fear that it could be used against them for their role in the Stamp Act protest of 1765. "Breaking Loose," 327. This seems unlikely, as those incidents were now three years old, and the House had no trouble passing a harsher version of this bill in 1770 when more sufficiently frightened by the Regulators. In other words, the dialogue of violence had not yet proceeded to the point that would justify such a harsh measure. See also the nearly simultaneous acknowledgement of the Council that the "People have been very Uneasy under the heavy Taxes . . . ; the Insurgents in particular made this one Article of their Complaints," and the Council therefore discontinued an old tax. Council Minutes for December 6, 1769, NCCR, 2d ser., 9:214.

6. For failed prosecutions, see Joshua Teague et al. to Harmon Husbands, September 14, 1769, NCCR 8:68–70; Diary of Waighstill Avery, entry for March 18, 19, 20, 1769, the Draper Manuscript Collection, North Carolina Papers (series KK), State Historical Society of Wisconsin (microfilm).

7. Tryon to Hillsborough, December 24, 1768, NCCR 7:885.

8. Diary of Waightstill Avery, April 12, 1769, the Draper Manuscript Collection, North Carolina Papers (series KK), State Historical Society of Wisconsin (microfilm).

9. Ibid., entry for March 18, 19, 20, 1769.

10. Council Journals, April 14, 1769, NCCR 8:26. For mention of the whipping of another sheriff in Anson County, see *Moravian Records*, 1:390.

11. Tryon to Hillsborough, April 25, 1769, NCCR 8:32.

12. Morgan Edwards's History of the Baptists in North Carolina [1772], NCCR 8:655.

13. For a more detailed discussion of the peaceful events of 1769 and 1770, including the Regulators' efforts at petitioning, prosecuting officials, and electing sympathetic assemblymen, see Kars, "Breaking Loose," 336–53.

14. Among others, Hermon Husband, John Pryor, and Thomas Person were elected in July 1769. See Ekirch, "*Poor Carolina*," 189–90.

15. The petitions are available in NCCR 8:75–80, 8:81–84, 10:1015–17, from Anson, Orange, and Mecklenburg counties, respectively.

16. The Regulators' enemies were swift to bring cases of slander against those who tried to bring them into court on corruption charges. This was an old tactic. George Sims, whose petition commenced chapter 2, was sued in this way, as were a number of Regulators over the course of the period. Kars, "Breaking Loose," 367; petition of inhabitants of Orange County, October 19, 1770, *Regulator Documents*, 268–72; Husband, "Impartial Relation," 257, 291.

17. The accounts of the riot are in a letter from Richard Henderson, the judge who presided during the court session, to Governor Tryon, available in NCCR 8:241–44, and three newspaper accounts derived from a single New Bern newspaper version of October 5, 1770, now lost. They are the *Virginia Gazette*, October 25, 1770; the *Evening Post* (Boston), November 12, 1770; and the *Annual Register* (London) 1770. They are conveniently available in *Regulator Documents*, 250–58. The newspaper accounts differ only slightly, the Virginia one waxing somewhat more rhetorical; it is unclear if it is a more exact reprint of the original New Bern version or if the Virginia editors tacked on phrases of their own. The original author in New Bern had clearly seen Henderson's letter, quoting it several times at length. Henderson fled the night of September 24, and his description of the events of the twenty-fifth depended on reports from others. A postscript to his letter indicates that he had received direct reports of the amount of damage done in Hillsborough before sending his letter on September 29. The Virginia reprint refers to another "eyewitness's" letter for the events of the twenty-fifth; the contrast between the two accounts is examined below. Also available are two depositions of other anti-Regulator eyewitnesses, Joseph Lyon and Ralph McNair; these are available in *Regulator Documents*, 249, 261–62. The Orange County Court records include a description of the events of the twenty-fourth, presumably inserted sometime after the event by Richard Henderson. The manuscript docket of trials for that day has survived with the annotations made by the Regulators. NCCR 8:236–40. Finally, there is a sworn statement by three Regulators denying certain reports about the stealing of money from Fanning's house. NCCR 8:260.

18. The contrast between Henderson's account and the rather inflated newspaper accounts begins already. The newspaper claimed that Regulators armed with rifles attempted to ambush Henderson and others on their way to Hillsborough to open the court. Somehow Henderson avoided this supposed ambush. While I cannot deny the possibility of the truth of this incident, it bears a remarkable similarity to the supposed attempted ambush of Fanning in 1769, which he avoided by taking another route. Diary of Waighstill Avery, entry for March 18, 19, 20, 1769,

the Draper Manuscript Collection, North Carolina Papers (series KK), State Historical Society of Wisconsin (microfilm). One wonders whether rumors of planned ambushes exceeded the fact. If not, the Regulators made pretty poor backwoodsmen. At any rate, Henderson himself did not mention the incident.

19. Again, contrast the eyewitnesses with the newspaper accounts. Henderson reported clubs, whips, and switches. McNair said he saw "wooden cudgels or Cow Skin Whips," while the newspaper made them into leaded or weighted whips.

20. This is all from Henderson's account. The newspapers completely ignored this portion of the day's events.

21. To clarify: the Regulators did not want to stop the court; they wanted it to continue under their auspices.

22. The trial docket from this day, complete with the Regulators' comments inserted, survives. It is reprinted in NCCR 8:236–40.

23. Some Regulators later denied taking any of Fanning's money during the wrecking of the house. NCCR 8:260.

24. The effigy, the church bell, and the threat to the church were mentioned only in the newspaper version. Those details ring true, however, to the traditional forms and restraints of protest violence. The Virginia newspaper version, quoting a supposed eyewitness, claimed that "The merchants stores are broke and rifled, Mr. Cooke's house torn to pieces, and Mr. Edward's had not shared a better fate."

25. This is one of the details tacked on by the newspapers. *Virginia Gazette*, October 25, 1770; *Regulator Documents*, 250.

26. Henderson's letter reported the rumor that numbers of armed Regulators were posted outside of town, but he admitted that others denied it and that there was no evidence for it. Easterners found it easy to assume, however, that they were armed, as Samuel Johnston casually described the Orange Mob as again in arms. Johnston to Alexander Elmsley, November 7, 1770, NCCR 8:257.

27. McCulloh to John Harvey, July 24, 1769, NCCR 8:59. "Levelling" refers to the various groups of reformers or sectarians who emerged during the English Civil War and who propagated theories about "levelling" social and economic distinctions. The threat of levellers became one of the great remembered fears of the Civil War era in addition to that of a standing army. To briefly "turn the world upside down" in moments of carnival or festival was one thing, and in fact could serve as a form of social control through acting as a kind of relief valve. The levellers preached a permanent reordering of the world, something a gentry class could only fear. See Hill, *The World Turned Upside Down*.

28. *Virginia Gazette*, October 25, 1770, *Regulator Documents*, 250. See the immediately preceding notes for the line-by-line comparisons between Henderson's account and the *Virginia Gazette*'s version.

29. Deposition of Josiah Lyon, *Regulator Documents*, 249. The reference to the Pretender referred to the still-extant Stuart claim to the English throne. The last serious threat of a Stuart return to England had been the Scottish rising in 1745, but English fears of the Jacobites lingered on. To drink success to the Pretender

constituted treason. Tryon knew the value of this accusation as propaganda, and he made sure to mention it in his October 18 proclamation, which condemned the September riots. *Regulator Documents*, 266.

30. Peter Wood's book on South Carolina is the best treatment of the consequences of fear of slave rebellion on white attitudes. *Black Majority*. See also Rachel Klein, "Ordering the Backcountry," for a discussion of the role of such fears in motivating the South Carolina elite to repress the South Carolina Regulators. For a brief summary of fears of slave rebellions in North Carolina, where the black population was smaller but still significant, see Taylor, "Slave Conspiracies in North Carolina," 30–31. Also useful is Kay and Cary, *Slavery*. North Carolina's fears of slave rebellion should seem self-evident, but "proof," if you will, came in 1771, when Tryon wrote to the counties asking them to send militia to the rendezvous to march against the Regulators. He requested troops from virtually every county save Brunswick, where the potential for slave insurrection was by far the highest. The 1767 taxables list shows black taxables in Brunswick outnumbering white taxables almost five to one. Only New Hanover even approached that ratio at approximately three to one. *Regulator Documents*, 376; NCCR 7:539.

31. North Carolina had a long history of conflict with various Indian groups, and North Carolinians, whether in the east or west, were fully invested in the notion of Indian savagery. Whether such a fear had any basis in reality is not the question. Life in the colonies had provided a new salience to the rhetorical label of "savage." See Sheehan, *Savagism and Civility*, 5–8. See also chapter 4 for a fuller discussion of colonial responses to Indians. Ironically, several Massachusetts writers took exactly this approach, that is, describing someone in Indian-like terms, when they criticized Tryon's supporters in the months after the Battle of Alamance. *Boston Gazette*, September 9, 1771, printed in *TC* 2:831–32.

32. John Shy notes that colonial elites held a more precarious grip on authority than their English equivalents. He cites the right to vote, the dependence of colonial position on the British government, and the weakening of face-to-face methods of leadership by a rapidly growing, diverse, and dispersed society. "American Society," 76.

33. North Carolinians tended to build along river and creek lines in a way that militated against nucleated settlement. There was no lack of a sense of local community; settlement areas were often referred to by the name of the creek along which they were located. What they did lack was an instantly accessible centralized point for gathering and transmitting news. For discussions of this kind of community formation, see Bartholomees, "Fight or Flee," 8–9, 43–45; Nobles, "Breaking into the Backcountry," 649–50; Ramsey, *Carolina Cradle*, passim, especially 99ff.

34. Contrary to various attempts to claim the Regulators as generally one ethnicity or generally one religion, they were by all appearances a very mixed lot, as were their (local) opponents. A casual survey of the names in the various Regulator petitions reveals that the movement was far from being mostly Scottish,

mostly Scotch-Irish, or mostly English. It was a mixture of all of them with also some significant German participation (miscalled "Dutch"). See, for example, the petition signatures in *TC* 2:117. There is a much more complete list of Regulator names available at the visitors' center of Alamance Battleground compiled in 1974 by Jerry Cross, a researcher for the North Carolina Department of Cultural Resources. Kay notes that people of English descent formed the majority in Granville and probably Orange County, and a substantial part of the other western counties. "An Analysis of a British Colony," 173. For additional information on German participation, see Welker, "Early German Reformed Settlements in North Carolina," NCCR 8:740. Husband himself defended the movement from charges of being primarily Presbyterian, declaring "our Body to consist Promiscuously of all Sects." "Impartial Relation," 280. Denson and Kars deal extensively with the varying religious denominations' participation. As for black participation in the movement, Kay and Cary have noted that there was apparently none, whether slave or free. "Class, Mobility, and Conflict," 134.

35. The associators sent this document as a petition to the government. Military Collection, War of the Regulation, Box 1 (undated, but context indicates shortly after the September 1770 riot).

36. See Ekirch, "*Poor Carolina*," 196–200, for another discussion of the motivations for the eastern elite to repress the Regulators.

37. He described the pulling down of Fanning's house and the assaults as "amounting only to a riot." The threats to the court could be only a high misdemeanor, and the toast against the king might be treason, but the available evidence was inconclusive. He also noted that given the situation in the western counties, attempting to arrest anyone would probably prove fruitless. Attorney General Thomas McGuire's Opinion, October 18, 1770, *Regulator Documents*, 266–67.

38. Tryon called for a general muster in all the counties on October 19 in order to identify volunteers who would be willing to turn out in the event of a future emergency (that is, conflict with the Regulators). The proclamation reflected his relative lack of legitimate grounds to move against them violently. He could refer to the rioters only as "Outrageous & disordly [*sic*]," while rather lamely asking for witnesses to come forward. He was of course sure to mention the one thing that the Regulators did that might be taken to have violated the "form" of a riot, that is the toasting of damnation to King George and success to the Pretender. Tryon's Proclamation, October 18, 1770, *Regulator Documents*, 266, 272–73. Ekirch has pointed out the "imperial" demands on Tryon's decisions. Unlike most of the colonial elite, he had to worry about what London thought, and for them order came first. "*Poor Carolina*," 197.

39. Published in the *New York Gazette and Weekly Mercury* in August 1771 (reprinted from an unknown *North Carolina Gazette*), NCCR 10:1018–19.

40. See also Moravian accounts of the Regulators forming committees and summoning people before them, even sentencing some to be whipped (although one Moravian writer was mixing up North and South Carolina Regulators, the others were clear in their reference to North Carolinians): *Moravian Records*,

1:450, 451–52; 2:652. The specific instances referred to in the Moravian accounts were also from the post-September 1770 period.

41. The Regulators continued to organize and to try to extend their support, but they had not started any kind of backcountry war. The Moravian diaries, while full of their own fears, record only peaceful behavior by the Regulators, even if they were a bit loud in the taverns. *Moravian Records*, 1:416–18. The Regulators also continued to petition, something they would do right up until Alamance. Petition of the Inhabitants of Orange County, May 15, 1771, *Regulator Documents*, 453–54.

42. Council Journals, November 19, 1770, NCCR 8:258–66.

43. Ibid., NCCR 8:260; William Tryon to Richard Caswell, November 20, 1770, *Regulator Documents*, 275.

44. Tryon to the Assembly, December 5, 1770, NCCR 8:283–84.

45. The Assembly to Tryon, December 10, 1770, NCCR 8:311–12.

46. ——— to Barker, undated, Military Collection, War of the Regulation, Box 2, NCA. The letter writer was a lawyer, and context dates this letter to shortly after the imprisonment of Husband in New Bern (that is, late December 1770).

47. James Iredell to John Harvey, December 21, 1770, *Papers of James Iredell*, 1:57; Assembly Journals, December 17, 1770, NCCR 8:322. For the tabling of the bill, see Assembly Journals, December 15, NCCR 8:319. The editor of Iredell's papers and a number of other historians disagree with Iredell's assessment of the Assembly as being of "regulating principles," basing their argument on the subsequent passing of the very harsh Johnston Act. Kay calls the "pro-regulator" bills of the session "cooptive and repressive." "The North Carolina Regulation," 99. Kars suggests that many of the laws addressed specific grievances but failed to change the overall legal and economic structure in the colony. See her discussion for a full treatment of the eventual texts of the so-called pro-Regulator acts: "Breaking Loose," 384–91. See also Whittenburg, "Backwoods Revolutionaries," 402–6. It is important to note, however, that all of the at least nominally "pro-Regulator" bills were introduced and had passed their first reading in the House (unlike the Johnston Act) by December 28, most of them before Husband's ejection from the House on December 20 (see below). Assembly Journals, December 10 to December 28, 1770, NCCR 8:309–43. This chronology helps establish the early weeks of the Assembly as continuing to treat the Regulators within a traditional framework of riot and protest. Legitimate violence engendered at least a partially paternalist response. As we will see, when the rumors of a march on New Bern began to intensify, the Assembly returned to the Johnston Act and passed it. An act similar to the Johnston Act had been proposed and voted down in November 1768, as "expressly contrary to the sentiments of this House." Assembly Journals, November 30, 1768, NCCR 7:965–66.

48. Council Journals, December 20, 1770, NCCR 8:268–69.

49. Tryon to Colonel Joseph Leech, December 24, 1770, *Regulator Documents*, 296–98.

50. Assembly Journals, December 31, 1770, NCCR 8:345–46. See also Tryon

to Fanning, December 26, 1770, *Regulator Documents*, 298.

51. ——— to Thomas Barker, undated, Military Collection, War of the Regulation, Box 2, NCA (context dates this letter to shortly after the imprisonment of Husband in New Bern). The author further declared that he could no longer live there under such conditions and would shortly leave for Virginia and then England.

52. Ironically, the committee appointed to investigate the practices of local officials submitted its report on the same day. The report heartily condemned the fee system and the resultant "extorting, exacting and receiving greater fees than the Law allows." The committee also spoke against the actions of the Regulators, but with a noticeably restrained rhetorical tone. Unlike the governor's speech or the Assembly's response earlier in the session, here we find neither "barbarous," "savage," nor "traitor." Assembly Journals, January 2, 1771, NCCR 8:388–89.

53. The bill can be followed through the Assembly in NCCR 8:319, 390, 405, 353, 410, 356.

54. For the English Riot Act, see Gilmour, *Riot, Risings, and Revolution*, 140–41. For the text of the Johnston Act, see *Regulator Documents*, 327–32. See Kars, "Breaking Loose," 381–82, for a further discussion of its provisions and Samuel Johnston's background.

55. A North Carolina law of 1741 authorized local justices of the peace to proclaim that any slaves who had run away and had been "lying out" should turn themselves in. If they did not submit, it became "lawful for any Person . . . whatsoever to kill and destroy such Slave or slaves . . . without Accusation or Impeachment." NCSR 23:201–2. See also Kay and Cary, *Slavery*, 74–75; NCSR 23:975.

56. Additional Instructions . . . , February 6, 1771, NCCR 8:516 (this portion of the royal instructions to Governor Martin was probably written later than the document's overall date of February 6); Royal Council Records, April 22, 1772, NCCR 9:285–86, 289; Earl of Hillsborough to Josiah Martin, June 6, 1772, NCCR 9:300–301.

57. Text of Johnston Act, January 15, 1771, *Regulator Documents*, 331–32.

58. For a similar two-handed response by a colonial governor, see Berkeley's response to the early stage of Bacon's Rebellion. Morgan, *American Slavery*, 259.

59. Assembly Journals, January 22, 1771, NCCR 8:450; quote from Council Journals, February 7, 1771, NCCR 8:497. Tryon had a separate problem with the Assembly over the issue of availability of currency. His calls for a resolution to raise troops were frequently met with a response that the currency prohibition must first be repealed. See, for example, Assembly Journals, January 25, 1771, NCCR 8:462–63.

60. Council Journals, February 7, 1771, NCCR 8:497–98; quote from Tryon to Colonels of Militia . . . , February 7, 1771, *Regulator Documents*, 341.

61. Dill, *Governor Tryon*, 149–50.

62. Tryon to Hillsborough, April 12, 1771, *Regulator Documents*, 396 (the epigraph at the beginning of this chapter is a fuller version of this quote).

63. This incident is described in a letter from one Regulator leader, Rednap Howell, to another (James Hunter), written on February 16. NCCR 8:537. Since the militias were ordered to stand down on February 20, the letter almost certainly refers to a muster called to prevent the suspected Regulator march on New Bern. Tryon had embodied the Craven militia in New Bern on the sixth and kept them three days in the town. Tryon to Hillsborough, April 12, 1771, *Regulator Documents*, 396.

64. Tryon to Hillsborough, April 12, 1771, *Regulator Documents*, 396. Tryon noted that no witnesses were available to testify to Husband's participation in the Hillsborough riots, so, on the advice of Chief Justice Howard, he tried the libel charge instead.

65. Colonel Caswell to Tryon, February 20, 1771, NCCR 8:500.

66. Tryon to Thomas McGuire, February 27, 1771, NCCR 8:695–96. Another account of Regulator activity during this period is less clear in the matter of restraint. The Moravians recorded that a group of Regulators "[went] to Mr. MacNally's house to regulate him, and after he had replied to their various accusations he raised a loaded pistol . . . and threatened to shoot the first man who attacked him . . . and they left without molesting him." *Moravian Records*, 1:450–51.

67. For sending the militia home, see the separate letters of Tryon to the various militia colonels, February 21, 1771, *Regulator Documents*, 349–51. The Council's response to Tryon's request is in NCCR 8:501–2. The Council's belief that the court could be held uninterrupted is evidence for a remarkable de-escalation of the Council's fears.

68. Estimates of their number vary from 250 to 500. Accounts of this meeting are in the deposition of Waightstill Avery, who was forcibly taken to the meeting by the Regulators (in order to provide witness to their intentions?) in NCCR 8:518–21. John Frohock and Alexander Martin, the Rowan County officials with whom the Regulators negotiated, wrote a letter describing the incident to Governor Tryon on March 18, NCCR 8:533–36. The description that follows is from these two accounts and, except for quotations, will not be footnoted further. The Regulators' "minutes" of the meeting, which include the text of the agreement between the two parties, are available in *Regulator Documents*, 357–58.

69. All quotes are from Avery's account, NCCR 8:520.

70. All quotes in this paragraph were from Frohock and Martin's account in their letter to Tryon, March 18, NCCR 8:533–53.

71. *Moravian Records*, 1:451. Other petitions and documented activities of the Regulators during this period reflect the greater sense of desperation engendered by the Johnston Act—some mentioning it specifically. Petition from Orange County Relative to Regulators, NCCR 8:543–44; *Moravian Records*, 1:452.

72. Tryon to Frohock and Martin, April 5, 1771, *Regulator Documents*, 394.

73. Tryon to Francis Nash, February 27, 1771, NCCR 8:693 (emphasis added).

74. See Kars, "Breaking Loose," 399–400, for more details on Tryon's packing the grand jury.

75. Jury described in *Virginia Gazette*, March 28, 1771 (bylined from New Bern, March 15).

76. Grand Jury Presentment, March 15, 1771, NCCR 8:528–30.

77. Fear of the Regulators was already making them into bogeymen. The news that Maurice Moore's kitchen had burned down, though a common enough occurrence, was blamed on the Regulators. Henry Johnston to Samuel Johnston, March 24, 1771, Hayes Collection, SHC.

78. One example: Tryon to Thomas Hart, March 16, 1771, *Regulator Documents*, 370.

79. Rednap Howell to James Hunter, February 16, 1771, printed in the Council Journals, March 18, 1771, NCCR 8:536–37.

80. Council Journals, March 18, 1771, NCCR 8:538.

81. There were actually two anti-regulator armies, a large one under Governor Tryon, and a smaller one composed of troops from the western counties under General Hugh Waddell. They are considered here together unless otherwise specified. There are four journals or order books surviving from the Alamance campaign. Tryon's army order book is in the PRO and has been reprinted in *Regulator Documents*, 417–50 (additionally, pages 410–17 reprint Tryon's general orders for the campaign). The Carteret County detachment's order book is reprinted from the manuscript in the North Carolina Archives in NCCR 8:574–600. This order book is virtually identical to Tryon's, with occasional omissions, and three extra days covering the period after Tryon's departure for New York. Tryon's journal of the expedition (original in the Bodleian Library at Oxford) is reprinted in *TC* 2:716–32. Finally, the order book of General Waddell's separate command is in NCCR 8:601–7. These are abbreviated hereafter, respectively: Army Order Book; General Orders of the Army; Carteret Detachment Order Book; Tryon's Journal (1771); Waddell's Order Book.

82. Rednap Howell to James Hunter, February 16, 1771, printed in the Council Journals, March 18, 1771, NCCR 8:536–37.

83. *Virginia Gazette*, March 28, 1771.

84. The Reverend Mr. Cupples to the Secretary, April 25, 1771, NCCR 8:551–52; Carteret Detachment Order Book, NCCR 8:588.

85. Tryon's Journal (1771), *TC* 2:717.

86. Tryon to Colonels Edward Vail and Edmund Buncombe, April 18, 1771, NCCR 8:708.

87. Return of Troops, September 22, 1768, *Regulator Documents*, 169; Troop request by county, March 19, 1771, NCCR 8:697; Roster of Troops, May 6, 1771, NCCR 8:607.

88. He did not request troops from Brunswick County. See Troop request by county, March 19, 1771, NCCR 8:697, for the numbers requested. See also Tryon to colonels of Militia, March 19, 1771, *Regulator Documents*, 379.

89. The numbers with Tryon can be found in *Regulator Documents*, 461. Pitt County does not appear on this list because its contingent was joined to the artillery section. In Tryon's diagram of the various contingents, Pitt's is comparable in

size to Onslow County's fifty. *Regulator Documents*, 418, 423. The numbers of the separate western army under Waddell are available in NCCR 8:607. At this point, some explanation must be given for the failure of the northern counties to send troops as requested. Financial matters in the colony were divided between a northern and southern treasurer. When Tryon made his call for troops, he instructed each treasurer to honor his warrants to issue funds to the various colonels to pay their troops. The northern treasurer, with a long-standing dislike of issuing currency, refused, and consequently very few of the northern counties raised any troops (the exceptions were Johnston, Orange, and Rowan counties, which obviously had a larger stake in the matter). For details on the controversy with the treasurer, see NCCR 8:650–51, 9:18, 9:12–13; *Regulator Documents*, 379. *TC* 2:796–97, shows the cancelled warrants. See also Ashe, *History of North Carolina*, 1:366, for a good discussion of the problem. Among the southern counties, Bladen, Duplin, and Hyde, although requested to do so, did not raise any troops.

90. *Boston Gazette*, August 12, 1771, NCCR 8:636–38.

91. A North Carolina militia private's pay in 1754 was 3 shillings per day, although that was considered exceptional. NCCR 5:110. The North Carolinians raised for the Yamassee War in 1715 received a £5 bounty (NCCR 2:180); the same £5 bounty was offered in 1759 (NCCR 6:34–35). Note that contrary to one historian's claims (*Regulator Documents*, xxii) that the 40 shillings bounty was offered after initially slow recruiting, Tryon actually communicated this amount in his first letter to the militia colonels on March 19. The Cherokee expedition pay is found in: Publick of North Carolina to John Nuckols, February 9, 1771, NCCR 8:517–18. The 1764 and 1766 garrisons' pay: NCCR 6:1148; NCCR 7:308. Governor Dobbs's comments about the necessary bounty: NCCR 6:257–58. The Alamance army's pay: 8:541–42. Compare also Titus's discussion of the necessity for a bounty to kick start recruiting in Virginia during the Seven Years' War. There a £10 bounty was issued, and that amount quickly filled the ranks. *Old Dominion at War*, 122.

92. NCSR 25:457.

93. Proceedings of the Provincial Congress, September 8, 1775, NCCR 10:203. The militia raised in 1761 for a seven-month tour with the British army outside North Carolina was offered a £5 bounty. NCSR 25:457.

94. Tryon to Hillsborough, January 19, 1769, NCCR 8:5–6.

95. North Carolina had a long history of extreme difficulty raising its militia or filling the quota of troops for service outside the state. For the Tuscarora War, see NCCR 1:838, 948. For the Seven Years' War, see NCCR 5:496–97, 570–72; NCCR 6:34–35, 111. In Wake County, Tryon, in leaving behind the Wake detachment to help the sheriff collect back taxes, made a point of exempting militia volunteers from having to pay those taxes. Army Order Book, *Regulator Documents*, 422.

96. Tryon to Hillsborough, March 12, 1771, NCCR 8:526. For the other laws designed to gain backcountry support and for Tryon's use of patronage to court

influential backcountry leaders, see Kars, "Breaking Loose," 388–90; Preyer, *Hezekiah Alexander*, 54–56, 72–73; and Husband, *Fan for Fanning*, 349.

97. Mecklenburg County sent only 84 men, although Tryon had asked for 300 troops. The county had provided 310 during the crisis of 1768. NCCR 7:889, NCCR 8:697, 607. When the Mecklenburg County troops under General Waddell, along with those of the other western counties, actually confronted a large Regulator force on May 9, they displayed such an unwillingness to fight that Waddell was forced to retreat. He was admittedly outnumbered, but he and his officers specifically cited the irresolution of their troops. Waddell's Order Book, NCCR 8:608; Tryon's Journal (1771), *TC* 2:719.

98. As indicated in the previous chapter, a comparison of Tryon's order book with that of Waddell, an experienced militia officer, reveals the extent to which Tryon emphasized European military formalism. This comparison is of course impressionistic but is based on a wide reading of many other militia, British, and Continental army order books. There are few "objective" ways to identify one army as being more formalistic than another. Briefly listed, Tryon worried a great deal more about color guards, flags, drums, honor companies, gambling, Sunday services, courts-martial regulations, garbage and sanitation, and order of precedence among officers and units. General Orders of the Army and Army Order Book, *Regulator Documents*, 410–50; Waddell's Order Book, NCCR 8:601–7. As noted above, Tryon actually used the army to surround the general muster of the Wake regiment to "encourage" enough of its members to volunteer. Tryon's Journal (1771), *TC* 2:717. At this point, he may have felt somewhat more desperate given the now apparent lack of turnout from the northern counties.

99. *Regulator Documents*, 378; NCCR 8:284. Farquhard Campbell of Cumberland County received a captain's commission for his efforts at raising a company of volunteers. *Regulator Documents*, 402. Tryon noted that they were mostly Scottish Highlanders and therefore probably raised by Campbell from his own clan. Tryon's Journal (1771), *TC* 2:724. Tryon, as in 1768, also continued to use ministers to provide the religious argument for supporting him. Tryon's Journal (1771), *TC* 2:719.

100. Tryon referred to them as "the Gentleman Volunteers." There were initially twenty of them, all from Granville and Bute counties. Tryon's Journal (1771), *TC* 2:719. After the battle, another small contingent of light horse arrived from Duplin County. Since they were the only troops from Duplin County, I have assumed that they too were "gentlemen." On May 22, their combined total was only twenty-three. *Regulator Documents*, 426, 431, 461. See also Samuel Cornell to Elias Debrosses, June 6, 1771, enclosed with Earl of Dunmore to Earl of Hillsborough, June 20, 1771, ER 13–10.

101. *TC* 2:747. When the North Carolina Provincial Congress of 1775 organized the first Continental regiments, the theoretical organization of 500 men and 34 officers reflected a ratio of 6 percent officers to 94 percent soldiers. Proceedings of the Provincial Congress, September 1, 1775, NCCR 10:186. Kay, "The North

Carolina Regulation," 91, claims that the 1768 army had a disproportionate number of officers, but it is unclear what he is comparing it to. Tryon's army in 1768 had 91 percent soldiers and 9 percent officers, although, as mentioned in chapter 2, it certainly had a disproportionate number of generals. Return of Troops, September 22, 1768, *Regulator Documents*, 169 (discounting surgeons, chaplains, and clerks).

102. Tryon to Hillsborough, August 1, 1771, NCCR 8:651.

103. The definition of "normal" in the phrase "larger than normal" is the key issue. Relatively few instances exist of a colonial militia army engaged in a civil war. But it is probably safe to say that gentry volunteers for service outside the colony (during the Seven Years' War for example) were a rare breed indeed. There was, however, a similar company of eighty gentlemen volunteers fighting for the Whigs in 1775 at the Battle of Moore's Creek Bridge. Colonel William Purviance to the Provincial Council, February 23, 1776, NCCR 10:465.

104. See chapter 4 for a discussion of the usual "way of war" of the North Carolina militia.

105. Most eighteenth-century European armies were composed of the lowest classes of society, often pressed into service, and never well remunerated; such men were a constant threat to desert. Frederick the Great's arrangements of his camp and his unwillingness to pursue a defeated enemy for fear of desertion are only the most well-known examples of the problem. Duffy, *Military Experience*, 172–73; Frey, *The British Soldier*, 72–73.

106. See chapter 4 for eighteenth-century expectations of military logistics.

107. Tryon to colonels of militia, March 19, 1771, *Regulator Documents*, 378. The commissaries, however, eventually had to requisition from the countryside (beginning as early as May 15). Army Order Book, *Regulator Documents*, 428. Tryon hoped that this measure would help contain his troops in camp, with the added benefit of preventing desertion to the Regulators. Tryon was also careful to issue receipts or pay cash for supplies taken during the march. See, for example, *Moravian Records*, 1:468.

108. General Orders of the Army, *Regulator Documents*, 413.

109. For May 13, Tryon's order book reads "His Excellency having been informed that the Army had committed outrages on the property of the Inhabitants settled on the Road contrary to his express commands. . . . He does once more strictly forbid every Person . . . from taking or disturbing the property of any Person whatever as they will on complaint receive the severest Punishment." Army Order Book, *Regulator Documents*, 427. Further examples of efforts to control the impact of the army on the countryside are found after the battle. Ibid., *Regulator Documents*, 439, 441. The Moravians at least were impressed with the discipline displayed by Tryon's army. *Moravian Records*, 1:432–33.

110. Letter from North Carolina, May 17, 1771, in *Boston Gazette*, August 12, 1771, NCCR 8:636–38.

111. Morgan Edward, History of the Baptists in North Carolina [1772], NCCR 8:656.

112. *Regulator Documents*, 454.

113. Letter from North Carolina, May 17, 1771, in *Boston Gazette*, August 12, 1771, NCCR 8:636–38 (emphasis added). A similar claim was made in another letter from a North Carolinian to a friend in New Jersey written July 24, 1771, and printed in the *Boston Gazette* on October 21, 1771 (reprinted in NCCR 8:647).

114. Kars claims that "the Regulators impeded the armies' marches as much as possible. They stole back horses and supplies, intercepted messages, destroyed bridges and barricaded roads." "Breaking Loose," 407. As this comment, in a powerfully argued work, directly contradicts my interpretation, it is necessary to look at her evidence more closely. Examining her references to TC 2:691, 718, 719, one finds three supposed incidents of resistance. The first was Tryon sending out pioneers to check roads and bridges; this was standard military practice. See Simes, *Military Guide*, 278. The second was the army's scouts discovering a "Regulator . . . laying in ambush with his Gun" on May 12. Few are the fools who will ambush an army on their own. It is far more likely that he was out in the woods with his gun and then tried to hide from the army's scouts. Finally, the disappearance of a few horses from the camp around Hillsborough hardly constituted significant resistance activity. Other supposed incidents (such as "Persons suppos'd to be Regulators . . . lurking about the Camp," *Regulator Documents*, 422) were more reflective of Tryon's fears than actual resistance. Possibly more serious is Kars's reference to *Moravian Records*, 1:455, 456, where there are hints that the Regulators intended to intercept a small militia contingent en route to join Tryon's army. If they so intended, they failed to do so.

115. Deposition of James Ashmore, June 22, 1771, NCCR 8:622–23; Wheeler, *Historical Sketches*, 2:65–67; Foote, *Sketches*, 481.

116. The obvious though not isolated comparison is the Boston Tea Party rioters' Indian dress. For the use of women's dress in European riot, see Davis, *Society and Culture*, 97–151. For examples in Great Britain, see Whatley, "How Tame Were the Scottish Lowlanders," 13; Thompson, "Moral Economy of the English Crowd," 115–17. Also recall how the Sugar Creek rioters blackened their faces. For other examinations of colonial rioters adopting Indian dress, see Smith, "Food Rioters," 6; Gilje, *Rioting in America*, 29, 31.

117. Deloria, *Playing Indian*, 6–7, 11–20, 25.

118. Petition of distressed inhabitants, undated, NCCR 9:98–99. Drunkenness was used as an excuse or mitigating factor, however, in crimes of personal violence. See, for example, the sentencing in Council Journals, May 28, 1725, NCCR 2:565.

119. Deposition of James Ashmore, June 22, 1771, NCCR 8:622.

120. A fuller discussion of an American "frontier" style of war is in chapter 4.

121. See above for some petitions and the continued efforts of the Regulators in March to hold meetings with local officials and resolve their grievances. The petitions written immediately prior to the battle are discussed below.

122. *Moravian Records*, 2:617. I say "even the Moravians" because, despite repeated instances of the Regulators refraining from actual acts of violence against the Moravians, they maintained a kind of paranoid fear of being attacked.

123. Ibid., 1:456.

124. Ibid., 1:466, also 2:653–54.

125. Tryon's Journal (1771), *TC* 2:719.

126. Waddell had dispatched a militia officer to scout the Regulators' numbers. Tryon further noted that many of Waddell's sentries had deserted to the Regulators. Tryon's Journal (1771), *TC* 2:719; Waddell's Order Book, NCCR 8:608.

127. *Moravian Records*, 2:619.

128. The term was common in documents of the era, but specific reference should be made to Malone, *Skulking Way of War.*

129. One could argue that the conventional eighteenth-century military ethos included the belief that an enemy defeated without fighting was even better than a battle won. It is unlikely, however, that the Regulators were operating on such fine distinctions.

130. Tryon expected the Regulators to oppose his passage of the Haw River west of Hillsborough. He supposed that the Regulators thought he would remain in Hillsborough until a representative had been elected in lieu of Husband in an election scheduled for May 13. Tryon thus hoped to cross the Haw without opposition by departing Hillsborough on the eleventh. It is difficult to judge if the Regulators really intended to confront him at the Haw. Tryon's orders for the tenth included the warning that the army would march the next day, and, as during the 1768 confrontation, the Regulators were usually well aware of the militia's plans and able to mobilize with great speed.

131. Tryon's fears of a night attack were possibly groundless. One Regulator's account written down many years later claimed that they knew nothing of Tryon's advance until the day before the battle. Account of Joseph McPherson, *Regulator Documents*, 569. Some of the leaders certainly knew, but that information apparently did not lead them to plan an attack or more of the men would have known of Tryon's proximity.

132. Petition of inhabitants of Orange County, May 15, 1771, *Regulator Documents*, 453–54.

133. These were the words that Governor Tryon had used in instructing the militia units he had deployed to resist an attempt to march on New Bern back in February. *Regulator Documents*, 341. Defensive force was always more legitimate.

134. Keegan, *History of Warfare*, 389–90. This term was first introduced by Hanson, *The Western Way of War.* This notion of decisive battle will be revisited in chapter 4.

135. It is significant to note how Tryon characterized the Regulators' behavior as "Indian-like." His journal's commentary on the retreat of Waddell says they used "many Indian shouts" to intimidate his men. Tryon's Journal (1771), *TC*

2:719. After the battle at Alamance, he would characterize them as a "desperate and cruel Enemy." *Regulator Documents*, 459.

136. Tryon's Journal (1771), *TC* 2:721.

137. For an example of attitudes to whipping of officials early in the Regulation, see the interview with former Regulator Joseph Macpherson, *Regulator Documents*, 565.

138. Ibid., 569.

139. Tryon acknowledged during a council of war that in their situation delay was dangerous, and that they should attack the Regulators as soon as possible. Samuel Cornell to Elias Debrosses, June 6, 1771, enclosed with Earl of Dunmore to Earl of Hillsborough, June 20, 1771, ER 13–10. After the victory at Alamance, Tryon received a letter from some citizens in Wilmington who had heard of the battle but were unclear of the exact results. They requested that he send an official account of the battle: "if government has had the advantage, it will inspirit many to inlist whose doubts at present make them backward." Archibald Maclain, William Hooper, et al. to Tryon, May 23, 1771, *TC* 2:750–51. One of Tryon's accounts of the battle is his response to this "committee." The account he sent the committee differed significantly in his relation of the numbers of troops and the success of his artillery from the more pessimistic official one he sent to Hillsborough. Tryon to the Committee at Wilmington, published in the *South Carolina Gazette*, June 13, 1771, *TC* 2:740–41, and Tryon to Hillsborough, May 18, 1771, *Regulator Documents*, 458–59. Arthur Benning claimed to have joined a group of gentlemen in a volunteer light horse organization raised in Wilmington after Tryon's departure, which was ready to assist "if occasion had required it." Loyalist claim of Arthur Benning (PRO AO13/117/20).

140. That such a perception was not Tryon's alone can be seen in a letter by one "Atticus" published in the *Virginia Gazette*, November 7, 1771 (reprinted in *Regulator Documents*, 517–26). The letter is in general highly critical of Tryon's conduct in inflaming the countryside and in his post-battle activities (discussed below) but acknowledges that, given the Regulators' assembling in arms, Tryon acted in the only way possible and had successfully "vanquished a Host of Scoundrels whom you had made intrepid by Abuse."

141. Tryon to the Regulators, May 16, 1771, *Regulator Documents*, 456. That this legal maneuvering was critical in establishing legitimacy for his later actions will be seen in the debate over Tryon's adherence to the "rules," which surfaced in the newspapers after the battle (see below). Tryon tried to send this response to the Regulators on the night of the fifteenth, but his courier encountered "unpleasantness" in the Regulator camp and returned without delivering it. Tryon's Journal (1771), *TC* 2:721. The one-hour provision was probably added in the version that Tryon delivered the next day, of which a copy survives.

142. There is significant variation in the accounts of the battle, particularly of the prebattle negotiations. The following is a composite of Tryon's journal (1771), *TC* 721–22; Caruthers, *Caldwell*, 147–66; Foote, *Sketches*, 60–61; Joseph

Macpherson's (a Regulator) account, in *Regulator Documents*, 569–70; Fitch, *Some Neglected History*, 185–232; Samuel Cornell to Elias Debrosses, June 6, 1771, enclosed with Earl of Dunmore to Earl of Hillsborough, June 20, 1771, ER 13–10; and a variety of newspaper accounts from the period, some of which purported to be letters from North Carolinians, most of which have been reprinted in *Regulator Documents*, 469–70, 471–72, 487–89, 501–3; also in NCCR 8:647.

143. The prebattle scuffles are described by Samuel Cornell, a participant in the militia army. Samuel Cornell to Elias Debrosses, June 6, 1771, enclosed with Earl of Dunmore to Earl of Hillsborough, June 20, 1771, ER 13–10.

144. Ibid.

145. There is little doubt about Thompson's death; the story appears in a number of sources. The question is whether this constituted a "first shot" that opened the battle. The armies were close enough that apparently many Regulators saw Tryon shoot Thompson.

146. Here again, there is a great deal of confusion on this point. A number of accounts accuse Tryon of firing before the expiration of the truce period. For us the interest lies not so much in whether he did break the truce, but in the fact that the question of his breaking the rules of war occupied so much attention in the post-battle discussion of his actions.

147. Some sources indicate that many of the Regulators had come unarmed. Caruthers, *Caldwell*, 147–48. But there were certainly sufficient armed Regulators to contest the battle for two hours.

148. The Regulators apparently asked James Hunter to take command, but he refused, saying "we are all freemen; and everyone must command himself." Caruthers, *Caldwell*, 163. Caruthers noted that one Montgomery acted as a captain, as did James Pugh (who was later hanged in Hillsborough). Ibid., 156, 166.

149. Again, note the difficulty between attempts to observe conventional forms and the actions of individuals either "ignorant of any signals or terms of war" or too inflamed by the moment to stop. Quote from *Virginia Gazette*, August 15, 1771, *Regulator Documents*, 501.

150. Tryon did not recount the incident in this way, though it is interesting to compare his description. He said "the Enemy took to Tree Fighting and much annoyed the Men who stood at the Guns which obliged Me to cease the Artillery for a short Time and to advance the first Line to force the Rebels from their Covering." Tryon to Hillsborough, May 18, 1771, *Regulator Documents*, 458–59.

151. Some sources contend that the Regulators retreated only when they had run out of ammunition.

152. This number was much debated at the time, but Tryon's return of troops dated May 22, 1771, seems fairly indisputable.

153. The various estimates of Regulator casualties are primarily in different newspaper accounts of the battle. See *TC* 2:740–41; *Regulator Documents*, 470, 471. Kay claims 17 to 20 Regulators killed without citing a source. "The North

Carolina Regulation," 103. Caruthers claimed only 9 Regulators were killed based on interviews with old Regulators. *Caldwell*, 157. A private letter from Samuel Johnston to Thomas Barker, June 10, 1771, listed the variety of casualty reports present in the rumor mill at that time, giving a spread for the Regulators' dead of 15 to 300. *Regulator Documents*, 476. Samuel Cornell, a militia participant, claimed 300 killed and wounded. Samuel Cornell to Elias Debrosses, June 6, 1771, enclosed with Earl of Dunmore to Earl of Hillsborough, June 20, 1771, ER 13–10. The Moravians recorded an eyewitness who claimed at least 13 dead Regulators with a number of other bodies found later. *Moravian Records*, 1:460.

154. Whether such decisiveness was real or apparent is not the issue. Contemporaries believed in the decisiveness of battle (see chap. 4). Gruber, "British Strategy," 22, 24; Duffy, *Military Experience*, 189–90; Conway, *War of American Independence*, 23, 34; Weigley, *Age of Battles*, xii, 536; Ostwald, "The 'Decisive' Battle of Ramillies"; Howard, *War in European History*, 70–71.

155. Recall that the very fact of battle in one sense released him from the legal requirements of the Johnston Act.

156. A survey of Tryon's correspondence shows that he referred to the Regulators as "insurgents" or the "people who style themselves regulators" right up to the battle. See, for example, *Regulator Documents*, 338, 340, 347; NCCR 8:538, 541–42. The use of "rebels" began in his post-battle proclamation to the troops and continued in his later correspondence. *Regulator Documents*, 430, 435.

157. *Moravian Records*, 1:458; *Regulator Documents*, 570; Caruthers, *Caldwell*, 158; *Boston Gazette*, October 21, 1771, NCCR 8:648; Tryon to Hillsborough, August 1, 1771, NCCR 8:651; letter of "Atticus" to Tryon in *Virginia Gazette*, November 7, 1771, *Regulator Documents*, 522; Kars, "Breaking Loose," 414. There is some controversy over why Few was hanged and whether a trial was held first. It seems clear, however, that it was an unnecessary, summary action.

158. Tryon to Hillsborough, August 1, 1771, NCCR 8:649–50; quote from Tryon to Fanning, May 24, 1771, NCCR 8:714; Tryon's Journal (1771), TC 2:724, 726–27; *Boston Gazette*, July 1771, NCCR 8:615; *Moravian Records*, 1:461.

159. *Moravian Records*, 1:462; letter of "Atticus" to Tryon, *Regulator Documents*, 524.

160. Tryon's Proclamation, June 9, 1771, NCCR 8:617.

161. TC 2:730, 840; *Boston Gazette*, July 22, 1771, NCCR 8:643; Tryon to Hillsborough, August 1, 1771, NCCR 8:650; Kars, "Breaking Loose," 420–22.

162. English authorities usually found ways to accuse many people, pardon large numbers of them, try a smaller number, convict yet a smaller number, and actually execute even fewer. Apparent exceptions were often remembered as unusually harsh, such as the "Bloody Assizes" following Monmouth's Rebellion. The crackdown in the Highlands after 1745 is another obvious exception but can be explained in terms of its ethnic dimension (the broader English support for the

1715 rising tempered judicial retaliation after that revolt). See Coward, *The Stuart Age*, 295; Lyle, *The Rebellion of Jack Cade*, 15; Woolrych, *Penruddock's Rising*, 21; Gilmour, *Riot, Risings, and Revolution*, 53, 69; Prebble, *Culloden*, 243–46. The application of mercy in a broader judicial context has been interpreted as a mechanism for the maintenance of authority by elites, allowing them the conspicuous use of mercy in the context of a severe penal code. While this is undoubtedly correct, the long tradition of its use had created a popular expectation of mercy; large-scale executions were still shocking. See Hay, "Property, Authority," 17–64, and a critique of his position in Langbein, "Albion's Fatal Flaws." For the similarly functioning legal system in Ireland and Scotland, see Connolly, "Albion's Fatal Twigs."

163. Tryon's Proclamation, May 17, 1771, NCCR 8:608; Tryon's Proclamation, May 21, 1771, NCCR 8:610–11; William Johnston to Mr. Bencham, June 7, 1771, NCCR 8:614. Tryon excepted a variety of people from this offer, including his current prisoners and other specified individuals. Tryon also repeatedly extended the deadline for taking advantage of the amnesty offer.

164. Martin to Hillsborough, December 26, 1771, NCCR 9:78. Governor Martin also recorded that they turned in between 700 and 800 stand of arms.

165. Martin to Hillsborough, December 12, 1771, NCCR 9:68–69; Assembly Journals, December 7, 1771, NCCR 9:169; Hillsborough to Martin, April 1, 1772, NCCR 9:274–75.

166. Martin to Hillsborough, October 18, 1771, NCCR 9:36; Hillsborough to Martin, December 4, 1771, NCCR 9:66. King George III also, on August 22, 1771, sent a proclamation to North Carolina announcing that he had heard of the abuses of public officials and listed several measures to be taken to prevent them. *Regulator Documents*, 508.

167. Assembly to Martin, January 28, 1773, NCCR 9:454.

168. Martin to Hillsborough, July 8, 1772, NCCR 9:311.

169. Ibid., March 8, 1772, NCCR 9:268–69.

170. NCCR 9:333–38.

171. Martin to Hillsborough, April 12, 1772, NCCR 9:278.

172. Martin describes the meeting in Martin to Hillsborough, August 30, 1772, NCCR 9:329–33.

173. Ibid., 330 (some punctuation inserted). Martin wrote a similar letter to Lord Dartmouth, November 28, 1772, NCCR 9:357–58.

174. The Moravian diaries indicate their worries along these lines. *Moravian Records*, 1:456–57, 459–60. Tryon's march around the countryside after the battle was calculated to prevent continued resistance. See also the letter of James Iredell to his father, June 15, 1771, in which he expressed a horror of "the miseries of civil war, but how much more horrid, to have property insecure, and lives held at the will of a parcel of Banditti." *Papers of James Iredell*, 1:71.

175. Tryon's Journal (1771), TC 2:723.

176. Ibid., 2:725. The Regulators also apparently stopped and searched some

Moravian wagons near the South Carolina border, but they were allowed to pass without violence. *Moravian Records*, 1:466, 2:653–54.

177. *Moravian Records*, 1:459–60.

178. Caruthers, *Caldwell*, 147–48.

179. Kars, "Breaking Loose," 416; *Moravian Records*, 2:461; Foote, *Sketches*, 63. Tryon's fears of further resistance appear in the account of Merrill's capture as well. Tryon believed that Merrill had been at the battle and had afterward tried to raise more troops. *TC* 2:727.

180. For Waddell's orders, see *TC* 2:777; *Moravian Records*, 1:469, 470.

181. Martin to Hillsborough, October 18, 1771, NCCR 9:36–37.

182. *Virginia Gazette*, May 30, 1771; *Virginia Gazette*, June 6, 1771; *Massachusetts Spy*, June 27, 1771; letter of a North Carolinian printed in the *Virginia Gazette*, August 15, 1771; *Boston Gazette*, October 21, 1771. Tryon's defenders deny this charge in *Virginia Gazette*, August 29, 1771 (bylined New Bern, July 27); *Virginia Gazette*, December 5, 1771; and *Virginia Gazette*, September 17, 1771. These newspaper accounts are extracted, respectively, in *Regulator Documents*, 469–70, 471–72, 491–92, 501–3; NCCR 8:647; *Regulator Documents*, 508–15, 529–33, 517–26.

183. See the sources in the previous note and also the letter of "Atticus" to Governor Tryon in *Virginia Gazette*, November 7, 1771, *TC* 2:820–23.

184. Letter of "Atticus" to Governor Tryon in *Virginia Gazette*, November 7, 1771.

185. *Massachusetts Spy*, June 27, 1771.

186. *Boston Gazette*, July 22, 1771.

187. *Virginia Gazette*, September 17, 1771; *Virginia Gazette*, August 29, 1771 (bylined New Bern, July 27).

188. Gould, "Collective Violence and Group Solidarity," 356–80.

189. Even Samuel Johnston, the author of the Johnston Riot Act, noted that the whole affair could have been avoided "had not the governor been influenced by some who had received personal insults from these people." Samuel Johnston to Thomas Barker, June 10, 1771, *Regulator Documents*, 476. Johnston's brother Henry also demurred from participating in the militia army marching against the Regulators, believing that it had been stirred up by the governor's circle, and that they should be the ones who had to deal with the consequences. Henry Johnston to Samuel Johnston, [March 1771], Hayes Collection, SHC. And we have seen how Governor Martin attributed the strong response of Tryon to the misrepresentations of the corrupt local officials.

190. The rapid military technological innovations of the twentieth century and the consequent speedy adoption of new forms of military violence constitutes an exception.

191. See the discussion in chapter 4.

192. The Regulators did not use demonization to initiate their movement. Their initial round of violence, as Roger Ekirch pointed out, was founded on a

country Whig ideology legitimizing resistance to a corrupt government. The patterns of that resistance were then determined by the legitimacy of form. Alternatively, the initial ideology of the Regulators could have been the "homestead ethic" suggested by Richard Maxwell Brown. Ekirch, "*Poor Carolina,*" 183–92; Brown, "Back Country Rebellions," passim.

Introduction to Part II

1. For a similar characterization of Anglo-American political culture, see Conway, "To Subdue America," 381.

2. Max Weber perceived that "if the institutions of the state do not succeed in attaining their prescribed goals within the limits of certain accepted rules, a loss of legitimacy of these institutions may result. . . . A loss of legitimacy of the state . . . is one of the fundamental conditions conducive to severe forms of political violence, crises and revolutions." Paraphrase of Weber by Zimmerman in *Political Violence,* 11.

3. Hanson, *The Western Way of War,* xv, 10.

4. I do not mean to privilege either the cultural or the rational as determinants of behavior in war. They coexisted. There is certainly a strong argument to be made that in war, "necessity" was the final law. I merely suggest that culture be reinserted in the equation. For another example of this problem in a different historiography, see Trigger, "Early Native North American Responses," 1195–1215.

5. Keegan, *History of Warfare,* 3, 5.

6. Dederer, *War in America,* 173–74. See a further discussion of providentialism in chapter 4.

7. Abler, "Scalping, Torture," 3.

8. Quote from Keegan, *History of Warfare,* 3.

9. Weinberg, *A World at Arms,* 124, 126, 217, 225, 232.

10. Dederer, *War in America,* 18–19.

4. Colonial Ways of War

1. Vattel, *Law of Nations,* 280.

2. Waterhouse, *A Declaration of the State,* 22–23.

3. For an excellent discussion of the earliest New England colonists' adaptation of the English militia to colonial requirements, see Breen, "The Covenanted Militia of Massachusetts Bay," 24–45.

4. The dates, origin, and nature of the military revolution are the subject of an expanding debate. Essays by exponents and opponents of the theory are collected in Rogers, ed., *The Military Revolution Debate.* See also important contributions by Parker, *Military Revolution;* Hale, *War and Society;* Black, *A Military Revolution?;* Downing, *The Military Revolution and Political Change;* and Eltis, *Military Revolution.*

5. For more detailed descriptions of sixteenth- and seventeenth-century European warfare on the continent, see Corvisier, *Armies and Societies in Europe*; Hale, *War and Society*; Anderson, *War and Society*; Parker, *Thirty Years War*; Lynn, *Giant of the Grand Siècle*; Black, ed., *European Warfare*.

6. Preston et al., *Men in Arms*, 116–20; Anderson, *War and Society*, 188, 196; Duffy, *Military Experience*, 10–13; Weigley, *Age of Battles*, 194–95.

7. See Gruber, "British Strategy," 14–31, for a discussion of the British variously favoring decisive battle or a "war of posts" (wearying the enemy). For decision in eighteenth-century battle, see Conway, *War of American Independence*, 23, 34; Duffy, *Military Experience*, 189–90; Weigley, *Age of Battles*, xii, 536–37; Ostwald, The 'Decisive' Battle of Ramillies"; Howard, *War in European History*, 70–71.

8. Weigley, *American Way of War*, 18–21.

9. For eighteenth-century military practice in general (in addition to the sources cited above), see Ropp, *War in the Modern World*, 40–59, 76–97; Strachan, *European Armies and the Conduct of War*, 8–37; Jones, *The Art of War in the Western World*, 267–319; Lynn, "Food, Funds, and Fortresses," 137–60; Van Creveld, *Supplying War*, 5–39. To the set of generalizations offered here, there are of course a host of exceptions. Defining those exceptions has created its own historiography. An excellent discussion of the development of European military practice and its influence on America is in Dederer, *War in America*, 85–111.

10. Parker, "Early Modern Europe," 41.

11. Parker explains the acceptance of these conventions as a result of the increasingly national character of armies, the decline of religion as an issue in war, the revulsion of the previous era, and the spread of reciprocity. Ibid., 51–55. These are all motivations for accepting and using the conventions. My list describes the sources for the conventions themselves.

12. For studies of the medieval development of the laws of war, see Johnson, *Ideology*, 26–80; Meron, *Henry's Wars and Shakespeare's Laws*, passim; Keen, *Laws of War in the Late Middle Ages*, passim; Contamine, *War in the Middle Ages*, 260–92. See also J. R. Hale's study on the impact, or lack thereof, of public opinion on the way of war in the fifteenth and sixteenth centuries: "War and Opinion," 18–33.

13. Dederer, *War in America*, 89–90, 164–65; Johnson, *Ideology*, 150–255; Johnson, *Just War Tradition*, 174–79.

14. Victoria, *De Indis Et De Jure Belli*; Grotius, *Law of War and Peace*; Vattel, *Law of Nations*. Victoria was published (posthumously) in 1557. Grotius was originally published in 1625, in English in 1654. See Donagan, "Atrocity," 1143, for a history of Grotius's appearance and influence in England. See Lepore, *The Name of War*, 107, for Grotius's influence in New England. Vattel's work was originally published in 1758.

15. Parker, "Early Modern Europe," 41.

16. A better term might be the "War of the Three Kingdoms." A recent trend in English historiography has rightly emphasized that the English Civil War was very

much a British and Irish event. Given the population of Scots and Scotch-Irish in North Carolina, it is appropriate that we too consider it as a War of Three Kingdoms. For the political implications of the three monarchies and how their divisions helped lead to war, see Russell, *The Fall of the British Monarchies*. For a reminder that there was more than one "kind" of war, depending on who the combatants were, see Carlton, *Going to the Wars*, 260–64.

17. Donagan, "Atrocity," 1137–66; Donagan, "Codes and Conduct"; Donagan, "Did Ministers Matter?"; Donagan, "Prisoners in the English Civil War"; Carlton, *Going to the Wars*; Roy, "England Turned Germany."

18. Roy, "England Turned Germany," 127–29; Donagan, "Codes and Conduct," 68–73; Donagan, "Atrocity," 1154. Donagan outlines the "classic" atrocity narrative, which began with an insistence on the fact of massacre, and then emphasized its cold-blooded nature (hot-blooded acts carried less guilt). Such narratives then related circumstantial details peripheral to the main act such as particularly egregious individual horrors or counterclaims that it was in reprisal for other deeds. There are many such published narratives. For one vivid example, see Cranford, *The Teares of Ireland*. For discussions of atrocity narratives from the 1641 rebellion in Ireland, see Barnard, "Crises of Identity," 50–53; Canny, "What Really Happened in Ireland in 1641?" 24–42.

19. Donagan, "Codes and Conduct," 71–73. Another motif that emerges in the Irish atrocity narratives was the stripping of women and children "naked" and turning them out of doors. See, for example, Cranford, *Teares of Ireland*, 21, 24. It did not at first occur to me as a motif, because it did not seem as flagrant as the other violent acts in the narratives. Upon reading the Loyalist claims from after the Revolution, however, it was intriguing to note the persistence of this phraseology in many of their descriptions of what had happened to them at the hands of the Whigs (see chap. 7).

20. Roy, "England Turned Germany," 134–41.

21. Donagan, "Atrocity," 1138. In Donagan's examples, the conventions were as yet "uncodified" in England because Grotius's work, for example, did not appear in English until 1654.

22. Donagan, "Atrocity," 1146, 1154–55.

23. The following discussion of codes of conduct during the English Civil War is based on Donagan's excellent articles, which will not be cited further except in the case of direct quotes.

24. Karen Kupperman has documented one example of how powerful that concern for the proper treatment of prisoners could be. In 1640, the English officials of the Providence Island Company ordered the arrest and return of the acting governor of the Providence Island Company when they learned that he had executed Spanish soldiers who had given themselves up on the promise of free quarter. The company called it "a crime so heinous, so contrary to religion and to the law of Nature and Nations that it ought not to escape without punishment." *Providence Island*, 292, 294.

25. Even in the case of a stormed city, some limitations were observed.

Donagan writes that in the case of a stormed city, "anything short of rape or mutilation was permissible." "Atrocity," 1149.

26. By the eighteenth century, this point of no return became associated with the approach of siege trenches to a certain distance from the walls. The completion of those trenches usually led the attacker to offer surrender terms. Several examples of this tradition can be seen in the conduct of the British and American forces during the Revolution, discussed in chapters 7 and 8.

27. Donagan, "Codes and Conduct," 80. The understanding of the legitimacy of retaliation did not *necessarily* include a provision for revenge in only equal measure. In 1638, when the magistrates of the Massachusetts Bay Colony considered the case of Sequin, an Indian who it appeared had used the Pequots to help him avenge himself against English colonists at Weathersfield and thus set off the Peqot War, they allowed that his was a just revenge. They noted "that, if the cause were thus, Sequin might, upon this injury first offered by them [the colonists at Weathersfield], right himself either by force or fraud, and that by the law of nations; and though the damage he had done them had been one hundred times more than what he sustained from them, that is not considerable in point of a just war; neither was he bound (upon such an open act of hostility publicly maintained) to seek satisfaction first in a peaceable way; it was enough, that he had complained of it as an injury and breach of covenant." Winthrop, *Journal of John Winthrop*, 252.

28. [Charles I], *Proclamation for the better government.*

29. See especially Donagan's case study of Lostwithiel in "Codes and Conduct," 81ff.

30. Grotius wavered on this issue. While he tried to make "natural law" his criterion, which theoretically would encompass all of humanity, he allowed that natural law had been developed by civilized practice. He thus qualified its applicability to "all those that are more advanced in civilization." *Law of War and Peace*, 1:42. See also Donagan, "Atrocity," 1139; Lepore, *The Name of War*, 11; Sheehan, *Savagism and Civility*, 3. Sheehan's definitions are discussed more completely below.

31. Leach, *Custom, Law, and Terrorist Violence*, 27 (emphasis in original).

32. Carlton, "Going to the Wars," 33–36, 260–63. Donagan, "Did Ministers Matter," 152, notes the different quality of the war in Ireland but believes that "professional prudence or reciprocal obligation and honor" prevented the wholesale killing of prisoners.

33. Parker, "Early Modern Europe," 56.

34. Vattel, *Law of Nations*, 293.

35. Common soldiers, although unfamiliar with Grotius, were well acquainted with the articles of war. In the Parliamentary army, for example, they were read aloud at every pay and at the general rendezvous. Donagan, "Codes and Conduct," 84.

36. See Donagan, "Atrocity," 1139, for commentary on the importance of the reliability of the given word.

37. Johnson, *Just War Tradition*, 188–89. See also Starkey, *European and Native American*, 47, and Duffy, *Military Experience*, 13, for further discussion of real fears both of enraged peasantries and of undercutting their own food supply through the mistreatment of civilians.

38. Anderson, *War and Society*, 191–94; Robson, "The Armed Forces and the Art of War," 163–74; Duffy, *Military Experience*, 10–13. Although not discussed specifically below, the official British Articles of War from James II's articles of 1688 through those of 1765 reflected the increasing precision of military law, some of which was designed to protect noncombatants. They are reprinted in Winthrop, *Military Law and Precedents*, 920–46.

39. Samuel Bever and Samuel Johnson, *The Cadet*, quoted in Gruber, "British Strategy," 21.

40. Simes, *Military Guide*, 2, quote from p. 108.

41. Bland, *Treatise*, 237. See also his discussion of "Party-Blews," ibid., 186–87.

42. Stevenson, *Military Instructions*, 69–70, 117.

43. Ibid., 102, 119.

44. Ibid., 119, 152.

45. *Orderly Book—Expedition to Martinique, November 15, 1761 to January 18, 1762.*

46. Bowler, "Logistics and Operations," 69. Bowler thought that British commanders felt the same way, but see the important article by Conway, "To Subdue America," 381–407, for a look at the conflict of opinion among British officers over whether to prefer a scorched earth over a "hearts and minds" policy. For colonial views on foraging, see Higginbotham, "Early American Way of War," 291.

47. Bland, *Treatise*, 152; see also Simes, *Military Guide*, 158–65, for a lengthy treatment of the steps of negotiating terms during a siege.

48. Simes, *Military Guide*, 152.

49. On another level, the destruction of fruit trees and orchards was considered significantly worse than the burning of other arable crops. Mintz, *Seeds of Empire*, 137; Martin, *Ordinary Courage*, 74; Bland, *The Souldier's March*, 26; Vattel, *Law of Nations*, 292–93.

50. Johnson, *Just War Tradition*, 208. See also Christopher Duffy's interpretation of the limited extent to which the eighteenth century was an improvement over earlier eras in *Frederick the Great*, 295. Recently there have been a number of important works on the subject: Starkey, "War and Culture"; Starkey, "Paoli to Stony Point"; Conway, "'The Great Mischief Complain'd of'"; Conway, "Military-Civilian Crime"; and Geoffrey Parker's and Harold Selesky's contributions to Howard et al., eds., *Laws of War*, 40–58, 59–85.

51. Adams, *Grounds of Confidence*, 4 (emphasis in the original).

52. Dederer, *War in America*, 170–71; John Drayton to North Carolina Governor Thomas Burke, July 6, 1781, NCSR 15:511; Brown, *The Good Americans*, 102.

53. Since our concern is with violence *in* war, just war theory remains peripheral to this discussion. It did, however, develop in conjunction with the rules about conduct in war, and we will see some of its impact in the beginning of the American Revolution.

54. For a theory on how Western culture came to accept the dominance of the battle form as its way of war, see Hanson, *The Western Way of War*, xv, 10. See also Keegan, *History of Warfare*, 389–90.

55. Drayton to North Carolina Governor Thomas Burke, July 6, 1781, NCSR 15:511–12. Similarly, the Plymouth colony in June 1676 announced that they would not execute any Indian prisoners who "killed his enimie in the feild in a souldier like way." Shurtleff, ed., *Records of the Colony of New Plymouth*, 5:205.

56. Vattel, *Law of Nations*, 338. The legitimation of a rebellion by virtue of its own success has become enshrined in modern international law. Rebels can now achieve status as "belligerents," and therefore protection under the international law of war, by meeting several criteria. One of those criteria is the occupation of a substantial part of the national territory in dispute. As Heather Wilson writes, international recognition now hinges on "the military and political success of the movement and the degree to which it resembled a sovereign State." Wilson, *International Law and the Use of Force*, 23, 25. See also Andreopoulos, "The Age of National Liberation," 197–98; U.S. Department of the Army, *The Law of Land Warfare*, 9, 25.

57. For rebels' lack of rights under the laws of war, see Grotius, *Law of War and Peace*, 1:139. But note the argument in Johnson, *Ideology*, 212–13, that Grotius did not intend to grant complete freedom from regulation.

58. Donagan, "Atrocity," 1140–41.

59. Cited in Parker, *Military Revolution*, 100.

60. Lloyd, *A Discourse of God's Ways*, 20.

61. Ibid., 50. Lloyd went on to differentiate between a conquest made in a just cause versus an unjust cause, and the possibility that conquered subjects might have to distinguish between them. For the power of providentialist views of war in colonial America, see Anderson, *A People's Army*, 196–223; Stuart, "'For the Lord is a man of Warr,'" 528; Lepore, *The Name of War*, 106 ff; Fischer, *Paul Revere's Ride*, 271. See also the contrary view in Endy, "Just War."

62. Hill, *Celtic War*, 1–6, for the continuity of a "celtic" style of war, which included a tradition of guerilla warfare.

63. Brown, *Bloodfeud in Scotland*, 258. The bloodfeud continued to be recognized in the Scottish court system until the 1640s.

64. This and the following discussion of the Scotch-Irish are based primarily on Leyburn, *Scotch-Irish*, 105, 114, 120, 123–25; and Miller, "Non-Professional Soldiery," 320–26. David Fischer makes a broader argument about the Scotch-Irish representing a "borderer" culture, more militarily inclined, although less than conventionally "European" in its practices. In fact, Fischer rests much of his construction of the culture of the Scotch-Irish and the borderer communities upon

their experience of endemic violence. *Albion's Seed*, 617–18, 629. Maldwyn A. Jones notes that in Ireland, the Scotch-Irish lived in a hostile environment, with resultant "profound psychological effects. . . . [They] lived in [Ulster] in scattered settlements protected by castles, bawns, and fortified houses but surrounded by the dispossessed and resentful native Irish, whom they despised." "The Scotch-Irish in British America," 290–91. See also McWhiney's *Cracker Culture* and his "Ethnic Roots," and Nobles's discussion of those works in "Breaking into the Backcountry," 651–52.

65. Leyburn, *Scotch-Irish*, 114.

66. Ibid., 24; see also Carlton, *Going to the Wars*, 33–36. The 1641 rebellion inspired a tremendous outpouring of atrocity narratives in England.

67. Leyburn, *Scotch-Irish*, 127.

68. Axtell, *The European and the Indian*, 273.

69. Hirsch, "Collision of Military Cultures," passim. See also Abler, "Scalping, Torture," passim; Lepore, *The Name of War*, 96, 112; Starkey, *European and Native American*, 25–31, 101ff.

70. For native tactical styles, see Mahon, "Anglo-American Methods," 259–60; Malone, *Skulking Way of War*, 9, and passim; Corkran, *Cherokee Frontier*, 207–21; Eid, "'A Kind of Running Fight,'" passim; Starkey, *European and Native American*, 22; Way, "The Cutting Edge of Culture," passim.

71. There are a number of sieges described in Steele, *Warpaths*: Powhatan's siege of Jamestown in 1609 (43), the Cherokee siege of Fort Loudoun in 1760 (231), and the sieges of Fort Detroit, Fort Pitt, and Fort Niagara in 1761 (238). See also Keener, "Iroquois Assault Tactics." The question of casualties or relative intensity in Indian warfare is disputed. See below and Jennings, *Invasion of America* 150–51; Richter, "War and Culture," 535; Ferling, *Wilderness*, 36–38; Hirsch, "Collision of Military Cultures," 1190–91; Vaughan, *New England Frontier*, xix–xxii; Lepore, *The Name of War*, 116ff.

72. Richter, "War and Culture," 535; Hirsch, "Collision of Military Cultures," 1191. John Lawson described Indian warfare in early-eighteenth-century North Carolina as mostly "Ambuscades, and surprizes, which methods are commonly used by the Savages; for I scarce ever heard of a Field-Battle fought amongst them." *A New Voyage to Carolina*, 208.

73. Hirsch, "Collision of Military Cultures," 1190, 1191.

74. Governor Robert Johnson to Board of Trade, December 15, 1732, NCSR 11:22.

75. See, for example, Wright, *Study of War*, 1:58, 71, 77–78, 82; Turney-High, *Primitive War*, passim, 205–7. There are good short reviews of this ongoing debate in anthropological circles in Krech, "Genocide in Tribal Society," 14–15; Keegan, *History of Warfare*, 84–94; Milner, "Warfare," 108–9. See also Ewers, "Intertribal Warfare," 397–410; Ferguson and Farragher, *The Anthropology of War*, iii–iv; Ferguson and Whitehead, eds., *War in the Tribal Zone*, passim. My thanks to Elizabeth Fenn for discussions on this issue.

76. Keeley, *War before Civilization*. His use of statistics has inspired some criticism. See Meilinger, "Review," 598–602.

77. George Milner has recently surveyed the archaeological evidence for precontact warfare in North America and argues for a range of possible severity in primitive war, from low-casualty ritualized war to large war-party assaults resulting in many deaths. Milner does point out, however, that "single catastrophic attacks" resulting in the deaths of most or all of a community have not been recorded in the eastern woodlands area (there is evidence for such attacks in the plains). "Warfare," passim.

78. Richter, "War and Culture," 537. Rountree supports this general notion of war restrained by population loss in "Summary and Implications," 221. Some scholars have estimated that disease wiped out more than three-quarters of the eastern Indian population in the sixteenth and seventeenth centuries. Cronon, *Changes in the Land*, 85–91; Cook, "The Significance of Disease," 501.

79. Richter, "War and Culture," passim; Starkey, *European and Native American*, 25.

80. As noted in Rountree, "Summary and Implications," 221; Jennings, *Invasion of America*, 150–51; Hirsch "Collision of Military Cultures," 1191.

81. There is a whole literature growing around this subject, but see, for example, Steele, *Warpaths*, 189–90; Duffy, *Military Experience*, 268–79; Russell, "Redcoats in the Wilderness"; Paret, "Colonial Experience." See also Beattie, "The Adaptation of the British Army," 82, for a restatement of the position that conditions in North America probably influenced even the regular, professional portions of the British army but more certainly added a whole new set of auxiliary troops.

82. Starkey, *European and Native American*.

83. Mahon, "Anglo-American Methods," passim; Weller, "Irregular but Effective," 120, 126–27; Axtell, *The European and the Indian*, 300–302. See also Way, "The Cutting Edge," 132–33, 138, 142, for the readiness with which European regulars fighting in America adapted some native practices of war.

84. Robert Jones, Jr., to Edmund Fanning, July 25, 1765, Fanning-McCulloh Papers, NCA.

85. This is not to say that all Indian groups had the same cultural conception of war, merely that they were all different from the European conception.

86. See, in particular, Hirsch, "Collision of Military Cultures," passim; and Abler, "Scalping, Torture," passim (although as Ronald Karr has pointed out, Hirsch has ignored the Irish precedent: Karr, "'Why Should You Be So Furious,'" passim). Also essential to this discussion are Dederer, *War in America*, 127, 129–36; Malone, *Skulking Way of War*, passim; Ferling, *Wilderness*, 29–54; Rountree, "The Powhatans and the English," 173–205; Gleach, *Powhatan's World*, 157–69. See also Neil Whitehead's discussion of M. Taussig, *Shamanism, Colonialisms, and the Wild Man: A Study in Terror and Healing* (Chicago: Chicago University Press, 1987). Whitehead notes that the "projection of wild and savage qualities

... onto the colonised leads to the mimetic reflection of that projection in the acts of brutality of the colonisers. Indian 'savagery' or Caribbean 'cannibalism' thus justify Spanish massacres and punitive raids *a fuego y sangre.*" Ralegh, *The Discoverie*, 38.

87. Richter, "War and Culture," 529–35; Anderson, *Chain Her by One Foot*, 169–78; Jennings, *Invasion of America*, 152. The practice of adoptive war among southern Indian groups has not been as well explored. For the southeastern Algonquian groups, see Rountree, *Powhatan Foreign Relations*, 50, 221. There is some scattered evidence that the Cherokees, members of the Iroquoian language group, also practiced adoptive war. See Hatley, *The Dividing Paths*, 150–51.

88. As part of the wider disagreement about just how "savage" Indian war was, there is some argument as to whether Indians routinely killed women and children. See Ferling, *Wilderness*, 35, versus Jennings, *Invasion of America*, 151, and Hirsch, "Collision of Military Cultures," 1191. There is fairly strong agreement, however, that the eastern tribes did not rape captive women. See below.

89. Evidence for the English sense of outrage at this practice was the long-lived demand for, and popular interest in, the return of female captives who had married into a tribe. Demos, *Unredeemed Captive*. James Axtell believes, in fact, that after about 1753 Indians focused their capture efforts on women and children because they were the most likely to be successfully adopted (Axtell does not distinguish between different Indian groups in this article). Axtell, "White Indians," 58.

90. Seaver, *A Narrative of the Life*, 27–28. See John Demos's discussion of the internal logic of this "ruthlessness" in the face of harsh conditions and a long march. *Unredeemed Captive*, 24, 29, 33, 38–39.

91. For detailed discussion of the torture rituals practiced in adoptive war, see Richter, "War and Culture," 533–34; Anderson, *Chain Her by One Foot*, 169–78. The first English colonists in New England were not immediately in contact with the Iroquois tribes who practiced adoptive war, but they were well aware of the practice (if inflated by rumor) as early as 1634. Wood, *New England's Prospect*, 75–76. Even Roger Williams, usually sympathetic to the New England Indians, almost a cultural relativist, displayed a distinct anxiousness when it came to cannibalism. *A Key into the Language*, chapter 7.

92. For an attempt to catalog and categorize eastern torture rituals, see Knowles, "The Torture of Captives." One sample selection of captivity narratives that includes torture tales is available in Drimmer, *Captured by the Indians*. For a non-Englishman's viewpoint, see Gallup, trans., *Memoir of a French and Indian War Soldier*, 107–10. Corkran asserts that the Cherokees also practiced ritual torture and cannibalism on their captives. *Cherokee Frontier*, 10. See below for other accounts of torture in early North Carolina.

93. Abler, "Scalping, Torture," 9, 12.

94. For a seemingly definitive answer to the scalping controversy (who started scalping, the Europeans or the Indians?), see Axtell, *The European and the Indian*, 207–41. See also Abler, "Scalping, Torture," 6–7. For an early depiction of a South

Carolina tribe scalping and dismembering enemy dead, see the widely disseminated late-sixteenth-century drawings of Jacques De Morgues in *The Work of Jacques Le Moyne De Morgues*, 2:plates 107 and 123.

95. Sheehan, *Savagism and Civility*, 58–59.

96. Rosenberg, "The Moral Order of Violence," 52, 55–56, 66–67, 107–9, 125, 265–84; Cox, "'A Proper Sense of Honour,'" 188.

97. Linebaugh, "The Tyburn Riot"; Ladenheim, "'The Doctors Mob.'"

98. Steele, *Betrayals*, 184.

99. Way, "Cutting Edge," 134.

100. Axtell, "White Indians," 67; Rowlandson, *The Sovereignty and Goodness*, editor's comments, 107n.82; Abler, "Scalping, Torture," 13; Dowd, *A Spirited Resistance*, 9–10.

101. Hirsch, "Collision of Military Cultures," 1200.

102. Underhill, *News from America*, 42–43.

103. William Shea argues that the feed fight was an innovation of early Virginia settlers born of inability to catch the Indians themselves. *Virginia Militia*, 20, 33. Malone, in contrast, argues that the early-seventeenth-century settlers of New England were merely practicing the "total war" style familiar to them from the religious wars. *Skulking Way of War*, 102. See also Karr, "'Why Should You Be So Furious,'" 179; Starkey, *European and Native American*, 41; Way "Cutting Edge," 135–36.

104. Jennings, *Invasion of America*, 153; Malone, *Skulking Way of War*, 103–4.

105. Lepore, *The Name of War*, 10; Sheehan, *Savagism*, 45.

106. Sheehan, *Savagism*, 1–3; Morgan, *American Slavery*, 18–20; Nash, "Red, White, and Black," 1–5. See also Karen Kupperman's recent argument for the many grounds of similarity between early-seventeenth-century English culture and Indian culture. *Indians and English*, passim.

107. The depth of this expectation can be seen in a North Carolina court's sentencing of "George Seneka an Indian Man of Bertie precinct," who had killed a woman and two children with an ax in 1726. He pleaded guilty, and in pronouncing the sentence the justices began with the standard legal phraseology: "not having the fear of God before his eyes but movd by the instigation of the Devil," but then added: "& his own Cruel Feirce & Savage nature." NCCR 2:664–65. It is only fair to note that this was a European perception; Indian warfare actually was structured elaborately, with its own internal rationality. See Gleach, *Powhatan's World*, 157–69, for a look at the different perceptions of the Indians and of the English on the events of 1622 in Virginia.

108. Steele, *Betrayals*, 155; *South Carolina Gazette*, February 14, 1774. See also Lepore's discussion of Indian attacks as atrocity narratives. *The Name of War*, 71–75. "Smashing children" was a recurrent trope from the English atrocity narratives of the seventeenth century. See Cranford, *Teares of Ireland*, 55, 68.

109. This was in part due to the Euro-Americans' repeated inability to distin-

guish between tribes. Reports of Indian violence often led to retaliation against the nearest Indians. The Paxton Boys (discussed below) were hardly an isolated example. See, for example, Lepore's discussion of the English treatment of the "Praying Indians" during King Philip's War. *The Name of War*, 140–41, 157. Other examples can be found in Knouff, "Soldiers and Violence," 177–78; Morgan, *American Slavery*, 259.

110. Lepore, *The Name of War*, 10, 16, 45. Hirsch, "Collision of Military Cultures," believed the Pequot War was the critical moment, while others have cited the Powhatan attack on Jamestown in 1622. Vaughan, "'Expulsion of the Salvages,'" 57–84; Shea, *Virginia Militia*. My sense is that it was a developing process, but one that was certainly in full force by the eighteenth century.

111. Solomon Stoddard to Governor Dudley, October 22, 1703, *New England Historical and Genealogical Register* 24 (1870): 269–70. See also John Leverett's comment that King Philip had attacked "without any just cause, or provocation given them" and then fought unfairly, perpetrating "many notorious barbarous and execrable murthers, villanies and outrages." John Leverett to "All People," September 12, 1676, cited in Lepore, *The Name of War*, 108.

112. Cited in editor's introduction to Wood, *New England's Prospect*, 12.

113. For other examinations of this process, see Nash, "Red, White, and Black"; Vaughan, "From White Man to Redskin"; Knouff, "Common People's Revolution," 248, 255.

114. Cited in Way, "Cutting Edge," 134.

115. First quote from Morgan, *American Slavery*, 233; second from Lepore, *The Name of War*, 112.

116. Percy, "'A Trewe Relacyon,'" 272.

117. Ibid., 272–73.

118. Shea, *Virginia Militia*, 36. There are other similar uses of pretended parleys to murder Indian representatives. See, for example, Morgan, *American Slavery*, 251.

119. Council to Virginia Company, April 4, 1623, and January 30, 1623/4, cited in Shea, *Virginia Militia*, 37; emphasis in original. Shea notes that the Virginians had been enraged by a massacre, an ambush and the killing of male prisoners, all committed by the Indians.

120. Benjamin Franklin, "A Narrative of the Late Massacres," in *Papers of Benjamin Franklin*, 11:56. The events of the incident are discussed by the editor of Franklin's papers, 11:42–47.

121. For but a few examples, see Knouff, "Soldiers and Violence," 188; Johnson, *Militiamen*, 89; Mintz, *Seeds of Empire*, 134–35, 149. Other examples from North Carolina follow.

122. See Lefler, *Colonial North Carolina*, 67–76, for a full account of the Tuscarora War.

123. Graffenried's Memoir is reprinted in NCCR 1:905–86; his knowledge of the manner of Lawson's death is on 933.

124. Christopher Gale to his sister, November 2, 1711, NCCR 1:826. Lefler, *Colonial North Carolina*, 69, lists other rumors current in North Carolina about the manner of Lawson's death.

125. Lawson, *A New Voyage to Carolina*, 53.

126. Ibid., 207. In contrast, Knowles's survey of the records of eastern Indian torture found little evidence for its practice among the Chesapeake Algonquians or even among the coastal southeastern Iroquois peoples. He did find evidence of torture among the Yamassees of South Carolina and noted Lawson's account as well. Knowles concluded, however, that such techniques may have been picked up from the Europeans. "The Torture of Captives," 164–67.

127. Colonel Spotswood to the Board of Trade, October 15, 1711, NCCR 1:810–13.

128. For the reality of the Tuscaroras' grievances (which were numerous) and public knowledge of them, see Dill, "Eighteenth-Century New Bern: Part III," 299–300; Lefler, *Colonial North Carolina*, 67.

129. Sheehan, *Savagism*, 63. See another discussion of perception versus reality in the early colonial experience in White, "Discovering Nature," 874–91.

130. Christopher Gale to his sister, November 2, 1711, NCCR 1:826.

131. Barbara Donagan, "Atrocity," illustrations on pp. 1145 and 1153; Cranford, *Teares of Ireland*, 22, 23, 55, 68.

132. Christopher Gale's Memorial to the South Carolina Assembly, NCCR 1:827–29.

133. Graffenried noted that "instead of assembling one or two small bodies of troops to operate against the savages, and drive them out of the frontier, and from their dwellings or Plantations, every one pretended to keep and defend his own house,—and, of course, the savages had a good opportunity to destroy one plantation after the other." Graffenried's Memoir, NCCR 1:948. See also North Carolina Council, Governor, and Assembly to Governor Spotswood, n.d., NCCR 1:838; Governor Spotswood to the Board of Trade, May 8, 1712, NCCR 1:839.

134. Christopher Gale's Memorial to the South Carolina Assembly, NCCR 1:827–29.

135. Journal of Virginia Council, October 15, 1711, NCCR 1:809.

136. Governor Pollock to the Proprietors of North Carolina, September 20, 1712, NCCR 1:879; Graffenried's Memoir, NCCR 1:954.

137. Journal of Virginia Council, October 24, 1711, NCCR 1:815; Journal of the South Carolina Assembly, October 26, 1711, NCCR 1:821; Lefler, *Colonial North Carolina*, 72.

138. Barnwell, "Journal of John Barnwell," 5:391–402, 6:42–55.

139. Ibid., 5:396.

140. Ibid., 6:43.

141. Ibid., 6:46.

142. Ibid., 6:54 (emphasis added).

143. In another recognition of the utility of certain rules, the North Carolina

Council acted to preserve the rules governing the sanctity of heralds or ambassadors when they discovered that an envoy from the Senecas sent to "caution" the Tuscaroras had been captured by a Yamassee. The Council arranged to buy him back and ensure his safe passage home. Council Journal, January 9, 1713, NCCR 2:1–2.

144. Graffenried's Memoir, NCCR 1:954.

145. Ibid., 1:946.

146. Lefler, *Colonial North Carolina*, 78–79.

147. NCSR 23:3. The law remained in force until 1741.

148. North Carolina Lords Proprietors to the Board of Trade, July 8, 1715, NCCR 2:188; petition of South Carolina agents to the Board of Trade, July 18, 1715, NCCR 2:196.

149. Wood, *Black Majority*, 127–30; Merrell, *Indians' New World*, 66–68, 75–78.

150. See, for example, incidents or fear of incidents in 1716 (NCCR 2:246), 1722 (NCCR 2:458), 1740 (NCCR 4:472), and Bishop Spangenburg's discussion of the chronic levels of hostility between the Tuscaroras and the whites that continued as late as 1752, NCCR 4:1313.

151. Governor Dobbs to the Assembly, May 10, 1759, NCCR 6:97; Anson and Orange County petitions, April 1760, NCCR 6:369, 374; *Moravian Records*, 1:133, 141, 158, 169, 179–82, 188, 206, 209–11, 227–33, 236, 273, 358, 361 (these references refer to Indian-white violence in Rowan County from 1755 to 1767).

152. A sampling of accounts of North Carolina's role in the French and Indian War includes Ekirch, "*Poor Carolina*," 179; Lefler, *Colonial North Carolina*, 138–50; Hamer, "Anglo-French Rivalry"; Hamer, "Fort Loudoun"; Corkran, *Cherokee Frontier*.

153. The following account is derived from Hamer, "Fort Loudoun," 455–57, and Corkran, *Cherokee Frontier*, 219–21.

154. As one example, the post-siege ambush at Fort Necessity in 1754 is described in Gallup, trans., *Memoir of Charles Bonin*, 101–3.

155. Incidents from 1765 (*North Carolina Gazette*, July 10, 1765); 1768 (*Boston Chronicle*, November 7–14, 1768, NCCR 7:864–66); and 1773 (NCCR 9:541) serve as examples.

156. Corkran, *Cherokee Frontier*, 8, 10; Reid, *A Better Kind of Hatchet*, 9–10. Lawson made similar observations about the eastern Carolina tribes' emphasis on wars pursued for revenge. *A New Voyage to Carolina*, 208–9. Richard White pointed out that native desires for revenge were incurred even for deaths on the battlefield—a kind of killing that European culture generally acknowledged as legitimate. *The Middle Ground*, 80.

157. For discussions of the legal development of the militia, see Gobbel, "The Militia of North Carolina"; Wheeler, "The Role of the North Carolina Militia," 1–27; Wheeler, "Development and Organization"; Kay and Price, "'To Ride the Wood Mare'"; Bartholomees, "Fight or Flee," 60ff.

158. Exemptions under the 1715 act included Anglican ministers, physicians, and "Chirurgeons," members of the Assembly, clerks of the courts, marshals, constables, deputies, attorneys, secretaries, justices of the peace who were not militia officers, former militia field officers or captains, and of course the lords proprietors themselves. NCSR 23:29. The 1746 act required servants as well as freemen to enlist and added millers and ferrymen to the exemption list. NCSR 23:244–47. It also required an annual regimental muster (the general muster) and company musters four times a year (the "private" musters). The latter requirement was reduced to twice a year in 1749 (NCSR 23:330) but raised to five by the exigencies of the French and Indian War in 1756 (NCSR 25:334–37). The act also exempted overseers and justices of the Supreme Court (overseers with officer's commissions were not exempted). The 1760 act, amended, reduced private musters to three annually and added Presbyterian ministers to the exemption list (NCSR 13:518–22). After 1760, the exemption list expanded rapidly prior to the Revolution, eventually to include coroners, road overseers, branch pilots, schoolmasters, Quakers, all Protestant ministers (with churches), commissioners of roads, "searchers," and those acting under a commission of the peace (see Wheeler, "Development and Organization," 317). Compare to the Virginia militia exemptions discussed in Titus, *Old Dominion at War*, 2.

159. Authority to march the militia out of the colony first appeared in the 1746 Militia Act, although it specified only deployment to South Carolina and Virginia. NCSR 23:244–47. See also Governor Dobbs to the Assembly, November 26, 1759, NCCR 6:119; Governor Dobbs to Secretary Pitt, July 21, 1760, NCCR 6:266. See Wheeler's discussion of this controversy, "Development and Organization," 315 and n. 37.

160. *Moravian Records*, 1:237.

161. Dobbs to the Board of Trade, 1761, NCCR 6:614.

162. Wheeler, *Historical Sketches*, 1:45–46; Titus, *Old Dominion at War*, 31n.22.

163. That is to say, it was the "largest problem" from the point of view of needing an effective military force. To many colonists, the "largest problem" was the intrusion of musters into their daily lives. This is the thesis of Kay and Price, "'To Ride the Wood Mare,'" in which they demonstrate the regressive nature of militia service as a kind of tax.

164. Governor Gabriel Johnston to Assembly, September 22, 1736, NCCR 4:228.

165. Legislative Journals, November 29, 1744, NCCR 4:745.

166. Alexander Mebane to Governor Dobbs, [summer 1755], NCCR 5:365; Governor Dobbs to Secretary Pitt, January 21, 1760, NCCR 6:221; Governor Dobbs to the Assembly, May 17, 1759, NCCR 6:111.

167. Governor Tryon's "Sketch of the Polity," 1767, NCCR 7:490–91.

168. Legislative Journal, May 21, 1741, NCCR 4:594; Hertford and Wake County Militia returns, May 28, 1772, and October 6, 1773, NCCR 9:311–12, 689; Boyd, "The Sheriff in Colonial North Carolina," 179.

169. Dobbs was accused of appointing too many foreigners. He replied to the Board of Trade that he had made some appointments based on military experience and that efforts to get locals to accept subaltern positions had gone unrewarded, so he had appointed recent arrivals instead. Governor Dobbs to Board of Trade, August 3, 1760, NCCR 6:282–84.

170. Dobbs to Board of Trade, March 15, 1756, NCCR 5:570–72.

171. John Barnwell was accused of carrying off Tuscarora captives in 1712 and selling them as slaves. Governor Spotswood to Board of Trade, July 26, 1712, NCCR 1:862. But see Lefler, *Colonial North Carolina*, 78. Roger Ekirch narrates two incidents of officers using their units' pay for themselves. "*Poor Carolina*," 117–18. In 1764, North Carolina created a ranger organization to "range and reconnoiter the frontiers of this Province as volunteers at . . . their own expense." NCSR 23:601. Their motivation was to collect the £30 proclamation money bounty on Indian scalps or prisoners.

172. Shea, *Virginia Militia*, 15.

173. For example, Robert Halton, Esq., a member of the North Carolina Council, volunteered as a captain in one of the companies raised to join the British expedition to the West Indies in 1740. NCCR 4:575. Similarly, Governor Dobbs arranged for his son to be an officer in the North Carolina troops sent to Virginia in 1769, much as Governor Caswell would later arrange a Continental army commission for his son. For the generally wealthy character of senior militia officers, see Kay and Price, "'To Ride the Wood Mare,'" 385–88. For use of officership as social enhancements, see Isaac, *Transformation of Virginia*, 104–10; Boucher, "The Colonial Militia," 125–30; Mayer, *Belonging to the Army*, 52–53.

174. Governor Dobbs to Secretary Pitt, May 29, 1760, NCCR 6:257–58; Lord Egremont to Dobbs, December 12, 1761, NCCR 6:593; Council Records, March 30, 1743, NCCR 4:633.

175. County-level appointments, like militia officers, were nominally made by the governor, but the counties' representatives in the Assembly naturally had enormous influence over that process. Ekirch, "*Poor Carolina*," 52, 73, 176; Boyd, "The Sheriff in Colonial North Carolina," 179; and Tilley, "Political Disturbances," 348–49. Compare to Titus, *Old Dominion at War*, 32–36.

176. John Sallis to Governor Dobbs, September 6, 1755, NCCR 5:424–25. This long letter and its follow-up on March 3, 1756, NCCR 5:566–67, are revealing commentaries on the functions and machinations of the militia in the mid-eighteenth century.

177. John Sallis to Governor Dobbs, March 3, 1756, NCCR 5:566–67.

178. Governor Dobbs to the Board of Trade, March 15, 1756, NCCR 5:570–72, 574.

179. Fred Anderson describes how military punishment was mediated by the "relatively smooth gradation of social status between privates and commanding officers." *A People's Army*, 126. Harold E. Selesky finds a similar pattern in Connecticut. *War and Society*, 187. See also Titus, *Old Dominion at War*, 4.

180. Governor Dinwiddie to Governor Dobbs, October 10, 1755, NCCR 5:438.

181. Wheeler, "Development and Organization," 309; Isaac, *Transformation of Virginia*, 104–10; Boucher, "The Colonial Militia," 125. For a description of a North Carolina militia muster, see *Moravian Records*, 1:110 (quoted in full in chap. 2).

182. Similar conclusions have been made by other historians for other colonies' militias. See, for example, Malone, *Skulking Way of War*, 117–25; Ferling, *Wilderness*, 43–48; Starkey, *European and Native American*, passim. The following review of evidence in North Carolina should merely reinforce the point.

183. There is a very entertaining narrative of the militia parading at a muster in Wilmington in 1775 in Andrews and McClean, eds., *Journal of a Lady of Quality*, 190.

184. James Johnson argues that the relative importance of the three different military organizations in colonial Georgia (the militia, the rangers, and the British regulars) could be gauged by their presence or absence in the annual official festivities such as the King's Birthday. *Militiamen*, 55, 67, 84.

185. Barnwell, *Journal*, 6:52–53.

186. Governor Dinwiddie to Colonel Innes, June 1754, NCCR 5:126–28.

187. Starkey, *European and Native American*, 45–46; Higginbotham, *George Washington*, chapter 1.

188. Governor Martin to Lord Hillsborough, October 25, 1772, NCCR 9:349.

189. Pickering, *An Easy Plan*, introduction, p. 11 (Pickering repaginated each chapter).

190. When Governor Tryon surveyed the new boundary with the Cherokees in 1767, he took with him a fifty-man militia escort, which he described as follows: "What they wanted in discipline they made up by a strict observance and willing obedience to all orders delivered to them. Each man had his rifle gun, and their general uniform and appointments were a carters frock, indian match clouts (in lieu of breeches) moccasons (for shoes) and woolen or leather leggins [against the snakes]." Tryon to Earl Shelburne, July 8, 1767, NCCR 7:500. See also Waddell, *A Colonial Officer*, 62.

191. This pattern is clear both in the Tuscarora War and in the frontier fighting during the French and Indian War and the immediately succeeding Cherokee War. NCCR 1:843, 852; NCCR 2:39–40; NCCR 6:229–30.

192. Governor Dobbs to Secretary Pitt, October 14, 1759, NCCR 6:61. See also the discussion in chapter 5 of the Whig war against the Cherokees in 1776.

193. Shy, "A New Look at the Colonial Militia," 29; Martin and Lender, *Respectable Army*, 17–19. The best example of such a unit in North Carolina was the perpetually renewed, though tiny (ten to twenty-five men), garrison of Fort Johnston on the Cape Fear. See sample legislative renewals of their status in NCCR 7:901–2 and NCCR 8:412.

194. Dederer, *War in America*, 121–22. See also Titus, *Old Dominion at War*, 42–43.

195. Johnson, *Militiamen*, 9, finds a similar pattern in Georgia.

196. Governor Rowan to Board of Trade, June 3, 1754, NCCR 5:124.

197. As noted above, Peter Wood has identified significant black participation in the early South Carolina militia. *Black Majority*, 127–30. James Bartholomees's study of the revolutionary backcountry militia of North Carolina found very little black participation, and most of those did unarmed duty. "Fight or Flee," 68. Charles Neimeyer has shown, however, that there was significant African-American participation in the Continental army, including 42 out of a total of 670 men in the North Carolina Brigade in 1778. *America Goes to War*, 83.

198. The expeditionary unit of 500 "provincials" raised in 1761 for the Cherokee War, the troops sent to Virginia under Colonel James Innes in 1754, and the troops raised to assist in the West Indies expedition (to Cartagena) in 1740 were the groups that may have been the most unlike the peacetime militia organization. None served very long, however, and very few of the North Carolinians who went to Cartagena survived to return home. For the latter expedition, see Wheeler, "The Role of the North Carolina Militia," 19n.41.

199. Their draft instructions included the provision that they choose men who did not have the largest families. Council Journal, May 25, 1715, NCCR 2:180.

200. Council Records, March 30, 1743, NCCR 4:633.

201. Governor Dobbs to Board of Trade, August 24, 1755, NCCR 5:357; Tryon's Proclamation, July 16, 1767, NCCR 7:500.

202. Wheeler, "The Role of the North Carolina Militia," 19n.41; Gobbel, "The Militia of North Carolina," 45; *Moravian Records*, 1:230, 358.

203. See chapters 2 and 3. Further research into the social composition and organization of North Carolina militia expeditionary forces is needed.

204. For the wealth of work on this subject, referring here only to attitudes about the military, and not to the broader conceptions of republicanism as discussed by Caroline Robbins and Bernard Bailyn, see Cress, "Radical Whiggery," 43–60; Cress, *Citizens in Arms*; White, "Standing Armies in Time of War"; Dederer, *War in America*, chapter 8. For a survey of the development of anti–standing army prejudices in England, see Schwoerer, *No Standing Armies!* There is a useful collection of English and colonial pamphlets on the subject in Kohn, ed., *Anglo-American Antimilitary*. See also Don Higginbotham's cautious challenge to this dominant perspective in "The Early American Way of War," 279–82.

205. See Western, *The English Militia*, 73; Barnett, *Britain and Her Army*, 36, 171. For the role of the army in domestic disturbance, see (among others) Hayter, *The Army and the Crowd*; Palmer, "Calling Out the Troops."

206. Cress, "Radical Whiggery," 45.

207. Schwoerer, *No Standing Armies!*, 3, 8–18.

208. Francis Hutcheson, *A System of Moral Philosophy* (1750), in *Collected Works*, ed. Bernard Fabian (Hildeshiem, 1969), 2:323–25, quoted in Cress, "Radical Whiggery," 52.

209. Paraphrased, no date given, in Boucher, "Colonial Militia," 125.

210. Adams, *The Grounds of Confidence*, 12.

211. Fairfax County Committee of Safety Proceedings, [January 17, 1775], *Papers of George Mason, 1725–1792,* 1:212.

212. Governor Dobbs to the Council and Assembly, September 25, 1755, NCCR 5:496–97.

213. Stuart, *War and American Thought,* 13; Dederer, *War in America,* 18–19, 171–72.

214. Martin and Lender, *Respectable Army,* 32–33.

5. "A Fair Fight"

1. Cumberland Association Papers, SHC.

2. The terms "Whig," "Rebel," or "Patriot" militia are used here to distinguish it both from its prewar roots and from the rival Loyalist military organization.

3. For examples of studies of the military effectiveness of the southern militias, see Pugh, "The Revolutionary Militia"; Higginbotham, "The American Militia"; Ferguson, "Functions of the Partisan-Militia"; Ferguson, "Carolina and Georgia Patriot and Loyalist Militia"; Weigley, *Partisan War;* Weller, "Irregular but Effective"; Bartholomees, "Fight or Flee." There are similar studies for the militia war in the northern states. See especially the recent work by Kwasny, *Washington's Partisan War.*

4. Jerome Nadelhaft argues that in South Carolina there were many battles in the low country around Charlotte but that there was little of the kind of fratricidal violence associated with the backcountry or the swamps. *Disorders of War,* 64–66. Other historians who have emphasized the backcountry as the source of this kind of war include Crow, "Liberty Men and Loyalists"; Ekirch, "Whig Authority"; Escott and Crow, "The Social Order." As will become clear below, endemic violence and militia activity in North Carolina were hardly restricted to the backcountry.

5. Clyde Ferguson has pointed out that the differentiation that some historians have made between informal partisan organizations and the traditional militia is largely spurious. Ferguson, "Functions of the Partisan-Militia." Volunteer organizations frequently coexisted with, and had been incorporated into, more formal militia units. See also Wheeler, "The Role of the North Carolina Militia," 40, and the discussion of volunteers in the Alamance campaign in chapter 3 and below in chapter 7. Also note that in the first few months of the war, North Carolina's so-called Continental regiments were nearly indistinguishable from the militia.

6. Hoffman, "The 'Disaffected,'" 293.

7. Although contrast Henry Lee, who wrote in his memoirs of the war in the South that there had been some "great bitterness among the inhabitants" with "tragical scenes . . . on both sides" but that they were generally "confined to a few neighborhoods, and to a few instances." *American Revolution,* 928.

8. Greene to Samuel Huntington, president of the Continental Congress, December 28, 1780, *Greene's Papers,* 7:9.

9. Nadelhaft cites the initial period of violence created by Whig impositions and then turns to the actions of the British army. *Disorders of War*, 58–62. See also Frasche, "Problems of Command," 61–62; Weigley, *Partisan War*, 12–13.

10. For class tensions, see Hoffman, "The 'Disaffected,'" 312; Crow, "Liberty Men and Loyalists," passim; and Escott and Crow, "The Social Order," passim. For a contradictory opinion, see Ekirch, "Whig Authority," passim. For use of the militia as an agent of political enforcement, see Nadelhaft, *Disorders of War*, 58–62; Ferguson, "Carolina and Georgia," 175–76; Ferguson, "Functions of the Partisan-Militia," passim; Higginbotham, "The American Militia," 95.

11. Fowler, "Egregious Villains," 299–300; Knouff, "Common People's Revolution," 25ff. and passim; Brown, *The Good Americans*, 80; Selesky, "Colonial America," 85.

12. Fowler, "Egregious Villains," 21.

13. Maier, *From Resistance to Revolution*.

14. For works that focus on prerevolutionary violent protest, other than the vast number of works on specific disturbances (e.g., the Stamp Act riots or the Boston Tea Party), the best surveys are Maier, *From Resistance to Revolution*; Brown, "Violence and the American Revolution"; Reid, "In a Defensive Rage"; Wood, "A Note on Mobs"; Smith, "Anglo-Colonial Society and the Mob"; Slaughter, "Crowds in Eighteenth-Century America."

15. The Boston Port Bill became effective June 1, 1774. The Administration of Justice Act, May 20, 1774, exempted royal officials from local prosecution. The Massachusetts Government Act, May 20, 1774, essentially annulled the colonial charter.

16. The resolves of Rowan (August 8, 1774), Johnston (August 12), Granville (August 15), Chowan (August 22), and the town of Halifax (August 22) have survived. See NCCR 9:1024, 1031–41. When the North Carolina Convention met in New Bern on August 25, they too made an extended vow of loyalty to the Hanoverian line.

17. For example, Granville County resolved "That we know not how far our Brethren in Boston who destroyed certain Teas . . . may be justified, by Necessity, but such a Breach of civil Order; nevertheless, as the Constitution pointed out a Mode of Proceeding by which the [East India] Company might have obtained Redress, we must deem a late Act of the British Parliament, which arms the executive Magistrate with the Naval and Military Powers of the Nation . . . an open Attack upon the common Liberties of the Subject." Rowan County similarly resolved, "that the late cruel and sanguinary acts of Parliament . . . is a strong evidence of the corrupt influence obtained by the British Ministry in Parliament, and a convincing proof of their fixed intention to deprive the colonies of their constitutional rights and liberties." NCCR 9:1024 (Rowan) and NCCR 9:1035 (Granville).

18. The arrival of the news can be traced in Chowan County on May 3; Edenton on May 4; Beaufort County, Bath, and New Bern on May 6; Onslow County on May 8; and Wilmington and Brunswick on May 8. NCCR 9:1236–38.

19. Circular Letter to the Committee of South Carolina, June 30, 1775, published in the *Cape Fear Mercury*, July 28, 1775, NCCR 10:52.

20. Statement of "Twelve United Colonies by their Delegates in Congress to the Inhabitants of Great Britain," July 8, 1775, in NCCR 10:80; North Carolina Delegates to the Continental Congress to the Committees in North Carolina, June 19, 1775, NCCR 10:20–23.

21. Circular Letter to the Committee of South Carolina, June 30, 1775, NCCR 10:57.

22. Quote from McEachern, ed., *Wilmington Safety Committee Minutes*, 31. See also Jacob Blount's speech to a militia company in 1775, where he emphasized how "the hand of oppression . . . hath hastened over a once free and happy People and the many cruel and arbitrary Act[s] of Parliament that have been lately passed and calculated to . . . take from us our Liberty & Property & even our Lives." Speech to Militia, 1775, John Gray Blount Papers, NCA.

23. Quote is from Reginald Stuart's summary of colonial (puritan) theologians' views on just war theory. "'For the Lord Is a Man of Warr'," 524.

24. "Resolution of Massachusetts Congress, May 5, 1775," (Salem: E. Russell, 1775), broadside, Evans #14225.

25. Circular Letter to the Committee of South Carolina, June 30, 1775, NCCR 10:51. See also Fischer, *Paul Revere's Ride*, 273.

26. The various drafts of the declaration are in *JCC*, 2:128–57, especially 135, 139. See the discussion of the authorship of the declaration in Jefferson, *Papers of Thomas Jefferson*, 1:187–217.

27. Adams, *The Grounds of Confidence*, 5. See also James Iredell's (of North Carolina) argument that American resistance at Lexington and Concord was legitimate: "a very pretty story, that a Man may not give another a box on the Ear, who attempted his life." James Iredell to Joseph Hewes, June 28, 1775, in Iredell, *Papers of James Iredell*, 1:309.

28. *Pennsylvania Journal, Supplement*, May 24, 1775, quoted in Davidson, *Propaganda*, 151.

29. "A Bloody Butchery, by the British Troops . . ." (Salem: E. Russell, [1775]), broadside, Evans #13839; "Baltimore: April 26. We have just Received . . ." [Baltimore: Mary Katharine Goddard, 1775], broadside, Evans #13819; *JCC*, 2:136; Linn, *A Military Discourse*, 12. See Davidson's discussion of the use of Lexington as propaganda, and how some authors also focused on the sacrilegious behavior of the British. *Propaganda*, 151n.45. See also Purcell, "'*Spread* this *martial fire*,'" 633; Fischer, *Paul Revere's Ride*, 261–80.

30. Titus, *Old Dominion at War*, 142–43.

31. McDonnell, "Popular Mobilization," 952.

32. "Causes of the American Revolution," in *Papers of James Iredell*, 1:409.

33. John Stuart to Earl Of Dartmouth, July 21, 1775, NCCR 10:117–18. See also the letter of the North Carolina representatives to the Continental Congress to the North Carolina Committees, June 29, 1775, NCCR 10:20–23, which warned:

"Have you not . . . a dangerous Enemy in your own Bosom . . . [would the British] hesitate to raise the hand of the servant against the master? . . . Have we not been informed that the Canadians are to be embodied and the Indians bribed to ravage the Frontiers of the Eastern Colonies?" This letter was published in the *North Carolina Gazette* on July 7, 1775.

34. Richard Beeman cited the importance of the fear of Indians (and back-country outlaws) in motivating many backcountry inhabitants to join the Whig cause. He called it "negative-reference group behavior." "The Political Response," 230–31.

35. Snapp, *John Stuart*, 159–60, 175.

36. Henry Stuart's Account of his Proceedings with the Cherokees, August 25, 1776, NCCR 10:779.

37. For Alexander Cameron's pledge, see John Drayton, *Memoirs of the American Revolution*, 1:308–9. See also the extract from the *Cape Fear Mercury*, August 7, 1775, in NCCR 9:1219–20. Russell Snapp provides evidence of eventual British encouragement of the attack, and of John Stuart's ultimate complicity. *John Stuart*, 159–60, 166, 168–71, 177.

38. The Journal of the Committee of Safety for Rowan County, in Wheeler, *Historical Sketches*, 2:366.

39. Thomas Jones to James Iredell, July 23, 1776, in *Papers of James Iredell*, 1:415–16. In a similar vein, see General Charles Lee to the North Carolina Council of Safety, July 7, 1776, NCCR 10:659. Both sides would eventually make deliberate use of Indians as allies, demonstrating the role that perceived necessity could play in overcoming the rules. However, it is worth noting that the rules did allow retaliation in kind, and thus there was an early debate over who had used Indians first. General Gage, after seeing members of the Stockbridge tribe accompanying the Rebel militia near Boston in April 1775, wrote "We need not be tender of calling upon the savages, as the Rebels have shewn us the Example by bringing as many Indians down against us here as they could collect." Gage, *Correspondence of General Thomas Gage*, 1:404. See Neimeyer, *America Goes to War*, chapter 5, for a discussion of American efforts to gain Indian allies.

40. Ramsay, *History of the Revolution of South Carolina*, 1:160.

41. The role of southern fears of slave rebellion in contributing to the initial break with Britain has been long understood. For a recent exploration of the situation in Virginia, see Holton, *Forced Founders*, 133–63. For similar fears in Maryland (in 1754) and South Carolina (in 1775–76), see Stegmaier, "Maryland's Fear," and Olwell, "Domestic Enemies."

42. Martin to Earl of Dartmouth, June 30, 1775, NCCR 10:41–50.

43. Wilmington Safety Committee Minutes, June 20, 1775, NCCR 10:25.

44. Pitt County Safety Committee Minutes, July 1 and 8, 1775, NCCR 10:63, 87.

45. Colonel John Simpson to Colonel Richard Cogdell, July 15, 1775, NCCR 10:94–95.

46. Ibid., 95.

47. Andrews and McClean, eds., *Journal of a Lady of Quality*, 199–200.

48. For Whig adherents' early hints at the governor's complicity, see Letter to a Gentleman in New York from North Carolina, June 7, 1775, NCCR 10:11–12; entry for July 13, 1775, McEachern, ed., *Wilmington Safety Committee Minutes*, 43.

49. Entries for July 20, 21, 1775, McEachern, ed., *Wilmington Safety Committee Minutes*, 45, 47.

50. New Bern Committee Minutes, August 2, 1775, NCCR 10:137–38.

51. Deposition of James Cotton, August 13, 1775, NCCR 10:127–29. See also John Stuart to Henry Clinton, March 1776, in which he claimed that the Whigs' "pretended Discovery of an intention to Instigate Insurrections of the negroes and bring down the Indians . . . was assigned as the Reasons for arming the militia and for raising Troops." Quoted in Neimeyer, *America Goes to War*, 92.

52. Dunmore's proclamation, November 7, 1775, NCCR 10:308–9. For more details on Dunmore's actions in Virginia and how this news helped cement the opinions of some against the British, see Rankin, *North Carolina Continentals*, 23–24; Berger, *Broadsides and Bayonets*, 87–91.

53. North Carolina representatives to the Continental Congress to the North Carolina Committees, June 29, 1775, NCCR 10:20–23. See also the Statement of the Twelve United Colonies by their Delegates in Congress to the Inhabitants of Great Britain, July 8, 1775, NCCR 10:80.

54. For North Carolinians' specific references to military excesses in seventeenth-century England, see "Sermon against Plundering," in Samuel E. McCorkle Papers, DUSC (quoted in part above), and the petition of Samuel Richardson discussed at length in chapter 6.

55. The Journal of the Committee of Safety for Rowan County, in Wheeler, *Historical Sketches*, 2:366. See also General John Drayton to Governor Burke, July 6, 1781, NCSR 15:511, on fears of civil war.

56. "To the Non-Commissioned Officers and Privates, of the Several Companies . . ." [Philadelphia: Henry Miller, 1775], Evans #14507. For a similar appeal to military masculine virtue, see Linn, *A Military Discourse*, 13.

57. Davidson, *Propaganda*, 103.

58. Martin to Earl of Dartmouth, June 30, 1775, NCCR 10:44. See also Fischer, *Paul Revere's Ride*, 279.

59. Wheeler, *Historical Sketches*, 2:152–53. The Resolves appeared in the *North Carolina Gazette* of New Bern on June 16, 1775. See also the resolutions of the Cumberland County Association of June 20, 1775, sometimes called the Liberty Point Resolves, in Cumberland Association Papers, SHC.

60. Dederer makes a similar point about the image of the British redcoat as a symbol being a powerful motivator for those unmoved by "all the fine words" of revolutionary theorists. *War in America*, 182. See also Weller, "Irregular War," 125.

61. Samuel Johnston to Alexander Elmsley, September 23, 1774, Samuel Johnston Papers, NCA.

62. Proceedings of the Provincial Congress, April 12, 1776, NCCR 10:512.

63. The term is Charles Royster's from *Revolutionary People*, 25.

64. Many colonial statements of protest in 1775 and early 1776 continued their traditional assertion of loyalty to the king, blaming instead a corrupt ministry and Parliament. Some examples have already been cited above. See also the Pitt County Safety Committee Proceedings, July 1, 1775, NCCR 10:61; the Rowan County Committee of Safety Minutes, June 1, 1775, in Wheeler, *Historical Sketches*, 2:364; Governor Martin's Proclamation, June 16, 1775, NCCR 10:16–19.

65. William Hooper to Joseph Hewes, April 17, 1776, Hayes Collection, SHC. The reader will recall that the Regulators were compared to Hottentots in one version of the newspaper description of the September 1770 riot in Hillsborough. See chapter 3.

66. Fowler, "Egregious Villains," 290–91. As one other example, there is John Adams's characterization of the war as of 1778: "In spite of tomahawk and scalping knife; in spite of the numerous wicked and diabolical engines of cruelty and revenge, played off against us by the magnanimous and heroic, humane and merciful George the Third . . . and his wicked and abandoned soldiery." John Adams to Governor Richard Caswell, July 10, 1778, NCSR 13:456.

67. Nadelhaft, *Disorders of War*, 50ff., discusses South Carolina's use of the militia to suppress dissent. Weller, "Irregular War," 127–28, makes a similar point for the South as a whole, although I think his distinction between the "militia" and the "mob" (p. 127) may obscure the extensive overlap between the two. See also Wheeler, "The Role of the North Carolina Militia," 62–63.

68. For the militia as a disseminator of information, see the Journal of the Committee of Safety for Rowan County, July 18, 1775, in Wheeler, *Historical Sketches*, 2:365. For their use in bringing persons before the committee to take a test oath, see ibid., September 21, 1775, in Wheeler, *Historical Sketches*, 2:368–69; and the Wilmington Committee Minutes, December 20, 1775, NCCR 10:363.

69. The Journal of the Committee of Safety for Rowan County, September 23, 1774, and June 1, 1775, in Wheeler, *Historical Sketches*, 2:362, 364.

70. Depositions of Saml Williams, Jacob Williams, and James Cotton, August 12–18, 1775, NCCR 10:125–29.

71. Martin to Earl of Dartmouth, June 30, 1775, NCCR 10:48; Andrews and McClean, eds., *Journal of a Lady*, 192. Martin's account and Janet Schaw's (the journal keeper) are almost identical.

72. Andrews and McClean, eds., *Journal of a Lady*, 190.

73. Loyalist claim of Malcolm Love (PRO AO12/34/151).

74. Wheeler, *Historical Sketches*, 2:385.

75. Wheeler, "The Role of the North Carolina Militia," 32, 91–125.

76. Proceedings of the Provincial Congress, September 1, 1775, NCCR 10:186.

77. Ibid., September 7, 1775, NCCR 10:196–201.

78. Wheeler, "Development and Organization," 319. Some pensioners continued to refer to service in the minutemen in later years, but it essentially disappeared from official records.

79. NCCR 10:756; NCCR 10:881; NCCR 11:309. The council of safety directed that these books be distributed to the colonels of the various North Carolina Continental army regiments. A North Carolina printer advertised copies of *The Manual Exercise of the British Army from 1764* for sale in the *North Carolina Gazette*, June 27, 1777.

80. Proceedings of the Provincial Congress, August 20, 1775, NCCR 10:199.

81. The first traditionally "military" act of the Whig militia had been the unopposed taking of Fort Johnston in July 1775. The Whigs burned the fort, in an act that Governor Martin described as "done with a degree of wanton barbarity that would disgrace human nature in the most savage state and was an overt act of high treason." Proclamation of Governor Martin, August 8, 1775, NCCR 10:143. See also Rankin, *North Carolina Continentals*, 14–15; Wheeler, "The Role of the North Carolina Militia," 83–85; Deposition of Samuel Cooper, NCCR 10:130–31; Loyalist claim of Richard Wilson (PRO AO13/106/222).

82. The Journal of the Committee of Safety for Rowan County, November 8, 11, 1775, in Wheeler, *Historical Sketches*, 2:371–76.

83. McEachern, ed., *Wilmington Safety Committee Minutes*, 62.

84. Mrs. Pollock to Joseph Hewes, December 23, 1775, NCCR 10:1027–33; Samuel Johnston to Joseph Hewes, November 26, 1775, enclosed in the letter of Vice Admiral Graves, January 29, 1776, PRO CO5/123 transcript in ER 13–2; *North Carolina Gazette*, December 22, 1775.

85. Robert Nelson to Henry Nelson, October 20, 1775, PRO CO5/134, transcript in ER 13–7. It is worthy of note that as the rebellion became a war, tarring and feathering as a means of loyalty enforcement disappeared in North Carolina.

86. Loyalist claim of Daniel Maxwell (PRO AO13/121/567). Maxwell claimed that the major, James Bonner, was never punished.

87. In the case of the Pollock incident, there was a significant effort on the part of the Whig leadership to decry the violence against him, although no one was ever punished. See Don Higginbotham's comments in *Papers of James Iredell*, 1:341.

88. See the discussion of Weber in this context in Zimmerman, *Political Violence*, 11–12. Quote is from this discussion.

89. "Sermon against Plundering," Samuel E. McCorkle Papers, DUSC (emphasis in original).

90. The phrase is from Jack Green's exploration of what colonial Americans meant by "virtue." "The Concept of Virtue," 234.

91. White, "Standing Armies in Time of War," 91.

92. Adams, *The Grounds of Confidence*, 6–22, 26. There were many similar sermons exhorting soldiers to virtue. See Purcell, "'Spread this martial fire,'" 632.

93. Published in the *North Carolina Gazette*, June 6, 1778, NCCR 13:436.

94. Samuel Johnston to Governor Caswell, January 16, 1777, NCCR 11:355.

95. Stuart, "'For the Lord Is a Man of Warr,'" 519, 527, 531; Purcell, "'*Spread this martial fire,*'" 632.

96. Pickering, *An Easy Plan*, 10–11.

97. Cumberland Association Papers, SHC.

98. Drayton, *Memoirs*, 2:326–27.

99. Inglis, *The Christian Soldier's Duty*, 10–11.

100. Rankin, *North Carolina Continentals*, 22–23.

101. Murphey, *Murphey Papers*, 2:402.

102. Ferguson, "Functions of the Partisan-Militia," 246–47.

103. Murphey, *Murphey Papers*, 2:402.

104. See Ferguson, "Functions of the Partisan-Militia," 246–47.

105. Rankin, *North Carolina Continentals*, 23–27; Wheeler, "The Role of the North Carolina Militia," 143–48.

106. J. D. to Earl of Dumfries, January 14, 1776, PRO CO5/40 transcript in ER 12–13, NCA. See also the traditionally military correspondence that ensued between Colonel Robert Howe of North Carolina, Governor Dunmore, and British Captain Bellew over the exchange of prisoners, the removal of civilians from Norfolk, and other forms of truce negotiations. Letters between Howe and Bellew, NCCR 10:372; Howe and Dunmore, NCCR 10:365–69; Howe and the President of the Virginia Convention, NCCR 10:365.

107. Hugh Rankin has written a comprehensive study of the campaign, one version of which appears in *North Carolina Continentals*, 28–54. A nearly identical version was originally printed in the *North Carolina Historical Review* 30 (1953): 23–60, and has been reprinted in pamphlet form by the Eastern National Park and Monument Association, copyrighted 1986. Citations will be made to the pamphlet version, abbreviated Rankin, *Moore's Creek*. Since Rankin's coverage is so complete, I do not repeat a full narrative of the campaign but rather emphasize the incidents that relate to colonial norms of military violence.

108. Rankin, *Moore's Creek*, 4–7. The issue of the motivation of the Highlanders and the Regulators for supporting Governor Martin is a large subject, appropriate for a separate discussion. As a start, see Meyer, *Highland Scots of North Carolina*, 131–62; Johnson, "The War of the Regulation." Governor Martin, with the cooperation of authorities in England, had begun trying to encourage the Regulators to support him as early as May 1775. See Lord Dartmouth to Governor Martin, May 3, 1775, copied in Drayton, *Memoirs*, 1:344–45.

109. Martin's orders for raising the standard, January 10, 1776, NCCR 10:441–42.

110. Ibid.

111. Ibid.

112. There is a similar statement by the leader of the Loyalist forces, General Donald MacDonald. On two occasions in 1776, he tried to reassure the local populace that he would prevent violence against women and children, or to the persons and property of "His Majesty's subjects." He viewed "such outrages to be

inconsistent with humanity, and as tending . . . to sully the arms of Britons and of soldiers." NCCR 10:429–30, 443.

113. Grotius, *Law of War and Peace*, 1:139; Conway, "To Subdue America," 396–97.

114. In later years, the Whigs always referred to the Moore's Creek campaign as "the insurrection," differentiating it from the war against the British. See, for example, Cornelius Harnett to Richard Caswell, August 27, 1778, NCSR 13:212.

115. See Rankin, *Moore's Creek*, 7–14, for details of the raising of the Loyalist forces.

116. Ibid., 15; *Moravian Records*, 3:1049.

117. Rankin, *Moore's Creek*, 19.

118. Donald MacDonald was a native of Scotland and an officer in the British army who had been sent to North Carolina in 1775 by General Gage to help recruit Highland Loyalists. Governor Martin commissioned him to raise the royal standard, and he commanded the Loyalist force that gathered at Cross Creek. Moss, *Roster of the Loyalists*, 35; Rankin, *Moore's Creek*, 10.

119. Several letters of Moore and MacDonald, February 19–20, 1776, NCCR 11:276–79.

120. MacDonald to Caswell, February 26, 1776, Donald MacDonald Paper, NCA. The messenger carrying the ultimatum traveled under a flag of truce, and when a captain asked if he might kill the bearer of the flag, General Caswell "shook his head." Pension application of William Ward, in Camin, *North Carolina Pension Applications*, 3:331.

121. Caruthers, *Old North State*, 20; MacDonald's Report to the Continental Congress, May 29, 1776, in Force, *American Archives*, 4th ser., 6:613–14.

122. Rankin, *Moore's Creek*, 38. One North Carolina divine acknowledged the traditional right of soldiers to take battlefield plunder. He was equally aware of the legal notion that the state owned all such plunder, and allowing the soldiers to have it was considered, in his words, "a reward not of debt, but of grace." "Sermon against Plundering," Samuel E. McCorkle Papers, DUSC. See Grotius, *Law of War and Peace*, 3:672; Vattel, *Law of Nations*, 291–92.

123. Loyalist claims of William McQueen (PRO AO12/100/26), and Mary McCaskle (PRO AO13/91/189).

124. This in spite of the fact of the clear motivation to report as much loss as possible in hopes of restitution. Neill McGeachy, for example, was very specific in noting that his wife was able to keep their home intact until August 1781 (PRO AO12/36/62). Out of a sample of Loyalist claims, forty-seven of which were from individuals involved in the Moore's Creek campaign, only three made a clear indication that their property was plundered shortly after the battle (two others claimed property destroyed but were unclear about when). Admittedly, however, twenty-five of those persons claimed to have been held prisoner after the battle for long periods of time, or to have hidden out in the woods, and therefore may not have known of the fate of their property.

125. James Moore to Cornelius Harnett, March 2, 1776, NCCR 11:85.

126. Caruthers, *Old North State*, 163.

127. *Moravian Records*, 3:1029, 1095; Journal of the Council of Safety, July 31, 1776, NCCR 10:690.

128. *Moravian Records*, 3:1029.

129. Ibid., 3:1058.

130. Josiah Martin to Lord George Germain, September 15, 1777, NCCR 11:765–66; Caruthers, *Old North State*, 24; Letter from an Unknown Source, March 10, 1776, NCCR 10:486. The following discussion of the Whig categorization and treatment of prisoners is based on reading the Loyalist claims of numerous participants at Moore's Creek and on Moss's more systematic review of the fate of all of the identifiable participants in the battle. *Roster of the Loyalists*, passim.

131. Wheeler, *Historical Sketches*, 2:459. Slocumb was the wife of a Whig militia officer and was assisting in treating the wounded after the battle.

132. Caruthers, *Old North State*, 23–24.

133. Proceedings of the Provincial Congress, April 5, 1776, NCCR 10:503.

134. Loyalist claim of John Munro (PRO AO12/101/109).

135. See NCCR 10:559–60, 631, for a few of the many letters on the status of the prisoners.

136. NCCR 10:700–701.

137. Brown, *The King's Friends*, 197; Loyalist claim of John MacKenzie (PRO AO12/34/366). See also Robert Howe's letter of November 1, 1776, NCCR 10:887, trying to arrange for a Loyalist prisoner to have his parole as near as possible to his family, "where he might hear of his affairs frequently." For the clothing and cash allowance, see Proceedings of the Provincial Congress, December 4, 1776, NCCR 10:952; Council Journal, March 4, 1777, NCSR 22:916; Senate Journal, October 29, 1779, NCSR 13:870.

138. Proceedings of the Provincial Congress, April 27, 1776, NCCR 10:544.

139. Letter of Committee of Secrecy, War and Intelligence of North Carolina to John Hancock, April 22, 1776, NCSR 11:293–94; Senate Journals, May 6, 1777, NCSR 12:80–81, 95.

140. General MacDonald to the Secretary of War, September 6, 1776, NCSR 15:764–65. James Moore was promoted to general on March 1, 1776.

141. Rankin, *Moore's Creek*, 40–41.

142. Loyalist claim of Neill McGeachy (PRO AO12/36/62).

143. Caruthers, *Old North State*, 23. Caruthers says that fourteen men agreed to continue.

144. Rankin, *Moore's Creek*, 37.

145. Caruthers, *Old North State*, 23.

146. James Moore to Cornelius Harnett, March 2, 1776, NCSR 11:285.

147. [John] Johnston to James Iredell, March 17, 1776, *Papers of James Iredell*, 1:344–45.

148. Pension Record of Absalom Powell (R8401).

149. Brown, *The King's Friends*, 196. Wheeler, "The Role of the North Carolina Militia," 198–99, argues that the Whig militia struggled with the Tories throughout the summer of 1776. Most of his evidence, however, involves the continued use of the militia to enforce the loyalty oaths and so on and was not in response to actual Loyalist violence. The exception was the killing of Nathaniel Richardson discussed below.

150. Proceedings of the Provincial Congress, May 10, 1776, NCCR 10:574–75; NCSR 24:3–4. The penalty, however, was only £10 and liability for the item taken illegally.

151. Court-Martial of Captain Aaron Hill, August 8, 1776, Misc. Papers, Military Collection, NCA.

152. *Moravian Records*, 3:1036–37.

153. For a brief introduction to the history of the community, see Fries, "The Moravian Contribution."

154. See, for example, *Moravian Records*, 4:1708, 1570, 1767.

155. Ibid., 3:1049.

156. Ibid., 3:1044, 1052–53, 1073, 1077, 1093–94, 1099.

157. In this respect, it is interesting to compare the daily diaries to the yearly summaries. The latter tended to complain more loudly about the "pay" they received, because by the time the yearly summary was written the currency had depreciated to a greater extent than when the certificate or ticket was originally given. For the militia purchasing goods in 1776, see *Moravian Records*, 3:1044, 1028, 1029, 1035, 1052–53, 1074, 1121–26.

158. General Ashe to Council of Safety, August 13, 1776, NCCR 10:744.

159. Colonel Folsom to Council of Safety, October 8, 1776, NCCR 10:839–40; Proceedings of the Provincial Congress, November 26, 1776, NCCR 10:939. This is not the Samuel Richardson discussed in chapter 6.

160. Proceedings of the Provincial Congress, November 26, 1776, NCCR 10:933–35. In a separate incident, a party of Whig militia scouring Wake County captured and hanged one Tory. Rankin, *North Carolina Continentals*, 51.

161. *Moravian Records*, 3:1052–53; Journal of the Committee of Safety of Rowan County, May 8, 1776, in Wheeler, *Historical Sketches*, 2:376. The North Carolina Provincial Council, on March 2, 1776, recommended to the town and county committees that suspected persons be disarmed, and it resolved again on March 5 that suspected persons who had not taken up arms against the colony should be required to take an oath that they would not take up arms against the Whig government, nor aid the British. Copies of these resolutions are in *Moravian Records*, 3:1350 and 1351.

162. Compare this to the New Jersey Loyalists confiscating weapons in 1776, described in Fowler, "Egregious Villains," 68–70, 76–77.

163. Chapter 7 includes a full discussion of the notions of the house as immune from violence.

164. Weller, "Irregular but Effective," 123–24. For a similar observation comparing military violence against Indians to that against Tories, see Knouff, "Soldiers and Violence," 186.

165. Ganyard, "Threat from the West"; Hatley, *The Dividing Paths*, 191–203; O'Donnell, *Cherokees of North Carolina*, 13–22.

166. *Moravian Records*, 3:1064, 1105. See also Ganyard, "Threat from the West," 54.

167. *Moravian Records*, 3:1065. None of this is to comment on the relative grievances of the Cherokees versus the whites. This is merely an account of white perceptions at the outset of the campaign. For a brief look at the Cherokee grievances, see Ganyard, "Threat from the West," 51–53.

168. Charles Roberson and James Smith to ———, July 13, 1776, NCCR 10:665–66 (Roberson and Smith were passing along news from other men who had been in the Cherokee villages); NCCR 10:712.

169. Griffith Rutherford to the Council of Safety, July 14, 1776, NCCR 10:669.

170. Griffith Rutherford to William Christian, August 5 [?], 1776, NCCR 10:650–51; Ganyard, "Threat from the West," 56–57.

171. North Carolina Delegates to the North Carolina Provincial Council, August 7, 1776, NCCR 10:731.

172. Council of Safety to Rutherford, September 11, 1776, NCSR 11:351–52.

173. Pension Record of James Martin (W4728); Ferguson, "Functions of the Partisan-Militia," 250.

174. Council of Safety to Patrick Henry, October 25, 1776, NCCR 10:860–61; de Roulhac Hamilton, ed., "Revolutionary War Diary," 255–56; Colonel Williamson to General Rutherford, August 14, 1776, NCCR 10:745–47.

175. Sweeny, *Captain Thomas Cook*, 4 (a pamphlet version of Cook's pension record).

176. Pension Record of Archibald Houston (W295).

177. "Arthur Fairies' Journal," Lyman C. Draper Collection, series VV (Thomas Sumter Papers), State Historical Society, Madison, Wisconsin, 3:170–71. Fairies recorded another incident in which he suspected a group of militiamen of "helping . . . to her end" an elderly Cherokee woman whom they had captured. Ibid., 3:172.

178. De Roulhac Hamilton, ed., "Revolutionary War Diary," 255. Some of the army leadership apparently still encouraged restraint. When John Roberson "killed an old Indian prisoner," he "was put under Guard Tyed for it and marched into Aconolosta." Ibid., 256.

179. Captain William Moore to General Rutherford, November 18, 1776, NCCR 10:895–98.

180. Ibid., 898. In August 1778, the Cherokees complained to South Carolina that the North Carolinians, in contravention of the peace treaty, had sold as slaves some of their people who had not been returned. Rawl. Lowndes to Caswell, August 6, 1778, NCSR 13:204.

181. Two examples are the white-Indian conflict in western Pennsylvania described by Knouff, "Soldiers and Violence," and the Continental army expedition against the Iroquois in 1779, described by Mintz, *Seeds of Empire*; Fischer, *A Well-Executed Failure*; Graymont, *The Iroquois in the American Revolution*.

182. "Arthur Fairies' Journal," Lyman C. Draper Collection, series VV (Thomas Sumter Papers), State Historical Society, Madison, Wisconsin, 3:160–75. See James Axtell's discussion of this kind of psychological double standard in the white employment of Indian techniques of violence. *The European and the Indian*, 209. See also Knouff, "Soldiers and Violence," 180.

183. [Lee], *Strictures on a Pamphlet*, 11–12.

184. James Iredell to W. Thomas Jones, July 15, 1776, *Papers of James Iredell*, 1:414.

185. Rankin, *North Carolina Continentals*, 18–19. See also Russell, *North Carolina in the Revolutionary War*, 28; White, "Standing Armies in Time of War," 109–10.

186. In contrast, Michael McDonnell argues that the imposition of a European-style military discipline was part of an effort by the elite to impose social control on the lower sort who comprised the Virginia revolutionary military. "Popular Mobilization," 963.

6. Civil Consolidation

1. NCSR 13:188.

2. House Journals, January 22, 1779, NCSR 13:643–44.

3. *Moravian Records*, 3:1131. The General Assembly passed the Tax Act in April 1777. NCSR 24:6–9.

4. A check of four counties' records finds either a complete absence of court sessions between February/May 1776 and February 1777, or at most few and short sessions in 1776. See Cooper, ed., "Abstracts of Court Minutes," passim; Linn, ed., *Abstracts of the Minutes*; Haun, ed., *Johnston County Court Minutes, 1767–1777*; Moravian Records, 3:1048, 1128, 1141, 1150. The situation with the superior courts was more complex. A dispute between the colonial Assembly and Governor Josiah Martin had closed the superior courts in 1773. Civil cases remained pending while criminal cases were tried in special oyer and terminer courts in 1773, 1774, 1775, and 1777 (the latter ordered by the 1776 Provincial Congress). The first General Assembly, which met in April 1777 under the new state constitution, reestablished the district superior courts, and they began normal operation in 1778. Leary and Stirewalt, eds., *North Carolina Research*, 329–30; Haun, ed., *Hillsborough District*; DeMond, *Loyalists in North Carolina*, 27–30; NCSR 23:990–92; NCSR 23:992–96; NCSR 24:36–42; NCSR 11:xix.

5. Andrews and McClean, eds., *Journal of a Lady of Quality*, 198–99, hints at threats to Loyalists' property in 1775.

6. Proceedings of the Provincial Congress, April 6 and May 1, 1776, NCCR 10:504, 555.

7. Proceedings of the Provincial Congress, May 13, 1776, NCCR 10:585. On May 1, the Provincial Congress ordered that several estates of imprisoned Tories be inventoried, but that nothing be taken (save arms and ammunition), and further that the commissioners of the inventory should seek to restore to those estates anything already taken. Proceedings of the Provincial Congress, May 1, 1776, NCCR 10:554.

8. Council of Safety to Colonel Martin Armstrong, July 5, 1776, NCSR 11:308.

9. Proceedings of the Provincial Congress, May 3, 1776, NCCR 10:559. On May 9, the Congress examined Childers, let him off, and paid the victim £56 compensation.

10. DeMond, *Loyalists in North Carolina*, 153.

11. NCSR 23:985–86.

12. Ibid., 997–98. The law also provided that anyone who assisted a traitor could be found guilty of misprision of treason. It also allowed judges some latitude in providing for the families of those whose estates were forfeited by virtue of a high treason conviction.

13. NCSR 24:9–12. The definition of treason was repeated from an act of the Convention of December 1776. NCSR 23:997–98.

14. Thus, their property was not technically confiscated under this act, but the time allowed to sell was limited. They could hire an attorney to sell their real estate but even then were allowed only three months from their departure to do so, else it reverted to the state. NCSR 24:9–12.

15. *Moravian Records*, 3:1131–32. The assumption probably followed from the March 1776 Congress, which had resolved that all persons disarmed by the committees, or *suspected* of Loyalism, should be required to take an oath of allegiance. Proceedings of the Provincial Council, March 5, 1776, NCCR 10:476.

16. *Moravian Records*, 3:1144.

17. An exception was allowed if the person appeared before the Assembly after October 1778 and became a citizen. NCSR 24: 84–89.

18. *Moravian Records*, 3:1129.

19. Those who departed in 1779 are generally less specific about their motivations, but many of them went to join Lieutenant Colonel Archibald Campbell's expedition, which had landed in Georgia.

20. See, for example, the claims of Daniel McNeill (PRO AO12/35/59 and AO13/91/344); Andrew Riddell (PRO AO12/36/277); James Rogers (PRO AO12/35/144). All of these men were given multiple opportunities to take the oath. Alexander Brodie convinced his friend who was "chairman" of the county court to give him a certificate stating that he had taken the oath, which allowed him to remain until June 1780 (PRO AO12/100/204).

21. Cooper, ed., "Abstracts of Court Minutes," 4:93–96, 197, 201, 203. The Rowan County Court records show a similar progression of oath taking. The first oath was tendered in August 1777, and only sixty-five people took the oath in the whole of that year. Then in May 1778, the county initiated the general oath taking

process and even compiled a list of those who had failed to take it; the list totaled 577 persons in August 1778. Linn, ed., *Abstracts of the Minutes*, 22–46.

22. The 1779 act specified named individuals (usually wealthy) whose property was to be taken, and it weakened the provisions for widows and children. Actual confiscation based on this act began almost immediately. NCSR 24:209–13 (1778), 263–68 (1779). See also DeMond, *Loyalists in North Carolina*, 153–72, for a survey of the development of the Confiscation Acts up to 1779. For similar acts in South Carolina, see Nadelhaft, *Disorders of War*, 45, 77–81. For a look at confiscation around the continent, see Brown, *The Good Americans*, 127–31.

23. House Journals, February 12, 1779, NCSR 13:734e–734f.

24. David Fowler noted that property confiscation was among the most resented acts of the various Whig state governments. "Egregious Villains," 123.

25. Vattel, *Law of Nations*, 291–92.

26. Ibid., 309. Vattel's thinking reflected relatively recent development. Grotius was more cavalier in granting the state the right to redistribute private property, both movable and real, although he still tended to emphasize that real property devolved to the state and not to individuals. Grotius, *Law of War and Peace*, 3:672ff.

27. Memorial of the Merchants, Traders and Others residing at Cape Fear, rejected by the Assembly on May 2, 1780, NCSR 15:203.

28. House Journals, November 10, 1779, NCSR 13:991–92. The 1778 confiscation law (NCSR 24:211–12) specified that the wife and children of absentee Loyalists be allowed to inherit as if the said absentee had died. The text of the initial bill in 1779 provided for only one-third of the real estate to revert to the family. This provision led to the protest by some members of the House, and although the one-third provision was retained in the final act, there was also an amendment clause specifying that no provision of the act be construed as power to confiscate "any Household Furniture or Provision belonging to the aged Parents, Wives, Children or Widows of any person whose Estate is confiscated by virtue of this or any other Act passed in this State." The Senate voted 21 to 3 in favor of that amendment. Senate Journals, November 9, 1779, NCSR 13:897–98; NCSR 24:268. DeMond notes, probably correctly, that part of this effort to soften the Confiscation Act resulted from some members of the Assembly being personally connected to the wealthy Tories specified for confiscation. DeMond, *Loyalists in North Carolina*, 157–58.

29. Nadelhaft, *Disorders of War*, 77–81n.23. It must be admitted that some believed the Confiscation Act was not severe enough. The residents of Mecklenburg County petitioned the Assembly in October 1779, complaining that the 1777 act "inadequately punished & the public in no sort indemnified for the injuries it has sustained by his unatural guilt." Petition of Committee appointed by Inhabitants of Mecklenburg, October 1777, in October–November 1779, Joint Papers, Petitions to General Assembly, General Assembly Session Records, NCA.

30. At least 100 men in one Rowan County Company refused to take the oath,

publicly "huzzaeing" for the king. House Journals, August 17, 1778, NCSR 12:862. The Rowan County Court session of August 1778 determined that 577 persons had refused the oath. Linn, ed., *Abstracts of the Minutes*, 40–43. The Surry County militia, too, resisted the oath, causing fights at a general muster. *Moravian Records*, May 18, 1778, and May 27, 1778, 3:1232, 1234. On the social weight of oaths, see Brown, *The Good Americans*, 45.

31. Loyalist claims of Samuel Campbell (PRO AO12/35/4), Samuel Marshall (PRO AO12/3/218, PRO AO13/7/159). Both men admitted to taking the oath to avoid trouble. The majority of claimants made a point of saying that they had not taken the oath, perhaps from fear that their claim would be refused.

32. Deposition of George Redman, Criminal Action Papers, 1779, Salisbury District Superior Court Records, NCA.

33. As mentioned in chapter 5, Jeffrey Crow and Paul Escott have argued that Loyalist resistance was a class phenomenon rather than a political one. And while one might accept that huzzaing for King George served merely as a symbolic rallying cry of an oppressed class using loyalty to the king as a legitimizing tool of resistance, it does not explain why, for example, the Surry County militia would dissolve in fights over the oath if presumably they were all of the same class. Or why, in the case of Captain Johnston's company of Rowan militia, he could refer to the Whig portion and the Tory portion of his company, although the latter was apparently larger. (See note 30 above.)

34. To list only the large call-ups: a new Continental regiment in 1777 (700 men); a call to fill up the older regiments in 1777 (2,648 men); 1,200 men to march to South Carolina in 1777; 2,500 men to repel invasion; 2,000 men as nine-months recruits for the Continentals in 1778; 300 men to go to Georgia in 1778; 1,000 men in 1779; 1,000 men in 1779 to go to South Carolina. NCSR 12:iii–iv; NCSR 22:995; *Moravian Records*, 3:1249; NCSR 24:154–57, 198–99, 339. There were many other smaller call-ups of militia in this period, some of which will be mentioned below. Not all of these troops were raised, and some of those who were merely marched, countermarched, and went home. Nevertheless, such call-ups contributed to the overall sense of being oppressed by the requirement of military service.

35. James Scudieri claims that the British army rarely resorted to the press gang, and that none of the European armies fighting in North America during the Revolution (British, French, Hessian) "used a draft to obtain recruits." "The Continentals," 53. It is possible that some of the more recent immigrants to North Carolina were more used to this way of doing things and were therefore more thoroughly outraged by the draft than those more familiar with previous colonial militia drafts.

36. See, for example, NCSR 12:iii–iv; Recruitment Act, as printed in the *North Carolina Gazette*, May 8, 1778, NCSR 13:411–17; "Advertisement," March 16, 1779, NCSR 15:737–38.

37. NCSR 24:1; Bartholomees, "Fight or Flee," 63.

38. See, for example, *Moravian Records*, March 1, 1777, 3:1183, in which the third and fourth classes were called out simultaneously. The class system is discussed further in chapter 7.

39. NCSR 24:154–55.

40. *Moravian Records*, May 7, 1776, November 6, 1778, 3:1113, 1250; NCSR 12:iii–iv.

41. Petition of John Robinson, November 1, 1779, in October–November 1779, Joint Papers, Petitions to the General Assembly, General Assembly Session Records, NCA; Mr. Thomas Henderson to Governor Caswell, June 18, 1778, NCSR 13:446–47; House Journal, February 11, 1779, NCSR 13:729; Peter Mallett to Governor Caswell, November 15, 1778, NCSR 13:284–85; House Journals, August 17, 1778, 860–63; Remonstrance and petition from a number of inhabitants of the district of Salisbury, in April–May 1782, Joint Standing Committees, Propositions & Grievances—Report and Papers, General Assembly Session Records, NCA. These complaints came from Guilford, Beaufort, Orange, and Rowan counties.

42. Thos. Bonner to Governor Caswell, July 6, 1778, NCSR 13:188–89; Colonel W. Bryan to Governor Caswell, November 23, 1778, NCSR 13:295; Council Journals, July 3, 1779, NCSR 14:319; Governor Caswell to Colonel John Heritage, July 19, 1779, NCSR 14:169; Colonel Thos. Benbury to Governor Abner Nash, June 12, 1780, NCSR 14:850–51. These reports cover at least Edgecomb, Nash, Johnston, Dobbs, Halifax, and Chowan counties. See also Crow, "Liberty Men and Loyalists," 154–56.

43. Depositions in Inquiry on Drafting of troops in Anson County, Military Collection, Misc. Papers, NCA; Governor Caswell to Colonel Charles Medlock, June 6, 1778, NCSR 13:150–51, and follow-up letters on June 11, NCSR 13:158–59. Crow discusses this incident in "Liberty Men and Loyalists," 125–27. I believe he has partially misread the original document; the "ringleader" of this vote rigging did not suggest to the others that they could substitute other names of their choice, rather he threatened that he would substitute the names of those who refused to go along with him.

44. Senate Journals, August 13, 1778, and August 19, 1778, NCSR 12:775, 811.

45. Based on a reading of the pension records of 587 veterans of the North Carolina Rebel militia.

46. Dann, ed., *Revolution Remembered*, 186.

47. Pension Record of Archibald Houston (W295). See also Sweeny, *Captain Thomas Cook*, 4; and another scouring reported in House Journals, January 22, 1779, NCSR 13:643–44.

48. Pension Record of William Lenoir (S7137). The reader should remember this statement later when chapter 7 reviews the behavior of the Wilkes militia (to which Lenoir and Cleveland belonged) in the Moravian towns. Donagan notes that mock hangings were common in the English Civil War, including at least one

example of a half-hanging to extract information. Donagan, "Codes and Conduct," 66.

49. Ransom Southerland to the Council of Safety, July 13, 1776, NCSR 10:663–65 (apparently referring to Guilford County).

50. It is not possible to recount all the incidents and scares that occurred during this period, many of which fall under the category of draft resisters/associators discussed above. In addition to those discussed below, see, for example, NCCR 10:744 (death of Captain Richardson in Bladen County); Pension Record of James Martin (W4728) (capture of Colonel William Fields in Randolph County); NCCR 10:669 (reports of Tories in Anson/Cumberland); the two "salt scares" at Cross Creek, NCSR 11:527, 538, 546, 548–49, 554, 557–58, 560, 603–4, 630. The court records for this period are also vague on the extent of Tory activity. There are, for example, cases in the Salisbury District Court in 1777 for assault and/or housebreaking, but since the charges typically revolve around the taking of firearms, these may or may not have been Tory activities. If "banditry," their behavior was remarkably focused. Salisbury District Court Records (court of oyer and terminer), March 1777, printed in NCSR 22:501–13. "Treason" trials were also held in Salisbury, but of the ten treason trials in the Salisbury Criminal Action Papers for 1777 and 1778, eight were for treasonous words only. The remainder were for attempting to enlist others for the king. Criminal Action Papers, Salisbury District Superior Court Records, NCA.

51. Lieutenant Colonel Henry Irwin to Governor Caswell, July 16, 1777, NCSR 11:521. For a detailed examination of the conspiracy, see Crow, "Tory Plots."

52. J. G. Blount to Governor Caswell, NCSR 11:510–11; Jacob Blount to Governor Caswell, July 6, 1777, NCSR 11:513; Robert Smith to Governor Caswell, July 31, 1777, NCSR 11:551–52; General Allen Jones to Thomas Burke, August 6, 1777, NCSR 11:746–47.

53. Deposition of James Rawlins, Hyde County, August 6, 1777, quoted in Crow, "Tory Plots," 10.

54. *Moravian Records*, 3:1376, 1381.

55. Rutherford to Caswell, November 15, 1778, NCSR 13:282–83.

56. Observe how the writer of this petition complained of present "mischief" but was mostly worried about what was projected to happen, while the rest of the quote reads like hearsay. Petition of Jacob Alford and the Inhabitants, January 30, 1779, in January–February 1779, Joint Papers, Petitions, General Assembly Session Records, NCA.

57. Colonel Charles McLean to the General Assembly, February 6, 1779, NCSR 14:261–62; *Moravian Records*, 4:1880.

58. House Journals, February 12, 1779, NCSR 13:734b–734c; Caswell to General Locke, March 5, 1779, NCSR 14:27; Caswell to General Butler, March 5, 1779, 14:29; Caswell to General Jones, March 5, 1779, 14:31. Moore's rising led

the Assembly to pass the resolution (quoted above) allowing justices of the peace to seize suspected disaffected persons.

59. Caswell to General Locke, March 5, 1779, NCSR 14:27.

60. Examples from the summer of 1779 are found in Griffith Rutherford to Caswell, June 28, 1779, NCSR 14:132–33; Stephen Cobb to Caswell, July 26, 1779, NCSR 14:176–77; Caswell to Colonel John Heritage, July 19, 1779, NCSR 14:169–70. Rankin believes that the persistent rumors of Tory risings made it difficult to raise troops in response to the British moves in the South in 1779. *North Carolina Continentals*, 207.

61. Griffith Rutherford to Caswell, February 1, 1777, NCSR 11:372; Caswell to Thomas Burke, February 16, 1777, NCSR 11:393; *Moravian Records*, 3:1183.

62. For rumors of murders and so forth, from the spring of 1777 to the fall of 1778, see the *Moravian Records*, 3:1185, 1227, 1270, 1249; Charles Robertson to Caswell, April 27, 1777, NCSR 11:458–60. See also Rankin, *North Carolina Continentals*, 131. For Caswell's recognition of white encroachments, see Savanuca to Governor Caswell, April 14, 1778, NCSR 13:90; and Caswell's subsequent proclamation, May 5, 1778, NCSR 13:115–16. For the bounty law, see NCSR 24:15.

63. For 1779, see Wheeler, *Historical Sketches*, 2:450–51; and Senate Journals, January 20, 1779, NCSR 13:539. Robert Ganyard mentions the 1780–81 expeditions and provides more details for the incidents in 1777 through 1778. "Threat from the West," 64. The pension record of Samuel Riggs in Dann, ed., *Revolution Remembered*, 306–9, recounts the 1780–81 expedition. See also a letter from a Whig in Georgia, conveying intelligence about British intentions to raise the Indians in 1779. He wrote: "you may depend that there's 500 Indians on the Altamaha waiting to assist in their [the British] movement. . . . they expect all the Indians that Tate, Cameron and Stuart have Influence over to assist 'em on the frontiers of So. Carolina. I mentioned to the [British] General I thought it would be cruel to let the Indians loose, who would massacre indiscriminately, he told me they would be under the Command of White Men and meant more to divert the Army than to do Execution." Miscellaneous Papers, volume 2, NCA.

64. Several letters of Governor Caswell, all dated August 21, 1777, NCSR 11:583–85; *North Carolina Gazette*, New Bern, September 19, 1777, NCSR 11:774; Caswell to John Nelson, September 20, 1777, NCSR 11:775; *North Carolina Gazette*, New Bern, October 24, 1777, NCSR 11:787.

65. For the impending rumors of this British move into the South, see Russell, *North Carolina in the Revolutionary War*, 62–64.

66. Senate Journals, October 20, November 6, 1779, NCSR 13:835, 888; House Journals, October 9, 1779, NCSR 13:988.

67. Caswell to Colonel John Heritage, July 19, 1779, NCSR 14:170.

68. NCSR 24:3–4.

69. *Moravian Records*, 3:1253–54. For other examples of militia units keeping "strict order" in this period, see ibid., 3:1240, 1273.

70. Stephen Cobb to Caswell, July 26, 1779, NCSR 14:176–77. The governor sent the Third North Carolina Regiment under Captain J. Ballard, who apprehended several of the Basses. Ballard was unsure whether the prisoners fell under civil or military jurisdiction and referred the matter to the governor. Captain J. Ballard to Governor Caswell, August 3, 1779, NCSR 14:185; Stephen Cobb to Governor Caswell, August 5, 1779, NCSR 14:186.

71. The date of the poem is not certain but appears to be from this period, between 1777 to 1779. Burke, *The Poems of Governor Thomas Burke*, 9.

72. I have a photocopy of the original of Richardson's petition made some years ago by George Stevenson, an archivist at the NCA; as of this writing the original has not been relocated. Richardson's neighbors' supporting statement, dated September 29, 1779, is in the Draper Manuscript Collection, North Carolina Papers (series KK), State Historical Society of Wisconsin.

73. No will or tax assessment survives for Richardson, but he appears in the prewar Tryon County Court records several times as a grand juror, or a road juror, as well as one of those made responsible for verifying the sheriff's collection of taxes. He also held enough land to sell 157 acres of it in 1770. As late as 1778, he was still trusted enough to be appointed one of the tax assessors for a county district. Minutes of the Tryon County Pleas and Quarter Sessions, NCA (July 1769, April 1770, July 1770, August 1770, January 1772, April 1772, July 1772, April 1778).

74. NCSR 22:959.

7. "The Law of Retaliation"

1. Simcoe, *A Journal of the Operations*, 173. The question of firing at sentinels arose frequently during the war. See pension record of John Chaney reprinted in Dann, ed., *Revolution Remembered*, 230–31; Conway, *War of American Independence*, 74, 81; Knouff, "Common People's Revolution," 181, 204; Paret, "Colonial Experience," 47.

2. Dann, ed., *Revolution Remembered*, 189.

3. The chronological divisions used here in terms of violence escalation are appropriate to North Carolina. Similar stories with different chronologies could be told for Georgia and South Carolina.

4. The phrase is from Shy, "Hearts and Minds in the American Revolution," 178. See also Fowler, "Egregious Villains," 38ff.; Brown, *The King's Friends*, 58–61.

5. Deposition of Mathew Goodson, August 5, 1778, Salisbury District Superior Court Records, Criminal Action Papers, 1779, NCA. For Americans' almost legalistic recognition of the legitimacy of successful force combined with a realpolitik sense of wanting to be on the winning side, see Lee, *American Revolution*, 124, 452, 459; Gray's Narrative; Greene to Governor Burke, August 12, 1781, NCSR 15:605; Francis Marion to General Gates, November 21, 1780, Gates Papers (mi-

crofilm ed.); General Davidson to General Sumner, September 18, 1780, NCSR 14:773. Examples of Loyalists pursuing official commissions are discussed below.

6. Harold E. Selesky comments similarly on the relationship between the militias' style of war, the lack of institutional restraint, and revenge. "Colonial America," 85.

7. Typically when historians have reported on the Whig-Tory violence, they have highlighted quotes from generals and politicians who produced generic, if vivid, commentaries on the ongoing violence. Some standard examples include General Gates to the North Carolina Board of War, November 12, 1780, Gates Papers (microfilm ed.); Governor Burke's address to the General Assembly, June 29, 1781, NCSR 17:913; General Greene to Robert Howe, December 29, 1780, *Greene's Papers*, 7:17–18; General Drayton to Governor Burke, July 6, 1781, NCSR 15:511–13.

8. Remonstrance and petition from a number of Inhabitants of the District of Salisbury, April–May 1782, Joint Standing Committees, Propositions & Grievances—Report and Papers, General Assembly Session Records, NCA.

9. *Moravian Records*, 4:1657. Aaron Burr made a similar distinction: "Various have been the reports concerning the barbarities committed by the *Hessians*, most of them incredible and false. They are fonder of plunder than blood, and are more the engines than the authors of cruelty." Burr to Mrs. Edwards, September 26, 1776, Force, ed., *American Archives*, 5th ser., 2:551. See also a similar sense of the gradation of various kinds of military violence in Patrick Ferguson's "Proposed Plan for bringing the Army under strict discipline," in Rankin, ed., *An Officer out of His Time*, 2:336–42.

10. Petition of Sundry Inhabitants of Salisbury and Parts Adjacent, April–May 1782, Joint Standing Committees, Propositions & Grievances—Report and Papers, General Assembly Session Records, NCA.

11. Samuel Strudwick to Governor Burke, July 1781, NCSR 15:503–4.

12. Martin, *Ordinary Courage*, 69.

13. Samuel McCorkle, "Sermon against Plundering," in Samuel E. McCorkle Papers, DUSC.

14. Ettwein to Graff, February 18, 1777, *Moravian Records*, 3:1409. See also Foote, *Sketches*, 417.

15. As the currencies began to depreciate, yet another gradation developed between being paid with Continental currency, with North Carolina currency, and even occasionally in salt (the best). See General Greene to the Board of War, December 18, 1780, *Greene's Papers*, 6:598; *Moravian Records*, 4:1560, 1692.

16. Board of War to George Fletcher, September 23, 1780, NCSR 14:392. The board wrote to Thomas Polk in a similar manner that "if we do not feed the soldiers they must take care of themselves, and will do it at the point of the Bayonet. This must be avoided if possible." October 5, 1780, NCSR 14:405. General Gates gave almost identical instructions to several South Carolina militia officers whom he sent to gather provisions, further ordering that they ensure "leaving a sufficient quantity for the Support of each Family." Gates to Colonel Giles, Hicks

and Others, Circular, July 29, 1780, Gates Papers (microfilm ed.). See also Colonel Archibald Lytle to Governor Caswell, January 28, 1780, NCSR 15:329; Graham, *General Joseph Graham*, 312; Weller, "Irregular War," 135–36.

17. Greene to Morgan, December 16, 1780, *Greene's Papers*, 6:589–90.

18. For the best discussion of the eighteenth-century use of contributions, see Lynn, *Giant of the Grand Siècle*, 196ff., 213, 216. See also Vattel, *Law of Nations*, 292; Van Creveld, *Supplying War*, 8; Anderson, *War and Society*, 137–38; Lynn, "Food, Funds, and Fortresses."

19. Samuel McCorkle, "Sermon against Plundering," in Samuel E. McCorkle Papers, DUSC. The sermon is undated, but contextual clues place it probably in 1781. In general, this sermon provides a remarkable summary of attitudes toward the various kinds of plunder and the animosity that unregulated plunder could engender. McCorkle was a Presbyterian minister of the Thyatira (Rowan County) congregation.

20. An account of house burning in the *New Jersey Gazette*, August 5, 1778, makes this distinction clear: "Some have the effrontery to say, that the British officers by no means countenance or allow of burning. Did not the wanton burning of Charleston and Kingston in Esopus, besides many other instances, sufficiently evince the contrary, their conduct in Freehold I think may—the officers having been seen to exult at the sight of the flames, and heard to declare that they never could conquer America until they burnt every rebel's house, and murdered man, woman and child. . . . If the first officers in the British army are so far divested of honour and humanity, what may we not expect from the soldiery?"

21. Marshall to a member of the Unity's Elders Conference, June 21, 1781, *Moravian Records*, 4:1910. Marshall went on to give even more credit to the behavior of the Continental troops; see the epilogue.

22. Burke was responding to complaints that a Colonel Young of the militia had been complicit in plundering in Wilmington. Governor Burke to General Lillington, February 27, 1782, NCSR 16:527–28. See also *Moravian Records*, 4:1622.

23. Armand Armstrong to Governor Burke, August 20, 1781, NCSR 22:567–68. Similarly, though less plainly, General Butler to Governor Burke, August 10, 1781, NCSR 22:557.

24. State Military Orders, April 21, 1782, NCSR 16:268–69. Compare these accounts to the Loyalist groups in New Jersey early in the war, whose activities seemed mainly to consist of confiscating weapons. Fowler, "Egregious Villains," 66–70, 76–77.

25. Governor Burke instructed Major Hogg: "I need not to recommend to you to prevent, and if necessary, to punish all acts of plunder or inhuman or disgraceful violence, nor the having particular care that the families of those unfortunate people be not insulted or deprived of the means of subsistence." Included in this instruction was the assumption that Hogg's troops would be subsisting on the farms of the Tories in the area. March 1782, NCSR 16:231.

26. Colonel William Campbell's Orders of the Day, October 14, 1780, NCSR

15:118–19; Foote, *Sketches*, 417; Nestor, "To the Militia of Pennsylvania." For some North Carolina Rebel militia officers expressing their distaste for plundering, see General Harrington to the Board of War, November 3, 1780, NCSR 15:140; Major Nathaniel Morris to General Gates, October 27, 1780, Gates Papers (microfilm ed.) (this letter refers to a militia officer who turned over some plundered horses not knowing what to do with them); Lieutenant Andrew Armstrong to General Rutherford, March 12, 1782, NCSR 16:538.

27. Samuel McCorkle, "Sermon against Plundering," in Samuel E. McCorkle Papers, DUSC.

28. Examples of payment or receipt are numerous, but see, for example, *Moravian Records*, 4:1530, 1635, 1638, 1728, 1743. Even when paid or given certificates, however, the Moravians still had much to complain about, given the depreciation of the currencies.

29. Ibid., 4:1644–45.

30. Ibid., 4:1685. For other Moravian accounts of direct intervention or punishment by officers in cases of attempted illicit plundering, see ibid., 4:1683, 1655, 1677, 1681, 1684.

31. Ibid., 4:1562, 1632, 1666, 1677, 1741, 1744.

32. Ibid., 3:1277–78.

33. Ibid., 4:1565.

34. First quote from ibid., 4:1684, second from 4:1666. See also 4:1701–2.

35. Ibid., 4:1645 (I have provided a "*sic,*" but it may be that the diarist reduced the number of miscreants from several to one). See also the reaction of a group of Virginia militia to the excess of some Continentals in September 1780, ibid., 4:1563.

36. Ibid., 4:1641. It is pointless to give page references for all such comments, either positive or negative. They fill the diaries for the years 1780–81. It is also interesting to note that there are many examples of the militia or the Continentals attending church services while camped near the Moravian towns, in some cases improving their behavior after those services. See ibid., 3:1073, 1283; 4:1562, 1627, 1644, 1666, 1682, 1691.

37. This observation applies only to those instances where the plunderers were recognizably constituted militia forces, and not mere gangs of robbers. This was a distinction that the Moravians were always careful to make.

38. Prewar controversies over landholding may have contributed to some animosity between the Wilkes County men and the Moravian communities. *Moravian Records*, 3:1241, 1208–9, and the editor's comments on 4:1792n.8.

39. Ibid., 4:1743.

40. Ibid., 4:1677.

41. Ibid., 4:1679. See also Joseph Graham's discussion of a group of plunderers whom he interrupted in the Moravian towns who claimed that the Moravians were Loyalists and "remonstrated that they had been plundered by Tories and had a right to make themselves whole." Graham, *General Joseph Graham*, 312.

42. Starkey, "Paoli to Stony Point," treats the question of quarter at length. See also the debate over the petition of Philip Alston, accused of killing a Tory. It was noted that he had been in command of troops and therefore could and should have taken the man prisoner. House Journals, December 24, 1785, NCSR 17:399–400.

43. Board of War to Colonel Ambrose Ramsey, September 18, 1780, NCSR 14:381. Similarly, Governor Martin's orders to Captain Gillespie on October 24, 1782, advised: "you will observe strict discipline and regularity, no marauding, plundering, beating prisoners or killing them but in the act of taking or making their escape, on the severest penalties." NCSR 16:717.

44. It must be assumed that many examples of surrendering men being killed on the battlefield have not appeared in the records. But, as the following examples indicate, there were also frequent occasions in which the Rebels took substantial numbers of prisoners, even in ambush and night attack situations that were traditionally considered to be moments when quarter was more doubtful. See Starkey, "Paoli to Stony Point," 24–26.

45. Davie, Revolutionary War Sketches, 12.

46. Pension Record of Thomas Cummings (S6780). For other, not isolated, examples of North Carolina militia forces taking prisoners, see the pension claims of William Ward, Peter Banks, and Daniel Merrit collected in Camin, North Carolina Pension Applications, 1:18, 2:217, 3:331.

47. Wheeler, Historical Sketches, 2:41.

48. Letter of Colonels William Campbell, Isaac Shelby, and Benjamin Cleveland, Virginia Gazette, November 18, 1780, NCSR 15:164.

49. Account of Robert Campbell, NCSR 15:103. See also account derived from interviews with Colonel Shelby, NCSR 15:108.

50. Colonel William Campbell to Colonel Arthur Campbell, October 20, 1780, NCSR 15:126–27. See also Arthur Campbell's later memoir of the battle, NCSR 15:134.

51. Graham, General Joseph Graham, 281–82. For detailed studies of the battle and the surrender, see Bailey, Commanders at King's Mountain; Draper, King's Mountain and Its Heroes; Henry, Narrative of the Battle of Cowan's Ford; Moss, The Patriots at King's Mountain; White, The King's Mountain Men.

52. See Knight's "Prisoner Exchange and Parole" and Metzger's Prisoner in the American Revolution for general studies of the subject.

53. See chapter 5. For the continuing relatively benign view of Loyalist prisoners in 1777, see Thomas Burke to Governor Caswell, March 2, 1777, NCSR 11:401–2.

54. J. Rutledge to Caswell, June 23, 1779, NCSR 14:130–31; Caswell to Rutledge, July 11, 1779; Major Armstrong to General Gates, November 19, 1780, NCSR 14:744; Colonel Jno. Armstrong to General Sumner, June 13, 1781, NCSR 15:481; Governor Burke to General Greene, March 28, 1782, NCSR 16:565–69; NCSR 16:345–47; State Military Orders for April 21, 1782, NCSR 16:266–67; Governor Burke to General Greene, May 5, 1782, NCSR 16:318; Judge Jno. Wil-

liams to Governor Martin, June 27, 1782. The Continental Congress had resolved as early as December 1777 that Tories captured in arms should be returned to the individual states for criminal prosecution. Actual practice in the field varied. Knight, "Prisoner Exchange and Parole," 203.

55. William Davidson and William Davie to General Sumner, October 6, 1780, NCSR 14:676.

56. Gray's Narrative. This document appears to have been composed sometime in 1782 while Gray was still with the British army in Charleston. See also Brown, *The Good Americans*, 105; Fowler, "Egregious Villains," 188–89.

57. Board of War to Colonel Martin Armstrong, November 14, 1780, NCSR 14:462–64; Senate Journals, February 3, 1781, NCSR 17:668; Governor Burke to General Greene, March 28, 1782, NCSR 16:565–69; Governor Burke to Major Lewis, April 5, 1782, NCSR 16:269; Governor Burke to General Greene, May 5, 1782, NCSR 16:318; Governor Martin to General Alexander Leslie, May 12, 1782, NCSR 16:685–86.

58. Governor Martin to Archibald Maclaine (n.d.) 1782, NCSR 16:416–18. See also Governor Martin to General Greene, May 12, 1782, NCSR 16:684.

59. General Gates to the Board of War, November 15, 1780, Gates Papers (microfilm ed.); Colonel Thomas Wade to General Gates, November 23, 1780, ibid.; Senate Journals, February 3, 1781, NCSR 17:668; Proclamation of Governor Alexander Martin, December 25, 1781, NCSR 17:1049; Governor Burke to General Greene, February 15, 1782, NCSR 16:511; Governor Burke to General Sumner, February 26, 1782, NCSR 16:522; Governor Burke to Major Hogg, March 13, 1782, NCSR 16:229–31; Governor Martin to Governor Matthews (of South Carolina), June 9, 1782, NCSR 16:689–90. A few advocated more unconditional pardons but again tended to preclude the excessively violent or those who had taken commissions. See Alexander Martin to Governor Nash, November 10, 1780, NCSR 15:151–52.

60. That said, it must again be admitted that there is also significant evidence for abuse and occasional cold-blooded killing of prisoners. We will see how such violations served to inspire retaliation.

61. We will refer here largely to the Whigs' and Tories' treatment of each other. British prisoners, once taken, in virtually all cases were treated relatively strictly according to the customs of war. That is, they were held until they could be exchanged, with at least casual concern for the conditions of their confinement. Metzger, *Prisoner in the American Revolution*, 1–2; Knight, "Prisoner Exchange and Parole," 202, 210ff., deals specifically with the situation in the South.

62. Cornwallis to Smallwood, November 10, 1780, Gates Papers (microfilm ed.). There is a similar statement of attitudes about the nature of prisoners and when their execution would be appropriate in a letter from Samuel Ashe to William Caswell, May 28, 1781, William Caswell Papers, NCA. Related to this letter is one from Major Craig to William Hooper, July 20, 1781, NCSR 15:553–55. Both are unfortunately too long and rambling to quote.

63. Pension Record of William Gipson in Dann, ed., *Revolution Remembered*, 188–89. For the traditional use of spicketing, or picqueting, see Scouller, *The Armies of Queen Anne*, 268, 390; Claver, *Under the Lash*, 12–13. Picqueting was still listed as a punishment in the North Carolina militia law in 1774. NCSR 23:943.

64. Elijah Alexander recorded that when his militia unit took over guarding some Loyalists, some "were whipped so soon as Court Martial was holden, others were sent to jail or headquarters." Elijah Alexander Paper, NCA. See also Caruthers, *Old North State*, 87, and the pension record of Robert Love, transcribed in the David Schenk Papers, NCA. The courts-martial, although certainly drumhead, were not purely formalities either; they did hand down differential sentences. See *Moravian Records*, 4:1564, 1643, 1626–28. See the pension claim of Peter Banks in Camin, *North Carolina Pension Applications*, 1:18, for a Tory found in a swamp hideout, taken to New Bern, tried, and shot.

65. Isaac Shelby's account of King's Mountain, NCSR 15:109.

66. Ibid.

67. In addition to Shelby's account, see the Pension Record of William Lenoir (S7137); Robert Campbell's account of King's Mountain, NCSR 15:103–4; a British account from the *Scots Magazine*, January 1781, printed in NCSR 15:183.

68. Wheeler, *Historical Sketches*, 2:444; Fanning, *Narrative*, 35. Fanning's narrative, although it must be read very carefully and in conjunction with the parallel Whig documents, is an extraordinarily valuable document for the nature of the late-war Whig-Tory violence. In general, although Fanning's narrative is explicitly exculpatory, many of his accounts of restraint and of military formalism can be confirmed by Whig documentation of the same events.

69. Both Fanning's narrative and Caruthers's *Old North State* are particularly replete with accounts of one "cold-blooded" killing being cited to justify another. Some examples are outlined below. Caruthers, expressing his own opinion from his early-nineteenth-century perspective, noted the difference between the execution of men after a trial, on a pretext (even if trumped up), and other less formal, though still cold-blooded, killings. Ibid., 83.

70. General Herndon Ramsey and others to Governor Burke, July 22, 1781, NCSR 22:550.

71. Petition of Henry Reed and others, [January 3, 1787?], November 1786–January 1787, Senate Joint Resolutions, General Assembly Session Records, NCA. The Assembly agreed to pardon him. See Senate Journals, January 3, 1787, NCSR 18:209; House Journals, January 4, 1787, NCSR 18:444.

72. Fanning, *Narrative*, 35, 36–37.

73. Petition of John Arnold to General Assembly, November 16, 1790, November–December 1790, Joint Standing Committees, Committee of Claims—Reports & Papers, General Assembly Sessions Records, NCA.

74. Pension Record of John Taylor, in Dann, ed., *Revolution Remembered*, 210.

75. Caruthers, *Old North State*, 86, 88, 96, 97, 101. See also militia captain James Devane's refusal to participate in the rounding up of Loyalist women and children and bringing them to Wilmington. He resigned. Pension claim of James Devane in Camin, *North Carolina Pension Applications*, 1:87.

76. *Moravian Records*, 4:1573ff.; Colonel Joseph Hawkins to Governor Nash, June 17, 1781, NCSR 15:487; Pension Record of Henry Kea (S8783); Captain Dun. McNicol to Caswell, May 31, 1777, NCSR 11:480; Senate Journals, October 29, 1779, 13:870. All of these citations refer to the state's efforts to provide cash allowances for or feed prisoners. Kea's statement is a simple note about how their orders were to bring prisoners in and turn them over to Continental officers. Additional support comes from the very many pensioners who recalled tours of duty doing nothing but guarding prisoners.

77. Fanning, *Narrative*, 76.

78. Ibid., 35, 45, 48, 51, 53.

79. See also examples of more straightforward granting of parole: NCSR 14:718, 719; Pension Record of John McMullen (W4287).

80. Petition of Henry Reed and others, [January 3, 1787?], November 1786–January 1787, Senate Joint Resolutions, General Assembly Session Records, NCA.

81. The most famous example is that of Governor Burke, who was captured by Fanning in 1781, delivered to the British in Wilmington, and then transferred to Charleston. While there he lived on his parole but felt that his life was threatened by resident Loyalists. He escaped and then spilled much ink defending that escape. For just a couple of examples, see Burke's speech to the Assembly, April 16, 1782, NCSR 16:15–16; William R. Davie to Governor Burke, February 23, 1782, NCSR 16:202; Rankin, *North Carolina Continentals*, 372. See also Matthew Ramsey's effort to defend himself against a charge of breaking parole, in Fanning, *Narrative*, 66.

82. Fanning, *Narrative*, 60–61. See also Foote's account of Humphrey Hunter, *Sketches*, 424–25.

83. In addition to the examples below, note the efforts of the Whig leaders of the volunteers who were marching against Colonel Patrick Ferguson in 1780 to request a Continental general to assume command of their force. Colonel Cleveland and others to General Gates, October 4, 1780, Gates Papers (microfilm ed.).

84. Fanning, *Narrative*, 37–38.

85. Ibid., 45.

86. Ibid., 50, 73–76, 64ff. Parole was discussed above. See also Fanning to Governor Burke, February 29, 1782, NCSR 16:205–8.

87. Fanning, *Narrative*, 62, 68.

88. Ibid., 64, 70.

89. Fanning to Governor Burke, February 29, 1782, NCSR 16:205–8. See also Fanning, *Narrative*, 64–71.

90. Rape is another crime potentially at the top of this hierarchy but is much

less visible in the records. Fanning's conclusion to his narrative is worthy of note in this regard. He quoted the pardon issued by the Assembly on May 17, 1783, which specifically excluded him and two other individuals, and any person "guilty of deliberate and willful murder, robbery, rape, house breaking." Fanning then wrote, "Many people is fools enough to think, because our three names is particular put in this Act, that we are guilty of the crimes set forth.—But I defy the world to charge me with rape, or anything more, than I have set forth in this Journal." Fanning, *Narrative*, 104. See Donagan, "Atrocity," 1149, for earlier European views on rape as a war crime. For an amused near-tolerance of rape by soldiers, compare Lord Rawdon's comment in 1776 that because of the British army's presence, "A girl cannot step into the bushes to pluck a rose without the most imminent risk of being ravished, and they are so little accustomed to these vigorous methods, that they don't bear them with the proper resignation, and of consequence we have the most entertaining courts-martial every day." Letter from Lord Rawdon, August 1776, Great Britain, Historical Manuscripts Commmission, *Report on the Manuscripts of the Late Reginald Rawdon Hastings* (London, 1934), 3:179, cited in Starkey, *European and Native American*, 28–29.

91. See Knouff's assertion along these lines in "Common People's Revolution," 187–88.

92. In all of the rhetorical expostulations justifying pursuing Tories, I have never seen one that cited their killing of someone in battle.

93. Examples of clear murder and attempted murder appear in *Moravian Records*, 4:1650; Wheeler, *Historical Sketches*, 2:114; Loyalist claim of Maturine Colville (PRO AO12/37/117); Pension Record of James Shipman (W17810).

94. *Moravian Records*, 4:1549.

95. Wheeler, *Historical Sketches*, 2:459–60.

96. Pension Record of Robert Kincaid (W26186).

97. For other examples of restraint from killing, see Wheeler, *Historical Sketches*, 2:451; Graham, *General Joseph Graham*, 226; Fanning, *Narrative*, 48; and the examples cited above.

98. Vattel argued that retaliation generally should be avoided but that if "he [the sovereign] is dealing with an inhuman enemy who frequently commits atrocities such as . . . [hanging prisoners without cause] he may refuse to spare the lives of certain prisoners whom he captures, and may treat them as his own men have been treated." *Law of Nations*, 280–81.

99. General Alexander Leslie to Greene, April 27, 1782, *Greene's Papers*, 11:128; Cornwallis to Smallwood, November 10, 1780, Gates Papers (microfilm ed.). See further discussion in the epilogue.

100. For discussion of retaliation in other states during the Revolutionary War, see Fowler, "Egregious Villains," 186–87, 194, 313–16; Shy, "American Society," 81. See also Bertram Wyatt-Brown's discussion of honor in southern history and its corollary of retaliation, *Southern Honor*, xv, 34; and Richard Maxwell Brown's studies of the vigilante tradition in America, *Strain of Violence* and *No Duty to Retreat*.

101. Gray's Narrative.

102. Governor Burke to Major Craig, June 27, 1781, NCSR 22:1028 (emphasis in original). Burke goes on to confirm the greater power of retaliation, noting that if Craig allows vengeance to be taken on the Whig prisoners he is holding, Burke will do the same to the Tories he had control of. Religious writers on retaliation authorized vengeance but demanded that it be public, not private, vengeance. Stuart, "'For the Lord Is a Man of Warr,'" 523; McCorkle, "Sermon against Plundering," Samuel E. McCorkle Papers, DUSC.

103. Foote, *Sketches*, 279. Forbes survived long enough to report who had kicked him. For a similar story of personal revenge, see Willcox, *John Willcox*, 208. Thomas Blount wrote during his operations around New Bern in 1781 that, despite having to retreat, "we brought off our Tory prisoners and should they have exercised any cruelties on their prisoners I will certainly retaliate on them." Blount, *Blount Papers*, 1:18–19. Similarly, a Whig militia company that had captured a small band of Tories "held a kind of court martial . . . and it was decided, that as they [the Tories] had shot Johnson, they should be shot next morning." Caruthers, *Old North State*, 87.

104. Pension Record of Jonathan Starkey (S7612). Similarly, see William Gipson's justifying his unit's torture and killing of some Tories because of their beating of his mother. Dann, ed., *Revolution Remembered*, 189.

105. Pension Record of Moses Hall, in Dann, ed., *Revolution Remembered*, 202–3.

106. Petition from the Inhabitants of Guilford Co., June 28, 1781, June–July 1781, Joint Papers, Committee of Propositions and Grievances, General Assembly Session Records, NCA.

107. Major Craig to William Hooper, July 20, 1781, NCSR 15:554. For further comments on the general sense of retaliation and its legitimate use, see Graham, *General Joseph Graham*, 355; Colonel Nathan Bryan to Governor Burke, September 6, 1781, NCSR 15:634; Governor Burke to the General Assembly, July 14, 1781, NCSR 22:1042; Fanning, *Narrative*, 61.

108. Most of the pardons discussed below were issued by the Assembly after the accused Whig had been brought to trial (in county or district courts) by friends or relatives of victimized Tories. The outcome of those trials either went against the accused or was considered in doubt enough to warrant petitioning the Assembly. A more thorough examination of postwar court records (which are relatively scanty) is warranted.

109. Senate Journals, June 29, 1781, NCSR 17:827.

110. Pardons issued for the killing of Alexander Shannon: NCSR 18:209; for Cleveland's killing of William Coyle and Lemuel Jones: NCSR 835, 888, 988 (the House vote on this pardon was close, 29–24); for Philip Alston's killing of a Tory, NCSR 17:399–400. As a parallel case, see the British court-martial of Loyalists accused of plundering, discussed in Conway, "Military-Civilian Crime," 87.

111. Petition of William Linton to General Assembly, October 3, 1783, April

20–May 18, Reports and Papers, Joint Select Committees, General Assembly Session Records, NCA. Other details of the Linton/Quinn case can be found in NCSR 22:1031; 15:518; 19:524. The Assembly recommended a pardon.

112. It proved impossible to measure this difference quantitatively. The subjective impression, however, is convincing.

113. Major Craig to Governor Nash, June 20, 1781, NCSR 22:1024.

114. Starkey, "War and Culture"; Conway, "To Subdue America"; Conway, "'The Great Mischief Complain'd of.'" The question of British policy has also occupied other historians; see, for example, Smith, *Loyalists and Redcoats*; Shy, "Hearts and Minds in the American Revolution"; Tiedemann, "Patriots by Default." Sylvia Frey argues that in South Carolina, Cornwallis vacillated back and forth between terror and restraint. *Water from the Rock*, 116, 129–30.

115. In South Carolina, there was also vacillation in British policy with regard to whether many former Whigs would be allowed to remain neutral or have to take up arms in Loyalist militias. The mixed messages followed by enforcement drove many Whigs who might have stayed quietly at home into the Rebel militia. This inconsistency did not have a significant impact on North Carolina Whigs, most of whom had never been forced to accept British parole. For the changes in British policy, see Nadelhaft, *Disorders of War*, 55–56; Frasche, "Problems of Command," 62; Weller, "Irregular War," 133; Weigley, *Partisan War*, 12–13. For the dates and content of the various proclamations of Clinton and Cornwallis, the reader is referred to the preceding secondary works. For some examples of popular responses to those changes, see Examination of William Allman, September 20, 1780, Gates Papers (microfilm ed.); Smallwood to Gates, October 27, 1780, Gates Papers (microfilm ed.); Graham, *General Joseph Graham*, 241–42; Tarleton, *History of the Campaigns*, 92.

116. Remonstrance and petition from a number of inhabitants of the district of Salisbury, April–May 1782, Joint Standing Committees, Propositions & Grievances—Reports and Papers, General Assembly Session Records, NCA.

117. Ibid.

118. It should be pointed out that the senior British leadership in the southern campaign seems to have been committed to controlling the soldiery. There were many efforts, particularly by Cornwallis, to try to enforce discipline restraining violence against civilians. Sylvia Frey has even argued that by this point in the war the British had greatly reduced the amount of pillaging by the army. *British Soldier*, 75–76. For specific examples of British attempts at control, see Tarleton, *History of the Campaigns*, 55–56, 297–98; *Moravian Records*, 4:1554; Newsome, "A British Orderly Book," 164, 293, 296–97, 368, 379; General Leslie to General Clinton, November 19, 1780, NCSR 15:301–2; Lee, *American Revolution*, 154. Conway argues that there was much less agreement or consistency within the lower ranks of the officer corps over whether to restrain or overlook the violence of the soldiery. "To Subdue America," passim.

119. For general comments and examples of the Whig use of atrocity propa-

ganda, see Bowman, *Morale of the American Revolutionary Army*, 100; Davidson, *Propaganda*, 365–75; Berger, *Broadsides and Bayonets*, 140–41. See Knouff, "Common People's Revolution," 181ff., 202–7, 211, for British misbehavior motivating Whigs in Pennsylvania.

120. *JCC*, 7:276–79, 8:565. This report may not have been actually published, but that was certainly the intent of Congress. For some sample published broadsides that are excellent representatives of the kind of vivid atrocity rhetoric often used against the British, see "Interesting Intelligence. By Mr. Joseph White"; "Extract of a Letter from an Officer"; "The Progress of the British." Narratives of captivity published during the war served a similar purpose; see, for example, Dodge, *A Narrative of the Capture*, 13–14; Allen, *A Narrative of Colonel Ethan Allen's Captivity*, 29ff.

121. Captain Cogdell to Governor Caswell, May 28, 1778, NCSR 13:140–41. See also Cornelius Harnett to William Wilkinson, December 16, 1777, NCSR 11:822.

122. *North Carolina Gazette*, October 31, 1777, NCSR 11:789–90.

123. Lee's and Tarleton's memoirs serve as the primary narratives for the incident. Lee, *American Revolution*, 164–65; Tarleton, *History of the Campaigns*, 30–33, 79–81. See also Abraham Buford to the Virginia Assembly, June 2, 1780, T. A. Emmet Collection, NCA; *Moravian Records*, 4:1544.

124. Thomas Person to Thomas Burke, June 21, 1780, NCSR 14:858.

125. Lee, *American Revolution*, 165.

126. There are too many to cite, but two examples bear mentioning. British Major Wemyss became infamous in the South for his burning of Presbyterian churches. See Weller, "Irregular War," 134–35; General Gates to Samuel Huntington, November 14, 1780, Gates Papers (microfilm ed.). Cornwallis was also accused of deliberately trying to infect the population with smallpox. General Sumner to General Gates, October 8, 1780, Gates Papers (microfilm ed.); *Pennsylvania Gazette*, November 14, 1781. See the work of Elizabeth Fenn on the nebulous status of biological warfare as a violation of the customs of war. "Beyond Jeffrey Amherst," 1573–80. Also see Nadelhaft, *Disorders of War*, 56–59, and Weigley, *Partisan War*, 12–13, for their discussion of British violations of the customs of war and reaction in South Carolina.

127. *Moravian Records*, 4:1675, 1742; Albertson, *In Ancient Albemarle*, 165–67. Cornwallis noted that "Great Complaints having been made of Negroes Stragling from the line of March, plundrg & Using Violence to the Inhabitants." Newsome, "A British Orderly Book," 296.

128. The British encouraged slaves to come into British lines and formed some service units from them. Frey, *Water from the Rock*, 81–142; Frey, *The British Soldier*, 76–77; Nadelhaft, *Disorders of War*, 62–64; Quarles, *The Negro in the American Revolution*, 135–52.

129. Graham, *General Joseph Graham*, 269. Conway, "To Subdue America," 396–97, notes that many officers also felt this way.

130. For example, Captain De Peyster, captured at King's Mountain, noted how it was their "misfortune of being taken by the militia" who did not treat them appropriately. Captain De Peyster to General Gates, November 3, 1780, Gates Papers (microfilm ed.).

131. Allen, *A Narrative*, 21. Disgust at Rebel sniping cropped up repeatedly. Conway, *War of American Independence*, 74, 81; Starkey, *European and Native American*, 112; Knouff, "Common People's Revolution," 181, 204.

132. The British soldiers were also frustrated by the sniping that their foraging parties underwent in and around Charlotte. They took out their frustrations on the town. Preyer, *Hezekiah Alexander*, 159.

133. It is true, however, that much of the latter-day historiography of the militia has been at pains to point out the valuable, peripheral services contributed by the militia. See, for example, Higginbotham, "The American Militia," 95.

134. King's Mountain, in fact, was hardly a conventional battle. The Rebel militia completely surrounded the British force and used the forest cover to snipe with rifles until the British surrendered.

135. This story is taken from the petition of John Evans, NCSR 15:236. See also *Moravian Records*, 4:1561, 1613.

136. Brown, "Back Country Rebellions."

137. Brown, *Bloodfeud in Scotland*, 22–23. According to the Oxford English Dictionary, *hamesucken* survives in Scottish law. John Prebble documented one example of its use to prosecute British soldiers in the immediate aftermath of Culloden. *Culloden*, 306.

138. Loyalist claims of Thomas Evans (PRO AO12/35/168); Neill McGeachy (PRO AO12/36/62); Alexander McLeod (PRO AO12/36/182); James Kerr (PRO AO12/36/270); Nicholas Welsh (PRO AO12/34/374); William McQueen (PRO AO12/100/26); Neil Colbreath (PRO AO12/101/82); Mary McCaskle (PRO AO13/91/189).

139. Marion to Gates, October 4, 1780, NCSR 14:666. In 1768, Governor Tryon put specific weight on crimes that threatened physical harm or the firing of a house. Tryon's Proclamation, April 29, 1768, NCCR 7:730–31.

140. Lepore, *The Name of War*, 75–76, 87. See also Bland, *The Souldiers March*, 15.

141. There was a very strong trend of individuals having multiple tours of duty in the North Carolina Rebel militia; thus the "experience of the institution" was the multiple repeat service of individuals within it. Ninety-one randomly selected militia pensioners served an average of 3.6 tours in the North Carolina Rebel militia. In reality, that average should be higher, because many of those pensioners lost count of their tours, and others combined one or two short militia tours with a long term in the Continentals. See also Bartholomees, "Fight or Flee," 66.

142. Graham, *General Joseph Graham*, 348.

143. Henry, *Narrative of the Battle of Cowan's Ford*, 18, 27.

144. See Tarleton's praise of Sumter, who, he said "was thoroughly sensible

. . . that to keep undisciplined people together, it is necessary to employ them." *History of the Campaigns*, 97. For the rapid desertion in Charleston in 1780 of the militiamen who were unwilling to endure a siege, see Rankin, *North Carolina Continentals*, 224. See also Babits, *Devil of a Whipping*, 54; and on the persistence of this tradition in volunteer units in the Mexican War, see Winders, *Mr. Polk's Army*, 86.

145. Graham, *General Joseph Graham*, 232. Sumter's force was composed of a considerable number of North Carolinians in addition to those from his native South Carolina.

146. Petition of Charles McLean, undated, NCSR 15:213 (the original is filed with the General Assembly Session Records for August–September 1780, NCA). McLean petitioned because he had taken control of the seized horses, sold them, and took bond to the governor for the amount. He had since been threatened with prosecution because of it.

147. John (?) Johnston to James Iredell, March 17, 1776, *Papers of James Iredell*, 1:344–45.

148. Many historians have pointed out this tendency. See, for example, Higginbotham, "The American Militia," 99; Weigley, *Partisan War*, 15, and passim; Brown, *The Good Americans*, 105.

149. Knouff, "Common People's Revolution," 178–85.

150. To note just a few examples where North Carolinians frankly acknowledged the necessity of resorting to partisan tactics when outnumbered, see General William Caswell to Governor Burke, August 17, 1781, NCSR 22:564; Board of War to Colonel Ambrose Ramsey, September 18, 1780, NCSR 14:381; Board of War to General Greene, January 4, 1781, NCSR 14:485.

151. Burke to Caswell, July 22, 1777, NCSR 11:529.

152. For accounts of the Battle of Ramsour's Mill, see Rankin, *North Carolina Continentals*, 239; Graham, *General Joseph Graham*, 216ff.; Lee, *American Revolution*, 167.

153. The Continental army also used such partisan tactics on occasion, for the same reasons of necessity. Washington's success at Trenton is the most famous. More commonly, however, Washington, and especially Greene, directed the militia in partisan tactics in support of the conventional efforts of the regular army. See Weigley, *American Way of War*, 3–36. See also Kwasny, *Washington's Partisan War*.

154. William R. Davie to General Sumner, October 1, 1780, Gates Papers (microfilm ed.). Davie's prediction proved correct. The militia severely harassed the British army during this period. See Gray's Narrative; Wheeler, *Historical Sketches*, 2:263–65; Tarleton, *History of the Campaigns*, 163; Graham, *General Joseph Graham*, 204–5, 313–15.

155. Pension Record of John Padgett (W2331). There are many other examples of this type of continual skirmishing in the Pension Records. See especially William Lenoir (S7137), Thomas Cummings (S6780), Joseph Graham (S6937). Also useful

are the reminiscences of William Davie in *Revolutionary War Sketches*. Fanning, *Narrative*, is also full of these kinds of incidents.

156. The tendency of night attacks to get out of hand is the subject of Starkey, "Paoli to Stony Point."

157. See, for example, Davie's ambush of a Loyalist force and the apparent killing of many seeking quarter in July 1780. Davie, *Revolutionary War Sketches*, 12.

158. Pension Record of Thomas Cummings (S6780). Pensioners were asked to list the engagements they were involved in as part of proving their service. Many of them who had been in the militia, therefore, remarked that they had not been in a "regular engagement" but had been in various skirmishes or scourings.

159. Pension claim of William Ward, in Camin, *North Carolina Pension Applications*, 3:331. Regulator Joseph Macpherson remembered that during the Battle of Alamance, some of the Regulators had fired on a white flag in ignorance of its import, although a former soldier who was present had tried to stop them. *Regulator Documents*, 569. A similar version of this story is in the *Virginia Gazette*, August 15, 1771, *Regulator Documents*, 501.

160. Knouff, "Common People's Revolution," 181, 204. For other accounts of sniping and the varying reactions of officers, see the epigraph at the beginning of this chapter.

161. See, for example, the volunteers who turned out in response to the Tory rising in Tryon County in 1779. Caswell to General Jones, March 5, 1779, NCSR 14:31. This was also especially true for troops raised against Indians. See, for example, Mintz, *Seeds of Empire*, 30–31, 97.

162. Metzger, *Prisoner in the American Revolution*, 152. Robert Graves observed this phenomenon in Britain during World War I. Graves, *Good-Bye to All That*, 202, 207.

163. Pension Record of Jonathan Starkey (S7612). See also those pensioners listed above who cited their desire to retaliate for injuries as their motivation for enlistment.

164. Foote, *Sketches*, 315. See also ibid., 326; Shelby's Account of King's Mountain, NCSR 15:105.

165. Pension Record of William Gipson in Dann, ed., *Revolution Remembered*, 187–88. The well-known South Carolina partisan leaders Andrew Pickens and Thomas Sumter are the most often cited examples of Whigs inspired to fight by their personal experience of British or Tory violence. Middlekauff, *Glorious Cause*, 452.

166. I am not trying here to enter into the large question of the motivation of Loyalists as a whole but merely noting that frequently Loyalist units appeared directly in response to violence.

167. I should reemphasize that we are talking here about the 1780–82 period. The Highlanders in 1776 were not of course motivated by a sense of revenge, although their ostensible allies, the Regulators, may have been so motivated from

the events of the Regulation. Holly Mayer's observation that refugees accompanying armies perhaps "heightened the sense of injustice" within the army may have brought a kind of home-front hatred into the camp with them. This would not apply to most militia forces in North Carolina but could apply very much to the Loyalist units accompanying the British army. *Belonging to the Army*, 12.

168. *Moravian Records*, 4:1643, and Marshall to Henry XXVIII, January 2, 1781, ibid., 4:1906.

169. Loyalist claims of Andrew Hamm (PRO AO12/35/155); Jonas Bedford (PRO AO12/34/309); Faithful Graham (PRO AO12/36/28, PRO AO13/4/270).

170. Rankin, ed., "An Officer Out of His Time," 2:294. It can only be speculated whether Ferguson's use of "mongrel" was an effort to inject race into his rhetoric. Contrast this to the much more moderate proclamation issued a few days earlier (September 27) by Cornwallis. Cornwallis's proclamation is reprinted in Preyer, *Hezekiah Alexander*, facing 156.

171. The Bass family of southeastern North Carolina likely constituted such a band of robbers taking advantage of the war. See Report on the petition of a number of inhabitants of Wayne, Duplin, and Dobbs counties, April–June 1784, Joint Standing Committees, Propositions & Grievances, May 13–26, General Assembly Session Records, NCA. What makes this petition so different is that it is able to make specific accusations against the Basses rather than generic comments about "Loyalist outrages." A similar case of retaliation as self-interest occurred when John Hinton, Jr., took some armed men to the house of John Struthers and seized Amos Thompson's slaves, who were there, claiming that Thompson had participated in the recent stealing of two of Hinton's slaves. Hinton stated that he would hold them until his were returned; he eventually attached them for damages, and the court ruled in his favor. House Journals, May 1, 1782, NCSR 16:78.

172. Greene to Samuel Huntington, December 7, 1780, *Greene's Papers*, 6:546n.9. Graham similarly noted that some, "when they found a man wealthy or possessing a property which they wished, would accuse him of Toryism." Graham, *General Joseph Graham*, 312.

173. *Moravian Records*, 4:1743; Cornwallis characterized Marion's militia as recruited "partly by the terror of his threats & cruelty of his punishments, and partly by the Promise of Plunder." Cornwallis to Clinton, December 3, 1780, NCSR 15:103. Recall the petition of John Evans, NCSR 15:236, who was shown a gallows and told to enlist. Virtually all of the Loyalists captured at King's Mountain ended up enlisting in the Whig militia, much to the dismay of the senior Whig leadership, who had hoped to exchange those prisoners. Greene to Washington, December 6, 1780, *Greene's Papers*, 6:542–45 and n. 16; Senate and House Journals, February 3, 1781, NCSR 17:668; *Moravian Records*, 4:1573.

174. For general studies of the logistical difficulties of the Whigs, see Bowler, "Logistics and Operations"; Carp, *To Starve the Army*.

175. William Davie, appointed Greene's commissary in January 1781, remembered that "without money and without credit, subsistence depended upon com-

pulsory collection and the transportation on the same uncertain and unpleasant means." Davie, *Revolutionary War Sketches*, 37, 41–42.

176. NCSR 24:344–47, 390–94. The tax in kind can be seen in operation in *Moravian Records*, 4:1623, 1629–30.

177. The Moravians made this problem explicit, complaining that the real blame for the impromptu demands made on them for provisions was that the Commissary did not "look after the soldiers and [did] not provide for them." *Moravian Records*, 4:1758. Two weeks after that comment, another militia company repaid the Moravians in food when their own supplies arrived. Ibid., 4:1759. Another pattern that is clear from the *Moravian Records* was the inability of the militia units to send a quartering officer in advance of the troops to request food. The Continentals and the British were much more successful in giving this kind of warning and consequently were more adequately fed.

178. Rankin, *North Carolina Continentals*, 353; Weller, "Irregular War," 135–36; Graham, *General Joseph Graham*, 352–53; Neimeyer, *America Goes to War*, 80.

179. Whitmel Hill to Burke, August 20, 1780, NCSR 15:56.

180. Mayer, *Belonging to the Army*. I would like to thank Holly Mayer for discussions on this difference between fraternity and community. It is possible that the lack of women accompanying short-service militia units contributed to their willingness to use illegitimate violence, although Mayer has pointed out that many of the women accompanying the Continentals could be quite bloodthirsty, with their own sense of grievances. Ibid., 12, and conversation with author, DLAR, June 26, 2000. For an example of how one woman viewed the appropriate role of women in restraining male violence, "polishing and improving the rough manners of men," see Kinnan, "A True Narrative," 326. Geoffrey Parker has argued that seventeenth-century European armies lacked a sense of corporate identity due to heterogeneous recruiting practices, high wastage rates, and mobility within ranks. *Military Revolution*, 60.

181. This is in contrast to some studies of other colonies' prerevolutionary expeditionary forces in which kinship networks and other loyalties were critical to recruiting. Anderson, *A People's Army*, 48; Selesky, *War and Society*, 170–72. Kinship and loyalty recruiting was evident in volunteer units in North Carolina, but those came with their own problems (see below). Sometimes relatives served as substitutes for those drafted, but their actual service was still removed from that kinship network.

182. Bartholomees, "Fight or Flee," 66, 70.

183. It should be noted that the standard tour was theoretically three months, but Whig desperation toward the end of the war led them to offer even shorter tours of six weeks or two months and give full credit for a three-month tour. See, for example, Graham, *General Joseph Graham*, 286–87.

184. Based on my survey of North Carolina Rebel militia pension records.

185. Pension Record of Robert Kincaid (W26186). Jesse Ausley similarly noted

of his tour that "there was very little Regularity as to officers." Pension Record of Jesse Ausley (W27520). The Wilkes County militia had a separate draft in 1778 to see which captain would get the command. Pension Record of Richard Allen, Sr., printed in NCSR 22:98.

186. Bartholomees, "Fight or Flee," 136. The Board of War advised General Smallwood, November 7, 1780 (NCSR 14:451), that he should be sure to place the volunteer companies under the formal direction of the commander in chief of the militia to help prevent their plundering. Smallwood himself wrote to Gates that "Plundering prevails to an amazing degree, by Persons who go under the denomination of Volunteers." Smallwood to Gates, October 31, 1780, Gates Papers (microfilm ed.).

187. One example has already been mentioned from 1776: Court-Martial of Captain Aaron Hill, Miscellaneous Papers, Military Collection, NCA. The Board of War ordered the court-martial of Captain Hardwick and other officers of Rowan County for plundering in 1780, but there is no record of an actual trial. Board of War to General Butler, November 25, 1780, NCSR 14:468–69. There are some records of other courts-martial of militia officers, but they were mostly related to graft or corruption rather than violent crimes. See Charles McDowell Papers, NCA (the entire collection is a record of his court-martial for "countenancing Tories"). It took a governor's order for a court-martial to be ordered for two officers in the state regiment who had encouraged disaffection. Council Records, September 9, 1779, NCSR 22:956. See also Court-Martial of Major Dennis, March 24, 1781, NCSR 15:431–32; House Journals, April 24, 1778, NCSR 12:712–13; General Lincoln to Caswell, February 6, 1779, NCSR 14:17; Provincial Journals, May 4, 1776, NCCR 10:560–63.

188. There are few surviving examples of these regular muster courts-martial from the revolutionary period. That they continued to occur, however, is clear. There are, for example, numerous references to them in petitions referring to irregularities in the draft process. See, for example, Petition of the freeholders and freemen of the District of Salisbury, December 1781, April–May 1782, Joint Standing Committees, Propositions & Grievances, General Assembly Session Records, NCA.

189. NCSR 23:943; NCSR 24:1–5.

190. Proceedings of the Provincial Congress, August 20, 1775, NCCR 10:199.

191. Governor Burke to the General Assembly, July 7, 1781, NCSR 22:1039–40.

192. Governor Burke to the General Assembly, April 16, 1782, NCSR 16:10.

193. *Moravian Records*, 4:1681, 1683.

194. Ibid., 4:1776.

195. Senate Journals, February 9, 1781, NCSR 17:689.

196. See epilogue.

197. Compare Anderson, *A People's Army*, 48, 185–94. This is also a main theme of Titus, *Old Dominion at War*. Skeen, *Citizen Soldiers*, 80–81, details the

continuing "democratical" nature of militia service in the War of 1812 (working with a broader base of surviving records).

198. The Guilford County militia petitioned against the cowardly and tyrannical behavior of their officers in 1776. Proceedings of the Provincial Congress, April 26, 1776, NCCR 10:541–42. There was a similar attempt by the New Topsail militia company to control who their captain would be in 1777. NCSR 11:658, 757; NCSR 13:4. While marching to Wilmington in the winter of 1776, the Bladen County militia turned out their captain for Toryism. Pension Record of James Shipman (W17810). See chapter 4 for a discussion of the prewar precedents.

199. Greene to General Knox, December 7, 1780, *Greene's Papers*, 6:547.

200. Pension Record of William Lenoir (S7137); Davie, *Revolutionary War Sketches*, 16.

201. Pension claim of William Ward, in Camin, *North Carolina Pension Applications*, 3:332.

202. Graham, *General Joseph Graham*, 369–70. The reader is also referred to the incident in the Moravian towns narrated above in which the captain was described as having "found pluck enough" to restrain his men from plundering once shamed into acting. *Moravian Records*, 4:1565.

203. Davie, *Revolutionary War Sketches*, 13. See also Bartholomees, "Fight or Flee," 74.

204. Pension Record of Landon Carter (W900), who remembered that they marched about "until we thought proper to return home all being volunteers."

205. Colonel William Davie to Governor Caswell, August 29, 1780, NCSR 22:777. See also how a group of Fanning's men forced him to spare a prisoner "much against his will." Similarly, note the Whig militiamen who forced their commander to go along with the execution of a Tory he would have preferred to spare. Both incidents are in Caruthers, *Old North State*, 86, 88.

206. There was still a strong tradition of socially prominent individuals who used their influence within the community to raise troops and then lead them. Such a man could on occasion use this ability to raise troops to help him avenge a personal grievance. See Graham, *General Joseph Graham*, 228–29. Conversely, soldiers committing non-customary violence could take comfort, as did rioters, in the legitimacy conferred upon them by the presence of a socially prominent officer. Alexander McLeod claimed that "no Men would follow any Man as a Leader unless he was possessed of Property." Loyalist claim of Alexander McLeod (PRO AO12/36/182). The loss of the leaders of the Guilford County Loyalists prior to the Battle of Moore's Creek Bridge led their followers to turn back. Rankin, *North Carolina Continentals*, 37. Leadership by the better sort conferred legitimacy of a kind, and if such a leader pursued excessive violence, then his followers could do so also with less fear of censure—a cultural version of "just following orders."

207. Quote from Senate Journals, February 7, 1781, NCSR 17:679. See also Clark's prefatory comments, NCSR 16:vi–vii; Proceedings of the Provincial Congress, September 7, 1775, NCCR 10:200; NCSR 24:2. The leaders of the King's

Mountain army requested that Gates send them a Continental general to take charge, but that he be one who could "keep up a proper discipline, without disgusting the soldiery." Colonel Cleveland and others to General Gates, October 4, 1780, Gates Papers (microfilm ed.). British leaders were similarly aware of that problem with the Loyalist militia. One noted that discipline and order had to be imposed with great caution "so as not to disgust the Men or mortify unnecessarily the Love of Freedom." Instructions of Clinton to Major Ferguson, May 22, 1780, in Rankin, ed., "An Officer Out of His Time," 358.

208. British Major Patrick Ferguson explicitly discussed this tension, noting that "some latitude" should be allowed for the lesser acts of plundering, in order to contribute to greater overall discipline. Ferguson's "Proposed Plan for Bringing the Army under strict discipline," in Rankin, ed., "An Officer Out of His Time," 337. James Edmonson makes a similar point in regard to desertion in the Continental army. "Desertion in the American Army," 30–31.

209. Snapp, *John Stuart*, 157–58; Ekirch, *"Poor Carolina,"* 187; Josiah Martin to John Burnside, May 28, 1775, in Loyalist claim of John Burnside, ER 3.

210. Pension Records of John McAlister (W1887); Archibald Houston (W295); Sweeny, *Captain Thomas Cook*, 6.

211. Frey, *British Soldier in America*, 4.

212. The tarring and feathering of Pollock was discussed briefly in chapter 5. See Don Higginbotham's comments in *Papers of James Iredell*, 1:341. Ekirch, *"Poor Carolina,"* 187. For further evidence of North Carolinians' antipathy toward Scots, see Archibald McClaine to Governor Burke, February 19, 1782, NCSR 16:200.

213. Anon., *The Crisis, Number IV*, 25–31. Charles Lee similarly demonized Scots but, aware of American fears of their martial capabilities, downplayed their numbers in the British army and described them as "not strong enough to carry packs." *Strictures on a Pamphlet*, 10.

214. This is a large field with roots in the earlier works of Jameson, *American Revolution Considered As a Social Movement*; Beard, *Economic Interpretation*; Jensen, *American Revolution within America*. More recent works of particular note are Nash, *Urban Crucible*; Young, ed., *American Revolution*; Young, ed., *Beyond the American Revolution*; Rosswurm, *Arms, Country, and Class*.

215. Crow, "Liberty Men and Loyalists"; Escott and Crow, "The Social Order." See also Hoffman, "The 'Disaffected.'"

216. Brown, "Back Country Rebellions," 75. Brown argues that this explains why urban riots, although caused by social division and strife, never erupted into full-fledged rebellions.

217. This is Ekirch's explanation for the Regulator movement, and Bailyn's explanation for the sources of the Revolution. Ekirch, *"Poor Carolina,"* 183–92; Bailyn, *Ideological Origins*. For the backcountry revolutionary violence in North Carolina, Ekirch asserts that the primary demand of the countryside was for order, and that they turned to the Whig government to provide it. "Whig Authority," passim.

218. Brown, "Back Country Rebellions," passim; Klein, "Frontier Planters," 68; Knouff, "Common People's Revolution," 1, 12–15; Countryman, "'To Secure the Blessings of Liberty,'" 128. See also Gilje's discussion of the role of class divisions in eighteenth-century American riots, *Road to Mobocracy*, 12.

219. Although see Nash, *Urban Crucible*, 124–25, 140, for his argument that class-based demonization had indeed entered into the political rhetoric of the urban northeast.

220. Pensioners and memoirists occasionally resorted to the justification of retaliation as well. That it does not dominate their accounts the way it does Fanning's or other petitioners immediately after the war is due, I would argue, to the *ex post facto* legitimacy of the Revolution in memory. Whig veterans writing thirty years after the war often simply did not feel the need to justify what they had done. That they occasionally did (as seen in the examples recounted in this chapter) is testimony to the power of the need to accommodate the social norm.

Epilogue

1. *Greene's Papers*, 8:349–50.

2. Kirkwood, *Journal and Order Book*, 159–60.

3. Washington, *Writings of George Washington*, ed. Fitzpatrick, 7:443.

4. Higginbotham, *War of American Independence*, 414; Shy, "The Military Conflict," 200–201.

5. Significant works for my purposes include Higginbotham, *War of American Independence*; Shy, "American Society"; Martin and Lender, *Respectable Army*; Scudieri, "The Continentals"; Wright, *Continental Army*; Royster, *Revolutionary People*; Rankin, *North Carolina Continentals*; Clodfelter, "Between Virtue and Necessity"; Neimeyer, *America Goes to War*; Wright, "'Nor Is Their Standing Army to Be Despised'"; Resch, *Suffering Soldiers*; Mayer, *Belonging to the Army*.

6. There was, for example, a significant exchange of correspondence between Washington and Gage (in 1775) and then Washington and Howe (in 1777) regarding the treatment of prisoners. In each case, both sides referred not only to the accepted humane practice of war but also to the potential for retaliation in case abuses were not corrected. For the Washington-Gage letters, see Washington, *Papers of George Washington*, Revolutionary War Series, 1:289–90, 301–2, 326–27; 6:76. For the Continental Congress, Washington, and Howe (1777), see Washington, *Writings of George Washington*, ed. Fitzpatrick, 7:1–5, 252–53; Washington, *Writings of George Washington*, ed. Sparks, 4:552–60 (Sparks's edition includes Howe's letters *to* Washington); *JCC*, 7:16, 135; abstracts of debates in Continental Congress, February 20, 1777, NCSR 11:381–82; *Pennsylvania Gazette*, January 28, 1778. See also Metzger, *Prisoner in the American Revolution*, 154–58, 160, 162. The Huddy-Asgill and Isaac Hayne controversies near the end of the war also exemplify circumstances in which Continental leadership very nearly resorted to actual retaliation for British actions but in the end withheld. Both incidents engen-

dered a large body of documents; for a short treatment, see Boatner, *Encyclopedia of the American Revolution*, 495–97, 529–30.

7. For a notable example of the accepting of quarter, see Armstrong Starkey's discussion of the Battle of Stony Point, "Paoli to Stony Point." See also Henry Lee's praise of Colonel Washington's restraint after the Battle of Cowpens when many of the soldiers wished to avenge the Waxhaws massacre. Lee, *American Revolution*, 165. For more details on the acceptance of the British surrender at Cowpens, see Davis, *Cowpens-Guilford Courthouse Campaign*, 38, 40; Babits, *Devil of a Whipping*, 122–23. Private Reuber of a Hessian regiment recorded several occasions when their Continental guards preserved them from popular resentment and was satisfied with his treatment while in confinement. Burgoyne, ed., *Enemy Views*, 131, 133–34. See also Metzger's extensive treatment of Continental efforts to provide for the prisoners. *Prisoner in the American Revolution*, 151–62.

8. Martin and Lender, *Respectable Army*, 129–30.

9. Americans were relatively unfamiliar with the experience of having to contribute to the maintenance of armies, and consequently they often referred to official Continental impressment as plunder, but they did recognize the gradations of legitimacy. Higginbotham, "Early American Way of War," 291.

10. Higginbotham, *George Washington*, 94–95; Carp, *To Starve the Army*, 77; Mayer, *Belonging to the Army*, 96.

11. Thomas Jefferson to General Greene, February 18, 1781, *Papers of Thomas Jefferson*, ed. Boyd and Cullen, 4:648; General Greene to the North Carolina Board of War, December 18, 1780, *Greene's Papers*, 6:598; Greene to Daniel Morgan, December 16, 1780, *Greene's Papers*, 6:589–90. These are just a few of the many examples of official, high-level communications expressing the need to restrain the soldiery and to procure supplies in an orderly manner. Actual efforts at restraining them are recounted below.

12. Scudieri, "The Continentals," 144. See below for some of the exhortations against plundering.

13. Marshall to a member of the Unity's Elders Conference, June 21, 1781, *Moravian Records*, 4:1910.

14. *Moravian Records*, 3:1282.

15. It should be noted that virtually all of the Moravian experience with the Continentals occurred in 1780 and 1781, a period of significant strain when perhaps the worst might be expected. *Moravian Records*, 3:1286, 1300–1301; 4:1554, 1569, 1571, 1572, 1672, 1691, 1692, 1696, 1880–81.

16. For examples of quartering officers arriving in the Moravian towns, see ibid., 4:1554, 1571, 1666–67, 1674. Such occurrences were vanishingly rare for the militia. See also Greene's order to a subordinate to make sure he did send such an officer: Greene to Jean-Baptiste, Vicomte de Lomagne, December 15, 1780, *Greene's Papers*, 6:577–78.

17. Even the notorious Wilkes County militia, which arrived on January 6, 1782, "very wild" and issuing threats, stayed quiet after they were given food, and some attended service. *Moravian Records*, 4:1787. See also chapter 7, n. 177.

18. Higginbotham, "The American Militia," 100. See also Higginbotham, *War of American Independence*, 375, 412–14.

19. Proclamation of August 4, 1780, Gates Papers (microfilm ed.).

20. "Sermon against Plundering," Samuel E. McCorkle Papers, DUSC.

21. Mayer, *Belonging to the Army*, 31.

22. Scudieri, "The Continentals," 293–95; Spaulding, "The Military Studies of George Washington," 675–80; Higginbotham, *George Washington*, 14–15, 78; Wright, *Continental Army*, 26–29, 140–42; General Greene to Governor Martin, March 28, 1783, NCSR 16:768.

23. Shy, "American Society," 78.

24. *Proceedings of a Court Martial*, 8. Henley was acquitted, but even the holding of this court-martial marked a significant departure from the practice of the North Carolina militia.

25. Duffy, *Military Experience*, 12, 74–80; Starkey, *European and Native American*, 54.

26. Martin and Lender, *Respectable Army*, 173. See also Higginbotham, *George Washington*, 52–53, 94–95; Hoffman, "The 'Disaffected,'" 310; Clodfelter, "Between Virtue and Necessity," 173; Selesky, "Colonial America," 75–76; Mayer, *Belonging to the Army*, 41.

27. Berlin, "The Administration of Military Justice"; Bradford, "Discipline." The Massachusetts Articles of 1775 and the Continental articles of 1775 and 1776 are conveniently reprinted in Winthrop, *Military Law and Precedents*, 947–52, 953–60, 961–71. Bradford, "Discipline," 4, discusses the minor alterations made to the 1776 articles during the remainder of the war.

28. Examples abound; a few include General Orders for July 25, 1777, Jacob Turner Order Book, 1777–78, NCA; entry for August 21, 1776, Gates' General Orders When in Command of the Northern Army, July 10, 1776–June 3, 1777, Gates Papers; November 11, 1779, 4th New York order book, in Lauber, ed., *Orderly Books*, 114–16; entries for August 6, 1780, and September 20, 1780, Copy Book of Orders Issued by Major General Gates While Commanding the Southern Army, July 26–December 4, 1780, Gates Papers (microfilm ed.).

29. Mayer, *Belonging to the Army*, 41.

30. James Neagles's extensive survey of courts-martial recorded in order books found 194 examples of soldiers charged with plunder or theft from civilians (7.3 percent of the total number of courts-martial). There were undoubtedly more, but the order books often did not include enough details to determine if certain offenses such as stealing were committed against civilians or other soldiers. Neagles, *Summer Soldiers*, 34. The Continental army also frequently used summary punishment for plunderers, occasionally even to include death. See entry for August 26, 1780, in Angell, *Diary of Colonel Israel Angell*, 108–9; Greenman, *Diary of a Common Soldier*, 168; Berlin, "The Administration of Military Justice," 140. It is worth noting that the very existence of such order books is an eloquent testimony to the more efficient military bureaucracy of the Continentals versus the militia.

There are no such surviving order books for the North Carolina militia, and they are rare for the other colonies.

31. Neimeyer, *America Goes to War*, 3–4, 8–9. Other historians believe Neimeyer goes too far here; see the review by Harold Selesky, *Journal of Military History* 62 (1998), 200–203. See also Resch's strong challenge to Neimeyer's general characterization of the Continentals in *Suffering Soldiers*, 13–46.

32. See Scudieri's excellent review of the literature on the social background of Continental recruits. "The Continentals," 26–27. Although it is more dated, see Martin and Lender, *Respectable Army*, 90–94. See also Shy, "American Society," 79. The recruiting in North Carolina for the Continental army has not been extensively analyzed, but a general pattern of a few volunteers, some draftees, and many hired substitutes seems fairly clear. See Bartholomees, "Fight or Flee," 65; Rankin, *North Carolina Continentals*, 129; Caswell to General John Butler, May 26, 1779, SR 14:105; Caswell to Allen Jones, July 5, 1779, SR 14:141–42; and the muster sheets in the Alexander Brevard Papers, NCA.

33. Scudieri documents the increasingly long service of Continental soldiers, noting that the "overwhelming majority of Continentals after 1776 were serving terms for the duration of the war or three years." "The Continentals," 45. The pension statements of Continental recruits from North Carolina also differ markedly from the militia in the number of officers under whom they served. Jarrot Crabb (S41499), in one nine-month tour, had two company commanders, and John Lock (S41782), over two and a half years, had only four. Compare these to the militiamen examined in chapter 7.

34. Neimeyer, *America Goes to War*, and Martin and Lender, *Respectable Army*, both argue that the Continentals were a restless group, who consistently expressed their grievances, both against the army leadership and against their perception of civilian indifference to their struggles. Neimeyer in particular argues that such disorder reflected the standard eighteenth-century popular response to a sense of their rights, or expectations, being violated, much as discussed here in chapters 1 and 2. See also Royster, *Revolutionary People*, 295–318; Martin, "A 'Most Undisciplined, Profligate Crew.'" For an enlightening parallel to Neimeyer's conclusions, see the accounts of the mutinies in the eighteenth-century British navy described in Rodger, *The Wooden World*, 119–24, 205–6; and Rodger, "The Naval World," 55–56. Rodger finds that the midcentury mutinies, provided they followed traditional forms and held traditional goals, often got what they wanted with little fear of punishment. By contrast, the mutinies at the end of the century were violently suppressed as a result of the officers having developed a class-based fear of disorder aaarising from their view of the French Revolution.

35. Royster, *Revolutionary People*, 295–307, 314–18.

36. Linn, *A Military Discourse*; speech of General Nash, July 21, 1777, An Original Orderly Book of a Portion of the American Army . . . [North Carolina Brigade, 2/7/71–8/13/77], Military Collection, War of the Revolution, Miscellaneous Papers (Box 6), NCA (original in the Brown University Library); entries for August 19 and September 5, 1777, in Kirkwood, *Journal and Order Book*, 150–

51, 159–60; entry for August 16, 1780, Order Book of the 4th New York Regiment, in Lauber, ed., *Orderly Books*, 879–80.

37. Martin and Lender, *Respectable Army*, 53–55, and contradictorily, 76–77; Rankin, *North Carolina Continentals*, 233; Middlekauff, *Glorious Cause*, 508; Lemisch, "Listening to the 'Inarticulate'"; Pension Record of Jonathan Libby. (Libby was a soldier in the Massachusetts line, and his pension record contains an imagined discourse on the justness of the war, reflecting his understanding of the ideological origins of the Revolution.) Scudieri, however, questions the influence of ideology on the Continentals, preferring instead to emphasize the economic motivation for initial recruitment, sustained by the solidarity of unit camaraderie forged in suffering. "The Continentals," 160–72.

38. Connecticut Papers (New York Public Library), 433f., cited in Davidson, *Propaganda*, 341. Davidson's footnote is unclear. The author of the letter was one Hezekiah Hayden, and there was a Sergeant Hezekiah Haydon in Huntington's Connecticut Continental regiment in August 1776. Connecticut General Assembly, *Record of Service of Connecticut Men* (Hartford: N.p., 1889), 102.

39. Martin and Lender, *Respectable Army*, 163. In many ways this also conforms to the notion of different violences appropriate for different venues. The mutiny was a kind of riot, and in a riot, it was necessary to restrain the kind of violence more acceptable in military situations.

40. Mayer, *Belonging to the Army*; Martin, *Ordinary Courage*, 45.

41. Neimeyer, *America Goes to War*, 163–64; Martin, "A 'Most Undisciplined, Profligate Crew,'" 119–40; Martin, *Ordinary Courage*, 62–63, 135.

42. Shy, "American Strategy," 133–62; Higginbotham, *War of Independence*, 93–94, 414; Fowler, "Egregious Villains," 320–21; Higginbotham, "Reflections on the War of Independence," passim. The recent work by Mark Kwasny would add nuance to this understanding, arguing that even Washington's strategy relied more heavily on partisan-style tactics than commonly admitted, but that even so, such actions were generally carried out by the militia. *Washington's Partisan War*, xiv.

43. This is compared to the examples elucidated in chapter 7, in which the frontier style of the militia created an environment more conducive to "illegal" killings. This difference was particularly clear in the negotiations conducted by the British and the Continentals for the surrender of besieged cities. In those cases both sides, adhering to tradition, negotiated in a spirit designed to prevent the excessive violence associated with the storm of a city. See Lee's account of the siege of Savannah in 1779. Lee, *American Revolution*, 138; *Articles of Capitulation*; Correspondence of Generals Lincoln and Clinton concerning the surrender of Charleston, reprinted in Kirkwood, *Journal and Order Book*, 31–45. This comment is of course dependent on the fundamental acceptability of battle. Battle itself was never "out of hand."

44. For Greene's revisionary approach to operational strategy as a combination of partisan war supported by conventional troops, see Dederer, *Making Bricks without Straw*; Weigley, *American Way of War*, 18–39.

Conclusion

1. One might be tempted to define the "public" as the white male masses. That would be a mistake. Women, while not always the violent actors (especially in war), play a significant role in transmitting cultural values, including those about violence. Edward Muir makes this point in his study of the vendetta of Renaissance Italy. *Mad Blood Stirring*, 191. See also Mayer, *Belonging to the Army*, 143–45.

2. There is a similar appraisal of modern protests in England in the editors' introduction to Quinault and Stevenson, eds., *Popular Protest and Public Order*, 20.

Bibliography

Included here are the sources and collections that had a material impact on this book. It is therefore something more than a "works cited" and something less than a "works consulted." Newspapers and manuscript court records are not listed but are given in complete citations in the text.

The bibliography is divided into five sections: manuscript and unpublished primary sources, published primary sources, European riot and charivari, European military traditions, and all other secondary materials. The two European sections include only those works that deal exclusively with violent phenomena as practiced in early modern Europe. Many works of colonial history provide some European background, but they are included in the "all other" category.

Manuscript and Unpublished Primary Sources

Elijah Alexander Paper. NCA.
John Gray Blount Papers. NCA.
Alexander Brevard Papers. NCA.
John Bush Orderly Book. SHC.
Richard Caswell Papers. DUSC.
William Caswell Papers. NCA.
Cumberland Association Papers. SHC.
Delamar, Marybelle, ed. *Legislative Papers Relating to Revolutionary Service.* 5 vols. Unpublished. Copy held at NCA.
William Dickson Papers. NCA.
Dobbs Papers. SHC.
Draper Manuscript Collection. State Historical Society of Wisconsin.
Early American Orderly Books, 1748–1817. New York Historical Society. Microfilm at DLAR.
Thomas Addison Emmet Collection. NCA.
English Records. NCA.
Fanning-McCulloh Papers. NCA.
James Fraser Papers. DUSC.
French, Christopher. Journal of Christopher French. Connecticut Historical Society. Microfilm at DLAR.
Horatio Gates Papers, 1726–1828. Microfilm edition prepared by the New York Historical Society and the National Historical Records and Publications Commission.
General Assembly Session Records, Joint Papers. NCA.

Granville District Records from the Marquis of Bath's Library in Longleat, Warminster, Wiltshire, England, 1729–80. Microfilm at NCA.

Gray, Robert. "Observations on the War in Carolina by Colonel Robert Gray, Officer of Provincial Troops." Military Collection, War of the Revolution, British and Loyalist Papers (a manuscript copy of an original "in the Chalmers Mss. Belonging to Mr. Bancroft"). NCA.

Hayes Collection. SHC.

Samuel Johnston Papers. NCA.

(John) Alexander Lillington Papers. SHC.

William Lytle Papers. SHC.

Donald MacDonald Paper. NCA.

Samuel E. McCorkle Papers. DUSC.

Charles McDowell Papers. NCA.

Military Collection. NCA.

Military Collection, War of the Revolution, Miscellaneous Papers, 1776–89. NCA.

Miscellaneous Collections, Granville District Papers, Land Office Records, 1744–63. NCA.

Miscellaneous Papers. NCA.

New Jersey, Revolutionary War: Damages by the British and Americans in New Jersey. Originals in New Jersey State Archives. Microfilm at DLAR.

Orderly Book of the 3rd South Carolina Regiment, 1778. South Carolina Historical Society. Microfilm at DLAR.

An Original Orderly Book of a Portion of the American Army . . . [North Carolina Brigade, 2/7/71–8/13/77], Military Collection, War of the Revolution, Miscellaneous Papers (Box 6). Original in the Brown University Library. Copy in NCA.

Papers of the American Loyalist Claims Commission, 1780–1835 (AO13). PRO, Great Britain. Microfilm at DLAR.

Records of the American Loyalist Claims Commission, 1776–1831 (AO12). PRO, Great Britain. Microfilm at DLAR.

Records Received from Other Than Official Sources (CR.X.). NCA.

Revolutionary War Pension and Bounty-Land-Warrant Application Files. National Archives, Washington D.C.

John Alexander Robeson Collection. NCA.

Griffith Rutherford Paper. NCA.

Griffith Rutherford Papers. SHC.

Saint Paul's Parish Records. SHC.

David Schenck Papers. NCA.

Jethro Sumner Papers. NCA.

Robert E. Troy Paper. SHC.

Jacob Turner Order Book, 1777–78. NCA.

Published Primary Sources

Adams, Zabdiel. *The Grounds of Confidence and Success in War, . . . A Sermon Preached . . . to a Detached Company of Militia.* Boston: Mills and Hicks, 1775. Evans #13789.

Allen, Ethan. *A Narrative of Colonel Ethan Allen's Captivity. . . .* Philadelphia: Robert Bell, 1779. Evans #16180.

Andrews, Evangeline W., and Charles McClean, eds. *Journal of a Lady of Quality.* New Haven: Yale University Press, 1939.

Angell, Israel. *Diary of Colonel Israel Angell.* Edited by Edward Field. Providence, R.I.: Preston and Rounds Company, 1899. Reprint, New York: Arno, 1971.

Anon. *The Crisis, Number IV.* Newport: S. Southwick, [1775]. Evans #13928.

"Articles of Capitulation, Made and Intered into between Richard Montgomery . . . and the Citizens . . . of Montreal." [Baltimore], Dunlap, [1775]. Broadside.

Barnwell, John. "Journal of John Barnwell." *Virginia Magazine of History and Biography* 5, 6 (1898): 391–402, 42–55.

Beasley, R. F. *The Battle of Elizabethtown.* Greensboro, N.C.: Guilford Battleground Company, 1901.

Benecke, Gerhard, ed. *Germany in the Thirty Years War.* London: Edwin Arnold, 1978.

Bever, Samuel, and Samuel Johnson. *The Cadet, a Military Treatise.* London: Printed for W. Johnston . . . , 1756.

Blackstone, William. *Commentaries on the Laws of England.* Edited by Stanley N. Katz. 4 vols. Facsimile reprint of 1765–69 ed. Chicago: University of Chicago Press, 1979.

Bland, Francis. *The Souldiers March to Salvation.* Yorke: Privately printed, 1647.

Bland, Humphrey. *Treatise of Military Discipline: In Which Is Laid Down and Explained the Duty of the Officer and Soldier, through the Several Branches of the Service.* 4th ed. London: S. Buckley, 1740.

Blount, John Gray. *The John Gray Blount Papers.* Edited by Alice Barnwell Keith. 3 vols. Raleigh, N.C.: State Department of Archives and History, 1952.

Bostwick, S. *An Address to Major-General Tryon, Written in Consequence of His Late Expedition into Connecticut.* [Hartford]: Privately printed, 1779. Evans #16212.

Boyd, William K., ed. *Some Eighteenth Century Tracts Concerning North Carolina.* Raleigh, N.C.: Edwards and Broughton, 1911.

Brown, A. S. "James Simpson's Reports." *Journal of Southern History* 21 (1955): 513–19.

Burgoyne, Bruce E., ed. *Enemy Views: The American Revolutionary War As Recorded by the Hessian Participants.* Bowie, Md.: Heritage, 1996.

Burke, Thomas. *The Poems of Governor Thomas Burke of North Carolina.* Edited by Richard Walser. Raleigh, N.C.: State Department of Archives and History, 1961.

Camin, Betty J., ed. *North Carolina Revolutionary War Pension Applications*. 3 vols. Raleigh, N.C.: Privately published, 1983.

Charles I. "Proclamation for the better government of His Majesties Army." November 25, 1642. Broadside.

Clark, Walter, and others, eds. *The State Records of North Carolina*. 16 vols. Winston and Goldsboro: Various publishers, 1895–1907.

Cooper, J. M. "Abstracts of Court Minutes—Pleas & Quarter Sessions of Chatham County, North Carolina, May 1774–May 1778." *North Carolina Genealogical Society Journal* 3–5 (1977): 52–61, 128–34, 187–91; 46–51, 87–96, 195–204; 31–36.

Cornwallis, Charles. *Correspondence of Charles, First Marquis Cornwallis*. Edited by Charles Ross. 3 vols. London: John Murray, 1859.

Cranford, James. *The Teares of Ireland*. London: A. N. for John Rothwell, 1642.

Dann, John C., ed. *The Revolution Remembered: Eyewitness Accounts of the War for Independence*. Chicago: University of Chicago Press, 1980.

Davie, William R. *The Revolutionary War Sketches of William R. Davie*. Edited by Blackwell P. Robinson. Raleigh, N.C.: Division of Archives and History, 1976.

Davis, James. *The Office and Authority of a Justice of the Peace*. New Bern: James Davis, 1774.

Davis, Richard Beale. "Three Poems from Colonial North Carolina." *North Carolina Historical Review* 46 (1969): 33–40.

De Morgues, Jacques Le Moyne. *The Work of Jacques Le Moyne De Morgues: A Huguenot Artist in France, Florida, and England*. London: British Museum Publications, 1977.

De Roulhac Hamilton, J. G. "Revolutionary War Diary of William Lenoir." *Journal of Southern History* 6 (1940): 247–57.

Dodge, John. *A Narrative of the Capture and Treatment of John Dodge, by the English at Detroit*. Philadelphia: T. Bradford, 1779. Evans #16262.

Drayton, John. *Memoirs of the American Revolution, From Its Commencement to the Year 1776, Inclusive: As Relating to the State of South-Carolina and Occasionally Referring to the States of North-Carolina and Georgia*. 2 vols. Charleston: A. E. Miller, 1821.

Drimmer, Frederick, ed. *Captured by the Indians*. New York: Dover, 1961.

"Extract of a Letter from an Officer of Distinction in the American Army." [Philadelphia:] John Dunlap, [1776]. Evans #14751.

Fanning, David. *The Narrative of Col. David Fanning*. Edited by Lindley S. Butler. Davidson, N.C.: Briarpatch Press, 1981.

Force, Peter, ed. *American Archives*. Washington D.C.: M. St. Clair Clarke and Peter Force, 1837–1846.

Ford, Paul Leicester, ed. *Orderly Book of the Maryland Loyalists Regiment, June 18–October 12, 1778*. New York: Historical Printing Club, 1891.

Franklin, Benjamin. *The Papers of Benjamin Franklin*. Edited by Leonard W. Labaree. 33 vols. New Haven: Yale University Press, 1967.

Friedman, Leon, ed. *The Law of War: A Documentary History.* 2 vols. New York: Random House, 1972.

Fries, Adelaide L., ed. *Records of the Moravians in North Carolina.* 11 vols. Raleigh: North Carolina Historical Commission, 1922–69.

Gage, Thomas. *The Correspondence of General Thomas Gage.* Edited by Clarence E. Carter. 2 vols. New Haven: Yale University Press, 1933. Reprint, n.p.: Archon, 1969.

Gallup, Andrew, ed. *Memoir of a French and Indian War Soldier: "Jolicoeur" Charles Bonin.* Bowie, Md.: Heritage, 1993.

Graham, Joseph. *General Joseph Graham and His Papers on North Carolina Revolutionary History.* Edited by William A. Graham. Raleigh, N.C.: Edwards and Broughton, 1904.

Greene, Nathanael. *The Papers of General Nathanael Greene.* Edited by Richard K. Showman, Dennis Conrad, Roger M. Parks, and Elizabeth C. Stevens. 9 vols. to date. Chapel Hill: University of North Carolina Press, 1976–.

Greenman, Jeremiah. *Diary of a Common Soldier in the American Revolution.* Edited by Robert Bray and Paul Bushnell. DeKalb: Northern Illinois University Press, 1978.

Griffin, Appleton P. C., ed. *Orderly Book of General George Washington, Kept at Valley Forge, 18 May–11 June, 1778.* Boston: Lamson, Wolffe and Company, 1898.

Grotius, Hugo. *The Law of War and Peace (De Jure Belli Ac Pacis).* Translated by Francis Kelsey. Classics of International Law. New York: Oceana, 1964.

Haun, Weynette P., ed. *Hillsborough District, N.C., Superior Court Minutes, 1768–1791.* Durham, N.C.: Published by the author, 1993.

———. *Johnston County Court Minutes, 1767–1777.* Durham, N.C.: Published by the author, 1975.

———. *Johnston County Court Minutes, 1778–1786.* Durham, N.C.: Published by the author, 1975.

———. *Johnston County North Carolina Record Book A#2, Johnston County North Carolina Court Martial Minutes, 1761–1779.* N.p.: Published by the author, 1983.

Hay, Gertrude Sloan, ed. *Roster of Soldiers from North Carolina in the American Revolution.* Baltimore: Genealogical Publishing Co., 1977.

Henderson, Archibald, ed. "Hermon Husband's Continuation of the Impartial Relation." *North Carolina Historical Review* 18 (1941): 48–81.

Henry, Robert. *Narrative of the Battle of Cowan's Ford.* Greensboro, N.C.: D. Schenck, 1891.

Holcomb, Brent H., ed. *Anson County, N.C., Deed Abstracts, Vol. 2: 1757–1766 and 1763 Tax List.* N.p.: Published by the author, 1975.

Holcomb, Brent H., and Elmer O. Parker, eds. *Mecklenburg County, North Carolina Deed Abstracts, 1763–1779.* Easley, S.C.: Southern Historical Press, 1979.

Hunt, Gaillard, ed. *Fragments of Revolutionary History.* New York: Historical Printing Club, 1892.

Husband, Hermon. "A Fan for Fanning and Touchstone to Tryon (1771)." In *Some Eighteenth Century Tracts Concerning North Carolina,* ed. William K. Boyd, 335–92. Raleigh, N.C.: Edwards and Broughton, 1927.

———. "An Impartial Relation (1770)." In *Some Eighteenth Century Tracts Concerning North Carolina,* ed. William K. Boyd, 247–334. Raleigh, N.C.: Edwards and Broughton, 1927.

Inglis, Charles. *The Christian Soldier's Duty Briefly Delineated: In a Sermon Preached . . . Before the American Corps Newly Raised for His Majesty's Service.* New York: H. Gaine, [1777]. Evans #15372.

"Interesting Intelligence. By Mr. Joseph White . . . May 20 [of British in Virginia]." Baltimore: M. K. Goddard, [1779]. Evans #16312.

Iredell, James. *The Papers of James Iredell.* Edited by Don Higginbotham. 2 vols. to date. Raleigh, N.C.: Division of Archives and History, 1976–.

Jefferson, Thomas. *The Papers of Thomas Jefferson.* Edited by Julian P. Boyd and Charles T. Cullen. 21 vols. Princeton: Princeton University Press, 1950–83.

Kinnan, Mary. "A True Narrative of the Sufferings of Mary Kinnan (1791)." In *Held Captive by Indians: Selected Narratives, 1642–1836,* ed. Richard VanDerBeets. Knoxville: University of Tennessee Press, 1973.

Kirkwood, Robert. *The Journal and Order Book of Captain Robert Kirkwood of the Delaware Regiment of the Continental Line. . . .* Edited by Joseph Brown Turner. Wilmington, Del.: Historical Society of Delaware, 1910.

Kohn, Richard H., ed. *Anglo-American Antimilitary Tracts, 1697–1830.* New York: Arno, 1979.

Lauber, Almon W., ed. *Orderly Books of the Fourth New York Regiment, 1778–1780, the Second New York Regiment, 1780–1783 by Samuel Tallmadge and Others with Diaries of Samuel Tallmadge, 1780–1782 and John Barr, 1779–1782.* Albany: University of the State of New York, 1932.

Lawson, John. *A New Voyage to Carolina.* Edited by Hugh Talmage Lefler. London: Privately printed, 1709. Reprint, Chapel Hill: University of North Carolina Press, 1967.

Lazenby, Mary Elinor. *Catawba Frontier 1775–1781: Memoirs of Pensioners.* Washington, D.C.: Compiler, 1950.

Leach, John. *A Journal Kept by John Leach, during His Confinement by the British, Boston Gaol, in 1775.* Boston: Privately printed, 1865.

[Lee, Charles]. *Strictures on a Pamphlet, Entitled "A Friendly Address. . . ."* Philadelphia: S. Southwick, 1775. Evans #14155.

Lee, Henry. *The American Revolution in the South.* Edited by Robert E. Lee. Originally published as: *Memoirs of the War in the Southern Department of the United States.* New York: University Publishing Company, 1869. Reprint, New York: Arno, 1969.

Lennon, Donald R., and Ida B. Kellam, eds. *The Wilmington Town Book, 1743–1778.* Raleigh, N.C.: Division of Archives and History, 1973.

Library of Congress. *Journals of the Continental Congress, 1774–1789.* 34 vols. Washington, D.C.: GPO, 1905.

Linn, Jo White, ed. *Abstracts of the Minutes of the Court of Pleas and Quarter Sessions: Rowan County, N.C., 1775–1789.* Salisbury, N.C.: Published by the editor, 1982.

———. *Rowan County, North Carolina, Deed Abstracts.* 2 vols. Salisbury, N.C.: Mrs. Stahle Linn, Jr., 1972.

Linn, William. *A Military Discourse Delivered in Carlisle, March the 17th, 1776, to Colonel Irvine's Battalion of Regulars. . . .* Philadelphia: Privately printed, 1776. Evans #14828.

Lloyd, William. *A Discourse of God's Ways of Disposing of Kingdoms, Part I.* London: H. Hills, 1691.

Martin, James Kirby, ed. *Ordinary Courage: The Revolutionary War Adventures of Joseph Plumb Martin,* 2d ed. New York: Brandywine, 1999.

Mason, George. *The Papers of George Mason, 1725–1792.* Edited by Robert A. Rutland. 3 vols. Chapel Hill: University of North Carolina Press, 1970.

McCorkle, Samuel E. *A Sermon on the Comparative Happiness and Duty of the United States of America, Contrasted with Other Nations, particularly the Israelites.* Halifax, 1795.

McEachern, Leora, and Isabel Williams, eds. *Wilmington–New Hanover Safety Committee Minutes, 1774–1776.* Wilmington, N.C.: Wilmington–New Hanover County American Revolution Bicentennial Association, 1974.

McPherson, Elizabeth. "Unpublished Letters from North Carolinians to Washington." *North Carolina Historical Review* 12 (1935): 149–71.

Melling, Elizabeth, ed. *Crime and Punishment: A Collection of Examples from Original Sources in the Kent Archives Office, from the Sixteenth to the Nineteenth Century.* Kentish Sources, 6. Maidstone: Kent County Council, 1969.

Murphey, Archibald D. *The Papers of Archibald D. Murphey.* Edited by William Hoyt. 2 vols. Raleigh, N.C.: E. M. Uzzell and Co., 1914.

Neagles, James. *Summer Soldiers: A Survey and Index of Revolutionary War Courts-Martial.* Salt Lake City: Ancestry Incorporated, 1986.

Newsome, A. R. "A British Orderly Book, 1780–1781." *North Carolina Historical Review* 9 (1932): 57–78, 163–86, 273–98, 366–92.

Nestor [pseudonym]. "To the Militia of Pennsylvania." [Philadelphia: Macdonald and Cameron, 1778.] Broadside.

Orderly Book of Lieut. Abraham Chittenden, August 16–September 29, 1776. Hartford, Conn.: Case, Lockwood and Brainard Co., 1922.

Orderly Book of the Three Battalions of Loyalists Commanded by Brigadier-General Oliver De Lancey, 1776–1778. Baltimore: Genealogical Publishing Co., 1972.

Peckham, Howard H., ed. *Sources of American Independence: Selected Manuscripts from the Collections of the William L. Clements Library.* 2 vols. Chicago: University of Chicago Press, 1978.

Percy, George. "'A Trewe Relacyon': Virginia from 1609 to 1612." *Tyler's Quarterly Historical and Genealogical Magazine* 3 (1922): 259–82.

Pickering, Timothy, Jr. *An Easy Plan of Discipline for a Militia.* Salem, Mass.: Samuel and Ebenezer Hall, 1775. Evans #14404.

Powell, William S., James K. Huhta, and Thomas J. Farnham, eds. *The Regulators in North Carolina: A Documentary History, 1759–1776.* Raleigh, N.C.: State Department of Archives and History, 1971.

Proceedings of a Court Martial . . . for the Trial of Colonel David Henley Accused . . . of Ill Treatment of the British Soldiers. London: J. Almon, 1778.

"The Progress of the British and Hessian Troops through New Jersey . . . December 14, 1776." [Philadelphia, 1776]. Evans #15037.

Ralegh, Walter. *The Discoverie of the Large, Rich, and Bewtiful Empyre of Guiana.* Edited by Neil L. Whitehead. Norman: University of Oklahoma Press, 1977.

Rankin, Hugh F., ed. "An Officer Out of His Time: Correspondence of Major Patrick Ferguson, 1779–1780." In *Sources of American Independence: Selected Manuscripts from the Collections of the William L. Clements Library,* ed. Howard H. Peckham, 2:287–360. Chicago: University of Chicago Press, 1978.

Riling, Joseph R., ed. *Baron Von Steuben and His Regulations Including a Facsimile of the Original.* Philadelphia: Ray Riling Arms, 1966.

Rowlandson, Mary. *The Sovereignty and Goodness of God.* Edited by Neal Salisbury. Boston: Bedford, 1997.

Saunders, William L., ed. *The Colonial Records of North Carolina.* 10 vols. Raleigh, N.C.: Various publishers, 1886–90.

Seaver, James Everett, ed. *A Narrative of the Life of Mary Jemison.* Canandaigua: J. D. Bemis and Co., 1824. Reprint, New York: American Scenic and Historic Preservation Society, 1932.

Shurtleff, Nathaniel B., ed. *Records of the Colony of New Plymouth.* Vol. 5. Boston: William White, 1856.

Simcoe, J. G. *A Journal of the Operations of the Queen's Rangers.* New York: Bartlett and Welford, 1844. Reprint, New York: Arno, 1968.

Simes, Thomas. *The Military Guide for Young Officers.* Philadelphia: Reprinted by J. Humphreys, R. Bell, and R. Aitken, printers and booksellers, 1776.

Smyth, John Ferdinand Dalziel. *Narrative or Journal of Capt. John Ferdinand Dalziel Smith, of the Queen's Rangers, Taken Prisoner by the Rebels in 1775. . . .* New York: Gaine, 1778. Evans #16072.

Steele, John. *The Papers of John Steele.* Edited by H. M. Wagstaff. 2 vols. Raleigh, N.C.: Edwards and Broughton, 1924.

Stevenson, Roger. *Military Instructions for Officers . . . Containing a Scheme for Forming a Corps of a Partisan. . . .* Philadelphia: R. Aitken, 1775. Evans #14475.

Sweeny, William M., ed. *Captain Thomas Cook (1752–1841): A Soldier of the Revolution.* N.p.: Privately printed, [1909].

Taliaferro, Benjamin. *The Orderly Book of Capt. Benjamin Taliaferro.* Edited by Lee Wallace. Richmond: Virginia State Library, 1980.

Tarleton, Banastre. *A History of the Campaigns of 1780 and 1781, in the Southern Provinces of North America.* Dublin: Colles, Exshaw et al., 1787.

Tryon, William. *The Correspondence of William Tryon.* Edited by William S. Powell. 2 vols. Raleigh, N.C.: Division of Archives and History, 1980.

Underhill, John. *Newes From America.* London, 1638. Reprint, New York: Da Capo Press, 1971.

Vattel, Emmerich de. *The Law of Nations.* Translated by Charles G. Fenwick. Classics of International Law. New York: Oceana, 1964.

Washington, George. *The Papers of George Washington.* Edited by Dorothy Twohig. Revolutionary War Series. 7 vols. to date. Charlottesville: University Press of Virginia, 1985–.

———. *The Writings of George Washington.* Edited by Jared Sparks. 12 vols. Boston: Russell, Odiorne, and Metcalf, 1834.

———. *The Writings of George Washington from the Original Manuscript Sources, 1745–1799.* Edited by John Fitzpatrick. 39 vols. Washington, D.C.: GPO, 1931–44.

Waterhouse, Edward. *A Declaration of the State of the Colony in Virginia.* London, 1622. Reprint, New York: Da Capo Press, 1970.

Wheeler, John H. *Historical Sketches of North Carolina from 1584–1851.* 2 vols. Philadelphia: Lippincott, Grambo and Co., 1851.

Willard, Joseph. *The Duty of the Good and Faithful Soldier. . . .* Boston: T. and J. Fleet, 1781. Evans #17438.

Willcox, George W. *John Willcox, 1728–1793.* Historical Research Co., 1988.

Williams, Roger. *A Key into the Language of America.* Edited by John J. Teunissen and Evelyn J. Hinz. London: Privately printed, 1643. Reprint, Detroit: Wayne State University Press, 1973.

Winthrop, John. *The Journal of John Winthrop, 1630–1649,* unabridged ed. Edited by Richard S. Dunn, James Savage, and Laetitia Yeandel. Cambridge: Belknap Press of Harvard University Press, 1996.

Winthrop, William. *Military Law and Precedents.* New York: Arno, 1979.

Wither, George. *A Collection of Emblemes, Ancient and Moderne.* Edited by Rosemary Freeman. London: Augustine Matthews, 1635. Reprint, Columbia: University of South Carolina Press, 1975.

Wood, William. *New England's Prospect.* Edited by Alden T. Vaughan. London: Thomas Cotes, 1634. Reprint, Amherst: University of Massachusetts Press, 1977.

Woodmason, Charles. *The Carolina Backcountry on the Eve of the Revolution.* Edited by Richard J. Hooker. Chapel Hill: University of North Carolina Press, 1953.

European Riot and Charivari

Alford, Violet. "Rough Music or Charivari." *Folklore* 70 (1959): 505–18.

Amussen, Susan. "'Being Stirred to Much Unquietness': Violence and Domestic Violence in Early Modern England." *Journal of Women's History* 6 (1994): 70–89.

Beloff, Max. *Public Order and Popular Disturbances, 1660–1714*. London: Oxford University Press, 1938.

Bindoff, S. T. *Ket's Rebellion*. London: Historical Association, 1949.

Bohstedt, John. "The Moral Economy and the Discipline of Historical Context." *Journal of Social History* 26 (1992): 265–84.

———. *Riots and Community Politics in England and Wales, 1790–1810*. Cambridge: Harvard University Press, 1983.

Brownlie, Ian. *The Law Relating to Public Order*. London: Butterworths, 1968.

Burke, Peter. *Popular Culture in Early Modern Europe*. New York: Harper and Row, 1978.

Charlesworth, Andrew. *An Atlas of Rural Protest in Britain 1548–1900*. Philadelphia: University of Pennsylvania Press, 1983.

Connolly, S. J. "Albion's Fatal Twigs: Justice and Law in the Eighteenth Century." In *Economy and Society in Scotland and Ireland, 1500–1939*, ed. Rosalind Mitchison and Peter Roebuck, 117–25. Edinburgh: John Donald, 1988.

———. "Violence and Order in the Eighteenth Century." In *Rural Ireland 1600–1900: Modernisation and Change*, ed. P. O'Flanagan, P. Ferguson, and K. Whelan, 42–61. Cork: Cork University Press, 1987.

Cunnington, B. Howard. "A 'Skimmington' in 1618." *Folklore* 41 (1930): 287–90.

Darvall, Frank Ongley. *Popular Disturbances and Public Order in Regency England*. Oxford: Oxford University Press, 1934.

Davies, C. S. L. "Peasant Revolt in France and England: A Comparison." *Agricultural History Review* 21 (1973): 122–34.

Davis, Natalie Zemon. *Society and Culture in Early Modern France*. Stanford: Stanford University Press, 1975.

Devine, T. M. "Unrest and Stability in Rural Ireland and Scotland, 1760–1840." In *Economy and Society in Scotland and Ireland, 1500–1939*, ed. Rosalind Mitchison and Peter Roebuck, 126–39. Edinburgh: John Donald, 1988.

Dickinson, H. T., and K. J. Logue. "The Porteous Riot: A Study of the Breakdown of Law and Order in Edinburgh, 1736–1737." *Journal of the Scottish Labour History Society* 10 (1976).

Dobson, Richard B. *The Peasants' Revolt of 1381*. London: Macmillan, 1970.

Donnelly, J. S. "The Whiteboy Movement, 1761–5." *Irish Historical Studies* 21 (1978): 20–54.

Fourquin, Guy. *The Anatomy of Popular Rebellion in the Middle Ages*. Translated by Anne Chesters. Europe in the Middle Ages, Selected Studies, vol. 9. Amsterdam: North Holland Publishing Co., 1978.

Fraser, W. Hamish. "Patterns of Protest." In *People and Society in Scotland*, vol.1, *1760–1830*, ed. T. M. Devine and Rosalind Mitchison, 268–91. Edinburgh: John Donald, 1988.

Friedrichs, Christopher R. *Urban Society in an Age of War: Nordlingen, 1580–1720*. Princeton, N.J.: Princeton University Press, 1979.

Gatrell, V. A. C. *The Hanging Tree: Execution and the English People 1770–1868*. Oxford: Oxford University Press, 1994.

Gilmour, Ian. *Riot, Risings, and Revolution: Governance and Violence in Eighteenth Century England*. London: Pimlico, 1992.

Hare, J. N. "The Wiltshire Rising of 1450: Political and Economic Discontent in Mid-Fifteenth Century England." *Southern History* 4 (1982): 13–31.

Harvey, I. M. W. *Jack Cade's Rebellion of 1450*. Oxford: Clarendon Press, 1991.

Hay, Douglas. "Property, Authority and the Criminal Law." In *Albion's Fatal Tree: Crime and Society in Eighteenth-Century England*, ed. Douglas Hay and others, 17–64. New York: Pantheon, 1975.

Hayter, Tony. *The Army and the Crowd in Mid-Georgian London*. London: Macmillan, 1978.

Herrup, Cynthia. "Law and Morality in England." *Past and Present* 106 (1985): 102–23.

Hill, Christopher. *The World Turned Upside Down*. New York: Penguin, 1972.

Holmes, Geoffrey. "The Sacheverell Riots: The Crowd and the Church in Early Eighteenth-Century London." In *Rebellion, Popular Protest, and the Social Order in Early Modern England*, ed. Paul Slack. Cambridge: Cambridge University Press, 1984.

Ingram, Martin. "Ridings, Rough Music, and 'the Reform of Popular Culture' in Early Modern England." *Past and Present* 105 (1984): 79–113.

Kent, Joan R. "Folk Justice and Royal Justice in Early Seventeenth Century England: A Charivari in the Midlands." *Midland History* 8 (1983): 70–85.

Leopold, J. "The Levellers' Revolt of Galloway in 1724." *Scottish Labor History Society Journal* 14 (1980): 4–29.

Linebaugh, Peter. "The Tyburn Riot against the Surgeons." In *Albion's Fatal Tree*, ed. Douglas Hay et al., 65–118. New York: Pantheon, 1975.

Logue, Kenneth J. "Eighteenth-Century Popular Protest: Aspects of the People's Past." In *The People's Past*, ed. E. J. Cowan. Edinburgh: John Donald, 1980.

———. *Popular Disturbances in Scotland, 1780–1815*. Edinburgh: John Donald, 1979.

Luebke, David Martin. *His Majesty's Rebels: Communities, Factions, and Rural Revolt in the Black Forest, 1725–1745*. Ithaca, N.Y.: Cornell University Press, 1997.

Lyle, Helen. *The Rebellion of Jack Cade, 1450*. London: Historical Association, 1950.

Manning, Roger. "Patterns of Violence in Early Tudor Enclosure Riots." *Albion* 6 (1974): 120–33.

———. *Village Revolts: Social Protests and Popular Disturbances in England, 1509–1640*. Oxford: Clarendon, 1988.

Muir, Edward. *Mad Blood Stirring: Vendetta in Renaissance Italy*. Reader's ed. Baltimore: Johns Hopkins University Press, 1998.

Mullett, Michael. *Popular Culture and Popular Protest in Late Medieval and Early Modern Europe*. New York: Croom Helm, 1987.

Nenadic, Stana. "Political Reform and the 'Ordering' of Middle-Class Protest." In *Conflict and Stability in Scottish Society, 1700–1850*, ed. T. M. Devine, 65–82. Edinburgh: John Donald, 1990.

Quinault, R., and J. Stevenson, eds. *Popular Protest and Public Order*. London: Allen and Unwin, 1975.

Richards, Eric. "How Tame Were the Highlanders during the Clearances?" *Scottish Studies* 17 (1973): 35–50.

———. "Patterns of Highland Discontent, 1790–1860." In *Popular Protest and Public Order: Six Studies in British History, 1790–1920*, ed. R. Quinault and J. Stevenson, 75–114. London: George Allen and Unwin, 1974.

Rogers, Nicholas. "Popular Protest in Early Hanoverian London." In *Rebellion, Popular Protest, and the Social Order in Early Modern England*, ed. Paul Slack, 263–93. Cambridge: Cambridge University Press, 1984.

Rosenberg, Philippe. "The Moral Order of Violence: The Meanings of Cruelty in Early Modern England, 1648–1685." Ph.D. diss., Duke University, 1999.

Rudé, George. *The Crowd in History, 1730–1848*. New York: John Wiley, 1964.

———. *Paris and London in the Eighteenth Century: Studies in Popular Protest*. New York: Viking, 1952.

———. "Protest and Punishment in Nineteenth Century Britain." *Albion* 5 (1973): 1–23.

Samaha, Joel. "Hanging for Felony: The Rule of Law in Elizabethan Colchester." *Historical Journal* 21 (1978): 763–82.

Shelton, Walter J. *English Hunger and Industrial Disorders*. London: Macmillan, 1973.

———. "The Role of Local Authorities in the Provincial Hunger Riots of 1766." *Albion* 5 (1973): 50–66.

Stevenson, John. *Popular Disturbances in England, 1700–1870*. London: Longman, 1979.

Thompson, E. P. "The Moral Economy of the English Crowd in the Eighteenth Century." *Past and Present* 50 (1971): 76–136.

———. "The Moral Economy Reviewed." In *Customs in Common*, 259–351. New York: New Press, 1993.

———. "The Patricians and the Plebs." In *Customs in Common*, 16–96. New York: New Press, 1993.

———. "Rough Music." In *Customs in Common*, 467–538. New York: New Press, 1993.

Tilly, Charles. "Collective Violence in European Perspective." In *Violence in*

America: Historical and Comparative Perspectives, rev. ed. Edited by Hugh Davis Graham, and Ted Robert Gurr, 83–118. Beverly Hills: Sage, 1979.

Underdown, David. *Revel, Riot, and Rebellion: Popular Politics and Culture in England, 1603–1660.* Oxford: Oxford University Press, 1985.

———. "The Taming of the Scold: The Enforcement of Patriarchal Authority in Early Modern England." In *Order and Disorder in Early Modern England*, ed. Anthony Fletcher and John Stevenson, 116–36. Cambridge: Cambridge University Press, 1987.

Walter, John. "'A Rising of the People'? The Oxfordshire Rising of 1596." *Past and Present* 107 (1985): 90–143.

Walter, John, and Keith Wrightson. "Dearth and the Social Order in Early Modern England." *Past and Present* 71 (1976): 22–42.

Watts, D. G. "Popular Disorder in Southern England 1250–1450." In *Conflict and Community in Southern England*, ed. Barry Stapleton. New York: St. Martin's, 1992.

Whatley, Christopher A. "How Tame Were the Scottish Lowlanders during the Eighteenth Century?" In *Conflict and Stability in Scottish Society, 1700–1850*, ed. T. M. Devine, 1–30. Edinburgh: John Donald, 1990.

Whyte, Ian D. *Scotland before the Industrial Revolution.* New York: Longman. 1995.

European Military Traditions

Anderson, M. S. *War and Society in Europe of the Old Regime, 1618–1789.* London: Fontana, 1988.

Andreopoulos, George J. "The Age of National Liberation Movements." In *The Laws of War: Constraints on Warfare in the Western World*, ed. Michael Howard, George J. Andreopoulos, and Mark R. Shulman, 191–213. New Haven: Yale University Press, 1994.

Andrews, William. *Old-Time Punishments.* Williamstown, Mass.: Corner House, 1977.

Barnard, T. C. "Crises of Identity among Irish Protestants, 1641–1685." *Past and Present* 127 (1990): 39–83.

Barnett, Corelli. *Britain and Her Army, 1509–1970.* New York: Morrow, 1970.

Beattie, Daniel J. "The Adaptation of the British Army to Wilderness Warfare, 1755–1763." In *Adapting to Conditions: War and Society in the Eighteenth Century*, ed. Maarten Ultee, 56–83. University: University of Alabama Press, 1986.

Black, Jeremy. "Eighteenth Century Warfare Reconsidered." *War in History* 1 (1994): 215–32.

———. *A Military Revolution? Military Change and European Society 1550–1800.* London: Macmillan, 1991.

———, ed. *European Warfare, 1453–1815.* New York: St. Martin's Press, 1999.

Brown, Keith M. *Bloodfeud in Scotland, 1573–1625.* Edinburgh: John Donald, 1986.

Canny, Nicholas. "What Really Happened in Ireland in 1641?" In *Ireland from Independence to Occupation, 1641–1660*, ed. Jane H. Ohlmeyer, 24–42. Cambridge: Cambridge University Press, 1995.

Carlton, Charles. *Going to the Wars: The Experience of the British Civil Wars, 1638–1651*. London: Routledge, 1992.

Claver, Scott. *Under the Lash: A History of Corporal Punishment in the British Armed Forces*. London: Torchstream, 1954.

Contamine, Philippe. *War in the Middle Ages*. Translated by Michael Jones. Oxford: Blackwell, 1984.

Corvisier, A. *Armies and Societies in Europe, 1494–1789*. Bloomington: Indiana University Press, 1979.

Donagan, Barbara. "Atrocity, War Crime, and Treason in the English Civil War." *American Historical Review* 99 (1994): 1137–66.

———. "Codes and Conduct in the English Civil War." *Past and Present* 118 (1988): 65–95.

———. "Did Ministers Matter? War and Religion in England, 1642–1649." *Journal of British Studies* 33 (April 1994): 119–56.

———. "Prisoners in the English Civil War." *History Today* 41, no. 3 (March 1991): 28–35.

Downing, Brian M. *The Military Revolution and Political Change: Origins of Democracy and Autocracy in Early Modern Europe*. Princeton: Princeton University Press, 1992.

Duffy, Christopher *The Military Experience in the Age of Reason*. New York: Atheneum, 1988.

Eltis, David. *The Military Revolution in Sixteenth-Century Europe*. New York: St. Martin's Press, 1995.

Frey, Sylvia. *The British Soldier in America: A Social History of Military Life in the Revolutionary Period*. Austin: University of Texas Press, 1981.

———. "Courts and Cats: British Military Justice in the Eighteenth Century." *Military Affairs* 43 (1979): 5–11.

Graves, Robert I. *Good-Bye to All That: An Autobiography*. Providence, R.I.: Berghahn, 1995.

Gruber, Ira D. "British Strategy: The Theory and Practice of Eighteenth-Century Warfare." In *Reconsiderations on the Revolutionary War*, ed. Don Higginbotham, 14–31. Westport, Conn.: Greenwood, 1978.

Hale, J. R. "War and Opinion: War and Public Opinion in the Fifteenth and Sixteenth Centuries." *Past and Present* 22 (1962): 18–33.

———. *War and Society in Renaissance Europe, 1450–1620*. London: Fontana, 1985.

Hanson, Victor Davis. *The Western Way of War*. New York: Knopf, 1989.

Hill, James Michael. *Celtic Warfare, 1595–1763*. Edinburgh: John Donald, 1986.

Howard, Michael. *War in European History*. New York: Oxford University Press, 1976.

Ives, George. *A History of Penal Methods: Criminals, Witches, Lunatics.* Montclair, N.J.: Patterson Smith, 1970.

Johnson, James T. *Ideology, Reason, and the Limitation of War: Religious and Secular Concepts, 1200–1740.* Princeton: Princeton University Press, 1975.

———. *Just War Tradition and the Restraint of War: A Moral and Historical Inquiry.* Princeton: Princeton University Press, 1981.

Jones, Archer. *The Art of War in the Western World.* Oxford: Oxford University Press, 1987.

Keegan, John. *A History of Warfare.* New York: Knopf, 1993.

Keen, M. H. *The Laws of War in the Late Middle Ages.* London: Routledge and Kegan Paul, 1965.

Lynn, John A., ed. *Feeding Mars: Logistics in Western Warfare from the Middle Ages to the Present.* Boulder, Colo.: Westview, 1993.

———. "Food, Funds, and Fortresses: Resource Mobilization and Positional Warfare in the Campaigns of Louis XIV." In *Feeding Mars: Logistics in Western Warfare from the Middle Ages to the Present,* ed. John A. Lynn, 137–60. Boulder, Colo.: Westview, 1993.

———. *Giant of the Grand Siècle: The French Army, 1610–1715.* Cambridge: Cambridge University Press, 1997.

Malcolm, Joyce Lee. *To Keep and Bear Arms: The Origins of an Anglo-American Right.* Cambridge: Harvard University Press, 1994.

McNeill, William H. *Keeping Together in Time: Dance and Drill in Human History.* Cambridge: Harvard University Press, 1995.

Meron, Theodor. *Henry's Wars and Shakespeare's Laws: Perspectives on the Law of War in the Later Middle Ages.* Oxford: Clarendon Press, 1993.

Miller, David W. "Non-Professional Soldiery, c. 1600–1800." In *A Military History of Ireland,* ed. Thomas Bartlett and Keith Jeffery, 315–34. Cambridge: Cambridge University Press, 1996.

Ostwald, Jamel. "The 'Decisive' Battle of Ramillies, 1706: Prerequisites for Decisiveness in Early Modern Warfare." *Journal of Military History* 64 (2000): 649–78.

Parker, Geoffrey. "Early Modern Europe." In *The Laws of War: Constraints on Warfare in the Western World,* ed. Michael Howard, George J. Andreopoulos, and Mark R. Shulman, 40–58. New Haven: Yale University Press, 1994.

———. *The Military Revolution: Military Innovation and the Rise of the West, 1500–1800.* Cambridge: Cambridge University Press, 1988.

———, ed. *The Thirty Years War,* rev. ed. New York: Barnes and Noble, 1993.

Pictet, Jean S., ed. *Commentary: Geneva Convention.* Geneva: International Committee of the Red Cross, 1952.

Prebble, John. *Culloden.* London: Secker and Warburg, 1961.

Preston, Richard, Alex Roland, and Sidney Wise. *Men in Arms: A History of Warfare and Its Interrelationships with Western Society,* 5th ed. Fort Worth: Holt, Rinehart and Winston, 1991.

Robson, Eric. "The Armed Forces and the Art of War." In *The New Cambridge Modern History*, vol. 7, *The Old Regime*, ed. J. O. Lindsay, 163–90. Cambridge: Cambridge University Press, 1966.

Rodger, N.A.M. "The Naval World of Jack Aubrey." In *Patrick O'Brian: Critical Essays and a Bibliography*, ed. A. E. Cunningham, 49–70. New York: W. W. Norton & Co., 1994.

———. *The Wooden World: An Anatomy of the Georgian Navy.* London: Collins, 1986.

Rogers, Clifford, ed. *The Military Revolution Debate: Readings on the Transformation of Early Modern Europe.* Boulder, Colo.: Westview, 1995.

Ropp, Theodore. *War in the Modern World,* new rev. ed. New York: Collier, 1962.

Roy, Ian. "England Turned Germany? The Aftermath of the Civil War in its European Context." *Transactions of the Royal Historical Society,* 5th ser., 28 (1978): 127–44.

Schwoerer, Lois G. *No Standing Armies! The Antiarmy Ideology in Seventeenth-Century England.* Baltimore: Johns Hopkins University Press, 1974.

Scouller, R. E. *The Armies of Queen Anne.* Oxford: Clarendon Press, 1966.

Strachan, Hew. *European Armies and the Conduct of War.* New York: Routledge, 1983.

Van Creveld, Martin. *Supplying War: Logistics from Wallenstein to Patton.* Cambridge: Cambridge University Press, 1977.

Weigley, Russell F. *The Age of Battles: The Quest for Decisive Warfare from Breitenfeld to Waterloo.* Bloomington: Indiana University Press, 1991.

Weinberg, Gerhard L. *A World at Arms: A Global History of World War II.* Cambridge: Cambridge University Press, 1994.

Western, J. R. *The English Militia in the Eighteenth Century: The Story of a Political Issue, 1660–1802.* London: Routledge and Kegan Paul, 1965.

Wilson, Heather. *International Law and the Use of Force by National Liberation Movements.* Oxford: Clarendon Press, 1988.

All Other Secondary Sources

Abler, Thomas S. "Scalping, Torture, Cannibalism, and Rape: An Ethnohistorical Analysis of Conflicting Values in War." *Anthropologica* 34 (1992): 3–20.

Adams, George R. "The Carolina Regulators: A Note on Changing Interpretations." *North Carolina Historical Review* 49 (1972): 345–52.

Albertson, Catherine Seyton. *In Ancient Albemarle.* Raleigh, N.C.: Commercial Printing Co., 1914.

Alden, John R. *The South in the Revolution, 1763–1789.* Baton Rouge: Louisiana State University Press, 1957.

Alexander, Jon T. "Colonial New England Preaching on War as Illustrated in Massachusetts Artillery Election Sermons." *Journal of Church and State* 17 (1975): 423–42.

Anderson, Fred. *A People's Army: Massachusetts Soldiers and Society in the Seven Years' War.* Chapel Hill: University of North Carolina Press, 1984.

Anderson, Karen. *Chain Her by One Foot: The Subjugation of Native Women in Seventeenth-Century New France.* New York: Routledge, 1991.

Ashe, Samuel A'Court. *History of North Carolina.* Greensboro, N.C.: Charles L. Van Noppen, 1925.

Axtell, James. *The European and the Indian: Essays in the Ethnohistory of Colonial North America.* Oxford: Oxford University Press, 1981.

———. "The White Indians of Colonial America." *William and Mary Quarterly* 32 (1975): 55–88.

Babits, Lawrence E. *A Devil of a Whipping: The Battle of Cowpens.* Chapel Hill: University of North Carolina Press, 1998.

Bailey, J. D. *Commanders at King's Mountain.* Gaffney, S.C.: E. H. Decamp, 1926.

Bailyn, Bernard. *The Ideological Origins of the American Revolution.* Cambridge: Belknap Press of Harvard University, 1962, 1992.

———. *Voyagers to the West.* New York: Knopf, 1986.

Bailyn, Bernard, and Philip D. Morgan, eds. *Strangers within the Realm: Cultural Margins of the First British Empire.* Chapel Hill: University of North Carolina Press, 1991.

Baller, Bill. "Kinship and Culture in the Mobilization of Colonial Massachusetts." *Historian* 57 (1995): 291–302.

Bartholomees, James Boone, Jr. "Fight or Flee: The Combat Performance of the North Carolina Militia in the Cowpens-Guilford Courthouse Campaign, January to March 1781." Ph.D. diss., Duke University, 1978.

Bass, Robert D. *The Green Dragoon: The Lives of Banastre Tarleton and Mary Robinson.* New York: 1957.

Bassett, John Spencer. "The Regulators of North Carolina, 1765–1771." *Annual Report of the American Historical Association for the Year 1894.* Washington, D.C.: American Historical Association, 1895.

Beard, Charles. *An Economic Interpretation of the Constitution.* New York: Free Press, 1986.

Beeman, Richard R. "The Political Response to Social Conflict in the Southern Backcountry: A Comparative View of Virginia and the Carolinas during the Revolution." In *An Uncivil War: The Southern Backcountry during the American Revolution,* ed. Ronald Hoffman, Thad W. Tate, and Peter J. Albert, 213–39. Charlottesville: University Press of Virginia, 1985.

Bellesiles, Michael A. *Arming America: The Origins of a National Gun Culture.* New York: Alfred A. Knopf, 2000.

Berger, Carl. *Broadsides and Bayonets,* rev. ed. San Rafael: Presidio Press, 1976.

Berkin, Carol Ruth, and Mary Beth Norton, eds. *Women of America: A History.* Boston: Houghton Mifflin, 1979.

Berlin, Robert H. "The Administration of Military Justice in the Continental Army during the American Revolution, 1775–1783." Ph.D. diss., University of California, Santa Barbara, 1976.

Bernheim, G. D. *History of the German Settlements and of the Lutheran Church in North and South Carolina.* Philadelphia: Privately printed, 1872. Reprint, Baltimore: Regional Publishing Co., 1975.

Blackwelder, Ruth. "The Attitude of the North Carolina Moravians toward the American Revolution." *North Carolina Historical Review* 9 (1932): 1–21.

Blethen, Tyler. *From Ulster to Carolina: The Migration of the Scotch-Irish to Southwestern North Carolina.* [Cullowhee]: Western Carolina University, 1983.

Boatner, Mark M. *Encyclopedia of the American Revolution.* Mechanicsburg, Pa.: Stackpole, 1994.

Bolton, Charles K. *The Private Soldier under Washington.* New York: Scribner, 1902.

Botein, Stephen. "The Making of a 'Respectable Army.'" *Harvard Magazine* (September–October 1978): 32–37.

Boucher, Ronald L. "The Colonial Militia as a Social Institution: Salem, Massachusetts, 1764–1775." *Military Affairs* 37 (1973): 125–30.

Bourdieu, Pierre. *Outline of a Theory of Practice.* Translated by Richard Nice. Cambridge: Cambridge University Press, 1977.

Bowler, R. Arthur. "Logistics and Operations in the American Revolution." In *Reconsiderations on the Revolutionary War,* ed. Don Higginbotham, 32–53. Westport, Conn.: Greenwood, 1978.

Bowman, Allen. "The Morale of Continental and Militia Troops in the War of the Revolution." Ph.D. diss., University of Michigan, 1941.

———. *The Morale of the American Revolutionary Army.* Washington, D.C.: American Council on Public Affairs, 1943.

Boyd, Julian P. "The Sheriff in Colonial North Carolina." *North Carolina Historical Review* 5 (1928): 151–80.

Bradford, S. Sidney. "Discipline in the Morristown Winter Encampments." *New Jersey Historical Society Proceedings* 80 (1962): 1–30.

Breen, T. H. "The Covenanted Militia of Massachusetts Bay: English Background and New World Development." In *Puritans and Adventurers: Change and Persistence in Early America,* 24–45. Oxford: Oxford University Press, 1980.

Brown, Kathleen. "Native Americans and Early Modern Concepts of Race." In *Empire and Others: British Encounters with Indigenous Peoples, 1600–1850,* ed. Martin Daunton and Rick Halpern, 79–100. Philadelphia: University of Pennsylvania Press, 1999.

Brown, Richard Maxwell. "Back Country Rebellions and the Homestead Ethic in America, 1740–1799." In *Tradition, Conflict, and Modernization: Perspectives on the American Revolution,* ed. Richard Maxwell Brown and Don E. Fehrenbacher, 73–99. New York: Academic Press, 1977.

———. *No Duty to Retreat: Violence and Values in American History and Society.* Oxford: Oxford University Press, 1991.

———. *The South Carolina Regulators*. Cambridge: Harvard University Press, 1963.

———. *Strain of Violence: Historical Studies of American Violence and Vigilantism*. New York: Oxford University Press, 1975.

———. "Violence and the American Revolution." In *Essays on the American Revolution*, ed. Stephen Kurtz and James H. Hutson, 81–120. Chapel Hill: University of North Carolina Press, 1973.

Brown, Wallace. *The Good Americans: The Loyalists in the American Revolution*. New York: Morrow, 1969.

———. *The King's Friends: The Composition and Motives of the American Loyalist Claimants*. Providence: Brown University Press, 1965.

Burton, Frank. *The Politics of Legitimacy: Struggles in a Belfast Community*. London: Routledge and Kegan Paul, 1978.

Calhoon, Robert M. "Civil, Revolutionary, or Partisan: The Loyalists and the Nature of the War for Independence." In *Military History of the American Revolution: The Proceedings of the Sixth Military History Symposium, United States Air Force Academy, 10–11 October 1974*, ed. Stanley J. Underal, 93–109. Washington D.C: U.S. Air Force Academy, 1976.

Carp, E. Wayne. "Early American Military History: A Review of Recent Work." *Virginia Magazine of History and Biography* 94 (1986): 259–84.

———. *To Starve the Army at Pleasure*. Chapel Hill: University of North Carolina Press, 1984.

Caruthers, E. W. *The Old North State*. Originally published in two volumes as *Revolutionary Incidents and Sketches of Character Chiefly in the "Old North State."* Philadelphia: Hayes and Zell, 1854–56. Reprint, Greensboro, N.C.: Guilford County Genealogical Society, 1994.

———. *A Sketch of the Life and Character of the Rev. David Caldwell . . . Including . . . Some Account of the Regulation*. Greensborough, N.C.: Swaim and Sherwood, 1842.

Cavanaugh, John C. "American Military Leadership in the Southern Campaign: Benjamin Lincoln." In *The Revolutionary War in the South: Power, Conflict, and Leadership*, ed. W. Robert Higgins, 101–31. Durham, N.C.: Duke University Press, 1979.

Clark, Murtie June, ed. *Loyalists in the Southern Campaign of the Revolutionary War*. Baltimore: Genealogical Publishing Co., 1981.

Clodfelter, Mark A. "Between Virtue and Necessity: Nathanael Greene and the Conduct of Civil-Military Relations in the South, 1780–1782." *Military Affairs* 52 (October 1988): 169–75.

Coldham, Peter Wilson. *American Loyalist Claims*. Washington D.C.: National Genealogical Society, 1980.

Conway, Stephen. "'The Great Mischief Complain'd of': Reflections on the Misconduct of British Soldiers in the Revolutionary War." *William and Mary Quarterly*, 3d ser., 47 (1990): 370–90.

———. "Military-Civilian Crime and the British Army in North America, 1775–1781." Ph.D. diss., University College, London, 1981.

———. "To Subdue America: British Army Officers and the Conduct of the Revolutionary War." *William and Mary Quarterly,* 3d ser., 43 (1986): 381–407.

———. *The War of American Independence, 1775–1783.* London: Edward Arnold, 1995.

Cook, Sherburne F. "The Significance of Disease in the Extinction of the New England Indians." *Human Biology* 45 (1973): 485–508.

Corbitt, David Lercy. *The Formation of the North Carolina Counties, 1663–1943.* Raleigh, N.C.: Department of Archives and History, 1950.

Corkran, David. *The Cherokee Frontier, 1740–1762.* Norman: University of Oklahoma Press, 1962.

Coulter, E. Merton. "The Granville District." *James Sprunt Studies in History and Political Science* 13, no. 1 (1913): 35–61.

Countryman, Edward. "'Out of the Bounds of the Law': Northern Land Rioters in the Eighteenth Century." In *The American Revolution,* ed. Alfred F. Young, 37–69. DeKalb: Northern Illinois University Press, 1976.

———. "The Problem of the Early American Crowd." *Journal of American Studies* 7 (1973): 77–90.

———. "'To Secure the Blessings of Liberty': Language, the Revolution, and American Capitalism." In *Beyond the American Revolution,* ed. Alfred F. Young, 123–48. DeKalb: Northern Illinois University Press, 1993.

Cox, Caroline Helen. "'A Proper Sense of Honour': The Status of Soldiers and Officers of the Continental Army, 1775–1783." Ph.D. diss., University of California Berkeley, 1997.

Cress, Lawrence Delbert. "An Armed Community: The Origins and Meaning of the Right to Bear Arms." *Journal of American History* 71 (1984): 22–42.

———. *Citizens in Arms: The Army and Militia in American Society to the War of 1812.* Chapel Hill: University of North Carolina Press, 1982.

———. "Radical Whiggery on the Role of the Military: Ideological Roots of the American Revolutionary Militia." *Journal of the History of Ideas* 40 (1979): 43–60.

Cronon, William. *Changes in the Land: Indians, Colonists, and the Ecology of New England.* New York: Hill and Wang, 1983.

Cross, Jerry L. "The Provincial Militia at Alamance Creek: A Roster of Citizen-Soldiers Serving under Governor William Tryon in the Campaign Against the Regulators, May 16, 1771." Historical Research Reports, ser. II, NCA.

Crow, Jeffrey J. "Liberty Men and Loyalists: Disorder and Disaffection in the North Carolina Backcountry." In *An Uncivil War: The Southern Backcountry during the American Revolution,* ed. Ronald Hoffman, Thad W. Tate, and Peter J. Albert, 125–78. Charlottesville: University Press of Virginia, 1985.

———. "Tory Plots and Anglican Loyalty: The Llewelyn Conspiracy of 1777." *North Carolina Historical Review* 55 (1978): 1–17.

———. "What Price Loyalism? The Case of John Cruden, Commissioner of Sequestered Estates." *North Carolina Historical Review* 58 (1981): 215–33.

Davidson, Chalmers G. *Colonial Scotch-Irish of the Carolina Piedmont*. Richburg, S.C.: Chester County Genealogical Society, 1978.

Davidson, Philip. *Propaganda and the American Revolution 1763–1783*. Chapel Hill: University of North Carolina Press, 1941.

Davis, Burke. *The Cowpens-Guilford Courthouse Campaign*. Philadelphia: J. P. Lippincott, 1962.

Dederer, John Morgan. *Making Bricks without Straw*. Manhattan, Kans.: Sunflower University Press, 1983.

———. *War in America to 1775: Before Yankee Doodle*. New York: New York University Press, 1990.

Deloria, Philip J. *Playing Indian*. New Haven: Yale University Press, 1998.

DeMond, Robert O. *The Loyalists in North Carolina during the Revolution*. Durham, N.C.: Duke University Press, 1940.

Demos, John. *The Unredeemed Captive*. New York: Vintage, 1994.

Denson, Andrew C. "Diversity, Religion, and the North Carolina Regulators." *North Carolina Historical Review* 72 (1995): 30–53.

De Van Massey, Gregory. "The British Expedition to Wilmington, January–November, 1781." *North Carolina Historical Review* 66 (1989): 387–411.

Dill, Alonzo Thomas, Jr. "Eighteenth-Century New Bern: Part III, Rebellion and Indian Warfare." *North Carolina Historical Review* 22 (1945): 293–319.

———. "Eighteenth-Century New Bern: Part VII, New Bern during the Revolution." *North Carolina Historical Review* 23 (1946): 325–59.

———. *Governor Tryon and His Palace*. Chapel Hill: University of North Carolina Press, 1955.

Dobson, David. *Scottish Emigration to Colonial America, 1607–1785*. Athens: University of Georgia Press, 1994.

Douglass, Elisha P. *Rebels and Democrats*. Chicago: Quadrangle, 1955.

Dowd, Gregory Evans. *A Spirited Resistance: The North American Indian Struggle for Unity, 1745–1815*. Baltimore: Johns Hopkins University Press, 1992.

Draper, Lyman C. *King's Mountain and Its Heroes: History of the Battle of King's Mountain October 7th, 1780, and the Events Which Led to It*. Cincinnati: Peter G. Thomson, 1881.

Edmonson, James H. "Desertion in the American Army during the Revolutionary War." Ph.D. diss., Louisiana State University, 1971.

Eid, Larry V. "'A Kind of Running Fight': Indian Battlefield Tactics in the Late Eighteenth Century." *Western Pennsylvania Historical Magazine* 71 (1988): 147–71.

Ekirch, A. Roger. "The North Carolina Regulators on Liberty and Corruption, 1766–1771." *Perspectives in American History* 11 (1977–78): 199–256.

———. *"Poor Carolina": Politics and Society in Colonial North Carolina.* Chapel Hill: University of North Carolina Press, 1981.

———. "Whig Authority and Public Order in Backcountry North Carolina, 1776–1783." In *An Uncivil War: The Southern Backcountry during the American Revolution,* ed. Ronald Hoffman, Thad W. Tate, and Peter J. Albert, 99–124. Charlottesville: University Press of Virginia, 1985.

Elliot, J. H. "Final Reflections: The Old World and the New Revisited." In *America in European Consciousness, 1493–1750,* ed. Karen Ordahl Kupperman, 391–408. Chapel Hill: University of North Carolina Press, 1995.

Endy, Melvin. "Just War, Holy War, and Millennialism in Revolutionary America." *William and Mary Quarterly* 42 (1985): 3–25.

Escott, Paul D., and Jeffrey J. Crow. "The Social Order and Violent Disorder: An Analysis of North Carolina in the Revolution and the Civil War." *Journal of Southern History* 52 (1986): 373–402.

Evans, Charles. *American Bibliography.* New York: Peter Smith, 1941.

Ewers, John C. "Intertribal Warfare As the Precursor of Indian-White Warfare on the Northern Great Plains." *Western Historical Quarterly* 6 (1975): 397–410.

Feierabend, Ivo K., Rosalind L. Feierabend, and T. R. Gurr, eds. *Anger, Violence, and Politics: Theories and Research.* Englewood Cliffs, N.J.: Prentice-Hall, 1972.

Fenn, Elizabeth, "Beyond Jeffrey Amherst: Biological Warfare in Eighteenth-Century North America." *Journal of American History* 86 (2000): 1552–80.

Ferguson, Clyde R. "Carolina and Georgia Patriot and Loyalist Militia in Action, 1778–1783." In *The Southern Experience in the American Revolution,* ed. Jeffrey J. Crow and Larry E. Tise, 174–99. Chapel Hill: University of North Carolina Press, 1978.

———. "Functions of the Partisan-Militia in the South during the American Revolution: An Interpretation." In *The Revolutionary War in the South: Power, Conflict, and Leadership,* ed. W. Robert Higgins, 239–58. Durham, N.C.: Duke University Press, 1979.

Ferguson, R. Brian. "Anthropological Perspectives on War." Unpublished paper delivered to the Triangle Institute for Security Studies, Chapel Hill, N.C., 1998.

Ferguson, R. Brian, and Leslie E. Farragher. *The Anthropology of War: A Bibliography.* New York: Occasional Papers of the Harry Frank Guggenheim Foundation, 1988.

Ferguson, R. Brian, and Neil L. Whitehead, eds. *War in the Tribal Zone: Expanding States and Indigenous Societies.* Santa Fe, N.M.: School of American Research Press, 1992.

Ferling, John. *A Wilderness of Miseries: War and Warriors in Early America.* Westport, Conn.: Greenwood, 1980.

Fischer, David H. *Albion's Seed*. Oxford: Oxford University Press, 1989.
————. *Paul Revere's Ride*. New York: Oxford University Press, 1994.
Fischer, Joseph R. *A Well-Executed Failure: The Sullivan Campaign against the Iroquois, July–September 1779*. Columbia: University of South Carolina Press, 1997.
Fitch, William Edward. *Some Neglected History of North Carolina*, 2d ed. New York: By the author, 1914.
Fogleman, Aaron Spencer. *Hopeful Journeys: German Immigration, Settlement, and Political Culture in Colonial America, 1717–1775*. Philadelphia: University of Pennsylvania Press, 1996.
Foote, William Henry. *Sketches of North Carolina: Historical and Biographical*. New York: Robert Carter, 1846.
Foster, Stephen. "The Godly in Transit: English Popular Protestantism and the Creation of a Puritan Establishment in America." In *Seventeenth-Century New England*, ed. David D. Hall and David Grayson Allen, 185–238. Boston: Colonial Society of Massachusetts Publications, 1984.
Fowler, David J. "Egregious Villains, Wood Rangers, and London Traders: The Pine Robber Phenomenon in New Jersey during the Revolutionary War." Ph.D. diss., Rutgers University, 1987.
Franklin, W. Neil. "Agriculture in Colonial North Carolina." *North Carolina Historical Review* 3 (1926): 539–74.
Frasche, Louis D. F. "Problems of Command: Cornwallis, Partisans, and Militia, 1780." *Military Review* 57 (April 1977): 60–74.
Frech, Laura Page. "The Wilmington Committee of Public Safety and the Loyalist Rising of February, 1776." *North Carolina Historical Review* 41 (1964): 21–33.
Frey, Sylvia. *Water from the Rock: Black Resistance in a Revolutionary Age*. Princeton: Princeton University Press, 1991.
Fried, Morton H., Marvin Harris, and Robert Francis Murray, eds. *War: The Anthropology of Armed Conflict and Aggression*. Garden City, N.Y.: Published for the American Museum of Natural History [by] the Natural History Press, 1968.
Fries, Adelaide L. "The Moravian Contribution to Colonial North Carolina." *North Carolina Historical Review* 7 (1930): 1–14.
Ganyard, Robert L. "Threat from the West: North Carolina and the Cherokee, 1776–1778." *North Carolina Historical Review* 45 (1968): 47–66.
Gilje, Paul A. *Rioting in America*. Bloomington: Indiana University Press, 1996.
————. *The Road to Mobocracy: Popular Disorder in New York City, 1763–1834*. Chapel Hill: University of North Carolina Press, 1987.
Gleach, Frederick W. *Powhatan's World and Colonial Virginia: A Conflict of Cultures*. Lincoln: University of Nebraska Press, 1997.
Gobbel, Luther L. "The Militia of North Carolina in Colonial and Revolutionary Times." *Trinity College Historical Society Papers* 13 (1919): 35–61.

Gould, Roger V. "Collective Violence and Group Solidarity: Evidence from a Feuding Society." *American Sociological Review* 64 (1999): 356–80.

Graham, Hugh Davis, and Ted Robert Gurr, eds. *Violence in America: Historical and Comparative Perspectives,* rev. ed. London: Sage, 1979.

Graham, Ian C. C. *Colonists from Scotland: Emigration to North America, 1707–1783.* Ithaca, N.Y.: Cornell University Press, 1956.

Graymont, Barbara. *The Iroquois in the American Revolution.* Syracuse, N.Y.: Syracuse University Press, 1972.

Green, E. R. R. "The Scotch-Irish and the Coming of the Revolution in North Carolina." *Irish Historical Studies* 7 (1950): 78–86.

Greene, Jack P. "The Concept of Virtue in Late Colonial British America." In *Imperatives, Behaviors, and Identities: Essays in Early American Cultural History.* Charlottesville: University Press of Virginia, 1992.

———. "From the Perspective of Law: Context and Legitimacy in the Origins of the American Revolution." *South Atlantic Quarterly* 85 (1986): 56–77.

Gurr, T. R. "Psychological Factors in Civil Violence." In *Anger, Violence, and Politics,* ed. Ivo K. Feierabend, Rosalind L. Feierabend, and T. R. Gurr, 31–57. Englewood Cliffs, N.J.: Prentice-Hall, 1972.

———. *Why Men Rebel.* Princeton: Princeton University Press, 1970.

Hadlock, Wendell S. "War among the Northeastern Woodland Indians." *American Anthropologist,* new ser. 49 (1947): 204–21.

Hamer, P. M. "Anglo-French Rivalry in the Cherokee Country, 1754–1757." *North Carolina Historical Review* 2 (1925): 303–22.

———. "Fort Loudoun in the Cherokee War, 1758–1761." *North Carolina Historical Review* 2 (1925): 442–58.

Hammer, Carl, Jr. *Rhinelanders on the Yadkin,* 2d ed. Salisbury: Rowan Printing Company, 1965.

Hanna, Charles. *The Scotch-Irish.* New York: G. P. Putnam's Sons, 1902.

Hatley, Tom. *The Dividing Paths: Cherokees and South Carolinians through the Revolutionary Era.* Oxford: Oxford University Press, 1995.

Hay, Gertrude Sloan, ed. *Roster of Soldiers from North Carolina in the American Revolution.* Baltimore: Genealogical Publishing Co., 1977.

Higginbotham, Don. "The American Militia: A Traditional Institution with Revolutionary Responsibilities." In *Reconsiderations on the Revolutionary War,* ed. Don Higginbotham, 83–103. Westport, Conn.: Greenwood, 1978.

———. "The Early American Way of War: Reconnaissance and Appraisal." In *War and Society in Revolutionary America.* Columbia: University of South Carolina Press, 1988.

———. "The Federalized Militia Debate: A Neglected Aspect of Second Amendment Scholarship." *William and Mary Quarterly,* 3d ser., 60 (1998): 39–58.

———. *George Washington and the American Military Tradition.* Athens: University of Georgia Press, 1985.

———. "Reflections on the War of Independence: Modern Guerrilla Warfare and the War in Vietnam." In *Arms and Independence: The Military Character of the American Revolution*, ed. Ronald Hoffman and Peter J. Albert, 1–24. Charlottesville: University Press of Virginia, 1974.

———. *War and Society in Revolutionary America: The Wider Dimensions of Conflict*. Columbia: University of South Carolina Press, 1988.

———. *The War of American Independence: Military Attitudes, Policies, and Practice, 1763–1789*. Boston: Northeastern University Press, 1983.

———, ed. *Reconsiderations on the Revolutionary War*. Westport, Conn.: Greenwood, 1978.

Higgins, W. Robert, ed. *The Revolutionary War in the South: Power, Conflict, and Leadership*. Durham, N.C.: Duke University Press, 1979.

Hirsch, Adam J. "The Collision of Military Cultures in Seventeenth-Century New England." *Journal of American History* 74 (1988): 1187–1212.

Hoerder, Dirk. *Crowd Action in Revolutionary Massachusetts, 1765–1780*. New York: Academic Press, 1977.

Hoffman, Ronald. "The 'Disaffected' in the Revolutionary South." In *The American Revolution*, ed. Alfred F. Young, 273–318. DeKalb: Northern Illinois University Press, 1976.

Hoffman, Ronald, Thad W. Tate, and Peter J. Albert, eds. *An Uncivil War: The Southern Backcountry during the American Revolution*. Charlottesville: University Press of Virginia, 1985.

Hofstadter, Richard, and Michael Wallace, eds. *American Violence: A Documentary History*. New York: Knopf, 1970.

Holton, Woody. *Forced Founders: Indians, Debtors, Slaves, and the Making of the American Revolution in Virginia*. Chapel Hill: University of North Carolina Press, 1999.

Isaac, Rhys. *The Transformation of Virginia 1740–1790*. Chapel Hill: University of North Carolina Press, 1982.

Ivers, Larry E. *British Drums on the Southern Frontier: The Military Colonization of Georgia, 1733–1749*. Chapel Hill: University of North Carolina Press, 1974.

Jackson, Carlton. *A Social History of the Scotch-Irish*. New York: Madison, 1993.

Jameson, J. Franklin. *The American Revolution Considered As a Social Movement*. Princeton: Princeton University Press, 1967.

Jennings, Francis. *The Invasion of America: Indians, Colonialism, and the Cant of Conquest*. New York: Norton, 1975.

Jensen, Merrill. *The American Revolution within America*. New York: New York University Press, 1974.

Johnson, Elmer. "The War of the Regulation." M.A. thesis, University of North Carolina, Chapel Hill, 1942.

Johnson, James M. *Militiamen, Rangers, and Redcoats: The Military of Georgia, 1754–1776*. Macon, Ga.: Mercer University Press, 1992.

Jones, Maldwyn A. "The Scotch-Irish in British America." In *Strangers within the*

Realm, ed. Bernard Bailyn and Philip D. Morgan, 284–313. Chapel Hill: University of North Carolina Press, 1991.

Jones, Mark Haddon. "Herman Husband: Millenarian, Carolina Regulator, and Whiskey Rebel." Ph.D. diss., Northern Illinois University, 1982.

Karr, Ronald Dale. "'Why Should You Be So Furious?'" The Violence of the Pequot War." *Journal of American History* 85 (1998): 876–909.

Kars, Marjoleine. "'Breaking Loose Together': Religion and Rebellion in the North Carolina Piedmont, 1730–1790." Ph.D. diss., Duke University, 1994.

Kay, Marvin L. Michael. "An Analysis of a British Colony in Late Eighteenth Century America in the Light of a Current American Historiographical Controversy." *Australian Journal of Politics and History* 11 (1965): 170–84.

———. "The Institutional Background to the Regulation in Colonial North Carolina." Ph.D. diss., University of Minnesota, 1962.

———. "The North Carolina Regulation, 1766–1776: A Class Conflict." In *The American Revolution,* ed. Alfred F. Young, 71–124. DeKalb: Northern Illinois University Press, 1976.

Kay, Marvin L. Michael, and Lorin Lee Cary. "Class, Mobility, and Conflict in North Carolina on the Eve of the Revolution." In *The Southern Experience in the American Revolution,* ed. Jeffrey J. Crow and Larry E. Tise, 109–51. Chapel Hill: University of North Carolina Press, 1978.

———. *Slavery in North Carolina, 1748–1775.* Chapel Hill: University of North Carolina Press, 1995.

Kay, Marvin L. Michael, and William S. Price, Jr. "'To Ride the Wood Mare': Road Building and Militia Service in Colonial North Carolina, 1740–1775." *North Carolina Historical Review* 57 (1980): 361–409.

Keeley, Lawrence H. *War before Civilization.* New York: Oxford University Press, 1996.

Keener, Craig S. "An Ethnohistorical Analysis of Iroquois Assault Tactics Used against Fortified Settlements of the Northeast in the Seventeenth Century." *Ethnohistory* 46 (1999): 777–807.

Kerber, Linda K. *Women of the Republic: Intellect and Ideology in Revolutionary America.* New York: Norton, 1980.

Kern, John. "The Politics of Violence: Colonial American Rebellions, Protest, and Riots, 1676–1747." Ph.D. diss., University of Wisconsin, Madison, 1976.

Kittrie, Nicholas N. *The War against Authority: From the Crisis of Legitimacy to the New Social Contract.* Baltimore: Johns Hopkins University Press, 1995.

Klein, Rachel N. "Ordering the Backcountry: The South Carolina Regulators." *William and Mary Quarterly,* 3d ser., 38 (1981): 661–80.

Knight, Betsy. "Prisoner Exchange and Parole in the American Revolution." *William and Mary Quarterly,* 3d ser., 48 (1991): 200–222.

Knouff, Gregory T. "'An Arduous Service': The Pennsylvania Backcountry Soldiers' Revolution." *Pennsylvania History* 61 (1994): 45–74.

———. "The Common People's Revolution: Class, Race, Masculinity, and Locale in Pennsylvania, 1775–1783." Ph.D. diss., Rutgers University, 1996.

———. "Soldiers and Violence on the Pennsylvania Frontier." In *Beyond Philadelphia: The Pennsylvania Hinterland in the American Revolution*, ed. John B. Frantz and William Pencak, 171–93. University Park: Pennsylvania State University Press, 1998.

Knowles, Nathaniel. "The Torture of Captives by the Indians of Eastern North America." *American Philosophical Society Proceedings* 82 (1940): 151–225.

Krech, Shepard III. "Genocide in Tribal Society." *Nature* 371, no. 6492 (September 1994): 14–15.

Kupperman, Karen Ordahl. *Indians and English: Facing Off in Early America.* Ithaca, N.Y.: Cornell University Press, 2000.

———. *Providence Island, 1630–1641: The Other Puritan Colony.* Cambridge: Cambridge University Press, 1993.

Kwasny, Mark V. *Washington's Partisan War, 1775–1783.* Kent, Ohio: Kent State University Press, 1996.

Ladenheim, Jules Calvin. "'The Doctors' Mob' of 1788." *Journal of the History of Medicine and Allied Science* 5 (1950): 23–53.

Leach, Douglas Edward. *Roots of Conflict: British Armed Forces and Colonial Americans, 1677–1763.* Chapel Hill: University of North Carolina Press, 1986.

Leach, Edmund. *Custom, Law, and Terrorist Violence.* Edinburgh: Edinburgh University Press, 1977.

Leary, Helen F. M., and Maurice R. Stirewalt, eds. *North Carolina Research: Genealogy and Local History.* Raleigh: North Carolina Genealogical Society, 1980.

Lee, Lawrence. "Days of Defiance: Resistance to the Stamp Act in the Lower Cape Fear." *North Carolina Historical Review* 43 (1966): 186–202.

———. *Indian Wars in North Carolina, 1663–1763.* Raleigh, N.C.: Carolina Charter Tercentenary Commission, 1963.

Lefler, Hugh T. *Colonial North Carolina: A History.* New York: Scribner, 1973.

Lefler, Hugh Talmage, and Albert Ray Newsome. *North Carolina: The History of a Southern State.* Chapel Hill: University of North Carolina Press, 1954.

Lefler, Hugh, and Paul Wager, eds. *Orange County, 1752–1952.* Chapel Hill: Privately printed, 1953.

Lemisch, Jesse. "Jack Tar in the Streets: Merchant Seamen in the Politics of Revolutionary America." *William and Mary Quarterly,* 3d ser., 25 (1968): 371–407.

———. "Listening to the 'Inarticulate': William Widger's Dream and the Loyalties of American Revolutionary Seamen in British Prisons." *Journal of Social History* 3 (1969): 1–29.

Lennon, Donald R. "'The Graveyard of American Commanders': The Continental Army's Southern Department, 1776–1778." *North Carolina Historical Review* 67 (1990): 133–58.

Lepore, Jill. *The Name of War: King Philip's War and the Origins of American Identity.* New York: Knopf, 1998.

Lewis, Jan. *The Pursuit of Happiness: Family and Values in Jefferson's Virginia.* New York: Cambridge University Press, 1983.

Leyburn, James G. *The Scotch-Irish: A Social History.* Chapel Hill: University of North Carolina Press, 1962.

Luebke, David Martin. *His Majesty's Rebels: Communities, Factions, and Rural Revolt in the Black Forest, 1725–1745.* Ithaca, N.Y.: Cornell University Press, 1997.

Mahon, James K. "Anglo-American Methods of Indian Warfare, 1676–1794." *Mississippi Valley Historical Review* 45 (1958): 254–75.

Maier, Pauline. *From Resistance to Revolution.* New York: Knopf, 1972.

———. "Popular Uprisings and Civil Authority in Eighteenth-Century America." *William and Mary Quarterly* 27 (1970): 3–35.

Malone, Patrick. *The Skulking Way of War.* Lanham, Md.: Madison, 1991.

Martin, James Kirby. "A 'Most Undisciplined, Profligate Crew': Protest and Defiance in the Continental Ranks, 1776–1783." In *Arms and Independence: The Military Character of the American Revolution,* ed. Ronald Hoffman and Peter J. Albert, 119–40. Charlottesville: University Press of Virginia, 1974.

Martin, James Kirby, and Mark Edward Lender. *A Respectable Army: The Military Origins of the Republic, 1763–1789.* Arlington Heights, Ill.: Harlan Davidson, 1982.

Maurer, Maurer. "Military Justice under General Washington." *Military Affairs* 28 (1964): 8–16.

May, Henry F. "The Enlightened Reader in America." *American Quarterly* 28 (1976).

Mayer, Holly A. *Belonging to the Army: Camp Followers and Community during the American Revolution.* Columbia: University of South Carolina Press, 1996.

McDonnell, Michael A. "Popular Mobilization and Political Culture in Revolutionary Virginia: The Failure of the Minutemen and the Revolution from Below." *Journal of American History* 85 (1998): 946–81.

McGeachy, Neill Roderick. *A History of the Sugaw Creek Presbyterian Church, Mecklenburg Presbytery, Charlotte, North Carolina.* Rock Hill, S.C.: Record Printing Co., 1954.

McWhiney, Grady. *Cracker Culture: Celtic Ways in the Old South.* Tuscaloosa: University of Alabama Press, 1988.

———. "Ethnic Roots of Southern Violence." In *A Master's Due: Essays in Honor of David Herbert Donald,* ed. William Cooper, Michael F. Holt, and John McCardell, 112–37. Baton Rouge: Louisiana State University Press, 1985.

Meilinger, Philip S. "Review of *Demonic Males,* by Richard Wrangham and Dale Peterson, *War before Civilization,* by Lawrence H. Keeley, and *A History of Warfare,* by John Keegan." *Journal of Military History* 61 (1997): 598–602.

Merrell, James. *The Indians' New World*. Chapel Hill: University of North Carolina Press, 1989.

Merrens, Harry Roy. *Colonial North Carolina in the Eighteenth Century: A Study in Historical Geography*. Chapel Hill: University of North Carolina Press, 1964.

Metzger, Charles H. *The Prisoner in the American Revolution*. Chicago: Loyola University Press, 1971.

Meyer, Duane. *The Highland Scots of North Carolina, 1732–1776*. Chapel Hill: University of North Carolina Press, 1961.

Middlekauff, Robert. *The Glorious Cause: The American Revolution, 1763–1789*. New York: Oxford University Press, 1982.

Milner, George R. "Warfare in Prehistoric and Early Historic Eastern North America." *Journal of Archaeological Research* 7 (1999): 105–51.

Morgan, Edmund S. *American Slavery, American Freedom*. New York: Norton, 1975.

———. "Conflict and Consensus in the American Revolution." In *Essays on the American Revolution*, ed. Stephen G. Kurtz and James H. Hutson, 289–309. Chapel Hill: University of North Carolina Press, 1973.

Morgan, Edmund S., and Helen M. Morgan. *Stamp Act Crisis: Prologue to Revolution*. Chapel Hill: University of North Carolina Press, 1953.

Moss, Bobby Gilmer. *The Patriots at King's Mountain*. Blacksburg, S.C.: Scotia-Hibernia Press, 1990.

———. *Roster of the Loyalists at the Battle of Moore's Creek Bridge*. Blacksburg, S.C.: Scotia-Hibernia Press, 1992.

———. *Roster of the Patriots in the Battle of Moore's Creek Bridge*. Blacksburg, S.C.: Scotia-Hibernia Press, 1992.

Nadelhaft, Jerome J. *The Disorders of War: The Revolution in South Carolina*. Orono: University of Maine at Orono Press, 1981.

Nash, Gary B. "Red, White, and Black: The Origins of Racism in Colonial America." In *The Great Fear: Race in the Mind of America*, ed. Gary B. Nash and Richard Weiss, 1–26. New York: Holt, Rinehart and Winston, 1970.

———. *The Urban Crucible: The Northern Seaports and the Origins of the American Revolution*, abridged ed. Cambridge: Harvard University Press, 1986.

Neimeyer, Charles Patrick. *America Goes to War: A Social History of the Continental Army*. New York: New York University Press, 1996.

Nelson, Paul David. "Horatio Gates in the Southern Department, 1780: Serious Errors and a Costly Defeat." *North Carolina Historical Review* 50 (1973): 256–72.

———. "Major General Horatio Gates As a Military Leader: The Southern Experience." In *The Revolutionary War in the South: Power, Conflict, and Leadership*, ed. W. Robert Higgins, 132–58. Durham, N.C.: Duke University Press, 1979.

Newlin, Algie I. *The Battle of Lindley's Mill.* Burlington, N.C.: Alamance Historical Association, 1975.

———. *The Battle of New Garden.* Greensboro, N.C.: North Carolina Friends Historical Society, 1977.

Nobles, Gregory H. "Breaking into the Backcountry: New Approaches to the Early American Frontier, 1750–1800." *William and Mary Quarterly,* 3d ser., 46 (1989): 641–70.

Norton, Mary Beth. *Liberty's Daughters: The Revolutionary Experience of American Women, 1750–1800.* Boston: Little, Brown, 1980.

Oberschall, Anthony. "Group Violence: Some Hypotheses and Empirical Uniformities." *Law and Society Review* 5 (1970): 61–92.

O'Donnell, James H., III. *The Cherokees of North Carolina in the American Revolution.* Raleigh: North Carolina Department of Cultural Resources, 1976.

Olwell, Robert A. "'Domestic Enemies': Slavery and Political Independence in South Carolina, May 1775–March 1776." *Journal of Southern History* 55 (1989): 21–48.

Palmer, Bryan D. "Discordant Music: Charivari and Whitecapping in North America." *Labour/Le Travailleur* 3 (1978): 5–62.

Pancake, John S. *This Destructive War: The British Campaign in the Carolinas, 1780–82.* Birmingham: University of Alabama Press, 1985.

Paret, Peter. "Colonial Experience and European Military Reform at the End of the Eighteenth Century." *Bulletin of the Institute of Historical Research* 37 (1964): 47–59.

———. "The Relationship between the Revolutionary War and European Military Thought and Practice in the Second Half of the Eighteenth Century." In *Reconsiderations on the Revolutionary War,* ed. Don Higginbotham, 144–57. Westport, Conn.: Greenwood, 1978.

Peckham, Howard H. *The Toll of Independence.* Chicago: University of Chicago Press, 1975.

Plant, Marjorie. *The English Book Trade: An Economic History of the Making and Sale of Books.* London: George Allen and Unwin, 1965.

Pocock, J. G. A. *The Machiavellian Moment: Florentine Political Thought and the Atlantic Republican Tradition.* Princeton: Princeton University Press, 1975.

Powell, William S. *The North Carolina Gazetteer.* Chapel Hill: University of North Carolina Press, 1968.

———. *The War of the Regulation and the Battle of Alamance, May 16, 1771.* Raleigh, N.C.: Division of Archives and History, 1976.

Preyer, Norris W. *Hezekiah Alexander and the Revolution in the Backcountry.* Charlotte: Heritage Printers, 1987.

Pugh, Robert C. "The Cowpens Campaign and the American Revolution." Ph.D. diss., University of Illinois, 1951.

———. "The Revolutionary Militia in the Southern Campaigns, 1780–1781." *William and Mary Quarterly,* 3d ser., 14 (1957): 154–75.

Purcell, Sarah J. "'Spread this *martial fire*': The New England Patriot Clergy and Civil Military Inspiration." *Journal of Church & State* 38 (1996): 621–39.

Quarles, Benjamin. *The Negro in the American Revolution.* Chapel Hill: University of North Carolina Press, 1961.

Ramsay, David. *The History of the Revolution in South Carolina.* 2 vols. Trenton, N.J.: Isaac Collins, 1785.

Ramsey, Robert W. *Carolina Cradle: Settlement of the Northwest Carolina Frontier, 1747–1776.* Chapel Hill: University of North Carolina Press, 1964.

Rankin, Hugh F. "Cowpens: Prelude to Yorktown." *North Carolina Historical Review* 31 (1954): 337–69.

———. *The Moore's Creek Bridge Campaign.* Conshohocken, Pa.: Eastern National Park and Monument Association, 1986.

———. *The North Carolina Continentals.* Chapel Hill: University of North Carolina Press, 1971.

———. *Upheaval in Albemarle: The Story of Culpeper's Rebellion, 1675–1689.* Raleigh, N.C.: Carolina Charter Tercentenary Commission, 1962.

Rapoport, Anatol. *The Origins of Violence: Approaches to the Study of Conflict.* New Brunswick, N.J.: Transaction, 1995.

Rediker, Marcus. *Between the Devil and the Deep Blue Sea.* Cambridge: Cambridge University Press, 1987.

Reid, John Phillip. *A Better Kind of Hatchet: Law, Trade, and Diplomacy in the Cherokee Nation during the Early Years of European Contact.* University Park: Pennsylvania State University Press, 1976.

———. "In a Defensive Rage: The Uses of the Mob, the Justification in Law, and the Coming of the American Revolution." *New York University Law Review* 49 (1974): 1043–91.

Resch, John. *Suffering Soldiers: Revolutionary War Veterans, Moral Sentiment, and Political Culture in the Early Republic.* Amherst: University of Massachusetts Press, 2000.

Richter, Daniel K. "War and Culture: The Iroquois Experience." *William and Mary Quarterly,* 3d ser., 40 (1983): 528–59.

Riling, Joseph R. *The Art and Science of War in America: A Bibliography of American Military Imprints, 1690–1800.* Alexandria Bay, N.Y.: Museum Restoration Service, 1990.

Robertson, Karen. "Pocahontas at the Masque." *Signs* 21 (1996): 551–83.

Robson, Eric. "The Expedition to the Southern Colonies, 1775–1776." *English Historical Review* 66 (October 1951): 535–60.

Rosswurm, Steven. *Arms, Country, and Class: The Philadelphia Militia and "Lower Sort" during the American Revolution, 1775–1783.* New Brunswick, N.J.: Rutgers University Press, 1988.

Rountree, Helen C. "The Powhatans and Other Woodland Indians As Travelers." In *Powhatan Foreign Relations, 1500–1722,* ed. Helen C. Rountree, 21–52. Charlottesville: University Press of Virginia, 1993.

———. "The Powhatans and the English: A Case of Multiple Conflicting Agendas." In *Powhatan Foreign Relations, 1500–1722*, ed. Helen C. Rountree, 173–205. Charlottesville: University Press of Virginia, 1993.

———. "Summary and Implications." In *Powhatan Foreign Relations, 1500–1722*, ed. Helen C. Rountree, 206–28. Charlottesville: University Press of Virginia, 1993.

Royster, Charles. *A Revolutionary People at War: The Continental Army and American Character, 1775–1783*. New York: Norton, 1979.

Russell, Phillips. *North Carolina in the Revolutionary War*. Charlotte, N.C.: Heritage Printers, 1965.

Sabine, Lorenzo. *Biographical Sketches of the Loyalists of the American Revolution*. Boston: Little, Brown, 1864.

Scudieri, James Domenic. "The Continentals: A Comparative Analysis of a Late Eighteenth Century Standing Army, 1775–1783." Ph.D. diss., City University of New York, 1993.

Selesky, Harold E. "Colonial America." In *The Laws of War: Constraints on Warfare in the Western World*, ed. Michael Howard, George J. Andreopoulos, and Mark R. Shulman, 59–85. New Haven: Yale University Press, 1994.

———. *War and Society in Colonial Connecticut*. New Haven: Yale University Press, 1990.

Shaw, Peter. *American Patriots and the Rituals of Revolution*. Cambridge, Mass.: Harvard University Press, 1981.

Shea, William L. *The Virginia Militia in the Seventeenth Century*. Baton Rouge: Louisiana State University Press, 1983.

Sheehan, Bernard W. *Savagism and Civility: Indians and Englishmen in Colonial Virginia*. Cambridge: Cambridge University Press, 1980.

Shy, John. "American Society and Its War for Independence." In *Reconsiderations on the Revolutionary War*, ed. Don Higginbotham, 72–81. Westport, Conn.: Greenwood, 1978.

———. "American Strategy: Charles Lee and the Radical Alternative." In *A People Numerous and Armed*, 133–62. Oxford: Oxford University Press, 1976.

———. "Hearts and Minds in the American Revolution: The Case of 'Long Bill' Scott and Peterborough, New Hampshire." In *A People Numerous and Armed*, 163–80. Oxford: Oxford University Press, 1976.

———. "The Military Conflict Considered As a Revolutionary War." In *A People Numerous and Armed*, 193–224. Oxford: Oxford University Press, 1976.

———. "A New Look at the Colonial Militia." In *A People Numerous and Armed*, 21–34. Oxford: Oxford University Press, 1976.

Skaggs, Marvin L. "North Carolina Boundary Disputes Involving Her Southern Line." *James Sprunt Studies in History and Political Science* 25 (1941).

Skeen, C. Edward. *Citizen Soldiers in the War of 1812*. Lexington: University Press of Kentucky, 1999.

Slaughter, Thomas P. "Crowds in Eighteenth-Century America: Reflections and New Directions." *Pennsylvania Magazine of History and Biography* 115 (1991): 3–34.

Smith, Barbara Clark. "Food Rioters and the American Revolution." *William and Mary Quarterly,* 3d ser., 51 (1994): 3–38.

Smith, Paul H. *Loyalists and Redcoats: A Study in British Revolutionary Policy.* New York: Norton, 1972.

Smith, William Ander. "Anglo-Colonial Society and the Mob: 1740–1775." Ph.D. diss., Claremont Graduate School, 1965.

Snapp, J. Russell. *John Stuart and the Struggle for Empire on the Southern Frontier.* Baton Rouge: Louisiana State University Press, 1996.

Spaulding, Oliver L. "The Military Studies of George Washington." *American Historical Review* 29 (1924): 675–80.

Spindel, Donna J. "Law and Disorder: The North Carolina Stamp Act Crisis." *North Carolina Historical Review* 57 (1980): 1–16.

———. "The Stamp Act Riots." Ph.D. diss., Duke University, 1975.

———. "Women's Civil Actions in the North Carolina Higher Courts, 1670–1730." *North Carolina Historical Review* 71 (1994): 151–73.

Spruill, Julia Cherry. *Women's Life and Work in the Southern Colonies.* New York: Norton, 1972.

Sprunt, James C. *Chronicles of the Cape Fear River, 1660–1916,* 2d ed. Raleigh, N.C.: Edwards and Broughton, 1916.

Starkey, Armstrong. *European and Native American Warfare, 1675–1815.* Norman: University Press of Oklahoma, 1998.

———. "Paoli to Stony Point: Military Ethics and Weaponry during the American Revolution." *Journal of Military History* 58 (1994): 7–27.

———. "War and Culture, A Case Study: The Enlightenment and the Conduct of the British Army in America, 1755–1781." *War and Society* 8 (1990): 1–28.

Steele, Ian K. *Betrayals: Fort William Henry and the "Massacre."* New York: Oxford University Press, 1990.

———. *Warpaths: Invasions of North America.* New York: Oxford University Press, 1994.

Stegmaier, Mark J. "Maryland's Fear of Insurrection at the Time of Braddock's Defeat." *Maryland Historical Magazine* 71 (1976): 467–83.

Stuart, Reginald C. "'For the Lord Is a Man of Warr': The Colonial New England View of War and the American Revolution." *Journal of Church and State* 23 (1981): 519–32.

———. *War and American Thought.* Kent, Ohio: Kent State University Press, 1982.

Taylor, R. H. "Slave Conspiracies in North Carolina." *North Carolina Historical Review* 5 (1928): 20–34.

Tiedemann, Joseph S. "Patriots by Default: Queens County, New York, and the

British Army, 1776–1783." *William and Mary Quarterly,* 3d ser., 43 (1986): 35–63.

Tilley, Nannie May. "Political Disturbances in Colonial Granville County." *North Carolina Historical Review* 18 (1941): 339–59.

Titus, James W. *The Old Dominion at War: Society, Politics, and Warfare in Late Colonial Virginia.* Columbia: University of South Carolina Press, 1991.

Trigger, Bruce G. "Early Native North American Responses to European Contact: Romantic versus Rationalistic Interpretations." *Journal of American History* 77 (1991): 1195–1215.

Troxler, Carole Watterson. *The Loyalist Experience in North Carolina.* Raleigh: North Carolina Department of Cultural Resources, 1976.

Troxler, George W. *Pyle's Massacre, February 23, 1781.* Burlington: Alamance County Historical Association, 1973.

Turney-High, Harry Holbert. *Primitive War: Its Practices and Concepts,* 2d ed. Columbia: University of South Carolina Press, 1991.

U.S. Department of the Army. Field Manual 27–10: *The Law of Land Warfare.* Department of the Army, 1956.

U.S. Department of Commerce. *Historical Statistics of the United States: Colonial Times to 1970.* White Plains, N.Y.: Kraus International Publications, 1989.

Vaughan, Alden T. "'Expulsion of the Salvages': English Policy and the Virginia Massacre of 1622." *William and Mary Quarterly,* 3d ser., 35 (1978): 57–84.

———. "From White Man to Redskin: Changing Anglo-American Perceptions of the American Indian." *American Historical Review* 87 (1982): 917–53.

———. *New England Frontier: Puritans and Indians, 1620–1675.* Rev. ed. New York: Norton, 1979.

von Clausewitz, Carl. *On War.* Edited by Anatol Rapaport. New York: Penguin, 1982.

Waddell, A. M. *A Colonial Officer and His Times, 1754–1773.* Raleigh, N.C.: Edwards and Broughton, 1890.

Watson, Alan D. "The Constable in Colonial North Carolina." *North Carolina Historical Review* 68 (1991): 1–16.

———. "Society and Economy in Colonial Edgecomb County." *North Carolina Historical Review* 50 (1973).

Way, Peter. "The Cutting Edge of Culture: British Soldiers Encounter Native Americans in the French and Indian War." In *Empire and Others: British Encounters with Indigenous Peoples, 1600–1850,* ed. Martin Daunton and Rick Halpern, 123–48. Philadelphia: University of Pennsylvania Press, 1999.

Webb, Keith. *Problems and Progress in Two Contemporary Theories of Conflict.* Collected Seminar Papers No. 30. London: University of London Institute of Commonwealth Studies, 1982.

Weigley, Russell F. *The American Way of War: A History of United States Military Strategy and Policy.* Bloomington: Indiana University Press, 1973.

———. *The Partisan War: The South Carolina Campaigns of 1780–82*. Columbia: University of South Carolina Press, 1970.

Weller, Jac. "Irregular but Effective: Partisan Weapons Tactics in the American Revolution, Southern Theater." *Military Affairs* 21 (1957): 119–31.

———. "The Irregular War in the South." *Military Affairs* 24 (1960): 124–36.

Wheeler, Earl Milton. "Development and Organization of the North Carolina Militia." *North Carolina Historical Review* 41 (July 1964): 307–23.

———. "The Role of the North Carolina Militia in the Beginning of the American Revolution." Ph.D. diss., Tulane University, 1969.

White, John Todd. "Standing Armies in Time of War: Republican Theory and Military Practice during the American Revolution." Ph.D. diss., George Washington University, 1978.

White, Kathrine Keogh. *The King's Mountain Men, the Story of the Battle, with Sketches of the American Soldiers Who Took Part*. Dayton, Va.: Joseph K. Ruebush Co., 1924.

White, Richard. "Discovering Nature in North America." *Journal of American History* 79 (1992): 874–91.

———. *The Middle Ground: Indians, Empires, and Republics in the Great Lakes Region, 1650–1815*. Cambridge: Cambridge University Press, 1991.

Whittenburg, James P. "Backwoods Revolutionaries: Social Context and Constitutional Theories of the North Carolina Regulators." Ph.D. diss., University of Georgia, 1974.

———. "Planters, Merchants, and Lawyers: Social Change and the Origins of the North Carolina Regulation." *William and Mary Quarterly*, 3d ser., 34 (1977): 215–38.

Wilson, Joan Hoff. "The Illusion of Change: Women and the American Revolution." In *The American Revolution*, ed. Alfred F. Young, 383–446. DeKalb: Northern Illinois University Press, 1976.

Winders, Richard Bruce. *Mr. Polk's Army: The American Military Experience in the Mexican War*. College Station: Texas A&M University Press, 1997.

Wokeck, Marianne S. *Trade in Strangers: The Beginnings of Mass Migration to North America*. University Park: Pennsylvania State University Press, 1999.

Wood, Gordon S. "A Note on Mobs in the American Revolution." *William and Mary Quarterly*, 3d ser., 23 (1966): 635–42.

———. "Rhetoric and Reality in the American Revolution." *William and Mary Quarterly*, 3d ser., 23 (1966): 3–32.

Wood, Peter H. *Black Majority: Negroes in Colonial South Carolina from 1670 through the Stono Rebellion*. New York: Norton, 1974.

Wright, Quincy. *A Study of War*. 2 vols. Chicago: University of Chicago Press, 1942.

Wright, Robert K. *The Continental Army*. Washington, D.C.: U.S. Army Center of Military History, 1983.

———. "'Nor Is Their Standing Army to Be Despised': The Emergence of the

Continental Army As a Military Institution." In *Arms and Independence: The Military Character of the American Revolution,* ed. Ronald Hoffman and Peter J. Albert, 25–49. Charlottesville: University Press of Virginia, 1974.

Wyatt-Brown, Bertram. *Southern Honor: Ethics and Behaviour in the Old South.* New York: Oxford University Press, 1982.

Young, Alfred F. "English Plebeian Culture and Eighteenth-Century American Radicalism." In *The Origins of Anglo-American Radicalism,* ed. Margaret Jacob and James Jacob, 185–213. London: George Allen and Unwin, 1984.

———, ed. *The American Revolution: Explorations in the History of American Radicalism.* DeKalb: Northern Illinois University Press, 1976.

———, ed. *Beyond the American Revolution: Explorations in the History of American Radicalism.* DeKalb: Northern Illinois University Press, 1993.

Zagorin, Perez. "Theories of Revolution in Contemporary Historiography." *Political Science Quarterly* 88 (1973): 23–52.

Zimmerman, Ekkart. *Political Violence, Crises, and Revolutions: Theories and Research.* Cambridge, Mass: Schenkman Publishing Company, 1983.

Index

Page numbers in italics are references to maps or figures.

Wayne E. Lee is assistant professor of history at the University of Louisville. He received his Ph.D. from Duke University and specializes in early American and military history.

Wayne E. Lee is assistant professor of history at the University of Louisville. He has published in the *Historical Journal, Hesperia*, and *North Carolina Historical Review*.